Operational Auditing

Internal Audit and IT Audit

Series Editor: Dan Swanson

PUBLISHED

Operational Auditing

Principles and Techniques for a Changing World

Second Edition

Hernan Murdock

CRC Press
Taylor & Francis Group
Boca Raton London New York

CRC Press is an imprint of the
Taylor & Francis Group, an **informa** business

Second edition published 2022
by CRC Press
6000 Broken Sound Parkway NW, Suite 300, Boca Raton, FL 33487-2742

and by CRC Press
2 Park Square, Milton Park, Abingdon, Oxon, OX14 4RN

© 2022 Taylor & Francis Group, LLC

First edition published by CRC Press 2017

CRC Press is an imprint of Taylor & Francis Group, LLC

ISBN: 978-0-367-56236-6 (hbk)
ISBN: 978-0-367-77142-3 (pbk)
ISBN: 978-1-003-09693-1 (ebk)

Typeset in Garamond
by MPS Limited, Dehradun

Contents

Author

Hernan Murdock, CIA, CRMA, is vice president, Content and Programming at ACI Learning. He has held positions as director of training for an international audit and consulting firm, and various audit positions while leading and performing audit and consulting projects for clients in the manufacturing, transportation, high tech, education, insurance, and power generation industries.

Dr. Murdock is a senior lecturer at Northeastern University where he teaches management, leadership, and ethics. He earned a DBA from Argosy University, Sarasota, Florida in 2007; a CSS from Harvard University, Cambridge, Massachusetts in 1996; and an MBA and BSBA from Suffolk University in 1992 and 1990, respectively. He also holds the following certifications: CRMA Certification in Risk Management Assurance (IIA), 2013; QAR Accreditation in Internal Quality Assessment/Validation (IIA), 2008; AchieveGlobal Leadership and Customer Service: Deliver and Develop Levels, 2007; IDC Certified Instructor (IIA), 2006; and CIA Certified Internal Auditor (IIA), 2001. He is the author of *Auditor Essentials: 100 Concepts, Tools, and Techniques for Success* (CRC Press, 2019), *10 Key Techniques to Improve Team Productivity* (The IIA Research Foundation, 2011) and *Using Surveys in Internal Audits* (The IIA Research Foundation, 2009). He has also written articles and book chapters on whistleblowing programs, international auditing, mentoring programs, fraud, deception, corporate social responsibility, and behavioral profiling.

Dr. Murdock has conducted audits and consulting projects, delivered seminars and invited talks, and made numerous presentations at internal audit, academic, and government functions in North America, Latin America, Europe, the Middle East, and Africa.

Dr. Murdock can be reached at Hernan.Murdock@gmail.com.

Chapter 1

Definition, Characteristics, and Guidance

Be a Product of the Product

What does it mean to be a product of the product? It's quite simple. Be a living example of what you sell, recommend or advise others. Personify what you preach. Show don't tell. Lead by example.[1]

John B. Petersen III

Introduction

Internal audit is undergoing a massive transformation. While its role to provide independent, objective assurance and consulting services to organizations in ways that improve their operations has remained constant for decades and remains true today, how this has been accomplished has changed over time.

Since the founding of the Institute of Internal Auditors (IIA) in 1941, the profession has evolved to adapt its personality, purpose, and approach to the changes taking place in the fields of management and organizational behavior. Universities and other academic institutions capitalized on the lessons of the industrial era and developed organization theories that created systems whereby centralization, a defined hierarchy, distinct authority levels and reporting lines, clear rules, and the division of labor were the norm.

Internal audit adapted to this approach and adopted it, so its methodologies were consistent with these theories. Standardization was the norm and organizations implemented rigid guidelines for how they functioned. Consequently, internal auditors did the same and implemented standardized approaches to audit their clients in those organizations. This search for consistency resulted in the proliferation of checklists, standard audit programs, and procedures. In the end, internal auditing evolved in a way that validated the organizations' hierarchy and structure, its centralization, assignment of rigid authority, discipline, rules, and the division of labor procedures against the standard model. The audit function, then, focused on assessing an organization's control or operational effectiveness with this standardization and could do so quickly by using checklists, prepared questionnaires, and reviewing the same documents year after year to verify consistency.

There was, and for those who continue to audit this way, a concealed risk. The focus on standardization limited the auditor's ability to be creative. Creative thinkers were not sought for nor gravitated toward the profession. Using the excuse, and the legitimate need for independence, internal auditors isolated themselves from the businesses they examined and were supposed to support. Some even abstained from making recommendations to improve the weaknesses they identified. This risk became apparent in the 1960s and lasted through the 1980s.

While internal auditors were protecting their independence, the businesses they served were changing due to globalization, technological advancements, relentless competition, and a new social, demographic, and financial landscape. Companies no longer operated using the standard model. Since manufacturing moved to different countries, it was impractical to have a single procurement function with a single manager overseeing all purchasing activities. Since customers were now located around the world, the approval of customer orders could no longer be handled expeditiously and competently by the sales manager. Purchasing and sales decisions were now being made by regional general managers at the countries where these activities took place. Approving and making adjustments to customer accounts, were no longer handled manually and personally by the company's controller. There was no need to. The local staff could handle that under the supervision of their local management team. The company's enterprise resource planning (ERP) system provided the necessary separation of duties and limited transaction processing to those authorized.

Many internal auditors missed these changes and were slow to adapt to the changing landscape, instead believing that the world still operated by the standard business model. The result? Many became irrelevant. Some internal auditors still used their standard checklists, asked the same questions, searched for the same documents, and applied the rules of the standard business model. They continued to insist that outdated procedures be followed, like having the sales vice president approve all customer orders and the corporate controller print out the credit memos and sign them.

There was little disagreement about the need for effective internal auditing. Broad consensus existed about the importance of having a strong and reliable internal control environment. Generally, management believed in the importance of having sound internal controls, but did not believe that the internal audit function was making an effective contribution to the company. Boards of directors and their management teams slowly lost confidence in an internal audit function that focused so disproportionately, and inflexibly, on traditional business models that they recommended changes to the business that were clearly out of step with how the company needed to function. The disproportionate focus on compliance led many auditors to focus on what they thought was important to the business and less on what was truly important to the business. Management became disenchanted with auditors who wanted to refrain from making changes, even when the internal and external environments demanded quick and judicious modifications to the business structure and its practices. Beyond the methodology, some managers even wondered why some audits were being performed in the first place.

As if that weren't enough, there was another problem. Internal audit in many ways evolved as an offshoot of external audit (i.e., public accounting) and excessively replicated external auditing by focusing on accounting transactions and the process of preparing financial statements. While the focus was generally more detailed and the materiality thresholds used by internal auditors was much lower, reviewing and reperforming accounting procedures seemed wasteful if the organization was already paying their external auditors to audit the accounting practices that led to the publishing of the company's financial reports.

Much has changed since then. Starting in the early 1990s, internal audit began a transformation process that is bringing it more in line with the true needs of the organizations it serves and the related stakeholders. The emergence of the stakeholder theory and topics about corporate governance, quality, and cycle time, in addition to the constant advocacy work of the IIA have brought many changes to the profession. The dot com meltdown in 2000/2001 and the enactment of the Sarbanes–Oxley Act of 2002 were wake up calls for the profession.

Today internal audit is achieving a healthier balance among operational, reporting, compliance, information technology (IT), fraud, and strategic topics. It is now looking beyond the immediate fiscal year and taking a closer look at longer term trends and the future implications of current dynamics. It is now identifying a wider set of essential skills, and finding that to succeed as a trusted advisor to the board and management, it must bring into its ranks people with a wider skillset, including broad business skills, strong communication skills, and familiarity with technology.

But there is still work to be done. The State of Internal Audit 2013 report from Thomson Reuters Accelus states that although internal auditors are beginning to evaluate more strategic-level risk management and monitoring activities, most internal audit departments continue to focus primarily on process assurance and monitoring activities. Respondents to the survey indicated there is a lack of skilled resources due to the changing role of internal auditors away from traditional quantitative assessments and toward becoming a qualitative assessor of the organization's goals and strengths. This condition remains true as this book goes to print. In this book, we discuss these dynamics and lay the foundation for effective operational audits.

We begin by defining and understanding the definition, role, and practices of modern internal auditing in general and the evolving world of operational auditing in particular. We examine the concept and manifestation of organizational risks and how internal auditors must adopt a risk-based auditing approach, which will allow it to better support the objectives of the organization.

Integrated auditing is a concept that has been in place for decades, yet many internal auditors still struggle to practice it effectively. We discuss key attributes of effective integrated audits and why it is essential for effective operational audits.

We end this chapter with a review of selected Standards for the Professional Practice of Internal Auditing (the *Standards*). But more than list them, we discuss their implications in the broader topic of operational auditing, and how these standards can be applied successfully.

Definition and Characteristics of Operational Auditing

Operational auditing is defined as "A future-oriented, systematic, and independent evaluation of organizational activities. Financial data may be used, but the primary sources of evidence are the operational policies and achievements related to organizational objectives. Internal controls and efficiencies may be evaluated during this type of review."[2]

The Business Dictionary defines operational audit as "A review of how an organization's management and its operating procedures are functioning with respect to their effectiveness and efficiency in meeting stated objectives. For example, a business might perform an operational audit if its senior management has become convinced that operational improvements can be made and need to be identified."[3]

I worked in banking operations for 6 years after graduating from college. Over time, one of my roles involved working with the marketing and IT departments to bring new product concepts to market and ensure their smooth implementation and operation. The work involved managing account creation and servicing of loan programs from account setup to payoff. There was a great deal of paper involved and the work was tedious, time consuming, and often stressful.

Due to the growth of the organization, the large volume of paper files and the related logistical difficulties of finding files at various stages of processing and storing documents, and manually reviewing each file to ascertain its credit worthiness, the company embarked on a reengineering project. I was invited to participate as a business partner during the reengineering and restructuring project and I gladly accepted the offer. The result was several months documenting existing processes while brainstorming how to make the processes faster, cheaper, and better for all involved.

We hired an external consulting firm and as I split my time between my regular work and the sessions with the consultants, I got an education on brainstorming, documentation, meeting facilitation, collaboration, negotiation, flowcharting, and time management, among many others. In the end, we successfully introduced a credit scoring system that reduced the amount of time and the number of people needed to process loan applications, we replaced paper records with scanned images for document safekeeping and underwriter review, and were able to provide faster and more accurate status updates about the loan application process and related disbursements.

I leveraged this experience when I subsequently left the bank to work as a business analyst in the insurance industry. For 2 years, I documented business requirements for software engineers, tested systems before rollout, and helped train end users. This involved facilitating workshops to define business requirements and system specifications, performing process design, mapping and analysis, and creating training materials. My role also involved writing client acceptance test procedures to verify that all requirements were included in the design. This experience taught me the intricacies of interviewing and working closely with computer programmers and operations personnel, facilitating meetings, documenting system layout and functionality, and training users. It also helped me to gain a more in-depth understanding of the nature of internal controls at various levels of system design, assessing the significance of system flaws, and postrelease reporting requirements.

My third career move was more directly related to my original career aspiration: work in international business. I wanted to take advantage of my professional experience, diverse personal background, and multiple language skills, so I contacted the internal audit department and asked for an informational interview. The internal audit manager who interviewed me asked many questions and appeared to be more interested in my experience documenting, analyzing, and improving business processes, than my degree in finance.

During our interview, we spoke about the importance of asking "who," "what," "when," "where," and "how" regarding the activities performed within a process, the people working within that process, and the systems supporting both the people and the process. One aspect of the conversation that still resonates with me was how animated she became when we discussed the importance of asking "why." While "who," "what," "when," "where," and "how" provide very valuable information to *describe* the process and understand how the process behaves, "why" provides even more valuable information because it pertains to the *purpose* of the activities performed.

As I knew then, and have come to observe repeatedly over the years, there are countless individuals in organizations working feverishly on activities with an unclear or undefined purpose. In some extreme cases, they perform activities that lack any purpose whatsoever, but they continue performing those activities "because we have always done things that way."

The interview was very productive and successful and I was offered a job within a few days. I promptly accepted the offer and so began my career working on the international team of a company that was rapidly expanding in Latin America. I became an internal auditor.

My relatives, friends, and business acquaintances were very supportive of my career decision, and I was very happy for their support. What I was not expecting, however, was the general lack of awareness about internal auditing as a profession, and what internal auditors did in particular. Some of their first words often became a statement along the lines of

"Oh, so you are going to work for an accounting firm?," or

"I didn't know you wanted to work for the IRS!," or the question

"Did you major in accounting?" or something along those lines.

Essentially, in the mid-1990s, internal auditing was generally unknown, and for those with some inkling about the profession, the tendency was to associate it with accounting, compliance, and tax-related work.

There was a general lack of awareness and while I was learning about internal auditing too, I knew that internal auditors did more than accounting, compliance, and tax work. I took the opportunity to explain as best I could the expanding role of internal auditors and how they helped management at multiple levels. I was doing my own advocacy work explaining the work of auditors in general and the exciting opportunities that this presented for me.

Since those days, the IIA has done an impressive job raising awareness through advocacy about internal auditing.[4] This effort was enhanced through the formidable work done by Cynthia Cooper, who with her staff unraveled the massive fraud at WorldCom; Sherron Watkins, who was instrumental in alerting others of the accounting irregularities in financial reporting at Enron; and Coleen Rowley, who documented the mishandling of information and failure to take appropriate action at the Federal Bureau of Investigation (FBI). In fact, their work was so instrumental in uncovering these problems, that they jointly received the *Time* Person of the Year award in 2002 as The Whistleblowers.[5]

As we take a closer look at internal auditing, it is helpful to review the definition of internal auditing as promulgated by the IIA. According to the IIA, the definition of internal auditing "states the fundamental purpose, nature, and scope of internal auditing"[6]

> Internal auditing is an independent, objective assurance and consulting activity designed to add value and improve an organization's operations. It helps an organization accomplish its objectives by bringing a systematic, disciplined approach to evaluate and improve the effectiveness of risk management, control, and governance processes.

Although this definition has been in place for years, it is still misunderstood by many nonauditors, and unfortunately, even by some internal auditors. The misunderstanding stems from a variety of reasons and heavily influenced by the legacy of auditors performing financial reviews and internal auditors having accounting backgrounds.

The definition reflects a modern view of the profession and positions auditors in such a way that they can provide much more valuable assistance to their organizations. The definition creates a variety of challenges and opportunities for internal auditors, who are no longer engaged in a static, routine, repetitive, and accounting/finance-focused activity, but instead admonishes internal auditors to review business programs, processes, and initiatives in innovative ways that can add tangible value to the organization.

The definition contains some key language that is important to note:

1. *Independence* has to do primarily with the position of internal audit within the organization's hierarchy. Internal audit should report to the audit committee (or its equivalent) on the board of directors so it receives advice and support to perform its duties. Furthermore, internal audit should not be under the control of those they audit. This direct reporting line to the highest authority within the organization will help internal audit reach its full potential, and also get the attention from those whose influence, recognition, and respect can compel corrective action of any anomalies identified by the auditors.

2. *Objectivity* is related to the auditors' frame of mind and their ability to examine documents, processes, and programs without a bias, without an agenda, with no other motive than to find the truth and communicate it accurately and promptly. Conflicts of interest are one of the biggest threats to objectivity, so internal auditors must be careful to balance maintaining healthy professional and social relationships with others in the organization without becoming too cozy with them.

3. *Assurance* relates to the auditors' ability to give confidence and make statements regarding the condition of matters within the organization. It is often considered a synonym to "compliance" as has been the traditional focus of internal auditors for millennia. Compliance audits focus on verifying conformity and adherence of a particular area, process, or system with policies, plans, procedures, laws, regulations, contracts, or other requirements that govern the conduct and actions of that area, process, or system.

Internal auditors provide reasonable assurance, not absolute assurance, because there are numerous variables to contend with constantly, but also because there are no certainties in life. However, this does not mean that internal auditors do substandard work knowing that they can't guarantee results. Internal auditors are expected to display competence, knowledge, and act with due professional care in all they do to provide the best assurance possible. Compliance can be driven by requirements that are internal or external, regulatory or not, explicit or implied.

I mention implicit, because the subject of corporate social responsibility (CSR), humane working conditions, and lower ecological impact is not always formally codified, but stakeholders are increasingly demanding compliance with higher ethical and moral standards of conduct. In fact, the Value of Sustainability Reporting study from the Boston College Center for Corporate Citizenship and EY (Ernst & Young) states that 68% of the 579 global organizations surveyed make a sustainability disclosure annually. Sustainability reports are becoming a leading business practice for large organizations worldwide.

There is increasing interest among organizations and investors in these types of reports as a way to make sure that environmental and social impacts are managed and as a way to assess the quality and commitment of management to economic, environmental, social, and governance topics. According to the report, there are four main reasons why organizations report:

a. Provide shareholders more transparency
b. Gain competitive advantage
c. Improve risk management capabilities
d. Respond to stakeholder pressure

The word "stakeholder" is a broad term used to denote any person or group that affects, or is affected by, an organization's policies, decisions, and actions. Stakeholders may be voluntary or involuntary, and either bear risks or share benefits. Since there is a strong, and ever more intertwined relationship between organizations and the environment in which they operate, there are shared interests and an interdependence that develops between any organization and other groups. Making sure that there is fair treatment and consistent, universal adherence to established social regulations are key objectives of compliance reviews.

Sustainability reports can be issued in accordance with the Global Reporting Initiative Guidelines[7] or another standard. Although it requires a great deal of work, the report indicates that the financial and social advantages outweigh the costs. In fact, half of the respondents indicated that sustainability reporting gave them a competitive advantage, so it implies that organizations should assess their sustainability practices and that these should inform corporate strategy.

CSR should function as a built-in, self-regulating mechanism enabling organizations to monitor and ensure compliance with laws, ethical standards, and international norms. The expectation is that CSR is deliberately included, and there is consideration of the public interest into corporate decision making. Organizations are expected to honor the triple bottom line: people (social), planet (environment/ecology), and profit (economic).

Since there are assurance implications involved, survey respondents indicated there are challenges too. These include availability of data, accuracy and completeness of data, and internal buy-in.

4. *Consulting* means giving advice to management and the board, and engaging in activities that helps the organization resolve nagging business issues. These engagements address performance, how to improve organizational programs, processes, and activities, and how to become more flexible, nimble, and responsive to business challenges. It also relates to the special projects that internal auditors sometimes work on. Lastly, consulting also relates to the way auditors do their work suggesting that the traditional mindset and role of the auditor as the corporate cop is being redefined and replaced by a more business-minded professional whose goal is to be respected more so than being feared.

5. *Designed to add value.* If you ask a gathering of internal auditors if they add value in their organizations, they unanimously raise their hands in agreement. If you pose the same question to nonauditors, the response is often far less enthusiastic. In fact, some may even argue that internal auditors are a necessary evil and an expense they can't do without because regulations, the board of directors, or other stakeholders demand the existence of an internal audit function. One of the goals of this book is to show how this goal of adding value can be achieved, and do so convincingly.

6. *Improve an organization's operations* is a very interesting statement because many auditors see their role as that of checking things and verifying the accuracy of various items and activities within the organization. But improve an organization's operations? Some would argue that this is a rather broad subject, a tall order, a complex goal, a challenging aspiration, and an insurmountable target. I believe it is not only achievable, but also expected of modern internal auditors.

Over the years, internal auditors have made many positive contributions to their organizations, but in some cases, they have become part of a problem: creating bureaucracy within organizations by recommending a never ending list of controls to mitigate risks, some of which are miniscule in their theoretical assessment and smaller yet if they were to materialize. Some audit teams operate under the mindset that they have to find something so they can produce a report, which inevitably will result in a series of recommendations for additional control procedures. In this book, we will examine ways in which internal auditors can help to improve operations to enhance efficiency, effectiveness, speed, and yes, reduce errors. By doing this, we will be better prepared to address business risks.

7. *Help an organization accomplish its objectives.* Many auditors practice what has been commonly referred to as controls-based auditing. In essence, they look for the controls within the process or program of their review, then check them to see if they are present and operating as expected. While this is important, they often forget to link those controls to the relevant risks, and link these risks to the business objectives that those risks threaten. All of this to say that the starting point for everything auditors do should be the identification of the relevant business objectives. With that in mind, then, internal auditors must do their work in ways that help the organization achieve its objectives by properly responding to the risks that threaten these objectives. By focusing on this, internal auditors can add value and the possibilities are almost endless.

During my early years in internal audit, one of my audit managers told me: "Think of yourself as running this department. Now, how would you then run it so it is successful?" With this in mind, I was told to prepare the audit program that would guide me and my team's work checking on the elements that should be there to improve their likelihood of success, and the roadblocks that could get in their way. Very wise words!

8. *By bringing a systematic, disciplined approach.* This refers to the approach followed when performing the work. This is encapsulated in the *Standards*, the Practice Guides and Practice Advisories, which provide a great deal of guidance on how to plan, execute, and communicate the results of the work done. Our methodology is quite extensive, and it provides enough direction and flexibility as a framework to examine virtually any aspect of an organization's operations.

9. *To evaluate and improve the effectiveness.* Our role as auditors goes beyond evaluating business dynamics and writing reports that merely lists the problems identified. The definition indicates that we evaluate, but also help to improve the organization's ability to achieve the goals and objectives related to:

   a. *Risk management.* This refers to the identification, measurement, assessment, and response to risks.
   b. *Control.* This refers to those activities that mitigate relevant risks and helps the organization avoid surprises.
   c. *Governance processes.* Corporate governance is a wide subject that includes matters related to organizational structure, reporting lines, span of control, resource allocation, accountability measures, discipline, and rewards mechanisms. Corporate governance relates to ethical behavior by directors and others charged with the creation and preservation of wealth for all stakeholders. The IIA's Position Paper on Organizational Governance states that since internal auditors are tasked with providing assurance on the risk management, control, and governance processes of their clients, they are one of the cornerstones of effective organizational governance. Auditors provide independent, objective assessments on the appropriateness of the organization's governance structures and the operating effectiveness of specific governance activities. They are catalysts for change, advising, or advocating improvements to enhance the organization's governance structure and practices.[8]

In my experience as an auditor, trainer, and consultant, I still find that too many auditors practice the traditional form of auditing that can be described as tick and tie. Another way to describe it is adding rows and columns on spreadsheets and reports to verify their mathematical accuracy. While this is important to verify accuracy and completeness, modern internal auditing is far more complex and while it presents numerous challenges due to its very expansive nature, it also provides countless opportunities to add value in new and innovative ways, also for internal auditors to demonstrate their abilities.

Internal auditors often have college degrees and many also possess master's degrees. They often have professional certifications ranging from Certified Public Accountant (CPA), Certified Internal Auditor, Certified Information Systems Auditor, and Certified Fraud Examiner (CFE), among many others. They typically have many years of experience and have a great deal of knowledge to tap into as they examine business activities. The new role of internal audit provides many opportunities to leverage this knowledge and experience for the betterment of their organizations.

By focusing on what I consider the "other parts of the definition," internal auditors would find that they can expand and enhance their work in ways that would create a much more positive and rewarding experience with management. Furthermore, it makes for a more exciting experience as auditors would not be limited by old practices and would have the freedom and flexibility to evaluate business risks in innovative ways.

After comparing the two definitions, operational auditing and internal auditing are indeed quite similar!

The Other Parts of the Definition

While many people focus on the accounting and compliance aspects of internal auditing, the definition mentions other aspects of the trade that are not as widely embraced and practiced by auditors. By this, I mean words like "consulting," which speaks more literally to the special projects that internal auditors sometimes embark on. While the definition refers to "assurance," which refers to traditional compliance work, I believe consulting refers to more than just special projects. It also includes the way auditors do their work.

I have found that by not only thinking of consulting as special projects, but also thinking in terms of the auditors' attitude, disposition, frame of mind, and working practices, it would go a long way toward living the intentions of "and consulting activity." For example, many internal auditors focus on one-on-one interviews and scantily practice facilitated sessions, where you bring together several employees for discussion, fact finding, problem identification, brainstorming solutions, and prioritizing alternatives. Another example is not being so afraid of scope creep that auditors fail to examine the root causes of business issues sufficiently. In this book, I present numerous tips, tools, and techniques to improve the interaction with audit clients and root cause analysis, among other critical activities.

Another aspect of the definition is "… improve an organization's operations." To me these words speak volumes about the importance of not only checking processes to make sure that control activities are performed according to procedures documentation, but also looking at the risk of bottlenecks, slowdowns, rework, and other operational dysfunctions that are the result of what I consider "the other types of risks." Internal auditors have focused disproportionately on accounting and financial risks, the risk of poor recordkeeping and classification, financial abuse, and theft. But many organizations thrive or fail based on their ability to manage the risk of inefficiency, ineffectiveness, rework, and delays better than the competition. The importance of managing these dynamics does not escape the nonprofit sector, as many NGOs, academic, and government institutions are increasingly operating with reduced budgets while struggling to achieve their mission and objectives.

So what is operational auditing?[9]

Operational auditing is a future-oriented, independent, systematic, and business-focused evaluation of management, and the organization's activities controlled by management and third parties. This is done to benefit the organization's stakeholders who trust internal auditors to identify anomalies, verify that resources are handled responsibly, and that the organization is structured and operating in ways that it is likely to succeed.

The purpose of operational auditing is to improve organizational profitability and the attainment of organizational objectives. These go beyond a review of internal control issues since management does not achieve its objectives simply by adhering to satisfactory systems of internal control. Instead, management must define its goals, set appropriate strategies, staff the organization with enough and competent workers, and execute effectively.

Operational auditing also involves evaluating management's performance, since they have a fiduciary responsibility toward the organization's owners and other relevant stakeholders. Over the past few decades, the expectations of stakeholders have increased monumentally creating a more challenging environment for managers and auditors alike. These expectations range from CSR, to acting ethically, safeguarding key information, and maintaining a positive reputation.

Another important aspect of operational auditing is that rather than merely verifying that employees are performing their duties according to established policies and procedures, internal auditors also verify a variety of qualitative aspects of the organization and its activities. Regarding procedures documentation, internal auditors are expected to verify that these documents are up to date, that they are relevant, that they reflect the best way to perform the work with regards to efficiency and effectiveness, that these documents are safe from unauthorized change, they are understood by employees, and that their location is known by employees so they can refer to them for guidance when there are questions.

Operational audits may also be concerned with the structure of the organization, since a poorly structured organization, or one where information does not flow accurately and promptly jeopardizes efforts to achieve objectives. Instead, poorly structured organizations tend to be disorganized, inefficient, have high employee, customer, and vendor turnover, and become wasteful. All of these manifestations of dysfunction erode the ingredients for success and an auditor who brings a fresh and objective perspective to the review can identify these weaknesses.

In the end, operational auditing is designed to evaluate the effectiveness and efficiency of business activities, processes, programs, functions, and units. The scope may be different from traditional fiscal-year scope periods, since achieving these objectives may require an analysis of multiple time periods to identify, analyze, and understand trends, patterns, outliers, and other positive or negative dynamics of interest.

These other risks are of importance to internal auditors, since our definition indicates that we are responsible for risk management, as stated in Standards 2010 (Planning), 2100 (Nature of Work), and especially 2120 (Risk Management).

The Risk-Based Audit

Engaging in risk-based auditing means that internal auditors must exercise and apply a broader view of organizational risks. Accounting and financial risks are only a limited number of the many risks organizations face. Other examples include the risk of delays, waste, inefficiency, poor customer service, excessive customer and employee turnover, poor quality data, and system failures. Although these risks actually characterize the working environments in many organizations, and affected employees readily describe the impact these risks have on profitability and the organization's ability to succeed, many auditors fail to identify, measure, and assess sufficiently the mechanisms in place to mitigate those risks.

Some organizations have come a long way in their attempts to correct this deficiency, such as hiring auditors with more diverse backgrounds. Over the past decade, I have met many auditors with diverse academic and professional backgrounds, such as engineering, nursing, geology, and biology degrees and backgrounds, among others. While hiring auditors without auditing experience poses some training challenges, it helps to bring into the unit a diversity of skills and mindsets that enriches the department and provides valuable insights into other risks affecting the organization. Furthermore, the drive to achieve diversity provides a competitive edge for the profession as we broaden our recruitment efforts and thrive to make sure that every auditor individually, and internal audit departments collectively, possess the knowledge and proficiency to perform their duties.

While traditionalists may find this expansion of auditor backgrounds puzzling, it is consistent with the guidance provided by the IIA. The IIA is the governing body of internal auditors worldwide. Founded in 1941, it counts more than 180,000 members in 180 countries[10] and has issued guidance for internal auditors in the form of the Standards for the Professional Practice of Internal Auditing (the *Standards*), Practice Advisories, Practice Guides, and Position Papers. These documents provide guidance on what internal auditors should do, and how.[11]

This concept of risk-based auditing is in contrast to what has been dubbed controls-based auditing. The latter is defined as audits that focus on identifying and evaluating internal controls without enough regard to their value to the process. This can happen because auditors take a preexisting work program without researching the nuances of the present audit scope sufficiently or even when they perform planning activities, their interviews and other research only focuses on identifying existing controls without fully understanding the key risks and objectives of the process under review.

Even when auditors perform interviews and walkthroughs, they could allow their accounting bias to steer the questions they ask and the documents they request for examination. When performing controls-based audits, the auditor then listens and searches for references to controls with the intention of verifying their existence and effectiveness. In effect, they are testing the controls in relative isolation, without fully understanding their connection to the underlying objectives and risks of the process or program under review.

Performing risk-based audits requires more brainstorming, more interactions with process owners, a more in-depth understanding of the organization's business, and a mechanism to address past, present, and future vulnerabilities and scenarios that threaten the achievement of business objectives. Since internal auditors are being asked to do more with less, they can't afford to review controls just because they are there. Internal auditors need to assess whether those controls are key to the achievement of objectives and only focus on those that are.

The IIA's publication on the 2015 Common Body of Knowledge (CBOK) global survey is entitled "Driving Success in a Changing World: 10 Imperatives for Internal Audit" and it confirms that the internal audit profession is making substantial progress in making itself relevant to business overall. There is still reference to the expectation gap between what stakeholders consider to be of value and what the internal audit function is delivering. But more than half of respondents now state that their activities are fully or mostly aligned with the strategic plan of their organization.

Chief Audit Executives (CAEs) report they will focus almost as much on strategic business risks (70%) as operational risks (72%). This shows the continued and fundamental shift away from the traditional approach of focusing on accounting/financial controls and instead moving closer to the review of the organization's primary objectives.

The report advises internal auditors to anticipate the needs of stakeholders, develop forward-looking risk management practices, and support the business objectives, identify, monitor, and deal with emerging technology risks and enhance audit findings through the greater use of data analytics. But the report also shows that many organizations are still struggling. In part this is because the environment in which they work is constantly changing; new regulations are constantly legislated and new risks evolve as the world itself evolves, particularly the world of data and technology.

Auditing Beyond Accounting, Financial, and Regulatory Requirements

With all of these matters in mind, it behooves internal auditors to look beyond traditional accounting, financial, and regulatory requirements. In the past, internal auditors predominantly had accounting degrees, graduated from university accounting programs, generally were recruited from external public accounting audit firms, and held CPA certifications. As such, their focus and experience was acquired in the accounting field and saw most audit matters through the prism of accounting requirements.

The other key focus area was compliance with regulatory requirements. In this case, auditors adopted a fairly binary approach to audits by attempting to understand the rules and regulations affecting a program or process. They then would apply a very effective methodology: Are they doing what the rulebook says? If "Yes," the test results were satisfactory. If "No," the results were documented and communicated as findings. In essence, a very predictable pass/fail approach to auditing. For many years, this became the standard operating practice of auditors and even today, some audits require a similar approach due to their regulatory and compliance focus, but we must be careful not to default to this approach when the expectation is broader.

Over time, business leaders and managers witnessed business failures caused by poor management decisions and practices. By poor management, I am referring to inadequate:

- *Operations management.* Some of the related issues are waste, inefficiencies, supplies that arrive late, poor customer satisfaction, and limited capacity to grow as opportunities arise or customers' demands change.
- *Human resources.* As evidenced by poorly supervised, trained, and evaluated employees who sometimes become unmotivated and unproductive.
- *IT.* Computer systems designed with an inaccurate understanding of the business needs and uses of these systems, poor data capture, and inadequate reporting mechanisms.
- *Marketing.* Mass marketing of products and services at a time when customers prefer to feel unique, or wasteful campaigns because they target the wrong audience.
- *CSR.* Issues range from child labor, sweatshop conditions, abusive management, and inappropriate waste disposal.
- Environmental Health and Safety (EHS) practices and conditions related to poor ventilation, excessive heat, extreme noise levels, and workplace hazards caused by chemicals, machinery, and workplace configurations, among others.

Another catalyst enhancing the role of internal auditors and moving it beyond compliance is the increase in stakeholder demands for advisory and consulting activities. Discussions within the

IIA to determine the nature of these activities, whether internal auditors should perform such activities, and to what extent they should allocate resources for this purpose, began in earnest in the 1990s. In many ways, the debate continues today.

By this, I am not suggesting that compliance is a failed effort, or that it does not provide some benefits. It does. Some of the benefits include process improvement, better controlled operations, greater reliability and protection of information, more stable, and predictable process.

The result in many ways is better integration of IT with the business, a greater understanding of the critical nature of management and IT functions and controls, higher funding and resources to improve information capture, analysis, use and security, and a reconsideration of outsourced business and IT functions with a number of companies bringing some of those responsibilities back in-house.

Advisory and consulting engagements are performed to take advantage of internal auditors' broad skillset and experience. Auditors have the unique ability to identify process improvement opportunities without sacrificing the control environment, assess how the related transactions are performed, and determine how risks affect them. Whether performing assurance or consulting activities, internal auditors are expected to act with independence and objectivity, and exercise proficiency and due professional care. High levels of financial, accounting, IT, management, and business analysis skills are typically required to perform these reviews.

The emergence of the conglomerate in the 1970s and the multinational corporation (MNC) in the 1980s has increased the size, reach, and complexity of many organizations. Outsourcing portions of company operations has become commonplace, as is responding to various risks through derivatives and contracting arrangements. Owning companies unrelated to the core business to diversify the revenue stream and being required to meet a plethora of ever-increasing performance expectations and regulatory requirements has become commonplace. The result is that what was a relatively straightforward logistics, supply chain, or treasury audit in the past is now a very complex endeavor involving multiple locations, languages, currencies, regulations, and computer systems.

In light of these dynamics, internal auditors have risen to the challenge by embracing a methodology that goes beyond accounting and more closely aligns itself with the recurring business risks and practices.

The Value Auditors Provide

Internal auditors are unfortunately not always regarded as highly as they should be. Seen as an obstacle, too many managers and employees fail to recognize that internal auditors provide a very valuable service to their clients—whether they are employees of the firm, or hired externally to provide internal audit services.

Internal auditors promote the efficient and effective use of resources. Since organizations operate with the funding received or authorized by their owners or contributors, it is imperative that the organization operates with this principle of financial fiduciary responsibility. The Cornell University Law School Legal Information Institute defines fiduciary responsibility as follows:

> A fiduciary duty is a legal duty to act solely in another party's interests. Parties owing this duty are called fiduciaries. The individuals to whom they owe a duty are called principals. Fiduciaries may not profit from their relationship with their principals unless they have the principals' express informed consent. They also have a duty to

avoid any conflicts of interest between themselves and their principals or between their principals and the fiduciaries' other clients.[12]

Recognition of the duties that all employees have to the principals is central to the proper discharge of their responsibilities as employees, who should always act in the interests of the main stakeholders of the organization. To this effect, internal auditors contribute to this process by making sure that these duties are defined, that structures are set to ensure behaviors are aligned with these objectives, and making recommendations to the board and senior management when there are discrepancies jeopardizing the success of these arrangements.

In the aggregate, internal auditors serve the public and common interests by making sure that owners receive the return on their investments that they are entitled to, and that the means of generating those profits are within the confines of the law. Beyond shareholders, however, internal auditors help the process of making sure that the interests of all relevant stakeholders are met. Stakeholders can be categorized as economic/primary and noneconomic/secondary.

Economic or market stakeholders are characterized by having a monetary exchange between them. They engage in transactions with the company as it carries out its primary purpose of providing society with goods and services. Consequently, employees, customers, creditors, and suppliers are economic stakeholders. They are sometimes referred to as primary stakeholders as well, because they are critical to the company's existence and activities (Figure 1.1).

A business's relationships go beyond those primary involvements to others. Secondary interactions occur when other individuals and groups show an interest in or concern about the activities of the organization. Noneconomic, nonmarket, or secondary stakeholders are people, groups, or organizations that though not engaging in direct economic exchange with the firm, are affected by or can affect its primary activities and decisions. The list includes communities, the general public, governments, social activist groups, the media, and business support groups (Figure 1.2).

An important aspect of the modern manager and auditor's job is to identify relevant stakeholders and to understand their interests. It is also important to understand the power they

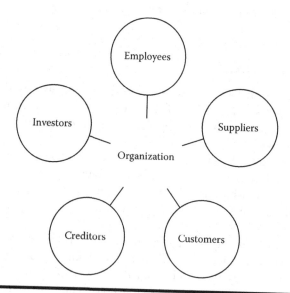

Figure 1.1 Primary (economic) stakeholders.

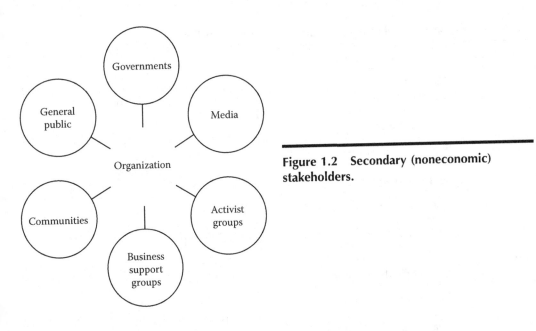

Figure 1.2   Secondary (noneconomic) stakeholders.

have to assert these interests. This process is called stakeholder analysis, which asks three fundamental questions:

1. Who are the relevant stakeholders?
2. What are the interests of each stakeholder?
3. What is the power of each stakeholder?

Since stakeholders refer to persons or groups that affect, or are affected by an organization's decisions, policies, and operations, it is important to identify those parties and document their interests. If stakeholders can facilitate the attainment of objectives, or make decisions regarding resources, it is imperative that auditors understand their role and influence. Since various stakeholders may have varying amounts and forms of power, it is also important to determine what influence they have and how the organization can make sure relations are positive and productive. Stakeholder power is the ability to use resources to make an event happen or to secure a desired outcome. In general, stakeholder power can be categorized as political power, voting power, economic power, and legal power. Mismanaging any aspect of this relationship can stymie the achievement of strategic, operational, compliance, and reporting objectives (Tables 1.1 and 1.2).

Conducting a stakeholder analysis is an important aspect of modern internal auditing, because it gives the auditor an appreciation for the various parties interested in the outputs and outcomes of the organization, its programs and related processes. Organizations are increasingly finding themselves mired in controversy because they didn't anticipate, or properly manage the expectations of these diverse constituencies. To the extent that internal auditors can help management identify, plan for, and respond effectively to the primary and secondary stakeholders, the organization will encounter less pushback and it will likely be able to operate with fewer disruptions. In addition, during the planning phase of any audit, planners should identify the internal and external stakeholders involved to make sure they seek their input as to what their objectives, concerns, and plans are for the area audited. This will result in more effective and value-added reviews.

Table 1.1   Primary Stakeholders, Nature of Interest, and Power

Stakeholder	Interest	Power
Employees	Maintain stable employment Receive fair pay Work in a safe, comfortable environment	Bargaining power Work actions, strikes, and lawsuits Publicity
Suppliers	Receive regular orders for goods/ services Be paid promptly	Refusing to meet orders Supplying to competitors
Customers	Receive value and quality for money Receive safe, reliable products	Purchasing from competitors Boycotting Refusing to pay
Creditors	Receive repayment of loans Collect debts and interest	Calling loans Use legal authorities to repossess assets
Investors	Receive a satisfactory return on investments Realize an appreciation in value	Exercise voting rights Ability to inspect company records and reports

Source: Adapted from Lawrence, A. T., Weber, J., and Post, J. E. 2011. *Business and Society: Stakeholders, Ethics, Public Policy* (11th ed.). Boston: McGraw-Hill Irwin.

Table 1.2   Secondary Stakeholders, Nature of Interest, and Power

Stakeholder	Interest	Power
Governments	Promote economic development Raise revenues through taxes	Adopting regulations and laws Issuing licenses and permits
Media	Keep the public informed Monitor company actions	Publicizing events that affect the public
Activist groups	Monitor company actions for ethical and legal behavior	Lobbying government for regulations Gaining public support
Business support groups	Provide research and information to improve competitiveness	Using staff/resources to help companies Providing legal political support
Communities	Employ local residents Ensure local development	Issuing/restricting operating licenses Lobbying government for regulations
General public	Minimize risks Achieve prosperity for society	Supporting activists Pressing government to act Praising or condemning companies

Source: Adapted from Lawrence, A. T., Weber, J., and Post, J. E. 2011. *Business and Society: Stakeholders, Ethics, Public Policy* (11th ed.). Boston: McGraw-Hill Irwin.

Identifying Operational Threats and Vulnerabilities

The traditional approach to internal auditing was to perform postmortem reviews to verify that what was done was done appropriately. This was a practice that followed in the footsteps of public accounting firms, which inspect transactions that occurred during the preceding fiscal year. Internal auditors need to go beyond inspecting transactions long after they were performed because the focus now leans toward an examination of future threats and vulnerabilities that can derail the organization's goals and objectives in the short, medium, and even the long term. In fact, focusing on future events and the future implications of present events would add more value to their organizations than reporting primarily on past events. When this happens, as has been common practice in the past, the organization dedicates itself on correcting past issues, which creates rework.

These future-oriented threats and vulnerabilities can be

Operational, such as maintaining operational capacity, speed of execution (i.e., cycle time), staffing levels, employee motivation, knowledge transfer, system development, and implementation

Technological, including protection of intellectual property and personally identifiable information, denial of service attacks, business continuity due to staff turnover, and system development

Strategic, referring to concerns related to strong customer and vendor relations, customer loyalty, building effective business partnerships, outsourcing arrangements, and mergers and acquisitions

Environmental, which may include reliable supply of water and electricity, achieving a lower carbon footprint, and reducing the amount of natural resources used during business activities

These threats and vulnerabilities can be evaluated in the medium and long terms, but also beyond the national borders of the organization's country of operations. As such, internal auditors are engaged in international auditing, evaluating home office and host country dynamics, finding out if local laws exist, whether they are enforced and how, and which requirements supersede which, if applicable. Even political issues, social unrest, and demographic shifts are of importance to today's auditors, since any of these changes can affect their organizations and their ability to achieve their objectives economically and in timely fashion.

All of these dynamics requires internal auditors to take a more futuristic view of their roles, be informed about dynamics in their industries, countries, and regions, and not only the microcosm of their organizations as they may have been doing in the past. The IIA's 2015 Global Pulse of Internal Audit, Embracing Opportunities in a Dynamic Environment states "The mandate to address emerging and evolving risks is clear. Risks are emerging at an unprecedented pace, and stakeholders' impatience with surprises is evident." (p. 8). The implications of this statement are profound. Internal auditors can no longer be content with reviewing the accuracy, completeness, and authorization of compliance and financial transactions. It is no longer enough to audit from the perspective of stated controls "ticking and tying" transactions from one source to a recorded entry, but most apply a far more dynamic and insightful methodology—one that is risk based.

The Skills Required for Effective Operational Audits

The paradigm shift in the work of internal auditing from being controls-based to risk based means that internal auditors must acquire and apply different skills to their trade from what they did in the past. Auditors must examine risk exposures and the measures in place to address more than accounting and financial risks. So what skills are helpful?

According to the IIA Research Foundation Core Competencies Report, the following are the top general competencies of internal auditors:

1. Communication skills, such as oral, written, report writing, and presentation skills
2. Problem identification and solution skills, such as conceptual and analytical thinking
3. Ability to promote the value of internal audit
4. Knowledge of industry, regulatory, and standards changes
5. Organization skills
6. Conflict resolution/negotiation skills
7. Staff training and development
8. Accounting frameworks, tools, and techniques
9. Change management skills
10. IT/CT[13] framework, tools, and techniques
11. Cultural fluency and foreign language skills

The three common core competencies identified in the report are communication skills, problem identification and solution skills, and keeping up to date with industry and regulatory changes and professional standards. These results highlight the importance of individual and team competencies and the role they play in team effectiveness.

In terms of behavioral skills, internal auditors should possess the following skills:

- Confidentiality
- Objectivity
- Communication
- Judgment
- Work well with all management levels
- Possess governance and ethics sensitivity
- Be team players
- Relationship building
- Work independently
- Team building
- Leadership
- Influence
- Facilitation
- Staff management
- Change catalyst skills[14]

How to acquire these skills should be done along two dimensions. One at the individual level and the other at the internal audit unit level.

At the individual level, internal auditors, like most professionals today, are expected to take ownership of their own training and development and not leave it to their employers to decide and implement. Whereas, in the past, it was common for employees to take a passive approach, waiting for their employers to tell them when, what, and why training would occur, today's auditors should take a more active and engaged approach to their training needs. They should

1. Reflect on their present competencies, identify their job needs, and perform a gap analysis to meet their current skill requirements
2. Define their career ambitions and chart a roadmap to acquire the skills and competencies needed in the future

Internal auditors should balance their training activities so they not only enhance their technical skills, but also their soft skills. I believe the term soft skills is a misnomer because they are as important as technical skills. In fact, they can be more important as anyone who has worked with a technically exceptional individual who can't explain what he is doing, did or plans to do, and why, knows.

Communication skills are also essential not only as it relates to fellow auditors, but also process owners and operators. All too often, internal auditors are unable to explain their activities, the reasons for testing certain items, or the implications of their findings to nonauditors. This inability to explain matters clearly diminishes the impact of their findings and the persuasiveness of their recommendations. This fact is supported by KPMG's Seeking Value through Internal Audit report which polled audit committee chairs and chief financial officers (CFOs). The report states that internal audit needs to improve communication skills (67%) and technology skills (62%).

At the internal audit unit level, the department should perform a skills analysis to identify their present skill repertoire, and those needed to perform audit and other reviews competently in the next 3–7 years. Organizations are increasingly performing multiyear risk plans to make sure their work is synchronized with the organization's strategic initiatives. This is a great opportunity to expand the identification of future work, but also determine how prepared the department is to meet those challenges.

The IIA Research Foundation Internal Audit Capability Model (IA-CM) can be used to assess the internal audit department's current condition and also as a visioning tool, helping to draft the course and expectations for the internal auditing function. The 5-level framework identifies conditions and practices that internal auditors should review, and use as a roadmap for continuous improvement from Level 1- Ad Hoc/Initial to Level 5—Optimizing/Change Agent (Table 1.3).

Integrated Auditing

Business changes, resources change, and risks change, so both operations and IT must adapt and continually improve to support the business and mitigate risks to acceptable levels.

Another important development over the past decades is the emergence of integrated auditing as a type of audit. These are characterized by the simultaneous inclusion of business and IT subjects in the review. Whereas in the past traditional auditors would perform a review of accounting/financial controls, and IT auditors would perform their assessment of IT risks and controls separately, during the 1990s this new practice, commonly referred to as integrated auditing, emerged.

Table 1.3   Internal Audit Capability Model (IA-CM)

Level	*Characteristics*
Level 5: Optimizing	Internal auditing recognized as a change agent Internal audit is recognized as a key change agent, continuously improving its professional practices, integrating performance data, global leading practices, and feedback to continuously strengthen the unit and the organization. It plans its workforce needs strategically and maintains effective ongoing relationships with other units within the organization to understand the organization's strategic directions, emerging issues, and risks
Level 4: Managed	Overall assurance on governance, risk management, and control Internal audit provides overall assurance on governance, risk management and control, contributes to the development of the organization's management, supports professional bodies, has a planning mechanism for its workforce, and uses quantitative and qualitative metrics. It coordinates its activities to be sufficiently comprehensive and provide reasonable assurance at a corporate level that GRC processes are adequate and functioning as intended to meet the organization's objectives
Level 3: Integrated	Advisory services Internal audit provides guidance and advice to management. These advisory services add value without the auditor assuming management responsibility. These services are directed toward facilitation rather than assurance and include training, system development reviews, performance and control self-assessment (CSA), and counseling. Internal audit focuses on team building and competency, developing a professionally qualified staff and effective workforce coordination within the unit and with other review groups. It uses output performance measures and tracks cost information. Internal audit is an integral component of the organization's management team
Level 2: Infrastructure	Compliance auditing The internal audit function focuses on compliance audits, which evaluate conformity and adherence with internal policies, laws, regulations, contracts, and other agreements or requirements that preside over the activities and goals of the area, process, or system being audited
Level 1: Initial	Ad hoc/isolated audits The internal audit function is unstructured and operates in an ad hoc manner. It performs isolated audits primarily examining documents and transactions for accuracy and compliance. The audit team is often part of a separate organizational unit with no established capabilities or infrastructure to support the function.

Source: Adapted from the 2009 IIARF Internal Audit Capability Model (IA-CM) for the Public Sector.

As we examine the approach employed by public accountants, their focus was centered on financial assertions, such as occurrence, completeness, accuracy, classification, existence, and valuation of accounting, and financial information, as inputs for the organization's financial statements. It is important to remember the key objectives of financial audits:

- Ascertain whether in all material respects, the income statement and the statement of cash flows accurately and reliably reflect the activities during the fiscal year
- Ascertain whether in all material respects, the balance sheet shows the condition of the organization as of the last day of the fiscal year

At the other end of the spectrum, we can place highly technical IT reviews, involving matters like database configuration and security, user authentication, operating system reliability, and network perimeter security. Between these two extremes, we can place IT general controls, such as physical security and environmental controls, backup procedures, user authorization, business process controls surrounding reconciliations, and exception reporting. Other areas of focus include production and change management, disaster preparedness and recovery, and business continuity.

This dynamic can best be shown as in Figure 1.3.

Financial and operational auditors are increasingly expanding their focus and incorporating IT applications and general IT topics in their reviews. Conversely, IT auditors, who have traditionally focused on IT technical subjects including general and application matters, are increasingly widening their view and including operational and financial elements to their review. This means that operational and financial auditors need to know the systems in use, and IT auditors need to know the business and how it uses the systems in place.

This approach is a refreshing departure from the previous practice of conducting financial audits, operational audits, and IT audits, all separate and at different points in time, of the same unit. This antiquated approach was disruptive to the organization, costlier due to the repeated reviews by different audit groups, and when communicating results, it did not provide a comprehensive view that linked process, finance, and IT in one audit report.

Furthermore, over time it became apparent that accounting/financial controls are increasingly dependent on computer systems. For example, exception reports, which identify transactions that do not meet preestablished criteria, are the result of a computer algorithm that defines rules. When these rules are not met, the transactions are noted on these reports for review and resolution. If traditional internal auditors don't understand the exception rules, and don't know how to review the code in the system to verify its accuracy, the reliance placed on the exception report could be misplaced.

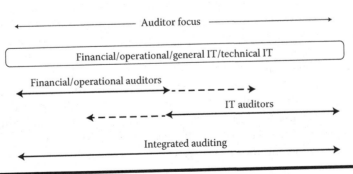

Figure 1.3 Integrated auditing.

Another example has to do with reports and reconciliations. As noted above, if the algorithm in the computer systems is not understood, and the procedures to check it are unknown, how can anyone rely on these reports? Both members of management and internal auditors could be relying on system-generated reports that contain unknown errors. If the auditors don't know how to review the underlying computer code, they could be signing off on faulty information, which would negatively affect the assurance they are supposed to provide to the board and management.

So, integrated audits are designed to address IT questions while simultaneously examining the business dynamics. In small organizations, it was, and may still be possible in some cases, to have individual auditors who have the depth of knowledge to examine both the accounting/financial and the IT aspects of business operations. As organizations grow in size and complexity, it is more common today to achieve integrated audits through team composition. These reviews require coordination so that auditors work from a single risk matrix that identifies all relevant objectives, risks, controls, and audit steps, the related documentation crosses over smoothly and the resulting report is comprehensive in its coverage of operational, financial, and IT subject areas.

The Standards

The IIA, which is the governing body of internal auditors worldwide, provides guidance for internal auditors on what should be done, how it should be done, and why. Adhering to the International Standards for the Professional Practice of Internal Auditing (*Standards*) is mandatory, while following the guidance provided in the Practice Advisories and Practice Guides is highly recommended and encouraged.[15] I have found these documents quite insightful and following their directives has enabled me perform numerous audits over the years with very positive client feedback. I have also learned that beyond the words and what the *Standards* state, it has been very beneficial to understand why these standards are in place.

The following passages and related commentary represent a selection of standards relevant to operational auditing and reflections on my experience implementing them in my work.

> *1210—Proficiency Internal auditors must possess the knowledge, skills, and other competencies needed to perform their individual responsibilities. The internal audit activity collectively must possess or obtain the knowledge, skills, and other competencies needed to perform its responsibilities.*

Internal audit is not a static profession, but rather one where its practitioners must remain proficient in terms of knowledge and skill to perform their duties effectively. Being qualified upon hire is one thing. Internal auditors must make sure they remain qualified throughout their career. This of course is a big challenge because business dynamics are constantly changing, but there is no alternative and we must keep up with the changes affecting our organizations. Internal auditors must adopt a learning mindset, continue to educate themselves, and stay up to date.

One of the greatest assets auditors have is their credibility. They earn this by delivering consistently accurate, useful, and timely communications that incorporate insightful opinions and recommendations when appropriate. Credibility cannot be achieved if the auditor lacks knowledge about the organization and the linkages between the issues noted, the causes of these issues, and an appreciation for the priorities and challenges of the organization. A deep understanding of the organization will make it possible to also understand the context in which issues are occurring.

This in turn will help to formulate pragmatic and business-appropriate recommendations that get to the root cause of the issues identified.

This knowledge base is important at the individual auditor level and at the department level. When there are skill deficiencies, the CAE must take action to recruit, train, and develop the auditors in the department so individually and collectively they have the ability to perform high quality reviews.

> *1210.A3—Internal auditors must have sufficient knowledge of key IT risks and controls and available technology-based audit techniques to perform their assigned work. However, not all internal auditors are expected to have the expertise of an internal auditor whose primary responsibility is IT auditing.*

> *1220.A2—In exercising due professional care internal auditors must consider the use of technology-based audit and other data analysis techniques.*

Organizations are increasingly relying on computer systems to capture, manipulate, and interpret data that helps guide them toward the achievement of their objectives. This means that internal auditors need to know how these computer systems are configured and operating to ensure accuracy and protection of the underlying data. It is also essential that the financial and nonfinancial reports generated from these systems be reliable. Furthermore, internal auditors must also know how to use technology-based audit techniques to better understand and evaluate the large volumes of data collected, how it is manipulated, and how the resulting information is disseminated to relevant stakeholders.

Using these technology-based audit techniques allows auditors to examine very large amounts of data that would be impossible or unfeasible to do manually. This is often referred to as computer-assisted audit tools and techniques (CAATTs). Those who have adopted this practice often reduce the amount of time and effort it takes to evaluate these large volumes of data as they automate the audit process. There are many tools available for auditor use, including ACL, IDEA®, Minitab, SAS, and many others. Microsoft Excel and Access are also very capable tools for a wide variety of tests.

These computer programs allow auditors to extract and analyze large volumes of information and build conclusions based on the entire population, instead of a limited sample of the population. This avoids the challenges of building conclusions based on a limited sample of the population.

Another important aspect of technology-based techniques is the use of electronic workpaper packages for workpaper and project management, document retention, and team collaboration. There are many benefits to keeping a centralized repository of audit workpapers. These include ease of storage and retrieval of current and past workpapers, backups of the documents, remote access, coordination among team members, and standardization of forms and procedures. Some commonly used tools include Teammate, Magique Galileo, Compliance 360, and Auditor Assistant.[16]

Acquiring these skills should commence upon hire and it applies to auditors of all specialties, not only IT auditors.

> *1220.A3—Internal auditors must be alert to the significant risks that might affect objectives, operations, or resources. However, assurance procedures alone, even when performed with due professional care, do not guarantee that all significant risks will be identified.*

While performing risk-based auditing, internal auditors must remember that the focus of their work is not limited to assurance considerations unless it is mandated as such, or the scope of the audit is defined that way specifically. Otherwise, reviews must also include the operational aspects of the program, process, or organization being examined. Success can be measured using a variety of criteria and success is not achieved only by meeting compliance expectations.

There are many organizations that experienced financial hardship, up to the point of bankruptcy, even though they adhered to generally accepted accounting principles and compliance requirements. This failure can be gradual or sudden and can happen in the short term or over a long period of time. General Motors, Chrysler, BlackBerry, CIT Group, Lehman Brothers, Kmart, Eastman Kodak, and Delphi are only a few examples of organizations whose difficulties were not due to compliance failures per se, but rather the poor management of operational and strategic risks.

> *2010—Planning. The CAE must establish a risk-based plan to determine the priorities of the internal audit activity, consistent with the organization's goals.*

The internal audit department's audit plan, which identifies the audits that will be performed by the internal audit function, must be based on the identification and measurement of risks to the organization. In the past, many internal audit departments developed and executed audit plans that followed other criteria and were characterized by cyclical and often repetitive reviews. Sometimes these audits were not the most needed based on past issues or organizational priorities, but were seen as safe and consistent with what internal auditors traditionally examined.

The result is that the auditors performed "safe" audits repeatedly, like expense reports, petty cash, accounts payable, and accounts receivable, which are not a bad idea in and of themselves. But I have witnessed cases where these same auditors had never examined key IT activities and IT development projects, bonus payouts, marketing activities, construction projects, treasury activities, customer fulfillment cycle times, and the management of outsourced activities, which represented far higher risks to the organization.

> *2120—Risk management. The internal audit activity must evaluate the effectiveness and contribute to the improvement of risk management processes.*

> By auditing what matters most, the limited resources available will be spent more wisely and the communications resulting from those reviews will be far more valuable to the board and management.

Among the responsibilities of the board and management is establishing a mechanism to identify, measure, and determine the best way to respond to relevant risks to the organization. Internal auditors for their part, should ascertain to what degree this mechanism and its underlying processes are effective. This assessment relies heavily on the determination that the organization's vision and mission are clear, provide a sense of direction, and are supported by the organization's structure and objectives. Also that significant risks are identified and assessed, and appropriate risk responses are selected that align risks with the organization's risk appetite.

There are very specific roles presented here that I want to reiterate: the board and management establish the structure and mechanism of the risk management processes, while internal audit evaluates, verifies the degree of effectiveness, and recommends improvements where appropriate.

A large number of organizations do not have risk management processes in place, and many that do, experience limited success with them. It behooves all involved to take action in this regard.

2120.A1—The internal audit activity must evaluate risk exposures relating to the organization's governance, operations, and information systems regarding the:

- *Achievement of the organization's strategic objectives*
- *Reliability and integrity of financial and operational information*
- *Effectiveness and efficiency of operations and programs*
- *Safeguarding of assets*
- *Compliance with laws, regulations, policies, procedures, and contracts*

2130.A1—The internal audit activity must evaluate the adequacy and effectiveness of controls in responding to risks within the organization's governance, operations, and information systems regarding the:

- *Achievement of the organization's strategic objectives*
- *Reliability and integrity of financial and operational information*
- *Effectiveness and efficiency of operations and programs*
- *Safeguarding of assets*
- *Compliance with laws, regulations, policies, procedures, and contracts*

I mention these two *Standards* together because they address areas of focus related to risk exposures (2120.A1) and controls (2130.A1), and share similar language. The focus of the internal audit activity is broad and complex. It must evaluate risk exposures related to the organization's governance, risk management, and compliance infrastructure, the design and function of its operations, and the reliability of its IT infrastructure. All of these elements must also be examined in relation to the organizations':

- *Strategy.* Organizations should have a plan of action, related policies, and a suitable structure so they increase the likelihood of achieving their mission and see their vision become reality.
- *Financial and operational information.* The quality of financial information has received a great deal of attention from external and internal auditors alike for many years. However, opportunities generally abound when it comes to operational information where I often find that it is insufficient, unreliable, or too generalized to provide the level of insight that managers and their staff need. Other common issues include the limited ability to generate needed reports from computer systems and the excessive restrictions on access to information, well beyond what segregation of duty considerations might dictate. This in many ways explain why so many organizations still rely disproportionately on spreadsheets to run the organization even though they spend heavily buying, configuring, deploying, and maintaining ERP systems.
- *Effectiveness and efficiency.* While most auditors perform tests to determine levels of accuracy, completeness, classification, and valuation of transactions, not enough emphasis has been given to the organization's ability to achieve its objectives (i.e., effectiveness). In fact, many organizations lack clearly stated, cascading, and interrelated objectives that begin at the enterprise level, and are sufficiently linked downward through the business unit, department, and process, and down to the individual level. On the other hand, efficiency has received limited coverage over the years from internal auditors, whose focus has been on

compliance and financial risks resulting in few findings that target long cycle times, waste, redundancies, bureaucracy, and rework.

■ *Safeguarding of assets.* External and internal auditors routinely examine the purchase, use, safeguarding, valuation, depreciation, and disposal of assets. In fact, for many auditors reviewing the existence, condition and accounting of land, buildings, machinery, vehicles, and inventory is part of every year's annual plan and these items receive the scrutiny they deserve. What may be also important to examine is whether there are other assets that have not received sufficient attention. For example, the expression "people are our greatest asset" has reached the level of being a cliché, but is true for many organizations. In fact, the knowledge, work discipline, creativity, motivation, and collaboration displayed by employees become the key wealth generator in many organizations. So we should ask ourselves, have we examined human resources from that perspective?

■ *Compliance.* I have already expounded on the pivotal role that compliance has had on the internal audit profession and this aspect of our role will remain important indefinitely. But when we consider compliance we should also pay close attention to the complexities that modern day organizations are exposed to. I am referring for example to cosourcing and outsourcing and the fact that this raises liability issues, performance management, and the safeguarding of data and personnel. Personal and data protection are becoming increasingly important as otherwise strangers have physical and logical access to data, facilities, assets, customers, and vendors.

The following are some questions to illustrate the complexities of modern day compliance:

– How do we know if these third parties are themselves further outsourcing our data and work?
– Are their values aligned with ours so there are no unethical practices in place?
– How exactly do they screen their employees before they begin working on our account?
– How quickly would they notify us if they experience financial or other forms of hardship so we are not surprised by business disruptions?
– Are they billing us accurately for the work they are doing?

2130—Control. The internal audit activity must assist the organization in maintaining effective controls by evaluating their effectiveness and efficiency and by promoting continuous improvement.

While internal auditors have focused on internal controls for decades, the IIA states that internal auditors must assist their organizations in maintaining effective controls. This means first of all, that the board and management own the internal controls and internal auditors assist them by verifying that the controls are effective. In addition, this standard also indicates that internal auditors should go beyond the effectiveness of these controls, but also examine their efficiency. In other words, avoid wasted resources, time, or effort while performing the control activity. Lastly, and in regard to promoting continuous improvement, while examining the current situation is pertinent, internal auditors must also help management embrace the practice of continuous improvement to always search for faster, cheaper, and better ways of performing control activities.

Because an action was effective in the past, it does not mean that it will continue to be effective in the future. In fact, stubbornly maintaining the status quo when conditions warrant modification can be costly and impair future success.

2201—Planning considerations In planning the engagement, internal auditors must consider:

■ *The objectives of the activity being reviewed and the means by which the activity controls its performance*
■ *The significant risks to the activity, its objectives, resources, and operations and the means by which the potential impact of risk is kept to an acceptable level*

This standard is one of my favorites. It states that while planning engagements we must consider the objectives of the entity, program, or process being audited and how management controls its performance, as well as the risk management procedures in place. Over the years, I have found that

■ A large number of employees have unclear or unknown objectives
■ The programs and processes they work in also lack clear objectives
■ When there are objectives, there are often few if any metrics in place to gauge the achievement of these objectives
■ Risk identification, assessment, and management procedures are limited or nonexistent, so there is no clear mechanisms to ascertain what the organization does to keep these risks at an acceptable level

Given these gaps, internal auditors have many opportunities to add value to their organizations while they work on meeting the requirements of this standard.

2220.A1—The scope of the engagement must include consideration of relevant systems, records, personnel, and physical properties, including those under the control of third parties.

When engaged in business reviews, internal auditors are encouraged to

■ Incorporate the elements of integrated auditing so auditors apply a holistic view during their work
■ Evaluate the people, processes, and technology relevant to the review being performed, and, examine third parties' systems, records, personnel, and properties under their control

These requirements are a reflection of the highly important role that outsourcing and co-sourcing have had on organizations over the last several decades, and that from all appearances will continue well into the future.

2310—Identifying information Internal auditors must identify sufficient, reliable, relevant, and useful information to achieve the engagement's objectives.

Internal auditors collect, analyze, and interpret data to prove/disprove hypotheses regarding the design and function of processes and systems as they relate to the achievement of objectives, and the effectiveness of risk management procedures. Internal auditors must also communicate their conclusions and this requires that their communications be persuasive. To accomplish this, communications must meet the requirements of

■ *Sufficiency.* This means that the auditor needs enough information, including quantifiable facts and figures.

- *Reliability.* Meaning that the information must be trustworthy and free from distortion.
- *Relevance.* This relates to the information being consistent with the objectives and scope of the review.
- *Usefulness.* This relates to the information helping the organization accomplish its objectives.

Quite often, when clients express confusion, disagreement, or skepticism about the internal auditors' communication, it is because the auditor has not met one or more of these four attributes.

> *2330—Documenting information. Internal auditors must document relevant information to support the conclusions and engagement results*

Internal auditors must make sure that in all aspects of their work, they base their conclusions and support their communications with facts. The rigor of their data collection activities, the sophistication of their analysis, and the maintenance of detailed records of the items examined and procedures performed, will increase the likelihood that management will accept the observations presented and be more inclined to accept the recommendations made. Any shortcuts are at the auditors' peril.

While intuition can be helpful in many situations, it can be a very problematic ingredient in the auditors' toolbox if it is not supported by facts and explainable procedures. All conclusion and results must be substantiated and referenced in the corresponding workpapers or the auditor's work could be in question.

> *2410.A2—Internal auditors are encouraged to acknowledge satisfactory performance in engagement communications.*

Internal auditors have traditionally provided exception-based reports. This term means that internal audit communications address what is abnormal or unexpected in the areas examined during the review. While there is a great deal of value in providing reports to the board and management that identify issues noted, the long term and continuous effect of providing exception-based reports is often less than positive. These reports are eventually interpreted by others as meaning that internal auditors only look at what is broken and embark on "gotcha!" expeditions. Furthermore, if an auditor examines 10 areas within their scope of work, and finds issues with two of these 10 areas and reports only on these, audit clients will wonder if the auditor even noticed that eight of the 10 areas examined met performance expectations. The reports could be perceived as being unfair and biased.

To address this misunderstanding, and the resulting halo effect that this would cause, internal auditors should acknowledge satisfactory performance in their communications. Over the years, I have done this in a variety of ways. If the report is relatively short, a sentence may suffice. For longer reports, I sometimes provide a full paragraph.

I once had a client that wanted a full section on best practices identified. This company built power stations and each site was a self-sustaining operation. Senior management knew that there was no need for an employee in one location to interact with that person's counterpart at another location, and best practices known by one was not likely to be known by another. Since internal audit traveled to multiple locations and was privy to operating practices, audit reports were shared among locations with two underlying messages for the staff involved:

1. Note what other facilities are doing well and emulate it if possible
2. Note what other facilities are doing poorly and make sure that is not happening in your location. If so, fix it before internal audit visits you

This was a well-run organization with enviable governance practices!

> *2420—Quality of communications. Communications must be accurate, objective, clear, concise, constructive, complete, and timely.*

One of the most important aspects of internal auditing is effective communications. Although internal auditors spend many hours planning, performing fieldwork, and writing the report, the client does not see most of this effort. Our product is the audit report, so it must impress the client.

Effective verbal communications are also essential for effective audits and overall success. They help auditors communicate the objectives for the audit and methodology that will be used. It also makes it possible to get the needed documents and win support for recommendations, while helping to build healthy relationships.

Effective communications, whether written or verbal, meet these seven attributes:

1. *Accurate.* There are no mistakes or errors in the information presented.
2. *Objective.* The auditor's work is focused on facts and informed judgment, there is no bias involved, and the results are neither inflated nor understated.
3. *Clear.* Easy to understand and interpret.
4. *Concise.* Brief by using only as many words as necessary—gone are the days of very lengthy reports.
5. *Constructive.* Serves the purpose of helping the organization improve its activities and promote advancement through excellence.
6. *Complete.* Nothing relevant or important missing.
7. *Timely.* Issued promptly because the value of the message decreases with time.

Summary

Internal audit is an evolving profession. The last few decades have brought an unprecedented number of changes to the operational, technological, economic, and social environment in which organizations operate and internal auditors must respond accordingly. The required adaptation involves redefining what we audit, how we audit, when we audit, who performs the audits, and even where the audits are performed.

The role of internal auditors has evolved so that we are now expanding our scope of work beyond accounting records and financial statements. Today, internal auditors are expected, in fact required, to examine how well the organization is organized, how efficient it is in its daily activities, and how effective it is in its pursuit of its stated mission, vision, and objectives. The internal auditors' review often means collecting and analyzing more than 1 year's worth of data and documents, talking to people outside the accounting and financial reporting offices, and literally interacting with everyone from the boardroom to the mailroom.

The skills requirements are increasingly diverse and go beyond accounting degrees and related experience. In fact, internal audit departments are increasingly searching for individuals who can "think risk," communicate effectively verbally and in writing, collaborate with others within and outside the organization, understand the connections linking operating units together, and understand process flows as much as they understand the systems that support them.

The guidance available to internal auditors is extensive and detailed. But having this guidance does not guarantee that auditors will apply them effectively. We must understand what the guidance says, why it must be followed, be able to adapt its implementation to fit the circumstances and maturity of our organizations, and articulate the merits to our clients. From design to execution, internal auditors must think outside the box and display leadership and adaptability. The past focus on compliance was too limited, because organizational success depends on far more than complying with rules and regulations. Organizational success depends on the effective implementation of governance mechanisms and structures, visioning and seamless execution, effective risk identification, hiring and deploying the best people possible, and exceeding the expectations of a diverse and demanding collection of stakeholders. The risks have never been higher. The opportunities have never been more promising. Internal auditors must rise to the occasion and assist the board and management meet these expanding responsibilities.

KPMG's Seeking Value through Internal Audit report states that in their survey it is clear that while companies want measurable impact from their internal audit functions, especially in the areas of risk and potential revenue enhancement, this does not constitute the primary concern of the audit committee chairs and CFOs polled. The study found that the most important factor is effectiveness and efficiency. This means that, while there is a call for measurable impact through a greater focus on risk, it should not come at the cost of reducing audit effectiveness and efficiency.

In response to the question: How important are the following to CFOs and audit committee chairs? The responses are shown in Table 1.4.

Metrics represent a great tool to measure performance and ascertain the degree to which goals are met. It is primarily a management tool, but we will also examine how internal auditors can use metrics to better gauge risks, the effectiveness of internal controls, and detect anomalies earlier than the traditional cyclical audit approach.

Finally, there is an indissoluble link between the processes designed to pursue the mission and goals of the organization, the people who work within those processes, and the systems that support both the processes and the people. In Chapter 2, we will examine this connection, its implications for internal auditors, and how to use this knowledge to perform more effective operational audits.

Table 1.4 How Important Are the Following to CFOs and Audit Committee Chairs?

Response	Percentage
Performance of effective and efficient audits	71
Measurable impact	63
Quality of IA reports	52
Commitment/technical excellence/quality	44
Appropriately qualified personnel	41
Clear standards/robust tools	35

Chapter 2 explores the objectives and characteristics of operational reviews and what internal auditors must consider when embarking on an operational audit of their own. We discuss the planning, fieldwork, and reporting phases, key considerations during each of these phases and how to navigate the multiple requirements of each more smoothly and effectively to achieve greater client satisfaction. It also explains the need for metrics to monitor business activities.

Effective business operations are the result of the deployment and coordination of resources for the pursuit of business objectives. Organizations exist to pursue a mission and processes are designed to that end. These processes are in turn staffed by people whose number and skillset advance the mission and are assisted by technology or machines. Consequently, success is the result of proper planning and the effective alignment of people, processes, and technology.

QUESTIONS

1. What is operational auditing and how can it add value to the organization?
2. Explain the importance of independence and objectivity and how having unfettered access within the organization impacts the internal auditors' ability to review any program, process, system, record, at any time and perform operational reviews.
3. Describe the difference between retrospective reviews that focus on past events and prospective engagements. List some of the future threats that internal auditors should include in their assessments.
4. What are five of the skills of internal auditors that have been identified as essential for success in the future? What can your internal audit department do to develop those skills among its staff?
5. Explain the five stages in the IA-CM and its implications for operational auditing.
6. Explain integrated auditing.
7. Describe the difference between controls-based and risk-based auditing.
8. Explain the importance of using business objectives while planning and performing operational audits, and how to use them when communicating the results of the audit.
9. What are the attributes of effective audit evidence outlines in Standard 2310 and what the implications for operational audits?
10. Explain how an organization could meet its compliance requirements but still fail over the medium and long term.

Notes

1 Quote from John B. Petersen III's blog Product of the Product at http://www.jbp3.com/blog/product-of-the-product
2 See https://daf.csulb.edu/offices/univ_svcs/internalauditing/audits.html
3 See http://www.businessdictionary.com/definition/operational-audit.html
4 To read more about the advocacy work of the IIA, see https://na.theiia.org/about-us/about-ia/Pages/About-IIA-Advocacy.aspx
5 To read the full article, see http://usatoday30.usatoday.com/news/nation/2002-12-22-persons-of-year_x.htm
6 The IIA's website www.theiia.org provides the definition of internal auditing in multiple languages and the full text of the Standards for the Professional Practice of Internal Auditing.
7 For more information regarding the Global Reporting Initiative, visit https://www.globalreporting.org/Pages/default.aspx

8 See IIA Organizational Governance Position Paper, July 2006.

9 Part of the definition is adapted from https://en.wikipedia.org/wiki/Operational_auditing and most of the commentary regarding operational auditing is based on my almost 20 years of being involved in the profession.

10 See https://na.theiia.org/membership/Pages/Membership.aspx

11 For details regarding the International Professional Practices Framework (IPPF), its components, and the requirements for internal auditors, see https://na.theiia.org/standards-guidance/Pages/New-IPPF.aspx

12 See https://www.law.cornell.edu/wex/fiduciary_duty

13 Information Technology/Information Communication Technology.

14 Full details are available in the 2010 Institute of Internal Auditors Global Internal Audit Survey: A Component of the CBOK Study report entitled: Core Competencies for Today's Internal Auditor (Report II) by James A. Bailey.

15 Starting in July 2015 and through 2016 and 2017, the IIA will be enhancing the IPPF and expanding both the Implementation Guidance and Supplemental Guidance. See https://na.theiia.org/standards-guidance/Pages/Standards-and-Guidance-IPPF.aspx

16 A list of software tools is available at https://www.iia.org.au/technicalResources/software-directory

Chapter 2

Objectives and Phases of Operational Audits

Out of clutter, find simplicity

Albert Einstein

Introduction

An operational audit involves a review of the activities performed in a program or process in the pursuit of its objectives by individuals, who are often supported by a variety of tools. Beyond that quick definition, lie a myriad of dynamics that can render that review a productive exercise for the organization or a frustrating waste of resources by all involved. The difference depends on a combination of factors involving the people engaged in the audit, the areas of focus established for the engagement, and the way that communication and coordination occurs among all involved.

In this section, we will examine the objectives of operational audits, how they are defined and what they mean for the audit. We will also examine the phases of operational audits and the dynamics associated with each phase. We will also discuss the role of data during operational audits and the impact of management practices on people, the process, and technology.

In many ways, operational audits share similarities to traditional accounting/financial reviews, yet there are some important differences worth examining. After the decision is made that either must be performed, both require the identification of the corresponding business objectives, and the life cycle of these audits can be encapsulated in three phases: planning, fieldwork, and reporting. Lastly, a follow-up will be performed at a time determined by the severity of the issues identified.

Let's begin with the definition of objectives.

Key Objectives of Operational Audits

Defining the objectives of any engagement is essential as an initial step to put it on the right footing for success. Without clearly defined, communicated, and understood objectives, all involved are

33

likely to drift during the course of the review by asking for irrelevant documentation, interviewing people unnecessarily, examining transactions, and analyzing process characteristics that are alien to the priorities embraced by the sponsors of the engagement. In the end, the auditors will communicate recommendations for improvement regarding topics of little importance to audit clients. In essence, not having clearly defined objectives will result in wasted time and money, frustration for all involved, and damage to the reputation of the internal audit function.

The objectives of the review will depend on several factors. First of all, we must determine whose objectives the engagement is intending to address. Internal audit should be careful not to define the objectives unilaterally. While this may be necessary in certain occasions, this should not be the prevailing practice, but rather, internal auditors should get management involvement as much as possible to make sure that the review will meet their needs.

The objectives for the review could be driven by

1. *New rules.* Rules can be established internally (e.g., policies and procedures) or externally (e.g., new or updated laws and regulations), or a combination (e.g., a contract signed by the organization and one or more external parties). Note that the new rule can also be the result of voluntary adoption like what we have observed with many aspects of CSR. While some argue that CSR is beyond the scope of internal audit, and highly regarded economists like Milton Friedman objected to business leaders spending time and resources on CSR initiatives, the growing consensus is that CSR is here to stay, and stakeholders are increasingly demanding greater involvement as it relates to the triple bottom line. Furthermore, as Deborah L. Rhode stated in the introduction to Warren Benis' book *Moral Leadership*, multiple studies have compared the social performance of companies with financial returns. Although results vary, a meta study (study of multiple surveys) of 95 surveys found that only 4 found a negative relationship, 55 found a positive relationship, 22 found no relationship, and 18 found a mixed relationship.

   A reputation for ethical conduct by organizations attracts customers, employees, and investors, and builds good relationships with government regulators. Evidence of the financial importance of ethical reputation is that in the year 2000, fewer than 75 socially screened funds existed. By July 2010, more than 150 traditional, open-end funds and 17 exchange-traded funds employed various social screens. The Social Investment Forum says that in the United States, socially screened portfolios, which include pension funds, endowments, and foundations, as well as mutual funds, held $2.7 trillion at the end of 2007. The 2014 Report on US Sustainable, Responsible and Impact Investing Trends states that assets in socially screened portfolios climbed from $3.74 trillion at the start of 2012 to $6.57 trillion at the start of 2014, an increase of 76%. These assets now account for more than one out of every $6 under professional management in the United States.

   Many of these investors are engaged activists, making demands on the companies they invested in. Notable institutional investors include Ariel Investments, Parnassus, Pax World, Calvert Funds, Domini, Gabelli, and Praxis.

2. *Poor performance.* Inefficiencies, waste, rework, or complaints from customers and vendors may trigger *management* involvement, resulting in their request to have the matter reviewed by internal audit.

3. *Compliance issues.* These can be the result of internal quality control initiatives that identify anomalies. In the case of regulators and inspector reviews that identify instances of noncompliance at other organizations, the internal audit department may investigate conditions at their organization to determine if a similar problem exists at home, help to

monitor the situation, and verify that follow-through on corrective actions take place in anticipation of future additional compliance reviews by external parties, such as regulators.

4. *Anomalous revenues or expenses.* While increases in sales is always welcome news, if these figures appear dubious, internal audit may review the related transactions to verify they are all legitimate, they have been recorded in the correct amount, and posted during the correct period. Similarly, unusually high or low, or otherwise questionable expenses, are likely to result in the request for a thorough review.

When defining the objectives, effective internal auditors examine the organization's infrastructure. The Merriam-Webster dictionary defines infrastructure as the underlying foundation or basic framework of a system or organization and the resources, such as personnel, buildings, or equipment required for an activity. As such, the objectives of an operational audit could include examining the collection of resources allocated to a program or process for it to accomplish its objectives. This may also include the entity's planning, budget, and technological systems.

The infrastructure could also include management reports because the extent, accuracy, proper distribution, and amount of detail contained in it weigh heavily on management's ability to perform its duties. Lastly, this infrastructure may also include the organizational structure and the assignment of responsibility and accountabilities. Placing responsibility in the hands of people without accountability, geographically disconnected, or burdened by cripplingly low staff, would impair performance.

Concerns over business risks, internal and external changes in the internal and/or external environment and dynamics affecting the organization's governance may also influence the objectives of an operational review. Among these governance and compliance elements are concerns over ethics, EHS, operational consistency in relation to existing policies and procedures as well as CSR expectations set by relevant stakeholders.

In general, the focus is on assessing and reporting on the efficiency, effectiveness, and economy of operations, activities, and programs; and conducting engagements on governance, risk management, and control. These are sometimes referred to as performance or value for money auditing, which cover the full spectrum of operating and business processes, the related management controls, and the results and outcomes achieved.

Technology may also influence the definition of objectives. Generally speaking, an organization or a program is comprised of processes designed to support the organization's program, processes, and units. To the extent that those systems are designed effectively, and operate as expected, they will support the achievement of objectives. Conversely, other conditions would work contrary to these ideals and become the focus of review.

> If you fail to plan, you are planning to fail!
>
> **Benjamin Franklin**[1]

Phases of the Operational Audit

Like traditional audits, operational audits are also structured in the traditional planning, fieldwork, and reporting phases. These provide a simple, effective, and time-tested approach to organizing, performing, and communicating the results of the work done. Following is a description of each of these phases, and some of the key activities that occur during their performance.

Planning

The planning phase includes scoping, budgeting, defining the population of interest, how testing will be performed, and announcing the audit. Planning is arguably the most important part of an audit. The proverb: "Failing to plan is planning to fail" comes to mind. More than mere words, experienced auditors know that poor planning leads to inefficient auditing practices as testing activities that can be combined or strategized, are instead done one at a time; selecting and reviewing transactions together is instead done as multiple steps, and rework is common as procedures are poorly initiated only to be rearranged and additional information examined later. Lastly, it also results in poor scheduling of meetings with process owners and other stakeholders.

So what are some of the key steps for effective planning? First, I must clarify that the planning process begins long before the actual audit begins. The starting point should be the performance of a risk assessment that allows the CAE to prepare an audit plan based on the results of an analysis of the organization's audit universe. The audit universe consists of all auditable activities such as accounts, processes, programs, and functions within an organization, and the risks associated with their ability to achieve their objectives. At this point, the risk assessment is done at the enterprise level.

This enterprise risk assessment should be done collaboratively with senior management and the board of directors. By involving them, the CAE will get their input about plans, concerns, and priorities. It will also be more likely to get their buy-in into the audit process, which will facilitate the execution of audits later. This risk assessment should then generate two key outputs: (1) a strategic plan impacting company operations for management use and (2) an audit plan.

The audit plan identifies what the internal audit function will review based on available resources and the needs and priorities of the organization. While an annual audit plan has been the norm for decades, CAEs are increasingly developing multiyear audit plans to facilitate future planning and identify resource needs. For example, if the CAE determines that an audit of treasury operations is needed and subsequent audits will be expected in the future, but the internal audit function lacks expertise on the matter, the action plan may have two components: (1) hire an outside firm to cosource the upcoming audit and (2) begin the process of recruiting an auditor with sufficient treasury experience who can then become the in-house resource for future reviews.

When performing each of the audits in the audit plan, the auditor in charge must perform a number of tasks. These include communicating with the corresponding process owner about the timing of the review, requesting needed financial and operational reports and documents, coordinating staff availability, identifying the systems in use, and defining the scope, objectives, work schedule, and budget for the engagement.

In addition to the enterprise risk assessment discussed above, a more tactical one should also be performed for each audit. At a more refined level, this risk assessment should identify auditable activities, relevant risk factors, and the relative significance/consequence and likelihood/probability of those risks.

As mentioned in Chapter 1, internal auditors should make sure to consider more than accounting and financial risks. Depending on the scope and objectives for the engagement, they should also consider other risks, such as operational, legal liability, corporate image (e.g., reputation), industry specific, compliance, and IT-related risks. The following questions can be very helpful when thinking about risk. I have found them particularly useful when planning audits and it has helped me brainstorm risks:

- What could go wrong?
- How could that unit fail?
- Are there any liquid assets that require special care and oversight?
- What physical assets are bought and used? How do they need to be protected and used for maximum effectiveness?
- What intellectual or digital assets are used and constitute a key success factor? These might include personally identifiable information, copyrights, and licenses.
- How could someone or something disrupt the operations?
- What are the objectives and how do we know if the unit is achieving them?
- Where are the people, processes, systems, or assets vulnerable?
- On what information do they rely the most?
- On what do they spend the most money?
- How do they bill and collect revenue?
- What activities are most complex?
- What activities are regulated?
- What is their greatest legal exposure?
- What decisions require the most judgment?
- How could someone steal from the unit?
- What systems are in use?
- Who has access to these systems and what activities can they perform using it?

What Must Go Right for Them to Succeed?

Internal auditors can help management achieve its organizational goals by focusing on the review of activities and other exposures with the highest significance and likelihood of harming the organization. But success is not achieved merely by avoiding calamity. Organizations must also excel at delivering, consistently, what the customer needs and wants.

Thoughts about risks often conjure images of what can go wrong. While this is acceptable and the standard default for these types of exercises, we can go further by drawing an analogy to sporting events where there is a widely accepted maxim: You can't win games just by playing defense. With that in mind, there is another question that I have found very helpful over the years.

It is also very helpful to identify priorities and help define how the organization should allocate its limited resources:

Internal auditors' position within their organizations' hierarchy, their adoption and use of a risk-based approach, their broad skillset and knowledge of their organizations, makes them uniquely qualified to add value. Proactive auditors will look beyond isolated negative events and also look for the interdependencies that management's strategic objectives and resources have. This means supplementing the risk of adverse events with the identification and management of the events that must go well so the organization's objectives can be achieved. Rather than merely focusing on what can go wrong, management's ability to achieve its objectives and those of their stakeholders will be enhanced when internal auditors help management determine what needs to go right and identify critical success factors, including the appropriate allocation of the organization's limited resources. The answer to this question helps to identify the priorities that drive this allocation of resources.

Consequently, risk assessments should not be limited to the identification of risks, but should also help to identify opportunities, determine the organization's preparedness, and identify those responsible for appropriately responding to those events.

Risk Factors

Risk factors play an important role during planning, and in particular, during risk assessments. Risk factors are conditions and other variables that in their present, or absence, as the case may be, either exacerbate or diminish the underlying risk. The presence of some factors increases the likelihood or impact of the underlying risks. On the other hand, the presence of some factors actually decreases the likelihood or impact of the underlying risks.

For example, a very important risk factor that Committee of Sponsoring Organization's (COSO) 2013 Internal Control-Integrated Framework (IC-IF) mentions multiple times is the competence of employees. As employees' competence increases, the risk of errors, omissions, and other operational problems decreases because they will be qualified to perform their duties, including control activities. To illustrate the dynamic, many experienced auditors have encountered situations where the person preparing bank reconciliations is not sufficiently knowledgeable about this control activity and they use "the plug" to ensure the "math works out" and the reconciliation zeroes out when in fact the discrepancy is due to missing transactions. A similar situation occurs with reconciling items, where the employee doesn't fully understand the importance of researching and correcting reconciling items rather than merely listing the open items on a log and allowing these to accumulate.

Another risk factor is the extent of judgment that can be exercised when performing relevant operational and control activities. As the extent of judgment increases, the underlying risk of error, abuse, and malfeasance increases. So these factors have an opposite effect on the underlying risks.

An example of a risk factor that moves in the same direction as the underlying risk is the number of transactions. As the number of transactions of interest increases, the risk of errors and omissions increases.

Other examples include: time since the last audit was performed, the geographical dispersion of the operations, level of motivation of employees, the ethical climate, complexity of operations, asset size, volume, liquidity, and pressure to produce or achieve organizational goals (Figure 2.1).

During planning meetings, internal auditors should engage in participative practices, involving process owners as much as possible to identify relevant activities, systems, people, and performance standards. When auditors do this, they are better equipped to define the scope more precisely. When auditors plan engagements in relative isolation, they often miss important aspects of the operation and the systems in use that may play an important role in identifying the risks that should be examined during the audit.

Risk factor	Risk profile	
	Increases	Decreases
Last time audited	X	
Major system change	X	
Complexity	X	
Geographical dispersion	X	
Liquidity	X	
Volume of transactions	X	

Figure 2.1 Impact of risk factors on the risk profile.

Internal auditors also benefit from reviewing prior audit workpapers as it provides insights into the operation reviewed, areas of concern, location of relevant data and documents, key individuals, amount of time various procedures took for completion, and verbal observations brought to the attention of process owners. Although reviewing prior workpapers is a highly recommended practice, caution is warranted as auditors must remember that each audit is the reflection of the objectives, scope, conditions, and expectations at the time it was performed.

Time required to perform procedures is a function of the competence and accurate record keeping of the auditors who worked on that engagement, and the speed of execution is affected by the degree of assistance, collaboration, and competence of the auditees at the time. All said, it is important to familiarize oneself with what was done previously and the results of that review.

While the amount of time spent planning, as a percentage of the entire audit will vary with each organization, type of audit, and experience level of all involved, spending less than 25% of the total time on planning is probably going to lead to execution problems during fieldwork. Good planning will prevent avoidable problems during fieldwork and good planning demands that a suitable amount of time be invested in these activities.

Typical audit steps for audit programs are shown in Table 2.1.

Other typical procedures include compare, prepare, obtain, verify, count, and recalculate.

In some ways, the entire suite of procedures and action words used to denote audit program steps can be summarized into one word: "verify." The board of directors, senior management, and middle management own the organizational strategy, objectives, risks, and controls of the areas under their responsibility. They establish the operating structure, performance activities, reporting lines, and information channels. They also assign resources, whether human, financial, technological or otherwise, and are also responsible for setting the performance metrics that allow them to assess the degree of completion and the quality of the work done.

With that in mind, internal auditors' duty is to verify that management, with the authority received from the board of directors, establish the structure, policies, procedures, and metrics to

Table 2.1 Audit Procedures and Their Meaning

Procedure	Meaning
Verify	Confirm, prove, or corroborate that a fact is true
Trace	This involves tracing a transaction from the source (e.g., a cash receipt, file creation) to its destination, which could be a financial, operational, or regulatory report
Vouch	This involves the "reverse-trace" of a transaction from the destination (e.g., financial, operational, or regulatory report) to its source (e.g., sales order, purchase, and time sheet)
Reconcile	Tie information from two separate sources to verify the accuracy or expected discrepancies
Foot	Add the items in a column
Cross-foot	Add the items in a row
Observe/tour	For an area of interest, observe and note physical conditions (e.g., fencing, temperature, cleanliness, and demarcation)

achieve the vision, mission, and objectives of the enterprise, and this should be done within the parameters of ethical behavior, legal requirements, and stakeholder expectations. So, every internal audit procedure could read: "Verify that..." For example:

> Verify that all deposits and withdrawals were recorded in the corresponding GL account, in the correct period, and were authorized by the appropriate manager.
>
> Or
>
> Verify that procedures are in place and are working effectively to process incoming customer calls promptly and provide accurate answers to customer inquiries.
>
> Or
>
> Verify that user access rights are revoked immediately upon termination.

The planning phase also involves estimating the amount of time tasks will take for completion. This can be done by examining the time logs from previous audits to provide an estimate about the possible time for the current audit. We should remember, however, that with each passing audit, the auditors should be a little faster than before because they should know how the work is performed, where to locate information, and who to contact to clarify doubts. Of course, if the process, workers, systems, or auditors have changed, time estimates would have to be updated, but unless there are changes, auditors reperforming a previous audit should expect to act with more expertise and speed with every subsequent review.

It is also important to remind auditors that because of the reliance placed on previous time estimates, underreporting the amount of time it takes to perform tasks is usually not a good idea. "Eating time," as this practice is sometimes called, will compromise the calculations and estimates for the work to be completed. Motivations for doing this vary from not wanting to exceed the number of hours agreed with the client, not wanting to appear to be working too slowly or because auditors are measured on how closely they meet the budgeted hours for the engagement. Regardless of the reason, the fact that the number of hours is underreported distorts the true amount of effort it took to complete the work and cheats the organization of the amount that should be recorded and charged for the work done. Everyone should follow this rule: If you did the work diligently, charge for it.

Fieldwork

The next phase in the engagement's life cycle is fieldwork. This phase is when most of the testing is performed, and it includes interviewing, documenting, applying testing methodologies, managing fieldwork, and providing status updates. It consists primarily of two things

1. Determining if the process or program under review is designed effectively so that the related goals and objectives are likely to be achieved
2. Verify that the controls in place are performing as designed by management

I get asked often during my seminars about the difference between planning and testing. The answer is not as easy as it might appear. During planning, the auditors obtain and review the documents received, analyze data, hold meetings with process owners, and may find there are obvious issues even at this stage. The question then must be asked: Is that planning or testing? The auditor may identify reportable conditions during the planning phase, even though identifying issues is usually considered an aspect of testing. In the end, it doesn't matter much. The anomalous condition should be documented. Separating the engagement into phases does not mean that the activities are necessarily exclusive of each other. Activities may straddle the category and even reportable conditions could be identified during the planning phase.

Therefore, we could find ourselves testing during planning, and planning during fieldwork. Planning during fieldwork may occur because after the testing begins, the auditor may discover that conditions were different than those anticipated, some of the work takes longer than anticipated or items that were considered low risks are actually bigger risks, and vice versa. When this happens, those managing the engagement need to evaluate the situation and decide how to rearrange the remaining work given the resources available. In general, auditors should make every effort to minimize the need to modify established, reviewed, and approved audit programs, timelines, and scope.

Types of Audit Evidence

Internal auditors are focused on verifying whether conditions are such that the operation or program under review is likely to achieve its objectives, and the procedures in place are working as designed. Deviations and concerns are then communicated through audit reports. During the review, auditors must substantiate their work, conclusions, and opinions on facts or information that support their beliefs and can be used to convince others than conditions and practices are as stated. In other words, auditors gather evidence to support their work and persuade others that conditions are satisfactory or not.

There are different types of audit evidence that auditors gather and evaluate during their reviews.

Testimonial

Testimonial evidence consists of verbal or written statements or assertions given by someone as proof regarding the matter being discussed. In the case of internal audits, anyone being audited may be asked to give testimonial evidence during interviews about a variety of topics. Examples include the steps performed while processing a loan application, how the employee pays incoming invoices, the procedures to record the purchase of inventory in the accounting system, or the steps followed when notified that an employee has been hired and access needs to be granted to the computer systems.

There are two types: testimony is what the individual states about his or her own personal knowledge about something, while hearsay is testimony based on what was heard about that topic, in other words, heard said by someone else. Auditors should be careful to corroborate verbal statements, especially hearsay because the individual could have misunderstood the facts or interpreted the information incorrectly.

Testimonial evidence doesn't have to be sworn during most internal audits, but during an audit, it is assumed that auditees are making truthful statements about their assertions. It should be clearly understood within the organization that false statements made to the auditor are grounds for disciplinary action.

Testimonial evidence is often obtained during interviews so it is typically verbal, but it can be written if provided in a questionnaire, as a result of an e-mail or when requested verbally, but the response is in writing. The opposite is also true for questionnaires; the respondent typically produces written evidence, but it can be verbal if the response is verbal (e.g., a meeting or phone call) in response to a written request.

Interviews are a very common form of evidence gathering and it often involves an auditor speaking with one or more individuals about matters related to the engagement. The most typical form is one-on-one interviews, but it is common for auditors, and especially new auditors, to conduct interviews in pairs. One of the key benefits of this practice is having a second auditor present to improve the quality and detail of the information gathered, and alternate roles as one auditor takes notes while the colleague asks questions, and vice versa.

An increasing variant of the one-on-one, or two auditors and one auditee arrangements, is to have two or more auditors and two or more auditees present during interviews. This is better described as a facilitated meeting than a typical interview and one of the key benefits is the amount and diversity of the information that can be gathered. I have found these meetings very productive as the statements of one individual may prompt another to elaborate or clarify a fact. By doing this in one meeting, I reduce the likelihood of having to conduct multiple meetings and potentially having to circle back to others to clarify information.

Observation

Auditors typically observe conditions and dynamics related to the subject of the review. The following are examples of items internal auditors may want to observe and why:

■ Observe the security measures to prevent unauthorized individuals from entering the facility
■ Observe the customer service area layout to better understand the flow of customers
■ Verify that machinery exists and is in working condition
■ Walk the perimeter of a construction site to confirm there is a fence that restricts access to only authorized individuals
■ Observe the way that trucks are loaded and unloaded in the warehouse to confirm adherence to safety procedures
■ Verify that the data center meets temperature and humidity guidelines

In general, auditors visually evaluate physical facilities, conditions, and practices to verify they exist, their condition, valuation, and protection.

The observation can be done in one of two ways:

■ The auditee knows that the auditor is observing
■ The auditee does not know that the auditor is observing

The quality of the information obtained could depend on whether the auditee knows, or does not know, that the auditor is taking note. When auditees know about the auditor's observation, there is a possibility that the individuals involved will modify their behavior so it is viewed favorably by the auditor. In a work site, there is a possibility that the laborers don't wear their safety equipment consistently, even if they are supposed to and they know they should. But when the auditor is present, they wear their gear and follow workplace procedures to avoid being discovered and reported. This behavior modification can result in false negatives, where the typical behavior is not displayed during observation.

This is similar to social desirability bias, which describes the tendency of survey participants to answer questions in a way that will be viewed favorably by others. During interviews, it can involve overreporting "good behavior" or underreporting "bad behavior," and its manifestation during observation is the behavioral change, sometimes also in the form of speeding up or slowing down as their interests are best served. So when auditors are observing working conditions, they should be mindful of this possibility and use the procedure that will give them the most reliable information.

Document Inspection

Another common way of collecting evidence is by reviewing documents. In fact, this is one of the most common procedures performed by auditors who examine documents to verify the date and amount of transactions, agreements made between various parties, evidence of authorizations and record of decisions made, among others. The documents can be internal or external.

The examples and their source are shown in Table 2.2.

Documents can be internal or external, financial or nonfinancial, and an auditor may be searching for specific items on the document. So, in the case of accounts payable payments, the auditor may want to look at the amount of each payment to compare it to the invoice received, the address where the payment should have been sent, and the name of the person who approved the payment to make sure the approver is authorized to do so.

Although internal auditors are not expected to be experts on altered or forged documents, they should pay close attention to each document in search of anomalous elements constituting red flags. If an invoice lacks a professional appearance, does not have what appears to be a corporate logo, phone number, street address, website, contact information, the print is slanted or has mathematical errors (e.g., tax rate or amount), the auditor should examine the document further. The prevalence of high quality printers make the creation of professionally looking documents easier than ever before, and possible segregation of duties or conflicts of interest within the organization can make the submission of fraudulent invoices a problem many organizations discover the hard way.

Recalculation/Reperformance

Mathematical recalculation is a form of audit evidence and it consists of checking the accuracy of documents or records. Sometimes auditors reperform the work of others to verify the accuracy and completeness of the work done, and to confirm that the amount is correct. For example see Table 2.3.

Table 2.2   Types of Documents

Internal	External	Combination
Invoices produced	Invoices received	Contracts
Memos	Bank statements	
Reports (e.g., production, inventory, and time sheets)	Confirmation statements	
	Certificates of insurance	
Policy statements	Credit reports	
Procedures documentation	Financial statements	

Table 2.3   Reasons to Perform Recalculation

Example	Objective of Recalculation
Depreciation expense	Verify that the assets were classified correctly and the appropriate depreciation schedule applied
Overtime hours	Verify that employees received the correct payment based on prevailing base and overtime pay rules
Billing amount	Confirm the accuracy of the price tables for items sold. In cases where the invoicing is done manually, it is even more important due to the increased possibility of human error

Another example involves the allowance for uncollectable balances, which are often based on a percentage of sales. The key premise for uncollectable balances is that a certain percentage of sales will enter the aging of accounts receivable and become bad debts eventually, so the organization can review its past experience and use the same percentage in the future to estimate those uncollectable amounts.

So if an organization records $12,000,000 of sales to hundreds of customers, and estimates based on historical experience show that 1.5% of these customers will not pay, it would need to record an allowance for uncollectable balances of $180,000 ($12,000,000 × 0.015). In this case, the auditors may verify the amount of sales, the historical information, and the entry made to the allowance account to make sure that this amount was recorded correctly.

Companies have been known to fraudulently modify their financial results by manipulating the amount they record for this allowance. Auditors look for this problem by comparing the amount of this allowance to gross sales over a period of time, to see if there are any changes in the proportion suggesting accounting irregularities.

Accounting staff often review the balance in the allowance for doubtful accounts as part of the month-end closing process, to make sure the balance is reasonable when compared to the latest bad debt forecast. For companies having minimal bad debt activity, a quarterly update may be enough.

An essential aspect of internal auditing is the gathering and analysis of evidence. Evidence is collected to support the results and conclusions derived from the engagement. Persuasiveness is defined as the confidence it gives the auditor when reaching a conclusion. Audit evidence should be as shown in Table 2.4.

The walkthrough is a useful mechanism to improve the quality of the audit and gain a better understanding of the completeness and accuracy of the data used when performing reviews. A signature alone is not enough evidence that a control occurred. Even if the procedures are explained to the auditor and include this step, and later if a signature is noted when inspecting documents, more is required. A walkthrough provides an additional level of evidence.

A walkthrough consists of the process of observing the flow of transactions from beginning to end (e.g., recording) and where applicable, disclosure in an organization's financial statements. It is a very useful tool to identify areas where errors and misstatements could occur and to test the overall design of the controls. The auditor begins the walkthrough at the initiation of a transaction and traces that transaction's authorization(s),

Table 2.4   Attributes of Persuasive Audit Evidence

Attribute	Meaning
Relevance	Evidence must be relevant to the related audit objectives and scope
Objective vs. subjective	Evidence is objective when two or more auditors, working independently, are very likely to arrive at the same result. Also when the parties involved are not influenced by personal feelings or opinions in considering and representing facts. For example, a physical count of inventory is more objective and persuasive than an estimate by the warehouse manager
Documentation	Documented evidence is more persuasive than undocumented evidence
Externality	Evidence obtained from a third-party is generally more persuasive than evidence from within the organization being audited
Sample size	Larger samples are generally more persuasive than smaller samples
Sampling method	Statistical samples are usually more persuasive than nonstatistical samples because they reduce the likelihood of sampling bias
Corroboration	Corroborated evidence is more persuasive than uncorroborated evidence
Timeliness	Recent items are typically more persuasive than older items or those produced after a delay
Authoritativeness	Authoritative evidence is more persuasive than nonauthoritative evidence. For example, a machine operator is usually more authoritative with regard to how well a particular machine works than the engineer who built the machine, or the manager who seldom or never actually uses the machine
Directness	Direct evidence is more persuasive than indirect evidence. For example, an original document is more persuasive than a copy
Adequacy of controls	Evidence from a well-controlled and reliable system is more persuasive than evidence from a poorly controlled or questionable system

processing, recording and when applicable, disclosing in the corresponding financial or operational reports.

The auditor can use a combination of procedures, including inquiry, observation, inspection, or reperformance techniques to assess the control design and effectiveness using the same documents and computer systems used by the organization. The auditor should also verify the accuracy and completeness of the data the organization used when performing the control.

In addition to examining what happens step-by-step, the auditor should also ask all involved personnel about any instances where normal procedures were not followed, management override took place, and unusual transactions, including fraud, took place.

Asking open-ended questions, that elicit a description or explanation, is more effective than close-ended (e.g., yes/no) ones. Also, by following a more dynamic approach rather than merely reading from a checklist, the auditor will gain a more detailed understanding of how the work gets done. While an important goal is for the auditor to understand the process and where errors or fraud may occur, it also provides a very useful mechanism for the auditor to identify weaknesses and recommend design improvements or additional review controls to mitigate these risks. It is also important to assess the level of competence of the individual performing the control, as lack of knowledge is a common reason for mistakes to be made, either by a processor or an approver. When a weakness is identified, it may call for deeper analysis. In addition, while performing the walkthrough, the auditor can verify that the related control(s) are operating as designed. With this in mind, auditors should balance the inquisitor nature of questions with conversational type dynamics. Not only does the conversational approach reduce stress and anxiety on the part of the auditee, but it also helps to foster a better relationship.

I am often asked how much evidence is needed when performing a review. The amount of evidence, testing, and rating of anomalies is generally a matter of professional judgment, informed by the amount of time since previous testing was performed, the effectiveness of the control when it was previously tested, any changes in the control since that last test (e.g., new computer systems and critical employee turnover) and the risk associated with the control (e.g., control over few, slow moving, and low value items).

Professional Skepticism

Although internal auditors are encouraged to use a conversational and participative approach when conducting their reviews, they must also remember that they are tasked with verifying the integrity of the information gathered and make sure their conclusions are sound. When obtaining and using evidence, internal auditors should display healthy professional skepticism and verify the quality of the information gathered and used. Internal auditors should be sufficiently suspicious of data received and reasonably verify that the information is free from manipulation or modification in ways that can compromise its quality. When there are doubts, the auditor must determine if those conditions make the evidentiary matter too unreliable for use. Similarly, internal auditors should approach interviews and meetings with sufficient skepticism, always attempting to verify the information provided, corroborate the testimony received, and observing behavioral changes that could indicate deceit.

Corroboration may involve obtaining supporting documentation to substantiate claims made or finding others to verify the accuracy of statements received. Another important source of information to ensure the auditor is working with reliable data is to obtain the assistance of a subject matter expert (SME). These individuals can provide a wealth of knowledge and assistance, in ways that the auditors may need years of diligent work and study to achieve.

SMEs can be internal or external to the organization. Previous audit experience is not required, but the SME must be willing to work with the auditor with a collaborative disposition and with the goal of seeking to find the true conditions within the scope review areas.

By this I mean, that although the SME may not always be as independent or objective as the auditor, there shouldn't be such limitations to these attributes that the auditor can no longer trust the SME's assistance. If that occurs, the assistance would not be helpful due to a lack of reliability.

The credentials of the SME are an important screening qualification as well. In most cases, the SME has superior and unquestionable academic and certification credentials. These are very helpful, but beyond conceptual or theoretical knowledge, the SME should also possess strong practical and experiential knowledge. The more substantial this experience is, the more useful the SME may be, since internal auditors should attempt to balance both theory and practice when working with SMEs.

In terms of evidentiary matter, it is also noteworthy to examine the source of the information. In general, the evidence will be useful if generated and provided by the client, but due to the possible lack of reliability as a result of fabrication or tampering, it is better if it were produced by a third party. The benefit derives from the greater likelihood that the third party won't have any reason to provide incorrect information to the auditor. Auditor self-generated evidence is the best, whether it consists of extracting data from computer records, observing workplace practices personally, or recalculating critical facts through the application of relevant formulas. But since this is not always possible or feasible, following the guidelines mentioned above will help to make sure that the information used is reliable.

There is a clear and critical difference between fact and opinion that internal auditors should understand. Facts are statements and information that can be proven to be true through verification. If a statement or piece of information is true, it is always true.

Opinions are subjective statements based on personal beliefs, so they are not always true for everyone. Opinions can be based on facts, but they are someone's personal interpretation of the facts and as such are open for debate.

Internal auditors should obtain as much reliable evidence as possible and base any opinions on the careful analysis of the related facts. Critical thinking is, therefore, very important to make sure that the opinions derived are accurate and consistent with the conclusion of an equally prudent, reasonable, and informed person.

> You are entitled to your opinion. But you are not entitled to your own facts.
> **Daniel Patrick Moynihan**

Workpapers

Workpapers are documents created by auditors to record the work done. They are a collection of evidentiary material showing the planning done, the fieldwork activities performed, and the support for all information mentioned in the audit report or other communication of results. They are also very useful during training and professional development, and as mentioned previously, also helpful while planning future engagements. Since auditors provide assurance regarding the conditions present during their review, the workpapers form the evidence that the audit was done according to the *Standards*.

Since workpapers are so important to the entire audit, they require review by the team leader to show there was proper supervision. The IIA has issued the following standard regarding audit workpapers.

> *2330—Documenting information: Internal auditors must document relevant information to support the conclusions and engagement results.*

The IIA's Practice Advisory 2330 states that the goal of workpapers are to

- Document the planning, performance, and review of audit work
- Provide the principal support for audit communication such as observations, conclusions, and the final report
- Facilitate third-party reviews and reperformance requirements
- Provide a basis for evaluating the internal audit activity's quality control program

Workpapers may include a wide variety of items, ranging from process narratives, flowcharts, copies of policies and procedures, checklists, organizational charts, management and financial reports, analysis of testing, correspondence, questionnaires, and pictures.

Narratives are one of the most common workpapers prepared by auditors. They consist of a description of a process or business activity and are usually prepared to explain how work is being done in an area being audited. They help the auditor understand the process. Some auditors show the controls in the process narrative or flowchart with one text color, and risks or weaknesses in the process with another text color. This provides an easy way to identify these critical elements.

Some advantages and disadvantages of narratives are shown in Table 2.5.

Flowcharts

Another common type of workpaper is the process flowchart. A flowchart is a diagram of the sequence of movements or actions of people or things involved in a process or activity. They illustrate a business process and virtually any process can be drawn in the form of a flowchart. Since the shapes are simple and visual, they are easy to understand.

To draw a flowchart, the first thing is to determine the boundaries of the process—in other words, where does it start and where does it end. It is fairly common for an auditor to spend unnecessary time and effort drawing portions of a process that are outside the scope of the audit being performed. Conversely, defining the portion of interest too narrowly can also create its own complications because it may not reflect the full scope of the review or highlight relevant strengths or weaknesses of the process.

Drawing a flowchart, or process mapping, is done to understand how the steps in a business process work together. This can be very helpful to understand where inefficiencies

Table 2.5 Advantages and Disadvantages of Narratives

Advantages	Disadvantages
Full detail of the area under review	Can be too detailed if the area is too complex
Good for small areas that do not need a flowchart	Difficult to visualize if the area or process is too complex
Simple to prepare with word processing software	May confuse the reader if it is too long

Action	Symbol
Start/begin and stop/end	⬭
A step in the process	▭
Decision	◇
Input/output	▱
Connector	⟶
File/database/storage device	⬢
Paper document	▢

Figure 2.2   Sample flowcharting symbols.

occur and how a process can be improved by reducing excessive hand offs, delays, and redundancies.

Ovals represent the starting or ending point of the process. Each step of the process is placed in a rectangular box. Decisions are indicated by a diamond and arrows are used to show the order and direction of the steps (Figure 2.2).

This is only a small sample of the symbols available for use when drawing flowcharts. I have found that I can draw most flowcharts with the symbols shown in the table, but others prefer to use more symbols to be more specific. That is a matter of preference. I suggest that auditors don't spend a disproportionate amount of time searching for symbols instead of actually drawing a flowchart that captures and conveys the message. A useful way to supplement the information on a flowchart is to write a companion narrative that provides additional details.

Over the years, I have observed many instances where the presenting problem is not caused within that unit, but it is rather only where the problem manifests itself. For example, incorrect data manually entered into a computer system can be either a data entry issue, or the accurate entry of incorrect information. In the case of the latter, the auditor should identify the source of the incorrect information, as the data entry activity is not the source of the problem, but rather the execution of an incorrect request.

Another example includes inventory audits. It has been customary to review the entry, safekeeping, and retrieval of inventory for use in manufacturing activities or for sale to customers. Inventory can be reviewed as a standalone activity or it can be examined as part of an entire cycle that begins with sales and manufacturing forecasting, the related purchasing activities, inventory acceptance and management, then the payment for the items bought. With this broader view of inventory, some organizations are moving away from auditing inventory, purchasing, or accounts payable activities in isolation, and auditing the purchase to pay process as described above instead.

Some of the key steps to follow when drawing a flowchart are

- Identify the steps through consensus
- Walk the process and arrange chronologically
- Draw using appropriate symbols
- Test for completeness (e.g., symbols, loops, dead ends, arrows, and direction)
- Look for problem areas as a team
- Get sign-off that the flowchart reflects the process

Table 2.6   Advantages and Disadvantages of Flowcharts

Advantages	Disadvantages
A teaching tool	May be more detailed than necessary
Managerial tool for discussion and analysis	
Errors may stand out and be obvious	
Provide flexibility	
Visual representation is best for some people	May take too much time to prepare
Easy to review	
Useful during discussions	Must learn many symbols if the organization decides to use a variety of them

In addition to flowchart, other names are process maps, value stream maps and when using swimming lanes to show the various departments or individuals who perform the activities, they are called cross functional process maps. Some use the terms interchangeably. In the end, however, the more information is added to the flow diagram, the more comprehensive the information will be.

Some advantages and disadvantages of flowcharts are shown in Table 2.6.

Internal Control Questionnaire

An internal control questionnaire (ICQ) helps to evaluate internal controls in specific areas by asking key questions. Internal auditors often use ICQs as a starting point and then supplement them with other information gathering and control evaluation techniques such as flowcharts and document reviews. They are used by process owners to help them assess their operation.

ICQs can also be very helpful when the auditor needs to collect large amounts of information. This can be the case when the audit involves multiple locations, or there are many individuals with information that the auditor needs, but interviewing each person individually and sequentially will delay the completion of the audit. In those cases, preparing and sending a questionnaire can be very helpful to collect large amounts of data quickly.

When preparing the ICQ, auditors should remember that respondents are only going to answer the question asked, so the questions should be worded clearly. Open-ended questions require the respondent to elaborate on the information provided. Closed-ended questions on the other hand, are designed to elicit a discrete answer, either in the form of a direct answer, such as "Yes," "No," an amount, name, date, or similar specific item. They can also consist of response choices from which the individual must choose to answer the question. This is the case with multiple-choice questions and the respondent chooses one answer or all that apply. It can also be a scale (e.g., degree to which the person agrees or disagrees with a statement). These are referred to as Likert scales or questions.

Examples of open-ended questions:

■ Please describe the process of processing customer payments
■ Tell me about the systems that you use to make purchases and who has access to it?

- What happens when a customer comes to the service window?
- Why did you choose to change vendors?

Examples of closed-ended questions:

- Does the receiving department enter the amount of items received immediately into the inventory system upon receipt?
- How many shipments of incoming materials do you receive per day?
- How many workers are on each crew?
- When was that sales office opened?
- Are all department personnel familiar with the company's requirements concerning the handling of private and confidential information?
- Do your computers/applications contain private or confidential information about patients?
- Does your area collect any individually identifiable private or confidential information on paper forms or records?
- If cash is accepted, are prenumbered receipts used to track payment?

Some advantages and disadvantages of ICQs are shown in Table 2.7.

Condition of Workpapers

Workpapers should be neat, easy to read, easy to review, and their appearance should be uniform. Most internal audit departments develop templates to standardize their appearance and key contents. In general, workpapers should include

- Objective of the procedure performed
- Source of the information evaluated
- Name of the auditor who performed the work
- Date when the work was done
- Name and date of supervisory review
- Details showing the work done
- Reference to other supporting documents, such as relevant objectives, risks, and controls
- Results of the testing procedure performed
- Conclusion

Table 2.7   Advantages and Disadvantages of ICQs

Advantages	Disadvantages
Brief	May not provide enough detail
Focuses on control techniques	May miss important or detailed information
Flexible	Could stifle creativity
Provides standardization	May miss control points
Easy to develop	

Table 2.8   Characteristics of High Quality Workpapers

Action	Purpose
Supervision	All workpapers must be reviewed by a supervisor and all review notes should be addressed as needed. The *Standards* require supervision of all engagements (Standard 2340), which provides evidence of compliance with the *Standards* but also serve as a training tool
Cross-referenced	Workpaper results should be referenced to the relevant supporting documentation to facilitate navigation, locate items of interest at a later date, and make sure there is support for all of the information in the audit report
Approved	The relevant audit supervisor should indicate approval of the workpapers and the date when this was done

Key steps to ensure workpapers are of high quality are shown in Table 2.8.

Any authorized reader should be able to understand what the auditor did, why, and how it was done. All workpapers should be clear enough so another person can reproduce or repeat the work done. The work done should be relevant to the audit and arranged logically. In the case of narratives and flowcharts, the description of the activities should flow based on chronological or process flow order so others can follow the sequence of events.

There are many ways that internal auditors can indicate the results of their work for transaction-based testing. Tickmarks show for each transaction whether the transaction met the criteria applied to the test. For example, if the auditor selects a sample of transactions, he will examine each of them to verify these four attributes:

1. The amount of the transaction was accurate
2. The transaction shows evidence that it was for a business-related activity
3. The transaction was approved before execution
4. The amount processed was recorded in the corresponding period

The following would illustrate the layout of a workpaper template.

In this illustration, the auditor would indicate the name of the organization, audit, process, and the source of the information/transactions reflected on the workpaper for the audit being performed. In the middle section, the auditor would indicate what transactions are being examined and the four attributes, as shown above, would receive tickmarks in the corresponding location. For tickmarks, I like to phrase the test intuitively, so the auditor would respond to the question in a conversational way. For example, the first question relates to a test to verify that the amount of the transaction is accurate. The auditor would compare the invoice received to the amount of the payment made to make sure the two amounts match. The auditor then has four ways of responding to this (Table 2.9).

The variance columns are a very useful addition to testing workpapers because they help the auditor keep track of the magnitude of the issue identified. In this illustration, this is how we would use these columns:

Table 2.9   Types of Tickmarks

Tickmark	Meaning	Interpretation	Action
Y	Yes	The amount of the payment is correct	The transaction passes the test
N	No	The amount of the payment is incorrect	This exception must flow onto the results, conclusion and be recorded as a reportable condition
N/A	Not applicable	The test is not applicable	Explain in the comments section
N/R	Not reportable	The transaction does not pass the test applied to it (i.e., amount is inaccurate), but this condition is not reportable	Explain in the comments section

Variance amount. A simple formula that subtracts the amount of the invoice from the amount paid; it should always show $0.00. If there is a difference, this amount is noted in the corresponding cell on this column. Upon completion of the test, the auditor can look at this column to quantify the extent of discrepancies noted during the entire test. Applying maximum, minimum, average, and total to this column would yield important insights into the issues.

Approved column. A similar analysis can be done as follows with the approved column. If the date of the approval is past the payment date, it shows that the activities are reversed and the control activity is being performed retroactively and potentially merely "to check the box," rather than as part of a well-functioning process.

Recording period. This would compare the recording date to the accounting period close and reporting date. Organizations are known to delay posting their liabilities because they subtract from their revenues. This is a case of financial statement manipulation in the worst case, but it can also be poor operating practices when done without malice. In either case, it underscores deficient performance. However, if it is indicative of intentional manipulation, then disciplinary action is warranted and if serious enough, could trigger the need to restate already published financial statements.

Electronic Workpapers

We use the term workpapers to denote the collection of documents related to the planning, fieldwork testing, and reporting worksheets that lead to the audit report. Many years ago, these items were paper documents, and consisted primarily of memos and accounting ledgers. These were large lined papers to document rows and columns of accounting transactions and with tickmarks, note that testing procedures were performed to verify among other things, the accuracy, completeness, and timeliness of entries.

More recently, workpapers have become electronic documents that are prepared using templates in a document management application. In other cases, the workpapers are prepared using common tools like Microsoft Word and PowerPoint, and then saved using standard folders. Even when source documents are physical documents, such as printed reports, invoices, packing slips, or bills of materials, these documents are often scanned and stored as electronic files, often in PDF (portable document format) or similarly easy to view formats.

Because workpapers can be so diverse, it is impossible to establish a single system, design, or template workpaper to be used in all situations by all companies. In this section, I have shared some common characteristics, but each organization should establish its own templates to facilitate record keeping and supervisory review with general elements and characteristics for uniformity. For some functional areas, such as cash receipts or accounts payable, and for repetitive/recurring audits, such as branch or program audits, the workpapers may have a more standardized format (Table 2.10).

The features and functionality of electronic workpaper systems has increased significantly and in many instances, the modules can be bought separately. In my experience, it is best to buy the entire suite of features rather than piece meal, because functionality absent from the application would then have to be managed externally. For example, not using the time tracking feature may force the internal auditors to log their time separately and internal management would then collect, collate, and analyze the information externally. However, when they need to link the hours to the specific activities associated with each audit, they may find that reconnecting the information is very difficult if not impossible (Table 2.11).

Table 2.10   Typical Features of Electronic Workpaper Systems

Access controls
Budget management
Data analytics
Integration with popular productivity tools
Document preparation and management
Findings documentation and tracking
Support multiple users
Report writing
Review notes
Risk and control assessment
Risk matrix
Task assignment
Time tracking
Version control
Online/offline functionality

Table 2.11   Examples of Electronic Workpaper Systems

ACL Exchange
Audit Pro
AuditWorks
Ease Beacon
Auto Audit/GRC
CCH TeamMate
Auditor Assistant
Galileo
GRC Cloud
ADM Plus
BWise
BPS Audit
MethodWare Pro Audit
CaseWare Working Papers
Pentana PAWS
Paisley Thomson Reuters Audit Manager

Access to workpapers should be limited, shared only upon request, and with the approval of the CAE. Backup copies of all of the information should be stored according to the organization's document retention policies and available for easy retrieval if needed. It is common practice, and highly recommended, that auditors planning a future audit, review at least the last audit's workpapers to familiarize themselves with what was reviewed, what data and reports were used, where that information was obtained, who provided it, what findings were reported in the report, and other nonreportable conditions and dynamics that may have been discussed with management at that time.

Reporting

The third phase of the audit is the communication of results, often referred to as reporting. It consists of communicating findings, observations, and best practices noted during the review, and developing recommendations for corrective action.

Findings are the documentation of deviations from what was expected and form the basis for the audit report. The term "finding" is in disuse by an increasing number of auditors who have found that their clients resent the label and prefer a term that is less controversial. As such, many auditors are calling these items "observations." Other auditors reserve the term "finding" for the more serious reportable conditions and refer to lower risk items as

Table 2.12   Attributes of Effective Audit Findings

Attribute	Meaning
Criteria	What was expected? It consists of what should exist or occur
Condition	What actually exists? What the auditor discovered as a result of the performance of audit procedures
Cause	The reason the condition exists and why it is different from the criteria. Auditors should focus on the root cause of the problem and avoid focusing on symptoms
Effect	Also referred to as the consequence. It consists of the impact of the condition
Recommendation	This is the action item necessary to correct the condition so performance is consistent with the criteria

"observations." For purposes of our discussion here, we use the term findings to refer to reportable conditions.

Findings have five attributes as shown in Table 2.12.

Over the years, I have found that capturing the information in the categories shown above provides a systematic, consistent, organized, and comprehensive way to capture the key attributes of audit findings. It provides a mechanism to assemble the features of the deficiency, so when the matter is discussed with management, the basis for the observation and the key facts are present.

As much as possible, internal auditors should quantify their findings by including amounts, values, time since when the condition has been occurring, how many individuals or organizations are affected, the age of assets involved, and do on. It also helps to quantify the effect or consequence of the finding in terms of monetary value or other relevant factors related to the finding. To the extent that the auditor documents the criteria, condition, cause, effect, and recommendation (CCCER) items, it will make it more persuasive and the reader will be more likely to be convinced that the problem requires correction.

There are two types of deficiencies:

- *Design.* These pertain to deficiencies in the design of the program or process. It means that the process or program is poorly structured and mechanisms to avoid problems from occurring are missing or found to be deficient. Recall that one of management's main responsibilities is to design the structures, processes, reporting relationships, and accountability frameworks governing the organization's operations. With this in mind, if the design is not conducive to the achievement of the organization's objectives and the enhancement of stakeholder value, then there is a design deficiency.
- *Operating.* These deficiencies are related to controls that are performing poorly and not acting as designed. Auditor testing procedures form the basis to determine if the control is working or not.

Findings should be discussed with the process owners and other relevant stakeholders before being included in the report. I have found process owners typically appreciate the courtesy afforded in this procedure, because it gives them an opportunity to discuss the facts and their implications. It also gives them an opportunity to prepare their response before their boss finds out about the problem. The third benefit of this practice is that it provides an opportunity to engage the process owner to discuss possible corrective actions for the issue.

While the CCCER model includes R for recommendation, this doesn't mean that the auditor has to formulate every recommendation every time. In my experience, telling our clients what to do presents two key problems:

1. *Dependency.* When told every time what to do, process owners don't develop the ability to think for themselves and identify some possible alternatives to correct the problem. Instead, they let the auditor do all the work, from problem identification to identification of alternatives, to the selection of the corrective action. Process owners should evaluate the conditions in their unit and formulate solutions to the problems presented.
2. *Lack of ownership.* I've encountered many instances over the years where after asking why certain practices are in place, the response is "the auditor told me to do it." Recall that management owns the programs, processes, their objectives, related risks, and controls. All activities performed should exist because they help achieve the program or processes' objectives. The auditor's role is to verify that the design and performance are conducive to the achievement of those goals. So, saying that the auditor told me to do it takes responsibility away from the process owner and presents the auditor as the de facto owner who has now instructed operators what to do. A recommendation is a suggestion or proposal and it is up to the recipient to accept it or not.

It is important to note that this discussion pertains to operational audits, because in the case of financial or compliance audits, the auditee seldom has the ability to reject a finding and the related instructions on the corrective action.

So, after presenting the facts surrounding the issue (the CCCE elements of the finding), I often ask clients "what do you think could or should be done to correct this?" The result is them having to think through the issue and formulate scenarios for corrective action. I can then determine if it will correct the issue, not correct the issue, or correct it partially. In the case of partial corrections, we then discuss alternatives and search for a satisfactory solution to the issue.

Follow-Up

After findings are reported, it is incumbent on both management and auditors to verify that the corrective actions are in fact applied and the problems fixed as expected. It does not serve the interest of the organization and its stakeholders for internal audit findings to be ignored after they are published in audit reports. Since findings should be significant enough to report them to senior management and the board, it is incumbent on the organization to take prompt corrective action.

The timeline for when the follow-up should occur depends on the risk associated with the finding. For some risks, management should take immediate action and auditors should check immediately as well. For example, if the organization's firewall is inoperative, the extreme risk that this represents warrants immediate corrective action. Similarly, if there is imminent risk to the safety of employees or the public, immediate corrective action is required. For most findings, however, the typical turnover time to implement remedial action and for the auditors to verify the effective implementation is several months to a year.

A follow-up review means that the auditor is checking to make sure the corrective action was performed, so it consists of checking what management did to address the issue reported. In cases where the severity of the observation was low, and the corrective action was administrative in nature (e.g., preparing or updating procedures documentation), a review of the item may suffice to close the observation in the findings database. If the finding is of medium or high severity, it may require a site visit, selecting a sample of records to test them, or analyzing 100% of the transactions to verify that a deficiency is no longer present.

Success for internal auditors consists of confirming, upon performing a follow-up review, that the issue has disappeared. While this positive outcome cannot be guaranteed, it is the goal that all auditors should pursue as it demonstrates that internal audit not only identified a problem, but also identified the root cause of the problem, and the agreed upon corrective action corrected the deficiency. Recurring findings indicate any of the following troublesome situations:

1. The reported finding was a symptom of something else. So, when corrective actions were applied, this addressed a symptom or only the affected records/files, but not the root cause.
2. The corrective action was only temporary and over time, behaviors and activities returned to their original state. This is caused by poor change management procedures.
3. There was no commitment to correct the issue and management failed to act on the observation.

The third item on the list above is arguably the worst-case scenario, as it shows that management did not take internal audit's work seriously. While on the surface it is egregious and cause for concern, internal auditors should make certain that an even greater and lamentable situation isn't occurring: that internal audit has no credibility and management ignores what was reported. This is an extreme situation and hopefully that is not the case.

As mentioned above, internal auditors are constantly searching for ways to demonstrate that they add value to their organizations. One approach seldom practiced is calculating preaudit statistics, such as error rates, yields, and cycle times when the audit is initially performed, then comparing these to postaudit statistics. This pre–post comparison and reporting can be a very valuable exercise and it can show the value internal audit's intervention has on the organization. A caveat on this action; auditors must make sure that any other variables that could also account for the improvements are considered so they are not taking credit for improvements that they did not cause.

Metrics

Metrics exist to assess the performance and provide a comparison between what should have been done and what was actually done.

People inherently want to do a good job and when properly led and rewarded, will deliver superior results. Metrics are a great tool to monitor performance and the achievement of organizational goals. As a result, what matters should be measured, and what is measured should matter. Unfortunately, many organizations lack reliable data and only use metrics to a small degree. This limits their ability to know how well or poorly they are doing, and to provide feedback to those stakeholders affected.

Since what gets measured gets attention, management should evaluate their programs and processes in light of the underlying objectives, and identify the metrics that will inform them about the related performance. People will generally ignore what isn't measured and focus on what is measured by taking action to improve those results. A good practice is to make these metrics visible, report, and monitor them publicly (within reason) and make sure that rewards mechanisms are aligned so employees understand the connection between measurable performance and rewards.

The focus should not be to produce metrics simply because the data are there and it can be packaged and reported in certain ways. Instead, the focus should be on the analysis and resulting action. The metrics should be used as a tool for decision making and by selectively choosing the ones that provide the most insightful information, so the organization won't be overwhelmed by this.

Since different stakeholders have different interests and needs, it is important to tailor the metrics to different audiences. This often means creating tiers, levels of detail, presentation modes, and distribution lists that cater to the recipient of the information. Similarly, the information should be acted upon, so accountability should be established to respond and correct deviations.

Having effective metrics in place, followed by their consistent review and corrective action is a key aspect of effective management. Furthermore, by applying the concept of the balanced scorecard, organizations are better equipped to gain a more comprehensive understanding of how well or poorly the organization is operating. This holistic approach, is superior to the one-metric-in-isolation approach, whereby metrics are merely independent measures, while the balanced scorecard consists of a collection of metrics.

Table 2.13 illustrates this concept when applied to a supply chain operation.

Metrics are important not only to ensure worker productivity but also management should simultaneously set the expectation that certain behaviors are expected, while others are unacceptable, from all employees. What is done is of importance, but how it is done is important too. Being solely profit driven will likely lead to unethical behaviors, so management is responsible for setting clear expectations about what is allowed and what is not, and avoid developing metrics-driven mechanisms that only focus on productivity, sales, and similar variables, without accounting for customer service, quality, ethics, respectful treatment, and compliance with legal and moral standards.

The Massachusetts Bay Transportation Authority (MBTA) provides mass transportation services in the Boston area. It is the oldest in the United States and the fourth largest in the nation. In 2016, it unveiled a new interactive website designed to provide easy to understand metrics about its performance. The site shows whether trains and buses have run on schedule, whether the agency is staying on budget, how many people are riding, and how happy or unhappy customers are. The Dashboard, as it is aptly named, provides data on

- *System reliability.* How dependable is the service?
- *Ridership.* How many trips are taken on MBTA bus and subway services on an average weekday?
- *Financials.* How is the MBTA tracking against the operating budget?
- *Customer satisfaction.* How do riders rate the MBTA?

Rachel Bain, assistant secretary for the Office of Performance Management and Innovation stated "A lot of performance reports the T has issued in the past can be so overwhelming that they miss the point. So much of our stuff ends up being, even to me, gibberish. The goal of the Dashboard is to

Table 2.13 Sample Metrics for a Supply Chain Process

Primary Results	Economic Value Added			
	Net Profit Margin	*Return on Assets*	*Gross Profit Margin*	*Revenue*
Subsidiary results metrics	Cost of goods sold (COGS) Cost per unit Direct labor Inbound freight Outbound freight Order fulfillment cost Order fulfillment lead time Overhead Total production cost	Fixed assets Asset turns Asset utilization Productivity Return on investment Working capital Finished goods (FG) carrying cost Inventory value Inventory carrying cost	Overall satisfaction Customer complaints	Revenue growth Percentage of sales from products introduced within the past 12 months Percentage of stock keeping units (SKUs) introduced during the last 12 months
Process metrics	Inventory turnsCost per delivery Percentage of transactions that are paperless	Percentage of production line just-in-time (JIT) Percentage of perfect orders Variability on delivery time Number of errors	Percentage of product line customized Percentage of cross-sale offered and completed Order to ship time Response accuracy Response time to enquiries	Time from feedback to innovation Total marketing cost

Source: Adapted from Jacoby, D. 2009. *Guide to Supply Chain Management: How Getting It Right Boosts Corporate Performance.* New York, NY: Bloomberg Press.

give our customers a way to easily understand how the T is performing." The "Performance Dashboard" was designed to be user-friendly and dynamic; users can look at the reliability of every bus route, commuter rail line, and subway line, users can also filter the data to show if trains and buses keep to their schedules on specific dates and during rush hour/nonrush-hour periods. The Dashboard is believed to be the first of its kind among major transit systems in the United States.

It is also important to remember that some metrics are somewhat indirect to the operation being examined, yet quite useful in assessing the quality, speed, or responsiveness of the process under review. Table 2.13 mentions customer complaints as an example of this, but other examples include the number of Six Sigma Black Belts employed at the organization and at key suppliers, the percentage of the workforce that has received the Six Sigma Green Belt, Yellow Belt, or other type of quality control and internal controls training, ratings on the organizations CSA evaluations, and survey results on motivation levels. I provide a more extensive list of metrics and analytical procedures in Chapter 10.

In my experience, all of these variables play an important role in the quality of operational activities and internal controls.

People, Processes, and Technology

Organizations should establish goals that drive their direction, prioritize the allocation of resources, give employees a sense of mission, and help the organization's vision become a reality. Consequently, there are processes designed to facilitate the achievement of these goals, there are people who work within these processes, and technology and other tools that support both the people and the processes. This relationship is unbreakable and unavoidable.

Unfortunately, all too often organizations fail to pay sufficient attention to the interdependency between these elements. A broken process will compromise the achievement of organizational goals. Unskilled or unmotivated employees will compromise the achievement of these goals. Inadequate or insufficient technology and tools will also compromise the achievement of these goals. When implementing new processes, or modifying existing ones, these three elements must be considered and addressed.

The reader may have witnessed instances when a dysfunctional process, characterized by errors, rework, delays, and other maladies, is "fixed" by introducing a new computer system. The reader may also have experienced the problem of noticing that the new system, however, expensive and well engineered, did not fix the problem. The reason is somewhat simple: a new computer system cannot fix a broken process.

Similarly, these same broken processes sometimes are "fixed" by bringing in more or new workers. This typically doesn't work either, or some metrics may improve, while unit cost, overall cost, motivation level, turnover rates, and other costs increase. Adding more workers to a broken process doesn't automatically fix the problems.

So, the process should be changed first or simultaneously with the new technological solution for the improvements to be effective and sustainable. With regards to the people, their needs must also be addressed and in the case of process improvements, this often means explaining why changes are needed, what benefits they and other stakeholders will derive from the improvements, and what training they will receive so they can contribute positively to the new and enhanced process.

So, these three items must be considered, addressed, and supported simultaneously for changes to be effective and sustainable.

Summary

Operational audits provide a great deal of versatility in the objectives they pursue. While financial reviews focus on whether financial statements faithfully reflect the activities during the period under review (e.g., income statement, statement of cash flows), or the condition as of the last day of the fiscal year (e.g., balance sheet), operational reviews focus on any or all aspects of business operations and attempt to identify opportunities for improvement.

The identification of risk factors plays a pivotal role in that exercise, because to the extent that negative events can hinder the accomplishment of objectives, they should be confronted. Likewise, identifying what must go right is also of high importance, because leveraging opportunities is as important for short- and long-term success; in fact, organizations can fail by not capitalizing promptly and fully on those opportunities before the competition does.

Audit evidence is essential to document the arguments made by the auditor, whether it is to support assertions about prevailing weaknesses, or to add credence to satisfactory conditions, internal auditors must gather, analyze, and interpret all evidence accurately. Metrics, consisting of data related to performance and risk indicators, provide quantitative and qualitative support, and help to determine the condition of the people, processes, and technology in use.

Chapter 3 examines risk assessments and their importance during the planning, fieldwork, and reporting of audit results. Risk assessments are central to the work of internal auditors, helping to define the audit plan, the individual audit programs, the amount of effort that should be exerted to verify the condition of workplace elements, and how best to communicate audit results. The preliminary risk assessment drives the approach for the operational audit, and risk-rating audit findings guide the auditor on how forcibly the audit results must be presented given the urgency of the problem discovered, when applicable.

Should the operation stay the course or change tack? The risk assessment is an invaluable source of information to answer that question.

QUESTIONS

1. List three reasons management may ask for an operational audit to be performed, and explain how the audit program would be impacted by each of them.
2. Explain the importance of identifying risk factors and using them during the planning phase.
3. Explain how an auditor would perform each of the following procedures:
   a. Trace
   b. Vouch
   c. Reconcile
   d. Foot
   e. Cross-foot

4. What is testimonial evidence and how is it gathered?
5. Give two examples where observation is a useful technique to examine operational risks and related controls.
6. Give two examples where document inspection is a useful technique to examine operational risks and related controls.

7. Explain professional skepticism and why it is important for all auditors.
8. Provide three benefits of drawing process maps (flowcharts or value stream maps, as some would rather call them).
9. What is an internal controls questionnaire and how can auditors use it during the planning and fieldwork phases of audits?
10. Explain the acronym CCCER.

Note

1 http://www.goodreads.com/quotes/460142-if-you-fail-to-plan-you-are-planning-to-fail

Chapter 3

Risk Assessments

A chain is only as strong as its weakest link.

Introduction

The theory of constraints adopts the common idiom "a chain is only as strong as its weakest link." This means that organizations, programs, processes, and even departments are vulnerable because the weakest element can always damage, break, or at the very least adversely affect the outcome. So, attention must be paid to performing an inventory of all the related components, assessing their strengths and weaknesses, performing a gap analysis, identify appropriate responses, implementing the best remedial action, and monitoring results. In many ways, this describes the risk assessment and management process.

There are many types of risks, ranging from strategic, operational, compliance, reporting, and IT related. Their consequences vary and are influenced by the types of vulnerabilities involved, the degree to which these consequences can be anticipated to deter or prevent their occurrence, the sophistication of the response mechanisms, and the flexibility of the organization to adapt as needed. This means that management must be aware, engaged, and knowledgeable to learn from history, understand the present, and prepare for the future.

Risk and CSAs are an effective mechanism to involve those who have ownership for risks and controls in the organization. By documenting processes, participants, and influencing variables, management can be better prepared to allocate resources appropriately, set priorities, establish accountabilities, and institute monitoring procedures.

The risk and control landscape has changed significantly over the past three decades. Operational changes, such as technological advances, globalization, outsourcing (domestic and offshore), complexities in financial markets, and demographic shifts, have all exposed organizations to a set of risk dynamics that require creativity and constant vigilance. Manual controls and procedures have limited value in an environment where conditions can change rapidly, and the relentless expectation of lower costs and higher quality require automation, speed, and accuracy.

In the midst of all these dynamics, internal auditors are uniquely positioned to help management and their boards of directors, and advocate for other stakeholders that don't have direct access to daily business events, but whose interests must be protected as well.

Risk Assessments

A risk assessment is the process of identifying, measuring, and analyzing risks relevant to a program or process. This assessment is systematic, iterative, and subject to both quantitative and qualitative inputs and factors. Furthermore, it is also dependent on the timeframe of the review.

Identification of Risks

A key aspect of any risk assessment is the identification of the relevant risks. This takes the form of a list of risks. Quite often this step is not exhaustive enough or performed by individuals with limited knowledge of the process being assessed. As a result, only some of the relevant risks are identified. This creates several limitations, the first and most important is the fact that all other actions related to the risk assessment will be limited as well. If a risk has not been identified, it won't be measured or analyzed either.

Internal auditors sometimes fail to identify relevant risks due to their lack of in-depth knowledge about the process being audited. This is understandable to a certain extent because they are external reviewers. At the same time, it highlights the importance of auditors doing sufficient planning and research so they have familiarity about the activities involved. Another reason for auditors' limited identification of risks is the bias that some may have as a result of the common training many have in accounting. If the auditor has been educated in accountancy, has had experience in accounting, and has focused primarily on accounting and compliance audits, the auditor is more likely to view most matters from an accounting and compliance prism. While this is also understandable, it is reason enough for auditors to be cognizant of this bias and make every effort to broaden their thinking into other types of risks.

To avoid these issues, it is useful to include in the risk identification exercise people with an extensive knowledge of the program or process that will be analyzed. This includes executives, employees with specialized technical skills, and those with long tenure in the organization. Their experience and expertise can be very helpful at this point in the process and it will be equally important in subsequent steps as well.

Another way to identify relevant risks is to use a prepared list. There are multiple templates and lists available, often organized by industry. COSO, ISO, Information Technology Infrastructure Library (ITIL), CVNET, and others have prepared lists that can help to identify some of the key risks that should be included in the assessment. When using them, auditors should always consider the peculiarities of their organizations and make sure that the list is adapted accordingly. While many of items on the prepared list will be relevant, that is not always the case.

The following are some of the common risks that operational auditors should consider during their risk assessments. Not all risks are applicable to every organization because differences in industry, business activities, geographic location, and size of organization make a difference. In addition, when performing operational reviews, auditors must examine a wider assortment of risks, and not just financial ones. For example, see Table 3.1.

It is imperative for internal auditors to remember that there are internal and external constraints in organizations. Internal constraints typically include

Table 3.1   Operational Risk Types

Type	Description
Capacity	■ Inability to produce as many units as required
	■ Process generating excessive amounts of waste
	■ Producing too many defective parts (i.e., error rate)
	■ Delivering ordered goods or services past the promised date
	■ Inability to provide high-quality service to every customer
Strategic	■ Failing to maintain beneficial relationships with customers'
	■ Computer system's inability to support the operating unit's needs
	■ Manufacturing lines being unable to keep pace with sales growth
	■ Lack of funding to finance business expansion
	■ Knowledge drain due to employee turnover
	■ Failure to respond to changing customer preferences
Compliance	■ Failure to meet external requirements (e.g., laws and regulations)
	■ Failure to meet internal standard operating procedure (SOP) requirements
	■ Failure to meet combined requirements (e.g., contracts)
Natural environment	■ Energy supply disruption
	■ Damage from fire, water, or natural disasters (e.g., floods, earthquakes, hurricanes, and tornadoes)
	■ Inability to secure needed resources (e.g., water and minerals)
	■ Dependency on carbon-based sources of energy
	■ Business interruption caused by disease
Political	■ Changes in legislation or regulation due to government changes
	■ Social unrest triggered by changes in government

Equipment. The types of equipment available and the ways they are used limit the ability of the process to produce more high quality goods and deliver services.

People. Lack of skilled and motivated workers limits the productive capacity of any process. Attitudes and other mental models (e.g., feeling defeated, victimized, or hopeless) embraced by workers can lead to behaviors that become a constraint on the process.

Policies. Written and unwritten policies can prevent the process from producing more of higher quality goods and services.

In addition, when evaluating internal dynamics and risks, internal auditors should be concerned about: (1) the slowest operation in a process, (2) the synchronization of activities within or between processes, and (3) robbing materials and other resources within or between processes or units. In my experience, a large number of operational issues are materialized due to one or several of these dynamics.

Measurement of Risks

After risks have been identified, they must be measured. The measurement process can be either subjective or quantitative, and either driven by facts or not. Subjective measures are driven by the participants' experience and intuition about the risks involved. Quite often, risks are measure using a three-point scale of high–medium–low. Using these measures, the impact of the risk, if it were to materialize, and the likelihood of the risk, if it were to occur, are rated. This can also be done using a five-point scale, with likelihood measures of rare–unlikely–possible–likely–almost certain. Impact measure may include insignificant–minor–moderate–major–catastrophic.

A key limitation of using these measures is that they are not based on explicit figures or facts. As such, one person's "minor" risk, could be someone else's "moderate," and so on. While this difference of opinion will always exist, the prevalence and magnitude of the differences generally increases when the process is predominantly subjective.

To improve on this, values can be attached to the assessment as shown in Figures 3.1 and 3.2.

Some argue that the probability values don't have to be linear and arranged in equally sized intervals. For example, Derbyshire in Northern England uses the following likelihood scale shown in Table 3.2.[1]

	Impact	Range ($)		
1	Negligible	0	to	50,000
2	Marginal	50,001	to	100,000
3	Critical	100,001	to	200,000
4	Severe	200,001	to	500,000
5	Catastrophic	1 million+		

Figure 3.1 Impact ratings by range.

	Likelihood	Range (%)		
1	Unlikely	0	to	20
2	Remote	21	to	40
3	Possible	41	to	60
4	Likely	61	to	80
5	Very likely	80	to	100

Figure 3.2 Likelihood ratings by range.

Table 3.2   Sample Nonlinear Likelihood Ratings

Level	Descriptor	Likelihood Over 5 Years	Likelihood Over 5 Years
1	Low	>0.005%	>1 in 20,000 chance
2	Medium–low	>0.05%	>1 in 2000 chance
3	Medium	>0.5%	>1 in 200 chance
4	Medium–high	>5%	>1 in 20 chance
5	High	>50%	>1 in 2 chance

Similarly, the impact ratings can be expanded to provide more detailed descriptions of the ranges for each. This may involve including variables such as the degree of disruption to the organization, bodily injury to workers and others, security, health and safety, social, economic, and environmental impacts (Tables 3.3 and 3.4).[2]

While this approach has been used extensively for many years by auditors and others, more precise quantitative approaches are emerging to link data to the measures shown above. These range from fairly simple ones to very complex ones based on extensive algorithms and historical data. Although many organizations are unprepared to adopt very complex approaches, the trend and expectation is that over time organizations will increase their sophistication, and incorporate more tangible, verifiable, and robust data. For example, when calculating the impact or consequence of a fire in a warehouse, the likelihood can be based on intuition and the level of concern over the items being stored and worked upon in the warehouse. A more quantitative approach would involve contacting insurance underwriters and actuaries who have statistical information about the incidence of fires in warehouses storing the materials in question.

If we consider the likelihood of delivery trucks having a roadside accident, the quantitative measure can be improved by looking at the National Transportation Safety Board and insurance industry data showing the accident rate of similar vehicles per 100,000 miles on the road. That figure can be adjusted for area density (urban vs. suburban vs. rural routes), weather conditions (e.g., snowy locales vs. rainy vs. arid), topography (e.g., hilly vs. flat), time (e.g., daytime vs. nighttime), and cargo weight (e.g., light vs. heavy loads).

Similarly, the impact to the organization and its operations should there be a fire in the warehouse can be based on beliefs and assumptions, or they can be based on the replacement value of the building and the average (or highest) value of the inventory stored in the facility. These figures can be adjusted periodically to make sure that the measurements are as accurate as reasonably possible. The same approach can be applied to delivery trucks, where the impact to the organization and others can be based on industry statistics and company history, average value and type of delivery items, and additional coverage for potential injury and damage to others.

Engineering specifications, industry statistics, and historical data can help organizations acquire the data for this approach. Scenario analysis, Monte Carlo analysis, and decision-tree simulations are examples of probabilistic modeling decision-making tools. They are outside the scope of this book, but increasingly being used to better assess exposures.

Table 3.3   Expanded Impact Ratings

Impact Rating	
Negligible—very low	Very little damage or harm. No disruption in operations. Insignificant number of injuries or impact on health. Insignificant number of people displaced and insignificant personal support required. Insignificant disruption to community services, or to the local economy
Marginal—low—minor damage or harm	No significant disruptions in operations. The event is less likely to cause any significant harm to staff or others and could be managed. Small number of people affected, no fatalities, and small number of minor injuries treated with first aid treatment. Minor damage to properties or displacement of a small number of people for less than 24 h and minor personal support required. Minor localized disruption to community services or infrastructure lasting less than 24 h. Negligible impact on local economy and the cost is easily absorbed. There is minor impact on environment with no lasting effects
Critical—moderate—significant damage or harm	Event may cause some very short disruptions to operations. Likely there is significant injury to staff and could result in moderate loss of assets, but event is manageable. Significant number of casualties, some requiring hospitalization and medical treatment. Damage that is confined to a specific location, or to a number of locations, but requires additional resources. Localized displacement of more than 100 people for up to 3 days. Disruption to infrastructure and community services. Limited impact on the local economy with some short-term loss of production and possible additional clean-up costs. Limited impact on the local environment with short- or long-term effects
Severe—high–serious damage or harm	May cause significant disruption or suspension in operations. May cause significant injury or death of workers or staff members. Could result in major loss of assets and finances and seriously jeopardize the company's abilities. Difficult to manage. Significant number of people in the affected area impacted with multiple fatalities, multiple serious or extensive injuries, and significant hospitalization. Significant damage requiring external resources to support local responders. 100–500 people in danger and displaced for more than 1 week. Significant impact and possible breakdown of delivery of some local community services. Significant impact on the local economy with medium-term loss of production. Significant extra cleanup and recovery costs. Significant impact on the environment with medium- to long-term effects

(Continued)

TABLE 3.3 (*Continued*) **Expanded Impact Ratings**

Impact Rating	
Catastrophic—very high—critical—extreme damage or harm	May result in long-term suspension of operations and possible office or program closure. Concern about imminent loss of life. Major loss or damage of assets and would be difficult to recover from. Very difficult or impossible to manage. Very large numbers of people in affected area(s) impacted with significant numbers of fatalities, large number of people requiring hospitalization with serious injuries with longer-term effects. Extensive damage to properties and infrastructure in the affected area requiring major demolition. General and widespread displacement of more than 500 people for a prolonged duration and extensive personal support required. Damage to infrastructure causes significant disruption to, or loss of, key services for a prolonged period. The community is unable to function without significant support and there is serious impact on local and regional economy with some long-term, potentially permanent, loss of production. Extensive clean-up and recovery costs. Serious long-term impact or permanent damage to the environment

The Risk Matrix

The risk matrix is a widely used and highly effective tool to record and analyze the objectives, risks, and controls in the program or process that is being audited as defined in the scope definition. The risk matrix is an essential ingredient when conducting risk-based audits, as they provide a means to capture and analyze these items.

The layout varies by organization, but it generally shows as seen in Figure 3.3.

Assessing Risk and Control Types

Risk assessment is a complex activity that some confuse with risk management. Risk assessment is a process, which means it is dynamic, and that in and of itself begins to highlight the lack of understanding that some have about this. For some, risk assessment consists of guessing how likely it is that something bad can happen, and if it did, guess what the impact might be. This some do merely to respond to a request from someone else so they can get this task off their "to-do" list.

Risk assessment is a process that is often done iteratively. The process begins by identifying potential hazards and analyzing those items to determine what could happen if the hazard were to occur.

There are many negative events that could occur, so the organization should consider the many hazards that the organizations and its stakeholders are or could be exposed to. These can occur depending on the magnitude, location, timing, velocity, and persistence of the hazard to cause damage to the organization, its stakeholders, and assets. An important aspect of risk assessment is identifying and quantifying the assets that are at risk.

Table 3.4   Expanded Likelihood Ratings

Likelihood Rating	
Unlikely–very low	The event is considered as not having a realistic probability of occurring against the organization under prevailing conditions. The organization has very little exposure to the threat
Remote—low—somewhat likely	The event is considered to have a reasonable probability of occurring and affecting the organization under prevailing conditions. The organization has some, but limited, exposure to the threat. This could also indicate some weakness in existing security measures
Possible—moderate—likely	The event is considered to have a fairly high probability of occurring and affecting the organization under prevailing conditions. The organization has a reasonable amount of exposure to the threat. This could indicate insufficient security measures
Very likely—high	The event is considered to have a very high probability of occurring and affecting the organization under prevailing conditions. The organization has a high amount of exposure to the threat. This could indicate very weak security measures
Certain or imminent—very high	The event is considered to be imminent and expected to occur. The organization has an extremely high amount of exposure to the threat. This could indicate the complete lack/absence of the appropriate security measures

Objectives		Risks												Controls				Audit program steps
Objectives	Risks	S	O	R	C	IT	F	Prob.	Imp.	Vel	Pers.		Control	P/D	A/M	X/D/W/M/Q	Audit steps
O1	R11												C111				AS1 (C111, C112, C113, C121)
													C112				
													C113				
	R12												C121				AS2 (C122, C123)
													C122				
													C123				
													C124				AS3 (C124)
	R13												-				
	-												C141				

Figure 3.3   Risk matrix.

While the word "asset" is usually associated with monetary resources, tangible goods (e.g., buildings, vehicles, machinery, and inventory), reputation, and both employees' and customers' health and safety are also of importance, because a poor reputation or injuries are a critical consideration of any risk assessment. Damage to company IT is also a key consideration, since a substantial amount of resources are typically invested in these items and interruption to their continued operation can cause severe disruption to the organization. The occurrence of a risk event could have a negative effect on the relationships that the organization has with its customers, suppliers, the surrounding community, investors, and other stakeholders. The loss of confidence in the organization, its leadership, its products, and services can be severe.

The conduct of a risk assessment means that we should look for weaknesses (sometimes referred to as vulnerabilities) that would make an asset susceptible to damage or loss from the hazard. When it comes to vulnerabilities, some common weaknesses are the age, condition, and location of buildings, and their contents (e.g., near coastal or seismic areas, critical systems on lower floors that are susceptible to flooding, shared office locations). To illustrate this, a warehouse without a fire sprinkler system could suffer a total loss, or at least far more extensive damage than a building with a fire sprinkler system that is professionally designed, installed, maintained, and inspected regularly. Similarly, an operation where customer payments are predominantly in cash is more susceptible to losses than another where payments are received electronically in a centralized location.

The Business Dictionary defines vulnerability as the "degree to which people, property, resources, systems, and cultural, economic, environmental, and social activity is susceptible to harm, degradation, or destruction on being exposed to a hostile agent or factor."[3] With this definition in mind, internal auditors can work with management to examine any aspect of the organization. The process of identifying the relevant events will be driven by the scope definition of the review, and can be done by following any of the following approaches.

Objectives based. Identify events that may hinder the ability of the organization to achieve its objectives partially or completely. In this case, brainstorming and the Adelphi method may be useful techniques to collect the relevant information and assess the impact of these events. Note that the event does not have to be negative in its immediate interpretation. For example, the rapid changes in the availability of broadband, apps, and the way consumers used cellphones changed industry dynamics limiting BlackBerry's market share, while Apple, Samsung, and LG leveraged these dynamics and grew rapidly. The event was the same, the impact on the organization was significantly different for the companies mentioned.

Scenario based. Create different scenarios or alternative ways of achieving objectives and determine how forces interact. A useful approach is to identify triggers that can start–stop different scenarios from occurring. By identifying and understanding the triggers caused or accelerated by these scenarios, the organization can better prepare itself to leverage opportunities and avoid negative consequences.

For either of these two approaches, management must consider the external and internal factors that can affect event occurrence:

> *External.* For example, economic, business, natural environment, political, social, and technological factors.
> *Internal.* Examples include infrastructure, personnel, processes, and technology.

To identify events, management must look into the past and the future to identify trends, shifting demographics, new markets, and competitor activities, among others. In many cases, these events are influenced by technological changes, economic development, increases in literacy levels, higher education attainment, natural events (e.g., floods and hurricanes), and demographic changes.

Events can have either a positive or negative impact representing risks and opportunities. These developments should be incorporated into the objective setting process and risk assessment.

Common-risk checking. Use a prefabricated list of common risks in your industry or area of scope. This technique is explained in more detail below.

Risk charting. Combination of above approaches consists of listing resources at risk and the threats to those resources. Identify the risk factors and the consequences. Hazards are of concern to the extent that they can result in some kind of loss to the program, process, or organization. The impact of these hazards and how to reduce them is the next aspect of the risk assessment process. This is referred to as mitigation.

There are many hazards that can threaten the safe and continued operation of an organization (Table 3.5).

The list of hazards is substantial, and the resources available to identify and incorporate them in the risk assessment have improved over the past few years as well. The following are but some of these resources available.

The Federal Emergency Management Agency provides the Mapping Information Platform and the Risk MAP (Mapping, Assessment, and Planning) to help organizations by delivering data that increases public awareness and leads to action to reduce the risk to property and life.[4]

The US Geological Service (USGS) has a great deal of seismic information to help organizations identify their vulnerabilities from fault lines, and incident history as a possible gauge to future activity through probability analysis based on location, time span, and radius from a designated location. The USGS also provides information related to landslides, volcanic activity, while the Occupational Safety and Health Administration of the US Department of Labor, also provides information about workplace hazards.[5]

The National Weather Service provides rain, hurricane, air quality, winter storm, flood, and marine weather information, which can have a substantial impact on the health, safety, and

Table 3.5 Organizational Hazards

Hazard	Examples
Natural	Floods, earthquakes, hurricanes, temperature, pandemic, and contamination
Human	Unintentional: poorly operated equipment, unsafe work procedures, fatigue, lack of training, and distractions
	Intentional: workplace violence, strikes, arson, and fraud
Mechanical	Poorly placed or installed equipment, outdated equipment, structural failure and mechanical breakdown, and hazardous materials
Technological	Loss of connectivity and corrupted data
Logistics	Supplier disruption and transportation interruption

operation of organizational process. Recall the impact that extreme cold and heavy snow fall had on the MBTA network during the 2015 winter season.[6]

Workplace violence has gained a great deal of attention as a result of several incidents affecting workplace safety, some of which have been fatal. The Critical Incident Response Group of the FBI published the *Workplace Violence: Issues in Response* manual. Workplace violence can be caused by a single or several disgruntled individuals (e.g., employees and customers), but also by organized groups (e.g., terrorists). The evolving nature of workplace violence requires management assessment to protect company facilities, employees, and visitors. While the threat of terrorism is increasingly on people's minds, these mass murders, while serious, are relatively infrequent. Instead, the threats, harassment, bullying, domestic violence, stalking, emotional abuse, intimidation, and other forms of behavior and physical violence can result in more serious violent behavior. This is especially true if there are no policies in place, they are inadequate or not enforced by supervisors and managers. Supervisors and managers should deal with these problems promptly, assertively, and consistently. The report states

> Employers have a legal and ethical obligation to promote a work environment free from threats and violence and, in addition, can face economic loss as the result of violence in the form of lost work time, damaged employee morale and productivity, increased workers' compensation payments, medical expenses, and possible lawsuits and liability costs.

The Environmental Protection Agency (EPA) provides information and assistance regarding harmful effects to human health or to ecological systems caused by exposure to any physical, chemical, or biological entity that can result in an adverse response (called stressors). In this case, of particular concern are how much of a chemical is present, how much exposure could or did occur, and the toxicity of the chemical. Consequently, the process of assessing human health risk assessment consists of the identification of hazards, followed by an analysis of the relationship between exposure and effects (i.e., dose–response assessment), exposure assessment to note what is known about the frequency, timing, and levels of contact with a stressor and lastly, risk characterization where the analysis involves examining how well the data support the nature and extent of the risk from exposure to the environmental stressors.

This process can be facilitated by asking a series of questions, for example

- What types of health problems may be caused by environmental stressors such as chemicals and radiation?
- What is the chance that people will experience health problems when exposed to different levels of environmental stressors?
- Is there a level below which some chemicals don't pose a human health risk? What environmental stressors are people exposed to, at what levels, and for how long?
- Are some people more likely to be susceptible to environmental stressors because of factors such as age, genetics, preexisting health conditions, ethnic practices, gender, etc.?
- Are some people more likely to be exposed to environmental stressors because of factors such as where they work, where they play, what they like to eat, etc.?[7]

The EPA, like the USGS, National Weather Service, and others, provide multiple databases, models, and other tools for the conduct of risk assessments.[8] The usage of these quantitative devices helps organizations avoid, or at least limit, the amount of guessing that is characteristic of some risk assessments so the calculation of likelihoods and impacts can be done more scientifically.

The answers to these types of questions help decision makers, whether they are parents or public officials, understand the possible human health risks from environmental media.

In technological circles, the common vulnerabilities and exposures (CVE) is a list of information security vulnerabilities and exposures that provides common names for known cyber security issues. Run by the US Department of Homeland Security, it is a free and public resource that makes it easier to share data across tools and services. The CVE list provides key information to the US National Vulnerability Database (NVD) to provide enhanced information for each identifier (also known as CVE names or numbers), such as corrective measures, severity and impact arranged by vendor, product, repository, product version, vulnerability type, and exploit information.

Since CVE provides information about multiple tools and the coverage provided by each, it enables organizations scan their intrusion detection system to determine if they have the appropriate safeguards to identify attempts to exploit specific vulnerabilities. Vulnerabilities in software can be used by hackers to gain access to a system or network, so having this information enables organizations to preempt possible attacks.

Through security advisories, organizations can check their databases, tools, and services to make sure they promptly identify any needed fixes from vendors' software products. So, if vendors and customers use the CVE standards and are CVE compatible, it is easier and faster to identify and correct vulnerabilities. In the end, organizations will know which tools are most effective for the organization's needs because they can link databases to find out where weaknesses exist. With this information, and the US NVD, business leaders can identify the remedies that will protect the organization's systems.[9]

When management is assessing their exposures to various risks, they must pay particular attention to data security. This goes beyond assessing the personally identifiable information that tends to be featured in many of today's headlines. Information at risk includes intellectual property, strategic corporate plans, communications (e.g., e-mail), and operational data used to make business decisions. It is important to ensure the organization focuses on the integrity and availability of the information and not only on the confidentiality of information. While it is important to focus on improving controls to hopefully prevent a cyber incident, it is also critical the organization improves its ability to monitor and identify whether it is experiencing a cyber incident. For this, they must have clear and effective cyber response plans and procedures in place.

If the impact can be significant, the organization should consider creating a mitigation strategy. If the impact is medium or low, then control activities are often enough. Hazards are relevant to the extent that there are assets that can be negatively impacted by these hazards. Assets include people, property, merchandise, and computer systems. Of great concert, and the reason why this exercise is important for auditors and business leaders alike, is the likelihood and magnitude of impacts to the organizations.

Impacts vary and include financial loss, property damage, fines, lawsuits, and loss of customers, among many others. Table 3.6 illustrates the relationship between these items.

The risk assessment, with the identification of hazards, assets at risk, impact analysis, and response activities can serve the organization well and increase the likelihood that goals and objectives will be achieved. The challenge today is greater than in the past, however, because in today's dynamic and highly competitive business and operating environment, organizations lacking the ability to adapt, and take advantage of opportunities proactively are as likely to fail as those that poorly manage the risk of adverse outcomes.

Table 3.6   Relationship of Hazards, Assets at Risk, and Organizational Impact

Hazards	Assets at Risk	Impact
Cyber attack	Property	Property damage
Supplier failure	People, property	Financial loss
Mechanical breakdown	Systems	Loss of customers
Utility outage	Machinery	Personal injury
Pandemic	Reputation, people	Contamination
Hazardous material spill	Environment	Fines and penalties
Terrorism	Property, people	Lawsuits, personal injury
Fire, explosion, structural collapse	Property, people, machinery	Loss of confidence in the organization, financial loss

Organizations must be resilient, so as much as anticipating adverse outcomes is key to success, the lack of flexibility to embrace new technologies, understand, and capitalize on new technologies, financial products, emerging markets, and social dynamics can be the cause of ruin. Organizations may find out all too late, that others have gained market share, obtained the necessary funding, and reduced their operating costs faster, rendering them uncompetitive.

The Importance of CSAs

Internal auditors have been proclaiming that management and the board "own" the programs and processes of the organization, the objectives of these programs and processes, the risks that jeopardize the achievement of these objectives, and the controls that mitigate their likelihood and impact. While this is true, my experience has been that far too many managers are not aware of this ownership. During my internal audit seminars, I often ask recent college graduates if they were required to take a class on internal auditing and while conditions are improving, all too often only accounting majors report they were required to do so. Consequently, if most business majors don't receive specific instructions on risks and controls, how much instruction would nonbusiness majors receive? This is of concern because many may later take on management responsibilities.

CSAs are designed to address this gap. They consist of questionnaires and other documents that process owners complete that identify the major activities in their programs and processes, the objectives, risks and controls, the individuals that perform key tasks and controls, and the major challenges affecting these programs and processes. CSAs require managers to think about the design and condition of their areas of responsibility, and assess the presence and quality of the related controls.

The adoption of CSAs is far from universal. In fact, when I ask seminar participants if there is a CSA program in place at their organizations, a significant number often state that their organizations do not have one in place, and they have not yet begun the process of implementing one. Those that have one in place, often share that the program is not living up to their expectations in terms of usage throughout the entire organization or the quality of the data captured in these documents.

I have found that success requires a great deal of work, but the rewards are worth the effort. The process should include internal auditors speaking to managers during their onboarding. Manager training should include topics related to internal controls. The information captured during the CSA process should also be subject to audit review and comparison between what the process owner indicated in the forms and what the internal audits identify in terms of risk and control effectiveness. Discrepancies should be analyzed and discussed with the corresponding manager and the initial assessment updated.

As subsequent cycles capture new data, the process repeats itself and by the third or fourth year, the quality of the data typically reflects existing conditions more accurately. Therefore, effective CSA programs require communication, linkage to corporate compliance and internal audit results, providing feedback on the gap analysis, and reinforcement. Control self-assessments can be very useful in helping organizations improve corporate governance. This often occurs as the process becomes embedded in the organization's practices and those who participate in the activities and are responsible for completing these documents, gain increasing knowledge about the organization's risks and controls, and how they relate to business objectives. These assessments also improve the quality of risk assessments as process owners gain competence on the linkages and incorporate this knowledge in operational and strategic decision-making. CSAs also help to improve accountability because the related documentation includes the roles of process owners, the identification of key control points and performers, the escalation process triggered when deficiencies are identified, and how remediation of issues is performed and evidenced. The result is better operational effectiveness as awareness, documentation, oversight, accountability, and follow-through improve. Internal auditors are encouraged to promote the implementation and promotion of CSAs, so their adoption is sustainable and the benefits can be realized.

Business Activities and Their Risk Implications

Organizations are engaged in a variety of activities and use a multitude of tools in their daily activities. It is essential that internal auditors have a general understanding of these practices, but also know how risk and opportunity affect these tools and actions. The following is a select list and discussion of business practices to provide a general understanding of the concept, the implications for internal auditors and where risk and opportunities lie.

Assemble to order. This is a type of production system where the material is prepared so it can be assembled quickly upon receipt of the customer request and is usually customizable to a certain degree. In general, the parts are already manufactured, but won't be assembled until the order is received. This strategy is between two other common manufacturing strategies: make to stock (MTS) and make to order (MTO). In MTS, products are manufactured in advance, while in MTO, the products are produced after the order is received. By combining the two strategies, organizations can get products to the customer quickly while allowing some flexibility to be customizable, so customers can quickly receive products based on their needs.

In this scenario, companies can sell a large number of different products from common parts. They maintain inventory for the common parts and sell customized products. Since the company doesn't have to anticipate every final product that a customer would want, they can have fewer items in inventory and use less storage space as well. Another benefit is that the organization can reduce the likelihood of errors by providing customers a list of ways the product can be assembled. So, components are made to stock and then assembled to order after the customer order is received.

While the concept is usually associated with manufacturing, such as computer systems, industrial equipment, and automobiles, it is also applicable in other environments, such as services, for example, corporate training.

MTO. This methodology involves manufacturing only after a customer's order is received, so the process begins when demand occurs. This is a pull-type supply chain operation because manufacturing is performed when demand is confirmed. In other words, it is being pulled by demand. The opposite business model is to manufacture products for stock MTS, which is push-type production.

There are various models for MTO. For example, in some cases, the process of assembling prepared parts starts when actual demand occurs. Or, in other cases, the production process starts with the obtaining of materials and parts, or further back from development designing (engineering).

MTS. When using this methodology, products are manufactured based on demand forecasts. Since the accuracy of the forecasts will prevent excess inventory on one end, and minimize the opportunity loss due to stockouts on the other, the issue for organizations is how to forecast demands accurately.

This methodology means to manufacture products for stock based on demand forecasts, which can be regarded as push-type production. In environments of mass production and mass marketing, the requirement for mass production urged standardization and efficient business management such as cost reduction.

Bottleneck. This term refers to a point in a process where there is limited productive capacity and the flow slows down. This constriction can slow or even stop the flow of work until some intervention occurs, or time passes allowing items to move through, while other incoming items continue to accumulate. When input comes in faster than the speed of the process, accumulation starts to occur. The blockage stalls production affecting the number of items produced, and has an impact on customer satisfaction since it leads to an increase in cycle time. Additional effects include supply overstock if the items are being produced faster than they are being sold. This situation can be frustrating for employees as well, who experience the lack of positive performance of the process, the likely complaints from customers and experience low morale as a result.

If the problem is short term or temporary (e.g., an employee takes a few days off), the impact is often not significant and customers often accept the explanation. However, internal auditors should always determine if the slowdown is acceptable and if a backup operator should provide coverage.

If the problem is longer term, then the impact is much more substantial and should be investigated further. A common mistake is to treat the delay(s) as temporary because an employee is out, but as other employees take their allowed time off, the cumulative effect could be that at virtually any point in time, the unit is experiencing bottlenecks somewhere. In the end, this impacts customer satisfaction and begs the question about backup coverage. Another form of long-term bottlenecks occurs when a machine cannot keep pace with the demand due to its inefficiency.

Eliminating bottlenecks is critical for improving efficiencies in any production line. Bottlenecks can be found by identifying the areas where accumulation occurs, evaluating the output of the process, assessing whether each machine used in the production process is being used to its full capacity, and finding the machine with the highest wait time. A similar problem occurs in case-work environment, so the auditor is encouraged to consider the concepts presented here and apply them to the appropriate environment being audited.

Collaborative inventory management. Consists of the cooperation between a buyer and a supplier to improve stock availability and reduce costs. This is often accomplished by sharing forecast information and using a single plan.

Consignment. This is an inventory management and replenishment method where a buyer only pays for the products held at a third party location when the items have been sold to the customer. Unsold products can usually be returned to the supplier as well. Wikipedia defines it as "the act of giving over to another person or agent's charge, custody or care any material or goods but retaining legal ownership until the material or goods are sold." It means sending goods to another party, but ownership of these goods remains with the sender.

This arrangement is often used to place products close to the customer to reduce shipping times. It can also reduce carrying and inventory costs because the other organization keeping custody of the items may warehouse the items at a lower cost than if the producing company did it itself by maintaining multiple storage facilities in various geographic locations.

This distinction is important because it means that the items remain on the owner's financial records as inventory until sold. Auditors need to make sure the items are counted regularly, reported accurately, and evaluated periodically to make sure their monetary value is accurate and that the items are not obsolete (i.e., unsalable). Conversely, if the organization is incurring high inventory carrying costs, maintains multiple storage facilities, and is unable to manage them effectively, or delivery times are being affected by long lead times, a consignment arrangement may be a useful recommendation for management.

Cycle time. Refers to the reduction in the time and related costs needed for a product or service to move through part or all of a supply chain. Internal auditors focused on financial and many compliance risks have paid little attention to this topic. However, as customer satisfaction gains increased importance to ensure first and subsequent sales, and to improve the organization's image, internal auditors do their organizations a disservice if they do not examine cycle time as a risk and opportunity. Furthermore, whenever a compliance requirement states "timely reporting…," the internal auditor should ask: "How do we make sure that we meet the reporting deadline every time?"

Cycle time compression is a related concept and relates to the reengineering of processes to reduce the cycle time. A word of caution is also warranted here. Some auditors may assume that whenever I mention supply chain that I am referring to manufacturing organizations and their related operations. That is not so. The concept of supply chain refers to the system of people, activities, information, and resources involved in creating and moving a product or service from the supplier(s) to the customer. With this in mind then, the concept also applies to service organizations, and within an organization, we can argue that there are many micro supply chains. For example, what does it take for an organization to hire a new employee? What are the steps in the supply chain that ensure an incoming invoice is paid according to the agreed upon terms?

Distribution center (DC) bypass or drop ship. This activity refers to circumventing the DC or entire distribution channel by routing freight directly to its destination. In other words, move products from the manufacturer directly to the retailer or end user without going through the typical distribution channels. This requires coordination with suppliers and customers to make sure there are sufficient items in stock and to address delivery frequencies required by customers.

While this practice can reduce cycle time and costs, it can create some risks to the organization as unscrupulous individuals could have items shipped to an unauthorized location for personal gain. Internal auditors should examine any such arrangements carefully to ensure that all shipments are authorized and legitimate.

Electronic data interchange (EDI). These consist of standardized sets of data transmitted between various business partners during business transactions. By using the same standard, two companies can exchange documents and reduce the reliance on paper, and reduce human interaction saving time and money. Another benefit is that with backed up electronic documents, these are more easily retrievable and storage costs are also reduced while being protected from natural hazards (e.g., fire, water, and deterioration).

In the case of a buyer and a seller, it makes possible the sharing of information regarding supply chain events, such as invoices, shipping notices, purchase orders, and requests for quotation. As more trading partners transmit information electronically, EDI has become a widely used mechanism to share information and enable faster and cheaper business transactions. For example, a seller can notify the manufacturer to ship from the warehouse to a retailer electronically and include in the transmission details about the receiving party such as the shipping address, billing address, specific items to ship, and quantity.

Beyond supply chain type of transactions, EDI is used to exchange many other types of information, such as medical records, laboratory results, transportation information (e.g., type of container and mode of shipment), and telecommunications. EDI requires there be an interface between each organization's internal systems and partners' systems. For an "inbound" document, the receiver needs to validate that the trading partner sending the file is a valid trading partner, that the structure of the file meets the EDI standards, and that the individual fields of information meet the agreed upon standards. Typically, software will create a file (e.g., fixed length, variable length, or XML tagged format) then convert and import the converted file or database into a format that can be imported into the receiver's business systems (e.g., ERP).

For an "outbound" document, the process consists of exporting a file (or read a database) from a company's information systems and convert the file to the appropriate format. The file is then validated to make sure it meets the standard agreed upon by the trading partners, converted into "EDI" format (adding the appropriate identifiers and control structures), and sent to the trading partner using the appropriate communications protocol.

An important aspect of EDI exchanges is the need to verify that all of the required steps were followed as the data and documents flow between trading partners. All transactions must be tracked to make sure they are not lost. For example, if the purchase order (PO) a buyer sends a vendor is lost, both parties will suffer negative consequences. The supplier does not fulfil the order, so there is a financial loss due to the lost business and the business relationship would be affected as well. For the buyer, which could be a retailer, they suffer a stock outage and lose sales, experience a reduction in customer service and satisfaction, and eventually have lower profits. Internal auditors can add value to their organizations by making sure that the relationships are formalized, that both parties follow the same standards, that outbound and inbound information is validated, and that transmissions are secure.

Inventory. Stock of raw materials, semifinished goods (e.g., work in process), or finished material held to protect the organization against unpredictable, uncertain, or erratic supply or demand with the objective of avoiding stock-out situations. While it is common practice to maintain inventory of various quantities and types, at different locations within a facility or multiple locations within a supply chain, managed by the owner of the items or by third parties, the concept of inventory management has changed over time.

For decades, JIT has been advocating zero or near-zero inventory levels. The idea is that the organization should only receive supplies it knows it will need, these items should arrive immediately when they are needed, and they should be moved forward toward the end user immediately. In effect, not hold any inventory but rather use pull systems. A pull strategy consists of the buyer "pulling" the goods or information they need (i.e., demand for their needs), while the suppliers "push" these items toward the consumers. In simple terms, push production is based on forecast demand and pull production is based on actual or consumed demand. The main premise is that inventory is the storage of company resources that could be used elsewhere for more productive purposes. Inventory also has carrying costs (e.g., storage and protection) and if the demand never materializes, the items may become obsolete.

There are a number of key aspects of inventory management that internal auditors should focus their attention on. For example, verifying that all inventories are accounted for and reflected accurately in the organization's financial statements and financial reports, making sure that inventories are still saleable, otherwise they should be treated according to excess and obsolete (E&O) guidelines and written off.

Future Challenges and Risk Implications

Organizations today face a myriad of different types of risks. While traditionally internal auditors focused primarily on accounting, financial, and compliance risks, today they are expected to assist their clients identify, assess, and properly respond to a far wider variety of risks. Looking into the future, organizations will increasingly be confronted with the following.

Increased outsourcing. This trend, which started getting widespread attention in the 1980s, accelerated in the 1990s, became commonplace in the 2000s and continues to grow into the 2010s. Initially, it was touted as a great mechanism to reduce expenses, boost productivity and efficiency, and free the organization, so it could focus on its core activities. This practice is consistent with the business strategy arguments posed by Michael Porter[10] related to competitive advantage and the ways that organizations can beat their competition: lower cost or differentiation. By seeking markets where labor and other production costs are lower, organizations can increase their profitability. However, this trend toward outsourcing, which began with low-skill repetitive activities being performed by lower cost third parties, has evolved to the point where companies are increasingly becoming more reliant on third parties to perform critical business functions.

Using offshore outsourcing firms carries risk and challenges, including different regulations, currency exchange exposure, language barriers, cultural differences, the risk of supply chain disruption, and poor quality. The consequences can be fines, regulatory sanctions, lawsuits, and reputational damage. In fact, KPMG's Internal Audit: Top 10 Key Risks in 2016 mentions third party relationships/vendor management as one of the top risks that firms should evaluate as part of their overall strategy, risk assessments, and internal audit plan. This is driven by increasing oversight of third party relationships and vendors and the need to prevent and detect risk management failures promptly at these organizations.

Internal auditors should make sure their organizations are practicing effective risk management on their third party relationships, including adequate due diligence, verifying that management has developed and implemented processes and controls to measure, monitor, and correct any deficiencies by these firms, and making sure that effective performance monitoring activities are in place. Since some of these third parties could have access to the organization's computer systems, the risk of a data breach increases as was evident in the massive data breach at Target where hackers used stolen credentials from a refrigeration contractor to plant malware that collected customer data.

Target discovered that hackers accessed customer debit and credit card information during the 2013 Thanksgiving and Christmas shopping season. Target reported that 110 million customers, who used a payment card at the company's point of sale (POS) devices at their stores had their payment card information copied for fraudulent purposes. The company faced at least three class-action lawsuits and more than 80 related lawsuits as a result of the breach, and the data breach cost shareholders $148 million.[11] In addition, sales decreased as a result of the data breach and on February 26, 2014 The *Wall Street Journal* reported that earnings fell 46%.[12] In December 2015, Target reported that it would pay a $39.4 million settlement to banks and credit unions who filed lawsuits against the retailer.[13]

Global sourcing. Whereas most companies used to work with, and obtain their raw and semifinished goods from local suppliers, it is commonplace now for organizations to search the globe for suppliers. This is driven by lower prices and the related savings, but also because the quality of foreign-sourced inputs has increased in most cases. While challenges remain, the quality of many foreign-sourced items is acceptable to western companies and in many cases, it is near that of western companies, or equal with lower production costs. China has become a good example of a country that has managed to cater to the needs of worldwide customers at most price points with matching quality. In fact, while poor workmanship and low quality where often attributed to Chinese-made goods, that is not always the case as China now manufacturers most of the world's household electronics and increasingly so, industrial ones as well. We saw a similar progression in Japan, where at first, they had a widely held reputation for shoddy exports. As a result, their companies explored new ways of thinking about quality and the transformation has been monumental.

Lower transportation costs, the enlargement and improvement in port facilities, lower trade restrictions, and fewer capital flow restrictions are also contributing to this shift. During the 1970s and 1980s, many trade restrictions were put in place limiting the flow of goods and capital between countries and regions. With the enactment of free trade agreements, like the North American Free Trade Agreement, Central America Free Trade Agreement, Mercosur, Asia Pacific Trade Agreement, ASEAN Free Trade Area, and others, global trade has increased making it easier for companies to source their products and sell to their customers around the world. The combination of lower cost, better logistics, and fewer regulations is promoting a movement toward global sourcing that is unparalleled in human history.

Margin compression. As competition has expanded to a more global environment, and some of the new competitors benefit from lower costs and even subsidies and protectionist practices in some countries, many organizations struggle to remain competitive under such conditions.

Technology. The number and scale of technological changes over the past two decades is immense. This includes, but is certainly not limited to, ERP systems with built-in supply chain management, product life cycle management, customer relationship management, supplier relationship management, document management, and project management functionality. They can also manage transportation, warehousing, billing, collections, staffing, and payroll. The migration from in-house or legacy platforms to internet-based data storage and processing, and even software as a service is transforming how data are obtained, manipulated, disseminated, and stored. Lastly, access to fast connectivity anywhere, anytime on ever-smaller devices using broadband and Wi-Fi connections, is revolutionizing how organizations operate.

Growth in Asia and other developing markets. The increasing purchasing power and wealth creation in emerging markets is opening new opportunities that many organizations cannot miss. This is resulting in the search for customers and the related adaptation of sales and marketing activities to address the different conditions in these diverse markets.

Improved customer analytics. In the past, organizations focused on mass production to drive down unit costs. Later, glocalization became commonplace as organizations adopted a global approach, while attempting to portray a local feel to their marketing of goods and services. This information is being gathered from credit card transactions, internet traffic, loan information, POSs devices, and other means, resulting in the accumulation of data that is increasingly being mined and analyzed by specialists. As we move further into the twenty-first century, it is increasingly apparent that the widespread availability and analysis of data captured everywhere will result is a better understanding of the customer, and continue to drive a closer identification of their needs and wants. As the reader may have concluded as well, this is also triggering a greater concern for the responsible use and proper safekeeping of this information.

Laws are being passed annually. The following are some examples from the United States:

- The Health Insurance Portability and Accountability Act (HIPAA)
- Financial Services Modernization Act, also known as the Gramm–Leach–Bliley Act
- Final Rule on Privacy of Consumer Financial Information, 16 Code of Federal Regulations, Part 313
- Fair Credit Reporting Act
- Fair Debt Collection Practices Act
- Driver's Privacy Protection Act

In Canada, Personal Information Protection and Electronic Documents Act (PIPEDA) and the Privacy Act are examples of laws that govern the collection, use, and disclosure of personal information. The United Kingdom and EU countries adhere to Article 8 of the European Convention on Human Rights, which requires respect for an individual's private and family life, home, and correspondence.

Data capture and transfer capabilities. Improvements in data storage, lowering the costs dramatically over the past three decades, improvements in networking capabilities (local area network [LAN], wide area network [WAN]) and the internet, and enhancements in wireless communications, such as radio frequency identification (RFID), make it increasingly easy and economical for organizations to obtain, analyze, and disseminate information real time or near real time. This allows organizations to know what is happening throughout their organizations and correct issues promptly. The widespread use of communication standards, such as XML will also facilitate collaboration and further reduce costs and surprises. As data are collected about customer shopping preferences and practices, such as Amazon's "memory," embedded chips in purchased items (e.g., automobiles) or postsale opt-in features (e.g., FitBit, iWatch/iPhone), will allow companies to offer valuable benefits and services postsale. The generation of this enormous amount of data carries risks and opportunities.

Environmental initiatives. Ecological considerations are increasingly becoming a key concern for organizations. Whether it is the sourcing of materials locally, sourcing them through fair-trade practices, reducing the amount of inputs and packaging used, lowering the amount of waste generated, manufacturing goods using recycled components, or producing items from reused ingredients, environmental considerations are affecting how organizations are perceived and in some cases even steering buying decisions.

The focus is not limited to what is produced, but also how items are produced and even under what conditions. Take for example the impact of placing solar panels on company rooftops, or lowering the amount of water consumed in the manufacturing and support offices, to the lower use of paper and electricity, using natural light more efficiently, increasing use of biofuels, and obtaining energy from renewable sources. All of these dynamics are influencing organizations and affects purchasing, manufacturing, transportation, office, design, and staffing decisions.

Government involvement. While the degree of acceptance of government involvement varies by country and changes over time, governments in general are increasingly becoming more involved in the support of private sector activities. This is the result of a greater understanding of the role that governments can play to facilitate trade, provide protection under the rule of law, educate populations, build needed infrastructure, provide favorable tax regimes, and reduce financial controls to facilitate the flow of capital. This is also evident in the number of trade agreements. As of January 1, 2015, the United States had 14 free trade agreements in force with 20 countries. The United States is negotiating the Trans-Pacific Partnership and the Transatlantic Trade and Investment Partnership.[14] These treaties affect commerce.

Due to infrastructure challenges around the world, organizations are likely to embark on public–private collaboration efforts through private investment, public policy, and shared infrastructure investment. Companies and governments will work to build, improve, and operate roads, ports, airports, and railroads.

Geo-political risks. The rise of extremism around the world threatens organizations' abilities to operate freely around the world. Some of this is related to bombings on the facilities of companies in the oil and gas and other extractive industries to attacks on the general population that frightens tourists and affects the tourism industry (e.g., airlines, hotels, restaurants, and museums). This also affects organizations' strategic plans, their strategic alliances, and their ability to deploy workers in places where conditions can change from peaceful to hostile almost overnight.

Corruption. Organizations, indeed entire economies, continue to suffer from the scourge of corruption. Defined as dishonest or unethical conduct by a person entrusted with a position of authority, often to acquire personal benefit, it includes many activities including bribery and embezzlement, though it may also involve practices that are legal in many countries, such as blatant favoritism and nepotism, discrimination, and largesse. It occurs when a government official or private sector employee acts in an official capacity for personal gain. It distorts the market by shifting resources to less productive purposes and increases the cost of doing business by forcing additional payments. It also creates skepticism and suspicion. In the public sector, it limits the welfare of the population and is often evidenced in substandard infrastructure, child labor, human trafficking, high child mortality, poor education standards, and environmental damage.

Transparency International (TI) publishes the annual Corruption Perceptions Index (CPI), which measures the perceived levels of public sector corruption worldwide. They report that although corruption is still rife globally, more countries improved their scores in the 2015 edition of TI's CPI than lowered them. However, two-thirds of the 168 countries on the 2015 index scored below 50, on a scale from 0 (perceived to be highly corrupt) to 100 (perceived to be very clean). The scale of the issue is huge. 68% of countries worldwide have a serious corruption problem. Half of the G20 are among them.

Business leaders, policy makers, internal auditors, and other stakeholders use this and other reports from TI as a gauge and input when performing risk assessments. Internal auditors should examine where their organizations operate, where their suppliers operate and where their customers reside, and evaluate the implications of their unique geographical network to their risk profile. Higher corruption indicators would naturally suggest the need for more robust audit procedures.[15]

Summary

KPMG's Seeking value through Internal Audit report states that internal audit departments are not delivering the value that audit committee chairs and CFOs are looking for. The reports refers to this as a "value gap," that is most evident on risk assessments and risk management practices, especially related to emerging risks. The report, based on a survey of audit committee members and CFOs, states that only 22% of them believe internal audit helps assessing risks and risk management practices. In addition, 57% of them said more insight on risk would be of most value to the organization. A similar gap exists with regards to emerging risks, where only 5% state that internal audit provides an informed perspective on emerging risks, while 36% consider this something valuable to receive.

Risk management, as a professional field, originated decades ago and most of it centered on insurance and reinsurance coverage. But it got a boost when COSO released the enterprise risk management (ERM) framework in 2004 and the International Organization for Standardization published ISO 31000 in 2009, both of which helped to promote the concept widely. Today, there are certifications like the Risk Management Professional, Certified Risk Manager, the Certification in Risk Management Assurance, the International Certificate in Risk Management, and even master's degrees in risk management. Internal auditors are encouraged to gain as broad and deep an understanding of risk management methodologies as possible because this will enable them to better assess the program in place, and make recommendations for improvement.

Chapter 4 examines the 8 Es—a collection of operational attributes that define successful organizations. It is easy to remember thanks to its simplicity, but takes organizations a long time to master because it encompasses organizational culture, structure, deployment, and execution within the organization and outside, across all stakeholders. It refers to effectiveness, efficiency, economy, excellence, ethics, equity, ecology, and emotion.

Embracing the 8 Es has catapulted some organizations into competitive stardom, created workplaces recognized as among the best places to work, and doomed those that have neglected one or more of these elements. Internal auditors should treat the 8 Es as an integral part of the themes they include in their audit plans, and as part of the topics examined during their reviews.

QUESTIONS

1. What are the benefits of the internal audit function establishing a risk-based plan when identifying the priorities of the internal audit activity?
2. Describe three ways that internal auditors can better identify the risks related to the area under review.
3. What are three internal and three external factors affecting a typical organization? How do these factors affect the future prospects of the organization?
4. Describe an event that has transformed or disrupted an industry and include: (1) An example of an organization that benefited from that opportunity and (2) an example of another organization that mismanaged it and suffered losses as a result.
5. List three organizations that provide lists of common vulnerabilities useful during a risk assessment.
6. List three of the benefits of CSA programs.
7. Describe three risks that are unique to each of the following two manufacturing approaches: made to order (MTO) and made to stock (MTS).
8. Explain why internal auditors should consider bottlenecks, long cycle times, redundancies, and reprocessing as operational risks.

9. What are the risk implications of outsourcing? Explain why management must remain vigilant even if a process and related activities have been outsourced to another organization.

10. What are some of the practices expected of organizations to fight corruption and support efforts to decrease institutional corruption?

Notes

1 See http://www.derbyshireprepared.org.uk/risks/risk_terminology/

2 This information is adapted from the Derbyshire Prepared, Local Resilience Forum and Other Solutions Ltd. At http://othersolutions.eu/

3 See http://www.businessdictionary.com/definition/vulnerability.html#ixzz3wnmuoCS7

4 For additional information, visit https://hazards.fema.gov/femaportal/wps/portal

5 For additional information, visit http://geohazards.usgs.gov/eqprob/2009/index.php, http://landslides.usgs.gov/, http://volcanoes.usgs.gov/, and https://www.osha.gov

6 For additional information, see http://www.weather.gov/ and http://www.wbur.org/2015/12/23/end-of-year-review-mbta-woes

7 For more information regarding human health assessments, see http://www.epa.gov/risk/human-health-risk-assessment

8 See, for example, http://www.epa.gov/risk/risk-tools-and-databases, http://www.weather.gov/informationcenter, and https://www.osha.gov/ (under Data and Statistics).

9 For additional information about the Common Vulnerabilities and Exposures, see http://cve.mitre.org/

10 Michael Porter is a leading authority and has written extensively on the subject of competitive advantage. His publications include the books *Competitive Advantage* (1985), *The Competitive Advantage of Nations* (1990), and *The Five Competitive Forces that Shape Strategy* (2008) in addition to many articles.

11 See https://www.privacyrights.org/data-breach-asc?title=target&=Apply

12 See http://www.wsj.com/articles/SB10001424052702304255604579406694182132568

13 See http://www.reuters.com/article/us-target-breach-settlement-idUSKBN0TL20Y20151203#qmGPWO0mR7raj6J0.97

14 See http://trade.gov/fta/

15 To read more about the CPI, the methodology used, and download the full report, visit http://www.transparency.org/cpi2015/

Chapter 4

The 8 Es

8 Es = Success

Introduction

As we examine how organizations operate, it becomes apparent that for many of them some things are not working out as they should. In general, there are more meetings but less communication. There are more tools at our disposal, but less time to get things done. There is more data, but less insight. Customers want to shop when they want to, for the items they want, get everything at a great price, and receive superior customer service during their entire experience. It is abundantly clear that organizations need to execute well every time because their customers demand it. If they don't execute well, the competition will.

With this backdrop, many organizations find themselves overwhelmed by the complexities of operating in today's ever-changing world and desperately need simple remedies to organize these complex quantitative and qualitative elements. I have found the 8 Es model very useful as a tool to organize the focus themes while planning operational audits. It is simple, yet it addresses some of the most important aspects of any organization. They are used to examine the short-term dynamics as well as the long-term ones. They are helpful when considering the structure of the organization and the operating practices of the organization. They highlight the responsibility that every organization should have toward its stakeholders, both internal and external. They also highlight the treatment of employees, suppliers, customers, lenders, and other stakeholders, even the environment. It reminds us of the importance of delivering everything, every time, to everyone, with high quality.

Internal auditors should remember that audits are conducted as a means to assess conditions within the client's organization. They are conducted with the objective of helping them improve their structure and their operating practices. Planning and performing and operational audit, then, should focus on management practices that facilitate or hinder the accomplishment of objectives. The 8 Es provide a simple, yet effective model to keep these essential concepts in mind.

The 8 Es

Operational audits often incorporate into their scope of work the 8 Es that play a key role in the success or failure of organizations. These Es, when used in the form of themes, can help the auditor add considerable value to the engagement and show audit clients that auditors are genuinely interested in helping the organization succeed. These 8 Es can then be incorporated into the planning process, making sure that interview questions, document reviews, goals and objectives, flowcharts, walkthroughs, and other activities performed during the audit, (1) probe for the presence of these attributes, (2) verify that these are functioning effectively, and (3) are considered when making recommendations for improvement.

The 8 Es are effectiveness, efficiency, economy, excellence, ethics, equity, ecology, and emotion. Let's examine each of them.

Effectiveness

First of all, every organization should have a mission and vision, and establish goals and objectives that drive employee actions toward their achievement. Without a mission and vision, the organization will move erratically like a ship without a clear destination. The mission should be clear and be communicated to all employees, providing a sense of direction, motivating, and sparking ambition toward its achievement. The mission is also long lasting, providing consistency to the long-term aspirations and actions of the entity.

Goals and objectives provide identifiable markers of the achievement of something, and help establish tactical actions to work toward. These are more immediate and facilitate the assignment of resources (e.g., budgets and projects) that can be aligned with the mission.

You are probably now starting to see where I am going with all of this. If during a review you ask yourself, how do we know that we are making progress in our efforts to achieve our mission? How do we know if we are achieving the goals and objectives set for ourselves? The answer lies in the concept of effectiveness.

Effectiveness is the process of evaluating the degree to which the organization, program, or process is achieving its goals and objectives. Effectiveness consists of comparing the planned outputs with the actual outputs. This can be expressed simply as achieving X percent of the goal. If the number is under 100%, the goal was not fully achieved, and conversely, if above 100%, the goal was surpassed.

Trending effectiveness metrics is a useful technique as well. It allows management, and auditors during their review, to ascertain the degree to which there is consistent accomplishment of goals. Furthermore, it provides context to metrics that in isolation may appear satisfactory. For example, if the organization has a goal of keeping scrap under 5% of total raw materials used in production, and at the time of the audit, the scrap yield was 4.7%, the auditor may conclude that while it is close to 5%, it is below the limit, so at best, she may make a verbal comment to monitor that figure.

On the other hand, if over the past 5 years, the scrap yield has been shown in Table 4.1.

Then, the assessment and opinion would differ substantially. In this illustration, the scrap yield has been increasing and the 4.7% is disconcerting due to the increasing trend line (Figure 4.1).

Internal auditors can make a substantial contribution for improvement in company operations by closely examining or even questioning the appropriateness, usefulness, and relevance of policies and procedures, which have a tendency to become outdated. Merely following

Table 4.1   Annual Scrap Yield Trend Line

Year 1 (%)	Year 2 (%)	Year 3 (%)	Year 4 (%)	Year 5 (%)
2.2	2.9	3.5	4.2	4.7

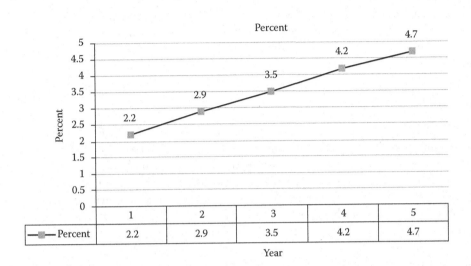

Figure 4.1   Annual scrap yield results.

existing policies and procedures is not enough. These must be appropriate and enable the achievement of objectives. If there is a discrepancy in this regard, internal auditors should question them.

Efficiency

Efficiency relates to the use of inputs and other resources toward the achievement of goals and objectives in some form of productive activity. Organizations must thrive to produce goods and services at or below cost levels. The ratio between the actual production (i.e., outputs) and the actual inputs (i.e., resources) constitutes the degree of efficiency of the organization's operations. You can think of it as the burn rate, or the rate at which the company's resources are used during its operations.

The pursuit of efficiency has been the rallying cry of many organizations for decades. As competition, lower budgets, the rising cost of some raw materials, and the lower availability of other inputs, organizations are forced to maximize the use of all of their resources. Furthermore, managers are hired to become stewards of the owners' invested capital. As such, managers are supposed to act responsibly and make sure that they extract the maximum utility from these resources.

In many organizations, in fact, in many countries, efficiency rates are abnormally low. This creates lower productivity, lower growth, and the waste of resources that if used more efficiently would result in higher rates of return. The key to higher efficiency and productivity lies in more education, and a better use of individual's skills and their tools at work.

In terms of employee skills, the organization should recruit individuals that meet the organization's skill requirements in the present and future. Then, these individuals must be placed in roles where they can use their skills best, and given the freedom, flexibility, resources, and encouragement to put their skills to maximum use. By creating a work environment that expects high results, and by rewarding the achievement of these goals, employees would be on their way toward greater efficiency.

The second contributing factor to greater efficiency is the role of technology. Regardless of the type of machinery, having modern machines with the capacity/capability to work effectively, and by training employees on how to use these machines effectively, organizations can boost their efficiency.

Economy

Economy refers to the price paid for organizational resources. Historically, the main criteria to assess economy was the price of goods and services used by the organization. While price is an important element, it has become quite apparent that buying shoddy merchandise or tools will most likely lead to having to buy replacements with greater frequency than if a higher quality item had been bought in the first place. The key is to buy based on value, not merely price, so company procedures should focus on the assessment of value when defining allowable purchases.

A better approach to assessing economy is to consider the entire value of the item. This includes warranties, replacement or repair guarantees, speed and reliability of delivery, expected useful life of the item, and so on. It is important to mention that this criteria apply to tangible goods like materials, machinery, equipment and tools, as well as financial inputs. For example, many organizations borrow funds for capital projects, expand their operations or as an integral part of their operations, as is the case with banks that obtain deposits, paying depositors interest, then these same banks lend the funds out to borrowers at a higher interest rate. A similar dynamic takes place with organizations that borrow funds to build a factory or increase the selection of products/ services available for sale. The cost of these inputs must be lower than the returns that the invested assets and related investment will produce. This also supports the objectives of economy.

Excellence

Another key aspect of organizational priorities is the performance of all work with high quality. In developed economies, and increasingly so in emerging markets as well, products and services are commoditized and differentiation based on price is a high-risk proposition. Relying on low costs only to secure customers is a race to the bottom, and some organizations find out that it can be very dangerous strategy as margins become increasingly smaller unless other activities improve results—such as efficiency and relentless cost cutting.

Instead, organizations are increasingly pursuing a strategy to gain differentiation based on quality. Differentiation is based on the perceived value that customers derive from the product or service and when developed and applied correctly, can result in higher profits. Furthermore, if customers perceive that what they bought is overpriced (i.e., the price paid is above the value obtained), the customer is likely to ask for a refund, or complain, including the use of social media. At some point, customers will likely abandon the organization and seek product or seller substitution.

Quality in all everyone does is essential for continued success. Measuring quality is essential to determine if it is being achieved and always remember that people do what is measured, repeat what is rewarded, and stop doing what is punished. Organizations may find the ISO 9000 quality management standards helpful. They are adaptable because they are not specific to any industry or organization size, yet they can help organizations effectively document quality management system (QMS) elements. By focusing on the customer, effective leadership, engaging people, having a process approach, continuously improving, making decisions based on evidence and promoting relationship management, organizations may significantly improve the quality of their products and services. The result is a framework to ensure organizations meet the needs of their customers and other stakeholders.

Quality is clearly an important value element when selling to customers. I have found it equally important for organizations to create and sustain a culture of providing quality to internal customers as well. Most people think of customer service, quality, and similar attributes as being related to external customers, but similar expectations should be created internally as well while promoting the understanding that anyone who receives something that you produce, is your customer.

Ethics

The Merriam-Webster dictionary defines ethics as the rules of behavior based on ideas about what is morally good and bad, it deals with what is good and bad behavior, what is morally right or wrong, and moral duty and obligation.[1] It is a critical subject for internal auditors because an individual's viewpoint regarding what is right and wrong will drive most aspects of decision-making and corporate behavior, including that related to the performance of control activities and treatment of others.

The *Standards* state "The internal audit activity must assess and make appropriate recommendations for improving the governance process in the promotion of appropriate ethics and values within the organization." (Standard 2110). As a result, internal auditors should have a familiarity with the underlying concepts that define ethical thought, and apply that knowledge to review and recommend improvements. After all, the lack of ethics is a key driver of inappropriate behavior and has significant implications in policy-making and organizational conduct.

Ethics is a broad field of study, and while exploring the many philosophical, practical, and historical elements driving its present understanding is beyond the scope of this book, it is important for internal auditors to know some fundamental elements about it, what it means, and its importance so they can better audit ethics.

Ethics is the study of moral values and the principles of conduct governing an individual or a group. Although many of the foundational elements of ethical thought are derived from religious beliefs, one of the challenges organizations face is that new circumstances and technologies create new problems and it is increasingly difficult, and rejected, to rationally tie our business ethics today to traditional sources and precedents. Some of these questions include

- Should organizations engage in CSR or should all resources and the resulting profits be directed toward maximizing the wealth of the owners of the organization (for many organizations: stockholders)?
- Should organizations engage in extreme tax avoidance strategies, or should they pay what is considered reasonable given stakeholder expectations and the pursuit of an image as being a good corporate citizen?
- Should organizations conduct animal testing for their products?

- What should organizations do if there are no local safety standards in an emerging market where they are operating or they are not enforced by the local authorities? Should they follow US/Canada/EU standards or operate at lower standards?
- If a failure to meet a regulation is unlikely to result in discovery, fines, or penalties, should the organization avoid compliance or comply based on its internal guidelines for adhering to prevailing laws and regulations?
- Should organizations demand that their contractors adhere to principles of human rights, safe work environment, and respectful treatment of workers? How about subcontractors?
- Should the organization only source its supplies from fair trade vendors and locations?
- How much effort should the organization exert to diversify its workforce and senior leadership ranks beyond basic compliance with antidiscrimination laws?
- What should the company do in countries where there are no religious, ethnic, gender, age, or disability protections for workers?

While we won't attempt to answer these and many other troublesome questions confronting organizations, let's take a look at some of the ethical principles and their implications for auditors.

Teleological or Prescriptive Approaches

These focus on the consequences of the act. They determine the morality of a decision based on the outcome or consequences. An example of this approach is utilitarianism, which seeks as its end the greatest good (or utility) for the greatest number of people and it is often performed through cost/benefit analyses—a common business tool that considers the most ethical decision the one yielding the greatest gain overall. While this can be a great mechanism to decide on the appropriateness of an act, it often fails to adequately measure certain elements. Since people place different values on objects or conditions, there is no way of knowing whose utility is maximized "by giving me the job or giving you the job." Similarly, there are difficulties measuring intangibles, such as health, happiness, and human life. Many costs and benefits cannot be predicted, hence cannot be measured reliably, such as basic scientific knowledge. Finally, another problem of measurement is deciding what to count as a benefit and what counts as a cost, given the different points of view of different people. For example, a loan officer confronted with a request for a loan to open a gambling casino.

The Ford Pinto fiasco illustrates the dramatic impact that the utilitarian approach can produce when intangibles are forcibly, and defectively, quantified. Ford attempted to address the company's loss of market share by developing a relatively lightweight (under 2000 pounds), low cost (under $2000) vehicle and bring it to market in 2 rather than the normal 4 years. Due to the time, design, and cost constraints, the fuel tank was placed behind the rear axle, where it was more susceptible to puncture during a rear-end collision, leaking fuel, and in the presence of stray sparks, the vehicle ignited.

Ford planned to build 12.5 million cars and the estimated cost to modify the gas tank was $137 million ($11 per car · 12.5 million cars). On the other hand, the potential damages to the company if the changes were not made were estimated at $49.15 million (based on the 180 estimated burn deaths, 180 burn injuries, and 2100 burned vehicles). At the time, the government officially valued a human life at $200,000, insurance companies valued serious burn injuries at $67,000, and the average residual value of subcompact cars was $700.

Since the Pinto met prevailing regulations and the $137 million estimated cost of modifying the gas tank would result in the prevention of customer losses valued at $49.15 million, Ford went ahead and produced the unmodified Pinto. Many people died or were severely burned, and the company's reputation and market share were subsequently damaged. Eventually, Ford discontinued the Pinto model.

Another concept is that of justice and the distribution of benefits and burdens fairly among people. Distributive justice is based on the concept of fairness and considers ethical decisions those that lead to the equitable distribution of goods and services. Hiring standards and discriminatory practices would challenge the principles of justice, but in many countries, laws are increasingly being passed to provide workplace antidiscrimination protections. But beyond legal requirements, another topic pertains to workers' wages. Should the organization pay the minimum wage only, knowing that for many that is not a living wage? Should the private sector lobby against minimum wage increases even when it limits the workers' ability to provide for themselves and their families?

The principle of distributive justice can be summarized in one simple statement: Never take any action that would harm the least among us, those with least income, education, wealth, competence, influence, or power. We don't have to help those people in the lower ranks of our society to any great extent; we just should never harm them.

Deontological Approaches

Other ethical systems are based on rules or principles that govern decisions under the premise that individuals should do what is right out of goodwill and duty, with no regard for the consequences of the decision. They refer to the duties or obligations of an individual or group.

Immanuel Kant formulated a widely regarded view on deontological ethics framed around two categorical imperatives. The first formulation of Kant's categorical imperative states that "I ought never to act except in such a way that I can also will that my maxim [reason for acting in a given way] should become universal law."[2] In essence, a person's reasons for doing something must be reasons that everyone would act similarly and be reversible; have others apply the same rule on oneself. If everyone on earth acted the way I was going to act, what would happen?

This is similar to the golden rule: "Do unto others as you would have them do unto you," which is a key principle of many Christian religions and inscribed in scripture "Therefore all things whatsoever ye would that men should do to you, do ye even so to them: for this is the law and the prophets" (Matthew 7:12—King James version) and again "And as ye would that men should do to you, do ye also to them likewise" (Luke 6:31—King James version). In fact, the golden rule is not only recognized in Christianity. It is found in the sacred writings of virtually all of the major religious and ethical traditions around the world.[3] Generally speaking, business decisions should incorporate this ethical screen and show respect for human life and basic rights, consider the dignity of those affected, and display good citizenship as a member of the local and world communities.

The second formulation of Kant's categorical imperative states that people should never be treated only as means, but always also as ends. This suggests that deception, force, and coercion are unethical because they fail to respect and provide for people's freedom to choose, unless the person freely agreed to have these acts performed on them. Plato, Aristotle, and many doctrines of religious belief promulgate virtue ethics, which focus on character. These ethical theories encouraged desirable traits like honesty, fairness, compassion, integrity, and generosity. Other virtues include temperance, self-control, friendliness, prudence, courage, truthfulness, and modesty.

Some of the guiding principles are shown in Table 4.2.

Pluralism and ethical relativism argue that what is considered moral or ethical in one culture may not be so in another. What one person considers appropriate, others may believe to be inappropriate or wrong. Examples abound, including the treatment of women and minors,

Table 4.2   Ethical Guiding Principles

Guiding Principles	
Rights and duties	What are the legal and moral obligations?
Justice	Guidance of fairness, equity, and impartiality
Utilitarian analysis	What is the greatest good for the greatest number?
Care	How will this action affect my relationships?
Virtue	How does this action affect my (or my company's) character?
Golden rule	Would you want the same treatment?

discrimination on the basis of religion or age, drinking alcohol, abortion, employment based on merit, connections, or appearance, etc.

Moral standards vary between groups of people within a given culture, between cultures, and over time. Cultural relativism argues that no culture's ethics is better than any other, which means that there are no international rights or wrongs. This condition is commonly described with the expression "When in Rome, do as the Romans do."

An unfortunate effect of ethical relativism is that it may be used as an excuse to engage in practices abroad that would not be tolerated, on moral or legal terms, at home. While ethical relativism can be very useful and is commonly applied in international business, it also possesses a weakness in that some local practices, like insider trading, pollution, and discrimination, may be considered acceptable while others would consider them damaging or injurious. The casual observer may conclude that some local practices occur because they are accepted, when in fact they are tolerated reluctantly and are the result of ineffective enforcement and inadequate regulations leading to behaviors that are clearly wrong (Table 4.3).

Being ethical is not the same as merely following the law. Being ethical is not the same as doing whatever society accepts. Being and acting ethically refers to abiding by well-founded standards of right and wrong that prescribe what individuals should do. It begins with a way of thinking about the world, and the societal environment in which the organization and individual operates. It is also concerned with the impacts the decisions and actions have on others in the short and longer term. Organizations are required to establish their ethical expectations, build support mechanisms to encourage adherence, and provide the means to monitor it all.

Equity

Equity relates to the treatment of others with dignity and respect. This should be done consistently, by everyone, always. Equity is often thought of in terms of fairness, reciprocity, and impartiality.

When discussing the subject of equity, most people think about it in the context of compliance with laws and regulations, and that is a reasonable assumption. In the United States, there are federally protected classes: race, color, religion or creed, national origin or ancestry, sex, age, physical or mental disability, and veteran status. Organizations should be careful not to engage in practices that can place them in a situation of noncompliance and trigger government fines and penalties. Furthermore, some employees negatively affected by discriminatory actions could seek

Table 4.3   Business Ethics Breakdowns

A Sample of Business Ethics Breakdowns	
Ford Pinto Defects and Fire Scandal	Turing Pharmaceuticals Daraprim Price Gouging
Union Carbide Air Contamination in Bhopal	Mortgage Loans Crisis of 2000s
Enron, WorldCom, Adelphia Fraud Cases	Stanford Financial Group Ponzi Scheme
Water Contamination in Flint, Michigan	Retail Sweatshop Conditions
Bernie Madoff's Ponzi Scheme	Veteran's Health Administration Hospitals
Canadian Food Inspection Agency and XL Foods	SNC-Lavalin Corruption Scandal
	Foxconn Workplace Conditions and Suicides
Peanut Corporation of America	Chinese Milk Contamination Scandal
Petrobras Corruption Scandal	HSBC Corruption and Money Laundering
Olympus Investment Losses Scandal	Banamex Fraud Scandal

recourse by hiring a lawyer individually, or collectively, seeking remediation through class action lawsuits.

To illustrate how damaging this can be, a look at the US Department of Labor (DOL) website shows there are many actions against organizations for noncompliance. However, equitable treatment goes beyond the direct relationship between one person and another, as there are some indirect impacts of equity or lack thereof. The consequences for noncompliance can include fines, penalties, and even lawsuits in some cases. While these are enough reasons not to allow these practices, there is also an economic argument to be made about the importance of equity. Take for example gender discrimination in promotions. If a woman is more qualified that the male candidate who is also up for promotion, but the promotion is nonetheless given to the man for arbitrary reasons, the organization is also going to suffer financial harm because they are typically accompanied by pay increases. Monetary compensation is an exchange of used talents and performance in return for some forms of compensation. If the male candidate is promoted through favoritism or nepotism rather than a more qualified woman, the organization is paying that male employee more than necessary, and getting less in return, than it would if it had promoted the more qualified woman instead. The direct impacts are clear and so are the indirect impacts because the damage goes further. Employees become demotivated when they see injustice done and those managed by this individual will perform less. Finally, upon questioning the opportunities for career advancement, qualified employees will likely leave the organization, leading to higher turnover. Finally, as turnover increases, productivity, quality, and customer service will be negatively impacted as well.

The same dynamic applies in the hiring process, and a similar process will develop if it is applied in the vendor selection process.

Work environments lacking equity and fairness experience motivation problems. When workers share the belief that promotions, bonuses, desirable special projects, and career advancement opportunities are beyond their reach, or are not earned based on merit, the desire to work hard will erode. They will ask themselves "Why should I work overtime when there is no reward for my sacrifice?" and "Why should I spend time thinking about ways to increase profitability or reduce costs when the organization won't recognize my contributions?"

The lack of equity is a problem whether it is in fact, or in appearance. If employees perceive a lack of equity and fairness, they will act as if it were so and reduce their level of involvement with the organization. Furthermore, as explained in the Fraud Triangle,[4] it may provide the grounds for them to rationalize fraudulent behavior to reimburse themselves and make themselves whole. This is a dangerous situation, so management must make sure that they provide their employees with enough information about their recruitment and compensation practices. Some key actions are

- Clearly state the job requirements, what is required and what is desirable
- Explain the impact of work experience in the selection process
- Provide clear performance evaluation criteria
- Require hiring managers to document the process followed during hiring and promotion decisions
- Publicize hiring and promotions actions

When considering the topic of equity, internal auditors should consider:

- Does the organization display the necessary care to develop and maintain productive relationships?
- Does the organization, through its policies and practices, establish trust through openness?
- Are there mechanisms in place to make sure that in theory and practice, the concepts of interdependence and collaboration are promoted and rewarded?
- Does the organization recognize the importance to nurture others and show compassion, while creating an expectation for hard work and discipline?
- Does the organization show respect toward its stakeholders and encourage dialog with them, rather than merely trying to exert power over them through opportunistic practices?

Ecology

Environmental concerns have reached high levels over the past years and will likely continue to garner much attention in the future. In addition, customers, employees, local communities, regulators, and other stakeholders increasingly expect organizations to act responsibly toward the environment.

While much of the emphasis has been in terms of environmental compliance, such as the Clean Air and Clean Water Act of the United States; the Canadian Environmental Protection Act, Transportation of Dangerous Goods and Hazardous Products Acts in Canada; the Environmental Protection Act, Countryside and Rights of Way Acts, Energy Act and Climate Change Acts in the United Kingdom; and the Water Framework Directive in the EU, proper disposal of hazardous waste materials and so on, many organizations are finding ecological product design, manufacture, and distribution an integral part of their business model. Similarly, service organizations are reducing their environmental impact through lower carbon footprint, lower resource consumption, and minimizing waste.

Beyond compliance, ecological awareness and stewardship can also have a positive impact on the organization's profitability. Companies can reduce their operating costs by limiting their water usage, lowering their consumption of electricity, and generating electricity themselves. Metrics related to ecology help to drive appropriate behaviors and provide a means to analyze, compare, benchmark, and improve results. Examples include amount of water used, electricity, and natural gas consumed in manufacturing and support activities, the amount of CO_2s generated during production, the amount of fuel consumed in transportation activities, and the amount and types of waste generated in manufacturing and support activities.

As an example, United Parcel Service (UPS) is leveraging the power of Global Positioning System (GPS) to map their transportation routes. Telematics have helped the logistics and package delivery companies determine their truck's performance and condition, and identify ways for drivers to adjust their behaviors to improve performance. UPS installed GPS tracking equipment and sensors in key areas such as brakes, the engine, and the trucks' exterior. With this equipment, the company can track the location of its delivery trucks, reduce idle time, and increase route efficiency. Some of the changes made include a reduction in the number of left-hand turns since these cause delays by forcing drivers to stop and wait for oncoming traffic to go by, it increases the likelihood of collisions, and results in greater fuel consumption. Other metrics captured and analyzed either real time or at the end of the day are speed, revolutions per minute (RPM), oil pressure, use of seat belts, number of times trucks are placed in reverse, and idling time.

The use of telematics in the United States enabled UPS to reduce idling time 15 min per driver per day, totaling 25 gallons of fuel per driver per year and a fuel reduction of 1.4 million gallons. While these amounts may seem small, these figures only apply to the program in the United States. When deployed worldwide, and affecting the entire global fleet of 90,000 drivers worldwide, the potential is enormous. The combination of data analytics, training, behavior modification, and driving patterns help to reduce fuel consumption, emissions, and maintenance costs. It also improves customer satisfaction and safety for both the driver and the public.[5]

While environmental stewardship is expected by all, some don't respond with equal fervor to altruistic goals. But these same individuals may respond favorably to the reduction of expenses that acting in an environmentally responsible way can produce. Walmart requires vendors to reduce the amount of packaging for their deliveries to reduce bulk. This reduces the number of containers to transport the same number of items, which requires fewer containers, fewer trucks and rail cars, fewer drivers, less fuel to move all of these items, less paperwork, and fewer transactions to prepare and monitor. So, one key initiative: reduce bulk, carries a large amount of benefits.[6]

Similarly, many organizations are finding that their strategic goals and ambitions can be well served by promoting environmental stewardship. Take for example General Electric (GE), which rolled out its "ecomagination" campaign to generate $20 billion in revenues through the sale of environmental products. Other companies that have achieved impressive results by embracing environmental strategies include those shown in Table 4.4.

There are many other organizations also engaged and heavily invested in environmental and sustainability initiatives. In fact, this trend is transforming the business model of many organizations, weakening some, and energizing others. The changes are so significant, that a *Harvard Business Review* article stated "Executives behave as though they have to choose between the largely social benefits of developing sustainable products or processes and the financial costs of doing so. But that's simply not true." The authors go on to say "sustainability is a mother lode of organizational and technological innovations that yield both bottom- and top-line returns. Becoming environment friendly lowers costs because companies end up reducing the inputs they use. In addition, the process generates additional revenues from better products

Table 4.4   Organizations Embracing Environmental Strategies

Company	Actions
Procter and Gamble (P&G)	Procter & Gamble (P&G) is working with UNICEF to sell NutriStar, which has a high nutritional content to combat malnutrition. The PuR product line consists of low cost water filters designed for emerging markets. P&G also changed the design of its bottles, saved over $500 million and 2 million tons of waste. Their European distribution program has saved them $25 million and 10 million kilometers of transportation
Starbucks	It has built most of its business model on fair trade and ethical sourcing of coffee, tea, and cocoa; engages in supplier diversity initiatives that started in 1997 by funding literacy programs in the United States and Canada. The Starbucks Foundation gave $13.1 million in 2014, making 144 grants to nonprofit organizations. Starbucks also promotes sustainable coffee farming (e.g., shade-grown coffee)
AREVA Solar	AREVA Solar designs, manufactures, and installs solar steam generators. Their focus is to reduce greenhouse gas emissions and have a portfolio of operations in four renewable energy segments: offshore wind, bioenergy, concentrated solar power, and energy storage
Grameen	Based in Bangladesh, it began operations providing micro credit to poor women without requiring collateral. Grameen Bank has grown into over two dozen enterprises, including trust, communications, energy, telecom, education, fisheries, business development, phone services, and others. The founder, Muhammad Yunus, received the Nobel Peace Prize in 2006 and micro lending is now offered by many organizations helping the poor around the world
Fair Trade	From Ten Thousand Villages and SERRV International, to Oxfam Trading, Siem Fair Trade, and Ben & Jerry's, there are thousands of organizations now engaged in fair trade. The World Fair Trade Organization (WFTO) reports that it operates in over 70 countries around the world and has established 10 principles that Fair Trade Organizations must follow in their day-to-day work. The WFTO carries out monitoring to ensure these principles are upheld. The principles are 1. Creating opportunities for economically disadvantaged producers 2. Transparency and accountability 3. Fair trading practices 4. Payment of a fair price 5. Ensuring no child labor and forced labor 6. Commitment to nondiscrimination, gender equity, and freedom of association 7. Ensuring good working conditions 8. Providing capacity building 9. Promoting fair trade 10. Respect for the environment

(continued)

TABLE 4.4 (*Continued*) Organizations Embracing Environmental Strategies

Company	Actions
Patagonia	This company designs, markets, and sells products produced under safe, fair, legal, and humane working conditions throughout their supply chain. Their mission statement reads "Build the best product, cause no unnecessary harm, use business to inspire and implement solutions to the environmental crisis." Their management support for this driving vision is legendary
Whole Foods Market	A chain of supermarkets specializing in natural and organic foods that also invests heavily in the markets where it operates
Ecolab	Ecolab is a global provider of water, hygiene, and energy technologies and services to the food, energy, healthcare, industrial, and hospitality markets. CRO magazine (formerly Business Ethics Magazine) recognized Ecolab in 2007 among the "100 Best Corporate Citizens." The award is based on an analysis of eight areas, including diversity, community, governance, shareholders, and the environment. Ecolab states their products are used for cleaning, sanitizing, food safety, and infection control and they operate in more than 160 countries
Coca-Cola	Coca-Cola's Global water stewardship program requires the company become more efficient in its water use by reducing the amount it uses per liter of product produced. The company recycles wastewater and states, "We promised to return 100% of the water we use to make our drinks. We met that goal and continue to regenerate more water than we use each year"[a]

Note
[a] To read more about Coca-Cola's water stewardship and other social and sustainability initiatives, see http://www.coca-colacompany.com/sustainabilityreport/world/water-stewardship.html#section-mitigating-riskfor-communities-and-for-our-system

or enables companies to create new businesses. In fact, because those are the goals of corporate innovation, we find that smart companies now treat sustainability as innovation's new frontier."[7]

Emotion

This relates to the emotional attachment and involvement that highly engaged employees show while working and interacting with others. When employees are emotionally invested in the organization and their work, they tend to work beyond the minimum requirements; they go the extra mile and strive in their efforts to delight the customer. Emotional identification with the organization's values, mission, vision, and objectives is motivating. Feeling that others in the organization are pursuing similar goals creates a stronger sense of community that binds employees to one another. The result is they support each other more, are more understanding and supportive of each other's shortcomings, and help each other along the way. Another important benefit of strong emotional ties is that employees will generally provide ideas for improvement and drive innovation, which help the organization move forward.

The opposite is often also true. When there is little emotional attachment, employees lack a sense of pride in the work done, which often translates into carelessness, apathy, and in more disruptive cases, even sabotage. Turnover is generally also higher because when there is little emotional attachment to the organization and its people, when "there is nothing to lose" in terms of friendships and professional alliances, employees lacking emotional connections are more likely to abandon the organization is search of another workplace providing that sense of community, belonging, and meaning.

Emotional attachment is also aligned with the concept of employee engagement, which generally posits that employees can be identified as being in one of three categories:

- Engaged: Characterized by being passionate and enthusiastic; sharing feelings of profound connectedness to the organization.
- Not Engaged: Sometimes described as employees having "checked out" and "sleepwalking". They may put in the time, but do not show energy or passion for the work.
- Actively Disengaged: These employees are a negative drag on the organization and its culture, they have no company loyalty, may undermine what engaged colleagues are doing and achieving, and may even sabotage company initiatives. They often think, and sometimes even verbally state that "it is not my job" when asked to perform certain tasks.

Emotion, therefore, is an important element that internal auditors should examine as it can enhance operational effectiveness when present and detract when absent.

Implications for Internal Auditors

Internal auditors should not think of the 8 Es only as a theoretical construct, but rather a framework to help them search for ways to add value to their organizations. While compliance is an integral component of what internal auditors do, and widely expected of auditors, a great deal of value can be added to organizations by incorporating the 8 Es into auditors' work programs. This can be done by making sure that whenever possible within the scope of the review, the auditor asks "how well is this program, process, or activity in terms of each of the 8 Es?" and "Are there opportunities for improvement along any of those dimensions?"

An internal auditor will certainly get management's attention when savings are identified or recommendations are made to accelerate a business process. Furthermore, by quantifying environmental benefits and linking these to increased revenue, lower waste, better public relations, and so on, internal auditors will demonstrate a strategic mindset that supersedes the tactical approach of traditional auditors.

Summary

Internal auditors can find themselves overwhelmed by the many activities that organizations are engaged in. While trying to identify and evaluate all of the dynamics affecting an organization, they can develop an overly complex and unmanageable audit scope. When they develop recommendations to address operating weaknesses, they can fail to sufficiently consider the value proposition for correcting the issues noted and embracing the recommendation made. After all, the purpose of fixing issues is not to appease the auditor; it is to make the organization more successful. This could mean doing the right things better, or avoiding the hardship caused by failing to do as expected.

The 8 Es can help auditors define themes for the scope and programs of their audit and consulting engagements. It is a great yet simple method to remind us about the eight key focus areas of all successful organizations:

- We must establish ambitious goals, and achieve them: effectiveness
- We must minimize the use of resources: efficiency
- We must only acquire what we need and do so at the optimal value point: economy
- We must do everything with high quality: excellence
- We must always act with integrity: ethics
- We must preserve the environment for ourselves and future generations: ecology

The eight elements are interconnected. By hiring workers based on merit (equity), we will staff the firm with the best individuals. Then, during normal business operations, we should treat workers, customers, and suppliers well and respectfully (ethics), which will also increase employees' feelings of well-being toward the organization and increase their attachment and investment (emotion). As an organization, we should only purchase what we need (economy, ecology) and operate carefully and scientifically (efficiency, excellence), which will generate less waste (ecology).

This model can help internal auditors to organize their thoughts, scope, programs, and define key elements of their findings and recommendations. For example

- Have we considered the 8 Es in our audit program?
- How many of the 8 Es are reflected in the recommendation?
- Did we address the 8 Es in our audit report?
- Which of the 8 Es shows the greatest weakness and what actions would restore balance?

Chapter 5 provides an overview of several internal control and other business frameworks. They help auditors and managers develop and execute internal controls better, provide greater cyber and physical security, realize greater cost savings, improve the opinion of stakeholders, avoid negative surprises, and in general, improve the quality of compliance, risk management, and corporate governance conditions.

These frameworks represent best practices relevant in a world of highly complex business dynamics, globalization, and information security. Effectively adopting these frameworks can enhance performance and make success something that is achieved in the short and longer terms. Sustainable success cannot be achieved if the organization suffers from design and operating deficiencies. Consequently, internal auditors are encouraged to help management implement, promote, and sustain any of the controls frameworks discussed.

QUESTIONS

1. List the 8 Es and explain how they impact organizational success.
2. How does the concept of effectiveness affect an organization's strategic and operating plans?
3. List three examples of how efficiency can be used as a competitive advantage.

4. Link the concept of excellence to the work of internal auditors and how it can be incorporated in audit programs.
5. How can failure in ethics affect organizational success? Is it something that can be audited?
6. Equity is often examined in the context of compliance with government employment and termination laws. Give three examples of how equity manifests itself in operations and the costs to the organization for failing to sustain these concepts.
7. Describe ways to monetize the concept of ecology, so we don't only rely on altruistic and emotional motivators, but also economic ones to encourage environmental stewardship.
8. Explain how an internal audit department can set goals and metrics, and incorporate the 8 Es in its annual performance report highlighting improvements within the organization.
9. How does the concept of excellence compare to criteria in the CCCER/5C Model used by internal auditors?
10. Give an example of how the 8 Es can be used when performing a site visit review.

Notes

1 See http://www.merriam-webster.com/dictionary/ethic
2 See Velasquez (2006, p. 97).
3 See Donaldson, Hosmer, and Hartman for additional information regarding the interfaith nature of this principle.
4 For a full description of the Fraud Triangle, see Murdock (2008).
5 Additional details about this program are available at http://www.automotive-fleet.com/article/story/2010/07/green-fleet-telematics-sensor-equipped-trucks-help-ups-control-costs.aspx
6 For more details about this program, see http://corporate.walmart.com/global-responsibility/sustainability/ and http://www.canadianshipper.com/features/wal-mart-launches-5-year-plan-to-reduce-packaging/
7 To read the full article, see https://hbr.org/2009/09/why-sustainability-is-now-the-key-driver-of-innovation

Chapter 5

Control Frameworks

Introduction

Today's business environment has resulted in a proliferation of vulnerabilities, risks, stakeholders, and activities much more complex than ever before. The blurring of national boundaries, intermingling of cultures, interfaces among computer systems, proliferation of e-commerce activities (whether B2B or B2C), and even the near irrelevance of time zones and geographic distances, have created a need for internal control frameworks. These are structures that organize, categorize, and sometimes prioritize an organization's internal controls. By definition, internal controls are practices put in place to create value for stakeholders and minimize risks, so frameworks make it easier to manage these diverging dynamics and evaluate the results more systematically.

There are several control frameworks in place and they are usually implemented voluntarily as a means to improve business results. COSO's Internal Control Integrated Framework (IC-IF) is arguably the most widely known internal controls framework in the world. IT controls are a subset of internal controls related to information technology (IT). IT control frameworks include Control Objectives for Information and Related Technology (COBIT), The International Organization for Standardization (ISO) 17799, and The Information Technology Infrastructure Library (ITIL). The Capability Maturity Model Integration (CMMI) is widely used in project management, process assessment, and performance improvement environments.

Control Frameworks

The COSO Frameworks: ICF and ERM

During the 1980s, a series of fraudulent acts affecting financial statements prompted the creation of a commission to evaluate the causes of the problems and prepare recommendations for corrective action. This National Commission on Fraudulent Financial Reporting, as it was called, was chaired by Mr James C. Treadway. Among the issues identified was the absence of a comprehensive internal controls framework containing a widely agreed-upon language that auditors, business leaders, regulators, and educational institutions could adopt. Consequently, among its recommendations was the need to create such a framework of internal control.

COSO of the Treadway Commission is a private sector initiative formed in 1985 to sponsor this National Commission on Fraudulent Financial Reporting. The National Commission was sponsored by five professional associations: The Institute of Internal Auditors (IIA), American Institute of Certified Public Accountants (AICPA), American Accounting Association (AAA), Institute of Management Accountants (IMA), and Financial Executives Institute (FEI), and also included representatives from industry, public accounting, investment firms, and the New York Stock Exchange (NYSE).[1]

COSO's goal was to improve the quality of financial reporting through a focus on corporate governance, ethical practices, and internal control. Emphasis is also given to ERM and fraud deterrence. COSO issued the IC-IF in 1992, which was revised and reissued in May 2013 and was effective from December 15, 2014.

The 2013 COSO IC-IF contains 17 principles representing the fundamental concepts associated with each component. COSO states that an entity can achieve effective internal control by applying all principles, which apply to operations, reporting, and compliance objectives. The COSO Framework is typically represented in the form of a cube showing the five components of internal control, the three categories of objectives, and the entity's structure, which is represented by the third dimension (i.e., depth).

The model and the related principles are aligned as shown in Figure 5.1.[2]

Talking about and acting ethically carries financial benefits.

Control Environment

This refers to the workplace environment, characterized by the way the organization is structured, the manner of leadership, the degree of openness, management's operating style, having and practicing the tenets of its code of ethics and statement of values. This also includes the tone at the top and the degree to which there is congruence between management's "talk" and its "walk." In other words, do managers practice what they preach?

The tone at the top is set and promoted by the board of directors and senior management, and it refers to the general attitude, integrity, and ethical practices of these individuals. It drives ethical conduct within the organization and helps to prevent unethical practices and fraud. When management formally communicates its principles and values, and its behavior is consistent with these pronouncements, it will influence the organizational culture and permeate the entire organization. Organizational culture is the collection of learned beliefs, traditions, and guides for behavior shared among members of the organization. It defines and expresses shared assumptions, values, and beliefs and it is manifested in many ways, including

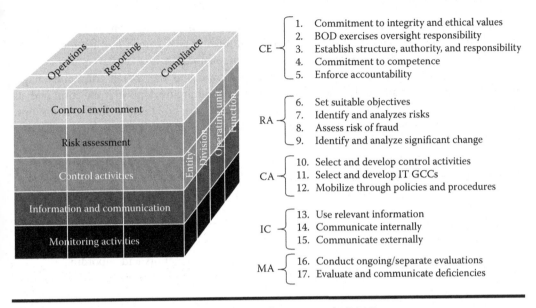

Figure 5.1   COSO Internal Control—Integrated Framework (2013).

formal rules and policies, norms of daily behavior, physical settings, and modes of dress, special language, myths, rituals, heroes, and stories. It is imperative that leaders pay close attention to organizational culture.

A healthy culture and ethical environment advances employee morale, and it also helps to improve productivity and efficiency. Organizations that set expectations and support doing the right thing, doing it well, and doing it for the right reasons tend to outperform other organizations in terms of customer satisfaction, employee satisfaction, and retention. After all, happy employees deliver higher quality customer services. Failure to retain an effective governance, ethics, and compliance program can jeopardize an organization's reputation, its bottom line, and even its existence as was evidenced in Enron, Barings Bank, Olympus, and Societé Générale. Ethics is also closely linked to quality, as evidenced in the Volkswagen emissions violations scandal. An auditor who fails to meet accounting standards can cause great damage to the firm and the client, as observed in the Xerox and KPMG cases.[3]

Similarly, a health care worker who fails to meet recognized ethical norms and standards is not delivering high-quality health care and while negligence can be claimed for a variety of reasons, malpractice lawsuits can be significant. In 2012, a $78.5 million verdict was handed down by a Philadelphia jury against Pottstown Memorial Medical Center, and in another case in 2014, $32.8 million was awarded in that case. Both cases are due to the delayed delivery of a baby who suffered brain damage and the two hospitals involved are owned by Community Health Systems of Franklin, TN.[4] So, failure to meet minimum quality standards increases ethical concerns, and can result in significant financial losses. Ethics and quality care can never be separated.

The control environment also includes the activities related to the competence and development of personnel, the assignment of authority and responsibility, and the organizational structure. Employee reporting lines and accountability requirements are also shaped by reporting lines, and these play an important role in the effectiveness of internal controls.

Another important aspect of the control environment is that management establishes a risk management philosophy and the entity's risk appetite, forms a risk culture, and integrates ERM with related initiatives. Many managers have come to the realization, after suffering financial and reputational damage, that the control environment is critical to the overall corporate image. Organizations are realizing that having a healthy corporate culture has a positive effect on sales as the number of customers who buy with their heart increases. It also affects vendor relationships, investor preferences, recruitment effectiveness, and stakeholder scrutiny. Talking about and acting ethically carries financial benefits.

It is important to remember that culture plays a key role defining the control environment. It includes the norms, values, rules, climate, and symbols. Organizational culture refers to the sum of perceptions that develop within an organization. According to Trompenaars, organizational culture includes three key elements:

1. The general relationship between employees and their organizations
2. The vertical or hierarchical system of authority defining superiors and subordinates
3. The general views of employees about the organization's destiny, purpose, and goals, and their place in it

These beliefs, values, and perceptions of employees, as defined in the code of ethics and other instruments, and promoted by management, can be distinct from the national culture. It is learned, and it is passed from one employee generation to another. Since new employees have to learn the organization's culture, it is critical that management act clearly and consistently in the promotion of proper conduct, follow ethical practices, and display the behaviors that encourage cooperation, adherence to company policies and procedures, and fair dealings internally and externally.

While acting with integrity and fairness generally characterizes ethical behavior, the following are some examples of unethical behavior that auditors should be on the lookout for:

Undue emphasis on bottom-line performance: While high expectations for generating a healthy profit, or operating well within the budget of the organization are to be expected, placing an unreasonable emphasis on this in ways that it becomes the main, if not the only true consideration, it is likely that unethical behaviors will be produced. The focus should be on satisfying the customer and keeping employees happy while managing costs. Organizations that put the customer and employees first often achieve superior results.

High-pressure sales tactics: An organization's revenues depend heavily on effective sales and marketing. However, when sales practices are more focused on extracting funds from customers, the mischaracterization of the company's products and services increases. Ruthless negotiations and failure to disclose to customers the true features of, and issues with, products and services will usually portend future problems.

Kickbacks or bribes: These consist of illicit payments made to someone who has facilitated a transaction or appointment. Most countries have laws forbidding these types of payments. The US passed the Foreign Corrupt Practices Act (FCPA) in 1977. It is a federal law that applies worldwide and has two key elements:

1. Forbids paying bribes, personal payments, or rewards to foreign government officials
2. Requires accounting transparency and record keeping to verify that illicit payments were not made

Table 5.1   Top Ten FCPA Fines

Company	Fine ($ millions)	Year
Siemens	800	2008
VimpelCom	795	2016
Alstom	772	2014
KBR/Halliburton	579	2009
BAE	400	2010
Total SA	398	2013
Alcoa	384	2014
Snamprogetti/Eni	365	2010
Technip SA	338	2010
JGC Corporation	218.8	2011
Daimler AG	185	2010

Consequences include high financial penalties. Note on the list of the top 10 biggest FCPA fines that the amounts are substantial, but also that since its inception, all the top fines/settlements occurred since 2008 (Table 5.1).

Other recognizable companies that have been fined recently include BHP Billiton ($25 million), Pfizer ($60 million), Bristol-Myers Squibb ($14 million), Hitachi ($19 million), BNY Mellon ($14.8 million), and Goodyear Tire & Rubber Company ($16 million).[5]

Communication, Consistency, and Belief in the Message

It is very important for management to communicate clearly, consistently, and often what is allowed and what is not. By setting clear expectations there is a better chance that they will be followed. But being followed depends to a large extent on management "walking the talk" and demonstrating through their actions that they believe in the messages. When there are inconsistencies between what management says is the expected behavior, and their own behavior, employees will see management as hypocritical. That is a sure recipe for trouble as employees will likely emulate their bosses.

The following quote from Ralph Waldo Emerson provides a very useful summary of the dynamics being described here:

"What you do speaks so loudly that I cannot hear what you are saying."

Having a code of ethics, code of conduct, and conflict of interest statement is very important to formally establish the expectations for proper conduct. Codes of ethics should act as a guideline or reference point for acceptable behavior and ethical decision-making. They should be values based, motivate employees to conduct themselves in ethical ways, support the questioning of authority when ethics are challenged, and hold employees accountable when rules are broken.

New employees should receive these documents upon hire and sign-off indicating they agree to abide by them. Training should also be required upon hire to make sure that employees understand fully what the documents mean. These should be followed by annual refresher training to remind employees of the importance of these topics, update them on any guidance that needs updating, and answer any questions. A common mistake organizations make is to expect that ethics will be on people's minds without ever talking about it.

Another useful activity that leading organizations practice is to have short articles, vignettes, scenarios, and surveys that are distributed periodically to all staff. This can be done through the company's newsletter, e-mail, and intranet posts. Running lunch and learn or brown bag lunch sessions is another helpful practice. These lunch and learn sessions are informal lunchtime events with a discussion topic allowing employees to hear a short presentation or video, have a short discussion, and engage a subject matter expert on topics related to risks and controls. Topics I have attended, facilitated, and heard about include

Harassment in the workplace
Bidding procedures
Hiring procedures
Travel and entertainment
Fraud awareness
Safety procedures
Health and fitness
IT security
Social engineering

Internal audit doesn't have to conduct these sessions, but it doesn't hurt either. By partnering with Human Resources, Legal, IT, and Loss Prevention, among others, the organization will see internal auditors also as educators and advisors. It is helpful for employees to hear from and about internal audit in other settings and not only when they are being audited.

Form over Substance

This consists of the management practices whereby on the surface it appears as though an essential activity has been performed, when in fact that is not so. This includes signatures that suggest transaction review and approval, when in fact the individual did not review the relevant documents as expected. Similar issues may apply to reconciliations where even the reconciliation form is completed, but upon closer inspection it is determined that the form is not mathematically correct, a "plug" has been entered to force the figures to tie, and reconciling items remain outstanding past the acceptable period for their clearance.

Principles underlying the control environment are

1. The organization should demonstrate a commitment to integrity and ethical values: In this regard, it is not enough for the organization to state that it believes in acting ethically, or even that it expects employees to conduct themselves ethically. The organization should show, through their actions, and by rewarding ethical behavior and castigating unethical behavior, that they are committed to integrity and ethical values. This also means that management cares not only about what is achieved, but also how those results were achieved. This means that the organization cares about how employees, customers,

communities, vendors, and other stakeholders are treated and it imposes prompt and appropriate sanctions on those that deviate from these expectations.

2. The board of directors demonstrates independence from management and exercises oversight of the development and performance of internal control: Passive boards of directors are a terrible thing for the quality of internal control because they display limited oversight over management actions. Some of the key responsibilities of a board is to provide a mission and vision for the organization, set expectations for management, authorize investments that show its priorities, and in general, look out for the interests of the company's owners. This is best accomplished when the board is independent of senior management and is not unduly influenced by it. If the entire board is not independent, at least the audit committee of the board should be.

3. Management establishes, with board oversight, structures, reporting lines, and appropriate authorities and responsibilities in the pursuit of objectives: While executing the priorities of the board of directors, management should establish an organizational structure that will facilitate the assignment of responsibilities, that will ensure the smooth flow of information down the chain of command and back in the form of feedback (e.g., performance results, concerns, and requests for needed resources).

4. The organization demonstrates a commitment to attract, develop, and retain competent individuals in alignment with objectives: The words "people are our greatest asset" is often emanating from the lips and keyboards of managers, but upon closer inspection is often evident that they don't treat employees in that way. As the primary means of production for many organizations, employee recruitment, selection, training and development, compensation, and promotion should be based on competence, proven potential, commitment, and performance. If people are truly assets, then they should be selected carefully, safeguarded once obtained, properly deployed, and maintained in good condition physically, emotionally, and technically. Those individuals that do not meet the technical and ethical expectations of the organization should undergo appropriate training and receive appropriate sanctions if they are being allowed to remain with the organization, or disciplined up to the point of termination if their infraction is severe enough. Failing to deal with performance and ethical breakdowns jeopardizes the organization's chances of achieving its objectives.

5. The organization holds individuals accountable for their internal control responsibilities in the pursuit of objectives: When control activities are assigned, it is imperative that management sets clear expectations that these activities must be performed. By setting accountabilities clearly, and enforcing compliance with them, the control environment will benefit from the discipline, follow through, and stability that internal controls provide. Objectives define the direction of the organization and the measure of its success, while controls provide protection that necessary activities will be carried out to mitigate risks and increase the likelihood that those objectives will be achieved.

Entity Level Controls

Entity level controls are used to determine if an organization's values, systems, policies, and processes would enable or dissuade fraud and encourage proper conduct. They refer to the entity's management style, as reflected in the corporate culture, values, philosophy, and operating style, the organizational structure, and policies and procedures in place. Auditing the entity's framework requires the examination of tangibles (e.g., policies, procedures, manuals, and rules) and intangibles (e.g., management philosophy, culture, and operating style). Review items also include human resources (HR) policies, the reporting structure with the assignment authority and responsibility, information flows, demonstration of a commitment to competence, and other types of checks and balances in the organization.

Typical areas of interest include

- Controls over management override
- The company's risk assessment methodology and techniques that identify both risks and owners of risk
- Extent and quality of controls over centralized processing, including shared service environments and outsource service providers
- Controls to monitor results of operations
- Controls over the preparation, review and communication of period-end financial and operational reporting, both internally and externally
- Policies that address significant business control and risk management practices
- The extent, accuracy, and suitability of policies and procedures related to governance, operations, risk management, control, and compliance expectations
- Hiring and retention practices
- Fraud prevention and detection controls, including analytical procedures
- The competence, scope, and depth of the work of the internal audit function
- Effectiveness of the whistle-blower hotline
- Adherence to the word and spirit of the code of conduct
- IT environment and organizations
- Results of organizational self-assessment reviews
- The depth of oversight of the company's disclosure committee
- The extent, competence, consistency, and extent of tone setting and oversight displayed by the board of directors, senior and middle management in their role as governance providers
- Assignment of authority and responsibility across all layers of the organizational structure
- Account reconciliations, variance analysis reporting, and related corrective measures
- Effectiveness of the mechanism to remediate control weaknesses
- Management triggers embedded within IT systems
- The establishment and reliability of physical and logical segregation of duties
- Effectiveness of change-management practices affecting the organization

The following are some illustrative questions internal auditors and business leaders can use to begin the process of identifying strengths and weaknesses in their entity level controls:

- Does the organization's code of conduct and other policies define acceptable business practices, conflicts of interest, and expected standards of integrity and ethics?
- Is disciplinary action sufficiently taken and communicated in the case of management, internal control, or ethical violations?
- How does management make sure that the organizational structure is appropriate to the achievement of strategic objectives?
- Have documented levels of authority and responsibilities been authorized and implemented in the policies and procedures documents, and systems, for all functions and departments? Are they current?
- Is relevant internal and external information available, obtained, and used about business financial and operational performance? Are exceptions addressed promptly?

- How does management know if the organization is meeting its compliance requirements?
- Are existing systems reviewed for efficacy and what is the status of recommendations for improvement?
- Is data and information complete, accurate, timely, and distributed to the correct individuals in management to use reliably?
- Are reports by the second line of defense (e.g., corporate compliance, quality control, and IT security) and third line of defense (i.e., internal audit) given the appropriate attention?
- Is there coordination within the organization's second line of defense units and among the organization's second and third lines of defense?
- Have plans been developed to share, mitigate, or avoid risks to assets, people, and the organization's reputation?
- How is management addressing the potential effects on the business of a loss or disruption of computing or operational facilities? Has a business continuity plan been developed and is it updated periodically as new threats emerge?
- Has the organization achieved national and international quality standard accreditations (e.g., ISO) and is management taking appropriate steps to make sure those accreditations are maintained?
- How does management measure the success of business operations against defined goals and objectives, including benchmarking results internally and externally?
- What is the process in place to make sure that all insurable risks are identified, assessed, and adequately covered?
- Is there a public and media relations policy in place and in the event of an emergency or crisis, what is the response plan? Has that response plan been tested within the past year?
- Does the organization have qualified accounting, tax, and operating personnel so all reports are prepared according to generally accepted principles and standards, and records maintained in accordance with current accounting and tax regulations and standards?
- What processes are in place to prevent the creation and distribution of inaccurate or invalid financial and operating information?
- Please describe the process to identify and manage operational risks, and not only financial, compliance, and legal ones?
- Please describe the onboarding process and how new employees are made aware of the organization's values, performance expectations, and disciplinary actions.

Internal auditors are encouraged to remember that a person's behavior is determined by the person and his or her environment. There are a number of different and competing forces that combine to result in the situation the individual encounters. In other words, a person's behavior may be different in unique situations, as the person acts in part in response to the environment. As a result, the person, who consists naturally of his or her past, present, and future, personality, and motivations, must be considered in conjunction with the environment.

This dynamic, developed by Kurt Lewin and known as Lewin's equation, states that behavior is a function of the person and the environment, and can be expressed in the formula:

$$B = f(P, \ E),$$

where B is the person's behavior, P is the person, and e is the environment.

What is the significance of Lewin's equation for internal auditors? Even though it was first published in Principles of Topological Psychology in 1936, most internal auditors are yet to fully understand and apply it in their work. Internal auditors are tasked with verifying that employees do what is appropriate to pursue organizational goals and this often implies they must follow internal and external policies, procedures and practices. In other words, they must behave in ways that further the company's stakeholders and the company's mission. However, employees don't always do this and the auditor is expected to communicate this deviation to senior management and the board. Why don't employees do what is expected of them?

The answer can be quite complex. I describe 13 reasons in Chapter 11—Change Management, but for purposes of this discussion, internal auditors must work with management to make sure there are clear standards of performance, that rewards and sanctions are clearly communicated, and that employees are managed and aligned effectively. John Kotter wrote in the Harvard Business Review article "What Leaders Really Do" that "Unless many individuals line up and move together in the same direction, people will tend to fall all over one another. To executives who are overeducated in management and undereducated in leadership, the idea of getting people moving in the same direction appears to be an organizational problem. What executives need to do, however, is not organize people but align them." Employees need a positive environment, where their leaders walk the talk, structures support what needs to be accomplished, and rewards are granted to those who act ethically to further the mission of the organization and act within the confines of internal and external requirements.

This dynamic highlights the importance of not only thinking about "bad apples" in the organization, but also to consider the negative effect of "bad barrels." The first scenario involves poor behavior caused by individuals who have a negative or opportunistic disposition and circumvent the rules for personal gain. The second scenario consists of good people who succumb to overbearing personal problems, such as excessive medical bills. While these personal matters do not justify the negative act, it describes a different situation where the pressure, in addition to the poor or missing controls, make it possible for this crime of opportunity to occur. The third scenario is one that auditors must also consider, and it relates to organizations where the collective practice and prevailing cultural more is that certain actions are acceptable, even when they are really not. In those cases, the weak control environment creates a bad barrel, where new and current employees may engage in the herd mentality and follow their peers and behave similarly.

Organizations need to work diligently to create, nurture, and indoctrinate employees on the organizational culture through socialization, education, formal/informal systems, and reinforcement. Creating a sense of family goes a long way toward creating a harmonious, productive, and ethical environment. This sense of family (or micro groupings that can sometimes occur) should not serve as a shield where unethical behavior is tolerated. In some dysfunctional environments, people are more loyal to the micro group than the entire organization, society, or even themselves, thus compromising their own ethics and those of the collective. Examples include not disclosing inappropriate actions, and embellishing performance reports as was observed with deadly results at the Veteran's Administration scandal.[6]

The focus on internal controls, with insufficient regard to the work environment, will result in many frustrating moments for the auditor. In fact, the term "tone in the middle" has been gaining a great deal of attention since many of the positive, and negative, behaviors, and the resulting impact on internal control and corporate performance occur "in the middle." So, what is the tone set by middle managers and supervisors? Are they reinforcing the guidance and expectations set by senior management, or are they encouraged, and rewarded for circumventing controls, taking inappropriate shortcuts, and engaging in self-serving behaviors?

Tone in the Middle

Deciding who becomes a manager is one of the most important organizational actions because employees judge their organization as ethical or not based on what they think their boss does. So when it comes to ethics, deciding who become managers is of critical importance. If employees think that their bosses treat them ethically, honestly, and fairly, that is what they will think about the company. The manager determines and reinforces the values, ethics, honesty, and workplace dynamics, also influences the process of getting customers and making sure they are happy. This means that the "tone in the middle" dictates workplace conditions leading to customer and employee satisfaction, turnover, profits, and the achievement of goals and objectives.

The workplace environment is in many ways determined by the level of employee engagement. There is a very big difference in results when workers are engaged, not engaged, or actively disengaged. Internal auditors should work with management to determine how engaged the workforce is.

Risk Assessment

The second component of the COSO framework relates to the identification, quantification, analysis, and management of organizational risks. Risks are those events that can jeopardize the organization's ability to achieve its objectives. In other words, they represent what can go wrong while engaged in business activities in the pursuit of organizational goals. In fact, COSO indicates in its 2013 IC-IF that the organization is subject to a variety of events; some positive while others are negative. Positive events are opportunities, while negative events are risks.

Risks are typically assessed along two dimensions

1. Likelihood, or the probability that these events occur
2. Impact, or the consequence if these events occurred

Establishing objectives is a precondition to risk assessment. A risk assessment is the process of identifying, assessing, and measuring risks to the organization, program, or process under review. It is imperative, however, before embarking on the risk assessment journey, that relevant objectives be identified. One of the key benefits of this approach is that it provides the context for the identification of risks. This is so because risks are only relevant to the extent that they jeopardize the achievement of objectives.

Larry Rittenberg, COSO's Chair Emeritus after serving as COSO Chairman from 2005 to 2009, stated in the book *COSO IC-IF: Turning Principles Into Positive Action* (p. 28):

> Internal auditing needs to understand—and consider—the link between objectives, risks, and controls. If objectives are not properly articulated (including a risk appetite and risk tolerances), then there is a deficiency in the control environment that should be brought to the attention of senior management and the board. There is another important lesson here: It is difficult to overcome a breakdown between senior management and board oversight. Focusing more on control activities cannot compensate for such a deficiency.

When risks have been identified, they should be linked throughout the organization. This process will provide a chaining mechanism to trace risks up and down the organization in terms of their likelihood and impact. For example, a risk that employees are not competent to perform their duties could be noted at any level of the organization, but to the extent that it is at the highest level (i.e., senior management), the repercussions could be catastrophic due to poor decisions on their part. If this risk is happening at the bottom of the organization, but it is pervasive, that fact should be identified, noted, and escalated to senior management because they should understand that this can impact day-to-day operations. Furthermore, remediating this issue could require a change in budgeted amounts for company operating units, a change in corporate policy regarding minimum training requirements, frequencies, and subjects, and the requirement that performance metrics be reassessed to determine progress made.

Risk assessment involves a dynamic and iterative process of identifying, analyzing, and deciding how best to respond to these risks in relation to the achievement of objectives. Due to the rapidly changing business environment, organizations are coming to the conclusion that this assessment must be done frequently and in some cases, near real time. Management specifies objectives within three separate but related categories:

> *Reporting*: Reporting considerations are arranged in four broad categories: internal/external and financial/nonfinancial. This is of importance to internal auditors who must remember that organizations must meet reporting expectations beyond external financial reporting. It includes the reliability, timeliness, transparency, or other terms set by regulators, the organization's policies or other recognized standard setters.
>
> *Compliance*: These are related to adherence to laws and regulations to which the organization is subject. Compliance requirements may also include compliance with contractual terms and conditions, service level agreements, voluntary agreements, like those involving corporate sustainability reports (e.g., Green Reports).
>
> *Operations*: These pertain to the effectiveness and efficiency of the organization's operations. This includes operational and financial performance goals, safeguarding assets against loss, damage or obsolescence, and making sure resources are obtained economically.[7]

Management must consider, specify, and analyze the degree to which objectives are aligned with their strategic priorities. This linkage is essential to ensure congruence and coordination between these objectives. I have observed numerous instances where operational, reporting, or compliance risks are not aligned with the entity's strategic risk, and the result is often competing interests, internal conflicts, priority dissonance, and poor performance. Note the following three examples:

1. An employee's objectives have a focus on cost reduction. As such, the employee decides to postpone equipment maintenance and this reduces costs. While this provides a short-term success, the equipment breaks down prematurely and the organization suffers from two outcomes: (1) the need to perform more expensive repairs including parts replacement and (2) the loss of revenues due to unplanned downtime.
2. The sales department's performance is measured on sales volume, but there are few safeguards to make sure that all sales are registered according to generally accepted accounting

principles, that the customers have the ability to pay for their purchases, and that the product features and related statements made to sales prospects are accurate. As a result, sales increase, but collections are subpar and accounts receivable write-offs skyrocket. Furthermore, disgruntled customers file a class action lawsuit for product misrepresentation and the company's reputation is damaged, further depressing future sales.

3. The manufacturing manager's goals are weighted heavily on lowering unit costs, so she increases production above and beyond projected sales figures. The excess production is then warehoused increasing carrying costs, raising concerns among investors, and depressing the company's stock price.

The examples above show the importance of aligning objectives with established laws, rules, regulations, and standards applicable to the organization and the marketplace. Neglecting these interrelated components can be a recipe for trouble and the consequences can be felt for many years. Furthermore, large-scale problems often invite regulator involvement and media attention, both distracting situations that can also become very expensive over time.

Any discussion about risk must consider that every entity faces a variety of risks from internal and external sources.

Business and Process Risk

This is the risk that the organization's processes are not effectively obtaining, managing, and disposing their assets, that the organization is not performing effectively and efficiently in meeting customer needs, is not creating value or is diluting value by suffering the degradation of financial, physical, and information assets.

- *Capacity risk*: Insufficient capacity limits the ability to meet demand in the short and long term, or excess capacity threatens the firm's ability to generate competitive profit margins
- *Execution risk*: Inability to produce consistently without compromising quality
- *Supply chain risk*: Being unable to maintain a steady stream of supplies when needed
- *Business interruption risk*: This risk stems from the unavailability of raw materials, IT, skilled labor, facilities or other resources that threaten the organization's ability and capacity to continue operations
- *Human resources risk*: A lack of knowledge, skills, and experiences among the organization's key personnel that threatens the ability to achieve business objectives
- *Product or service failure risk*: Faulty or nonperforming products and services that do not meet customer expectations can expose the organization to customer complaints, warranty claims, returns, field repairs, product liability claims, litigation causing lost revenues, lower market share, and damage to the business' reputation
- *Product development risk*: Ineffective product development threatens the organization's ability to meet or exceed customers' expectations consistently over the long term. This could be evidenced by developing products customers do not need or want, products and services that are priced at a level customers are not willing to pay or while the goods and services meet a need, they are late to market and a competitor reached first
- *Cycle time risk*: Unnecessary activities threaten the organization's capacity to develop, produce, market, and deliver goods and services in a timely manner

- *Health and safety risk*: Failure to provide a safe working environment for workers exposes the organization to compensation liabilities, loss of business reputation, and other costs
- *Leadership risk*: Workers are not being led effectively resulting in lack of direction, motivation to perform, customer focus, management credibility, and trust
- *Outsourcing risk*: Outsourcing activities to third parties could result in these third parties not performing in a way that is consistent with the organization's strategies, objectives, values, and behavioral standards and expectations
- *Competitor risk*: The risk that actions by competitors may threaten the organization's competitive advantage or even its survival
- *Catastrophic loss risk*: The risk that a catastrophe threatens the organization's ability to continue operating and provide goods and services
- *Industry risk*: Changing conditions that affect the attractiveness of the industry
- *Planning risk*: Lack of, unrealistic, irrelevant, or unreliable planning information could result in poor conclusion and decisions. This risk is often triggered when plans and budgets are unrealistic, not based on appropriate assumptions or performance metrics, are not relevant to organization goals, or unaccepted by managers and workers
- *Organization structure risk*: The organization's structure does not support change, flexibility, or the organization's strategies. An ineffective organizational structure can threaten its ability to change
- *Integrity and fraud risk*: Risk of management or employee fraud, illegal or unauthorized acts that could result in reputation loss. Management fraud is the intentional misstatement of financial and operational reports that negatively affect external stakeholders' decisions. Fraud could also be perpetrated by suppliers, customers, agents, and brokers against the organization for personal gain. Illegal acts committed by managers and employees can result in fines, penalties, sanctions, loss of licenses to operate, loss of customers, and reputation damage
- *Trademark erosion risk*: The erosion of a trademark or brand over time threatens the demand for the organization's products and services. It also limits its ability to develop and grow future revenue streams. Trademarks and brands usually help the organization build and retain demand for its goods and services. These include brand names, service, and certification marks/symbols
- *Reputation risk*: Risk of loss generally related to ethics, safety, security, quality, innovation, and sustainability causing lost revenue, higher capital and regulatory costs, lower stock price, or difficulties raising capital due to a potentially criminal event. Reputation risk may also cause loss of customers, profits, and the ability to compete
- *Data integrity*: Reliability and completeness of data flows, inbound and outbound from/to customers, vendors, regulators, investors, and other stakeholders. It also relates to the authorization, completeness, and accuracy of transactions as they are input, processed, and reported
- *Infrastructure risk*: Risk that the organization's IT infrastructure is obsolete, or lacks the IT infrastructure, such as hardware, software, networks, and people it needs to effectively support the information requirements of the organization to remain viable in the short and long term
- *Commerce risk*: Events that compromise B2B, and B2C financial and data flows, data integrity, and security
- *Access risk*: Failure to adequately restrict access to information could result in unauthorized use of confidential information. Conversely, overly restrictive access to information could limit the ability of personnel to perform their assigned responsibilities
- *Availability risk*: Unavailability of information when needed could threaten the continuity of the organization's operations and processes

Technological and Information Technology Risks

These risks relate to conditions where IT is not operating as intended, the integrity and reliability of data is compromised, and significant assets are exposed to potential loss or misuse. It also relates to the inability to maintain critical systems and processes. It includes

- *Data and system availability risk*: Uptime of systems, machines, and other tools to support the needs of workers, customers, suppliers, and other stakeholders of the organization. This involves data acquisition, maintenance, use, distribution, storage, and destruction
- *Data integrity risk*: Accuracy and consistency of data stored, processed, retrieved, and destroyed when it reaches the end of its life-cycle
- *System capacity risk*: Optimizing the amount of storage and computing ability systems possess
- *Data integrity*: Reliability and completeness of data flows, inbound and outbound from/to customers, vendors, regulators, investors, and other stakeholders. The authorization, completeness, and accuracy of transactions as they are input, processed, and reported
- *Infrastructure risk*: Risk that the organization's IT infrastructure is obsolete, or lacks the IT infrastructure, such as hardware, software, networks, and people it needs to effectively support the information requirements of the organization to remain viable in the short and long term
- *Commerce risk*: Events that compromise B2B, and B2C financial and data flows, data integrity, and security
- *Access risk*: Failure to adequately restrict access to information could result in unauthorized use of confidential information. Conversely, overly restrictive access to information could limit the ability of personnel to perform their assigned responsibilities
- *Availability risk*: Unavailability of information when needed could threaten the continuity of the organization's operations and processes

Personnel Risks

Personnel risks relate to conditions that limit the organization's ability to obtain, deploy, and retain sufficient numbers of suitably qualified and motivated workers. As organizations increasingly rely on their workforce to produce goods and services that add value to their customers, management is confronted with the risk that personnel shortages limit their ability to deliver consistently with high quality in the short and long terms.

- *Availability risk*: Sufficient workers and subject matter experts to support the organization's present and future needs
- *Competence risk*: Workers' ability to perform their duties efficiently and successfully
- *Judgment risk*: Workers' capacity to make sensible decisions based on relevant circumstances
- *Malfeasance risk*: Wrongdoing perpetrated by employees, contractors, suppliers, or customers
- *Motivation risk*: Demotivated workers fail to apply creativity and discipline to their tasks resulting in lower production, lower quality, poor service, and higher turnover and absenteeism

Financial Risks

Financial risks can result in poor cash flows, currency and interest rate fluctuations, and an inability to move funds quickly and without loss of value to where they are needed. Examples include

- *Resources risk*: Availability of funds when needed and their judicious use for business purposes
- *Commodity prices risk*: Fluctuations in prices expose the organization to lower margins or trading losses
- *Foreign currency risk*: Changes in foreign exchange rates can result in the economic loss of some of the value of the asset
- *Liquidity risk*: This is the loss exposure due to an inability to meet cash flow obligations, or the lack of buyers and sellers in a market (i.e., illiquid market)
- *Market*: Movements in prices, rates, and indices affect the value of the organization's financial assets and stock price. This could also affect its cost of capital and its ability to raise capital

Environmental Risks

Environmental risk relates to the actual or potential threat of negative effects on the environment by emissions, wastes, and resource depletion. This can be caused by an organization's activities and it influences living organisms, land, air, and water. Examples include

- *Energy and other resources risk*: Inability to obtain reliable supplies at a reasonable price
- *Natural disaster risk*: Events such as floods, earthquakes, fires, hurricanes, and tornadoes, also the lack of potable water and other resources needed in company facilities
- *Pollution risk*: Regulations and stakeholder demands affecting the source of energy supplies, and the quantity and manner of wastes allowable. Also excessive pollution that limit the organization's employees' health and safety. These activities can be harmful to the environment and expose the organization to liabilities for bodily injury, property damage, removal costs, and punitive damages, among others
- *Transportation risk*: Ensuring the availability of adequate means of transportation. Some depend on natural means such as navigable rivers, lakes, and coastlines, or are directly or indirectly affected by natural or human actions, such as having unobstructed roads and working railroads
- *Pandemic risk*: Bacteria or viruses that disrupt the organization's supply chain or availability of its workforce to perform its duties

Political

This is a type of risk faced by organizations, investors, and governments. It refers to the effects that political decisions, events, or conditions can cause when they affect the profitability of a business, or the ability to operate freely. It has to do with the complications organizations may encounter as a result of political decisions. Examples include

- *Regulations and legislation risk*: New or changes to existing regulations that limit the organization's ability to engage in its normal business activities
- *Public policy risk*: Stakeholder demands affecting the organization's operations
- *Instability risk*: Civil or military unrest that disrupts the organization's activities

Social Risk

Social risk relates to dynamics where an issue affects stakeholders who can form negative perceptions that can cause some form of damage to the organization. Social risk can be influenced by strategic and operational decisions management makes that affect issues stakeholders care about. The way society perceives organizations' ways of conducting business is becoming increasingly important and drives decisions related to climate change, obesity, workers' rights, poverty, and other social and environmental issues. Current and prospective customers are increasingly responding to these dynamics by buying more or less, commenting publicly through social media, or lobbying with power brokers to exert pressure on organizations to behave in ways that reflect their wishes.

Social risk is also influenced by societal dynamics affecting the workforce and target customers, such as their age, racial composition, national origin, and family structure decisions. Examples of social risks include

- *Demographics risk*: Changes that affect purchasing preferences, staff availability, or the cost to maintain a healthy workforce
- *Privacy risk*: Preferences that curtail the capture, storage, use, and dissemination of personal information
- *CSR*: Requirements for social involvement and investment that diverts time and other resources from the organization's primary activities
- *Mobility*: Dynamics that change the preferences of workers and customers to work, and live in ways that support the organization's needs and products

Risk assessment requires management to consider the impact of possible changes in the external environment and within their own business model that could make internal control ineffective. This includes focusing on clearly articulating objectives relating to operations, reporting, and compliance so any risks to those objectives can be identified and assessed. Also take into consideration the need to assess suitability of objectives to assess effectiveness. Effectiveness relates to the achievement of objectives and the degree to which these are achieved. Simply stating objectives is not enough.

For some internal auditors, identifying the business goals is a new frontier because they have always audited based on controls. For others it is a new frontier because they have never engaged in meaningful conversations with area managers about the operational goals of their departments. It is essential to begin with objectives in mind, and to obtain these from process owners during the planning phase. The IIA instructs internal auditors:

"In planning the engagement, internal auditors must consider:

- The objectives of the activity being reviewed and the means by which the activity controls its performance.
- The significant risks to the activity, its objectives, resources, and operations and the means by which the potential impact of risk is kept to an acceptable level" (Standard 2201).

When objectives are missing or undefined, internal auditors must engage with management and help them define goals. This is important because there are many issues that are likely to emerge when goals are not defined, ranging from confusion and lack of coordination, to a limited sense of purpose and outright waste while employees work aimlessly.

If the goals have been defined, but are inadequate, internal auditors should engage management to develop improvements. The IIA Standards state:

"Adequate criteria are needed to evaluate governance, risk management, and controls. Internal auditors must ascertain the extent to which management and/or the board has established adequate criteria to determine whether objectives and goals have been accomplished. If adequate, internal auditors must use such criteria in their evaluation. If inadequate, internal auditors must work with management and/or the board to develop appropriate evaluation criteria" (Standard 2210.A3).

Proactive efforts to define or help clarify goals will go a long way to helping managers perceive the value that internal auditors can bring to operational reviews. The decision about the exact objectives will clearly rest with management itself, but if people have been operating with clearly defined objectives for a long time, and the auditors can help them bring about that improvement, the results can be very positive. When considering risks:

"Internal auditors must be alert to the significant risks that might affect objectives, operations, or resources. However, assurance procedures alone, even when performed with due professional care, do not guarantee that all significant risks will be identified" (Standard 1220.A3).

The SMARTER model is very useful when developing organizational and personal goals. SMARTER is a mnemonic[8] that helps you remember the elements of well-developed goals. According to Wikipedia, George Doran first mentioned SMART goals in the November 1981 issue of Management Review. Table 5.2 shows the model in its entirety and the implications for internal auditors performing operational reviews. It is very effective, and two enhancements that add the letters "E" and "R" make it even more effective.

Specific

By being specific, goals become clearer and they avoid the ambiguity that can often impair goal-setting. Managers and employees know what they are expected to do and can focus their energy, resources, and priorities accordingly to accomplish them. Another important characteristic of specific goals is that they are easier to quantify and monitor for performance evaluations.

When formulating goals, process owners should consider the following questions:

■ What has to be to be accomplished?
■ Who is involved in getting this done?
■ What is its importance to me and the organization?
■ Where must this happen, if applicable?
■ Which requirements or restrictions apply, if any?[9]

Measurable

When goals are measurable it is easier to link their completion to the performance monitoring and rewards mechanism. Having a method to measure the degree of success accomplishing the related

Table 5.2   The SMARTER Model for Effective Goals

Letter	Major Descriptor	Related Descriptors or Minor Terms
S	Specific	Significant, simple, stretching, and sufficiently detailed
M	Measurable	Meaningful, motivational, and manageable
A	Achievable	Appropriate, assignable, ambitious, aspirational, attainable, agreed, actionable, and aligned
R	Relevant	Realistic and resourced
T	Time-bound	Timed, timely, time-specific, trackable, and tangible
E	Evaluated	Excitable, ethical, engaging, ecological, and enjoyable
R	Rewarding	Reevaluate, revisit, recordable, and reaching

Source: Murdock, H. 2011. *10 Key Techniques to Improve Team Productivity.* Altamonte Springs, FL: The IIA Research Foundation. (Retrieved from http://en.wikipedia.org/wiki/SMART_criteria on November 6, 2015.)

goal is essential. In fact, the lack of oversight and clear metrics to gauge performance is a common reason goals are ineffective and individuals fail to achieve them. Workers focus on what is measured, especially when the results affect their performance evaluations and compensation.

Process owners and workers in the corresponding process can benefit by asking themselves the following questions:

- What must be done to demonstrate progress?
- What is the quantitative and qualitative evidence that will show we achieved the goal?[10]

Achievable

Impossible goals do not motivate workers; they demotivate them. When the workers' viewpoint is that goals are unrealistic and unachievable, they feel impotent because the goal cannot be reached. Unachievable goals may also lead employees to fabricate financial and operational results in their attempts to appear to achieve their goals. This condition may have contributed to the Veterans Affairs (VA) Department Hospitals where allegations of treatment delays and falsified records involving secret lists were used to conceal long patient wait times for appointments.

According to PBS, "A former clinic director said up to 40 veterans died while awaiting treatment at the Phoenix VA hospital, even as hospital staff kept a secret appointment list to mask the delays. A VA nurse in Cheyenne, Wyoming, was put on leave for allegedly telling employees to falsify appointment records. A VA investigation in December found that staffers at a Fort Collins, Colorado, clinic were trained to make it appear as if veterans got appointments within 14 days, as VA guidelines suggest. Problems also have been reported in Pennsylvania, Georgia, Missouri, Texas, Florida, and others."[11]

Goals can be deemed achievable when they are aligned with the mission of the organization and the individual. Furthermore, by making them aspirational and ambitious, they build confidence and serve to motivate those involved to pursue something great. It also helps when the goals have milestones and checkpoints that will allow the person responsible for their completion to witness progress. Nothing promotes success like success!

Important questions include

- Does the goal carry specific parameters so it is tangible?
- Are there adequate resources available to work on the necessary task?
- Is there a strategy and/or plan to get this goal accomplished?
- Is there enough motivation propelling this endeavor?

Relevant

Goals should also be aligned with the mission and strategy of the organization, the process, and the individual. A common discovery when reviewing processes is that there are tasks performed that do not add value to the process or the customer. These are considered nonvalue adding activities, and they constitute a waste. Similarly, if the worker does not see how the task is relevant personally to their career or job description, it is very likely that they will be far less motivated to perform that task diligently.

Some useful questions for the process owner and the manager:

- How does this activity help to meet the needs of the customer?
- Is this activity essential?
- Is this the best way to perform this activity in terms of time, effort, and related tools (e.g., forms and data input)?
- What is the significance of this goal to my career and those of my team?

Time-Bound

"A goal without a deadline is nothing but a dream" is an expression often heard. It is quite simple, yet it is the root cause why many items on people's to-do lists never get completed. Setting deadlines require making a commitment to oneself and the person who oversees the completion of the goal. In the absence of a deadline, completion of the item is left to a classification of "ongoing," and that can carry on in near perpetuity due to procrastination or excuses.

Goals should precipitate a plan to accomplish the goal. The deadline should create a sense of urgency and time pressure. The combination of goals, plans, and deadlines brings out the talents in people and with proper management, synergies can be leveraged among all involved.

Important questions include

- Are there milestone dates that must be met in the interim to show we reached a significant change or stage of development in our work?
- When must the goal be achieved and what evidence is needed to prove it was done?
- What is the most efficient way of achieving the goal so we can accomplish it as quickly as possible?[12]

Evaluated

Goals must be evaluated to determine if they meet the SMARTER elements, but also to determine if they meet ethical and ecological considerations. While ethics is always important, unethical actions justified by saying "the manager insisted I do this" or "everyone else was doing it" are unfortunately commonplace in some locales. Similarly, ignoring the environmental impact of business actions is also unfortunate and something stakeholders are increasingly showing their disapproval about.

Excitable goals motivate workers and make stakeholders more willing to provide the needed resources and approvals. Goals must also extend the capabilities of those involved in working toward its completion. This means that the goal must be difficult to achieve and push those involved to work hard to achieve it, but not so difficult that it violates the other element: achievable. When goals are so easy to achieve that they are guaranteed, it can create opportunities for abuse. For example, salespeople compensated by the volume of their sales and who have abnormally low quotas, don't have to work too hard to achieve them and are guaranteed a bonus.

Some useful questions include the following:

- Are the metrics associated with this goal evaluated? How frequently?
- Does the goal infringe on my values, the organization's, and society's?
- Will there be negative environmental impacts while pursuing this goal?
- Who has to evaluate the appropriateness, timeliness, and other attributes of the goal?

> The results should be hard to achieve—they should require "stretching". They should be within reach. They should be meaningful. They should make a difference. Results should be visible and, if at all possible, measurable.
>
> **Peter Drucker in *Managing Oneself***

Rewarding

The rewards received should be commensurate with the effort exerted and the outcome achieved. If the amount of effort is greater than the reward, chances are that workers will eventually lower the amount of sacrifice made. Goals should also be reviewed by those involved in their formulation and performance toward their completion so everyone is clear about what the goals mean, what the implications are, and the short- and long-term benefits to the individual, organization, and customers.

Millennials[13] are often described as being idealistic and wanting to know why they are being asked to do things at work. Workplace satisfaction matters a great deal to Millennials and work-life balance is often seen as essential, sometimes more so than monetary compensation. They want to understand the big picture, and wish to feel that their work matters. With that in mind it is important then for managers to not only reward the successful completion of the tasks and the effort put into them, but also show how the work satisfies the needs of organizational stakeholders such as customers, local communities, and the employee.

Although this practice is described as being an important trait and preference of Millennials, it is important to note that this is also essential for internal auditors. One of the criticisms raised by process owners is that auditors do their own work and test what they think is important even though these tests may not be seen as particularly important for management. Internal auditors are sometimes blamed for asking for documents, testing transactions, presenting observations, and writing findings in reports with unclear connections to the priorities of the business.

To remedy this situation, internal auditors can practice something along the lines of what Millennials have been clamoring for: link the audit tests to the business objectives. In other words, why do we do what we do?

The simple answer is that everything that internal auditors do should be linked to a risk, which in turn is linked to a business objective. The sequence works as follows:

Business objectives are established by management and set the direction of the organization, the priorities of the program or process, the allocation of resources, and the focus of workers. These objectives are threatened by risks that hinder the achievement of objectives. To help ameliorate the potential likelihood and impact of these risks, management should put in place preventive and detective controls to protect the organization from these dangers. Internal auditors for their part, examine the functioning of programs and processes to make sure that the design and performance of these activities is as expected and make recommendations for improvement.

Consequently, anomalies detected during audit testing, should be presented in that context: "Noted control weaknesses allow risks to materialize, which jeopardize the successful accomplishment of a particular objective." This relationship can be represented as depicted in Figure 5.2.

By only presenting findings as control failures or weaknesses, internal auditors fail to link the situation to management priorities and the impact it has on the end users: the organization's customers, without whom there is no need for the organization to exist.

Important questions include

>
> What are the benefits to my customers for achieving this goal?
> What are the benefits to the organization for achieving this goal?
> What emotional, financial, and professional benefit will I enjoy?

The topic of fraud and corruption has garnered a great deal of attention over the past few years. This scourge has been a concern for decades, if not centuries, but over the past decade or so it has been the target of much attention by many governments, regulators, auditors, bankers, and economists. The IIA's *Standards* include specific reference to fraud:

> "Internal auditors must have sufficient knowledge to evaluate the risk of fraud and the manner in which it is managed by the organization, but are not expected to have the expertise of a person whose primary responsibility is detecting and investigating fraud." 1210.A2

Reports by many organizations provide some alarming statistics about fraud. For example, the Association of Certified Fraud Examiners state in the 2014 Report to the Nations that an estimated 5% of corporate revenues are lost to fraud with a median loss of $140,000 and more than one fifth of frauds involved losses of $1 million or more. The top high risk areas are accounting,

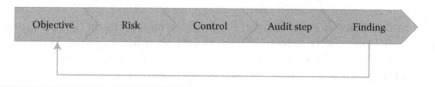

Figure 5.2   The link between audit findings and business objectives.

operations, customer service, sales, and purchasing. Upper management is also noted as high risk because high-level perpetrators cause the greatest damage to organizations.

Frustratingly, the same report states that the median time to detection is 18 months, highlighting the importance of internal auditors having sufficient knowledge to evaluate the risk of fraud and how fraud can be committed. Areas of focus related to fraud include material omission or misstatement of reporting, inadequate safeguarding of assets, and corruption.

In general, when discussing risks with operations management, the following are some useful questions:

- What would constitute failure and how do you look out for its indicators?
- Are there any liquid assets (e.g., cash) that are susceptible to loss?
- What assets need to be protected, including personally identifiable information (PII)?
- What must go right for this operation to succeed?
- How do we know whether the process is achieving its objectives?
- Where are the people, processes, systems, or assets vulnerable?
- On what information do you rely the most?
- What items constitute the largest expenditures?
- What activities are the most complex?
- What activities are regulated and where is the greatest legal exposure?
- What decisions require the most judgment?

Assessing risk on a formal and informal basis is essential for organizational success, and internal auditors can help to raise awareness merely by highlighting some exposures (Table 5.3).

It is essential to consider change when performing risk assessments. The magnitude and speed of change can undermine or enable the achievement of objectives. External change factors, such as demographic shifts, technological advances, and low interest rates can enable the achievement of business objectives. While the entrance of the Millennial generation into the workforce is seen by many as a challenge due to their behavior characteristics, they can also be a great asset. This generation is not only comfortable with technology but are technologically savvy, increasingly online, socially networked, and confident. They are tolerant of differences and generally embrace change as an almost natural part of their personal, social, and professional lives.

Similarly, technological advances like cloud computing, social media, and the widespread availability of broadband allow employees to work from virtually anywhere in the world, provide a means to

Table 5.3   Effects of Risk

- Loss of assets
- Negative publicity
- Erroneous decisions
- Customer dissatisfaction
- Fraudulent financial or operational reporting
- Erroneous record keeping and accounting
- Noncompliance with rules and regulations
- Purchase of resources uneconomically
- Failure to accomplish established goals

market and sell to customers in distant locations, and share information quickly. Those organizations that harness the benefits of change can beat their competition, reduce costs, and generate revenues in many ways, while those unable to adapt could be on their way to irrelevance in record time.

Control Activities

Done once, done right.

Controls are actions established through policies and procedures that mitigate the likelihood and/or impact of risks. Controls are performed at all levels of the organization, at various stages within processes and over the technological infrastructure of the organization.

Controls can be manual, which means they are performed by individuals and often using "hard, tangible" items, such as paper and locks. Whereas automated controls are performed by computer and electronic systems often without direct or exclusive human interaction.

Some controls are a combination of manual and automated, requiring both a system component and human follow-through. For example, exception reports capture transactions not meeting preestablished criteria, are generated by a computer system, and are distributed to individuals who are responsible for correcting the issue and making sure the transaction is reprocessed correctly. This means that for the control to be effective, both the computer system and the individual responsible for clearing the exceptions noted must do their duty. I have seen cases where exception reports are filed diligently, but the reconciling items shown on the reports take unacceptably long times to be remedied.

I have also seen cases with bank reconciliations, where the reconciler identifies discrepancies, but the items are not researched and resolved. Instead, the reconciling items are placed on a log containing reconciling items months or even years old. Those performing control activities, like the ones just mentioned, and their supervisors, should be taught about the importance of clearing these items promptly and how the anomalies can sometimes be an indicator of fraudulent activities.

The rate of dependence on IT has increased substantially over the past few decades and it is more integrated into business processes in virtually all organizations. In fact, most activities involve the use of computers to one degree or another and most organizations would not be able to operate for long if their IT applications were inoperable. While all systems are not equally critical to the continuous operation of the organization, they often do in the aggregate or as cogs in the interrelated assortment of systems in use that often must interface with each other to one degree or another.

Marketplace and regulatory forces have increased the focus on improving controls and led to a deeper understanding of how controls are designed and implemented. If controls are not designed effectively, it is highly unlikely they are going to operate effectively. Even if they are designed effectively, there is no guarantee of effective performance unless the implementation process addresses the relevant aspects of change management to ensure the sustainability of these measures. For example, it is fairly common for organizations to struggle with the lack of consistency in the performance of control activities because the implementation process is not aligned with performance evaluation measures and supervision, training, disciplinary actions, and rewards.

Control activities can be categorized as

Preventive: Preventive controls are those activities that act before the error or omission can occur and reduce the likelihood and/or impact of the event.

Detective: Detective controls identify errors or anomalies after they have occurred and alert the need for corrective action.

Directive: Directive controls are temporary controls that are implemented to redirect employee actions. They are sometimes referred to as corrective controls, because they are put in place when an undesirable action has occurred, even when there were preventive and detective controls in place. For example, if employees have received training instructing them to tether themselves to the handrail when walking on a scaffold more than 10 feet high, yet employees are found to ignore that requirement anyway, the breach in safety protocol may compel management to have everyone attend refresher training to reinforce the importance of that requirement and that it is expected of everyone, every time.

Another example could be employees who went through orientation and were told that sexual harassment is unacceptable, yet some engage in sexual harassment in the workplace anyway. In this case, all employees could be sent to sexual harassment training to remind them of the importance of adhering to the company's policy.

Compensating: Compensating or mitigating controls are those that are put in place when a control is not where it is expected as proper design would stipulate. For example, if there is a lack of segregation of duties, and more employees cannot be hired to address the weakness, then a supervisory review can be implemented to verify that all transactions performed are business appropriate. This could occur in a small office where an individual makes purchases, receives the items, and performs bank reconciliations. This employee could make inappropriate purchases without detection, so to mitigate this risk, the district manager could review all purchases periodically to make sure they were appropriate, the items were delivered to the company facilities, and were put into legitimate business use.

Table 5.4 shows control categories and some examples of each.

Generally speaking, preventive controls are preferable to detective controls because while detective controls are important and useful, they identify issues after the fact. When issues are identified after they occur, they must be corrected and transactions reprocessed, so they create rework. Preventive controls on the other hand, thwart problems from occurring so activities are performed one-time only. The general objective in all operating units and activities should be: "Done once, done right."

Internal auditors are generally tasked with verifying that processes, programs, and their related controls have been designed appropriately, and that those controls are operating as intended. When confronted with nonperforming controls, the natural question to ask is "why?" Reasons vary, but the following are some of the most common answers to that question:

■ *Inadequate knowledge*: Organizational effectiveness is the result of realistic goals, sound process design, sufficient resource allocation, and effective planning and execution.

Table 5.4   Examples of Internal Controls

Preventive	Detective	Directive	Mitigating
Segregation of duties	Supervisory review	Training programs	Supervisory review when there is a lack of segregation of duties
Authorizations	Exception reports	Policies and procedures	
Access passwords	Reconciliations	Required documentation	
Security cameras	Security cameras		
Competent employees	Confirmations		

Another key element is appropriate knowledge by workers. If those individuals performing any activity within the organization, control-related or otherwise, lack sufficient knowledge regarding the way to perform those duties, the outcome will be less than ideal. The requisite knowledge can be obtained elsewhere before employment or through classroom or on-the-job training. Employee competence is a key determinant of control effectiveness and this cannot be over-emphasized.

■ *Sabotage*: Disgruntled employees can act in ways that are very negative to their organizations. Their actions are deliberately damaging and when they involve control activities they may result in omission of key responsibility or dereliction of duty, fraud, and intentional disregard for the protection of company assets. Sometimes their unhappiness is triggered by poor management practices or the perception that they have been disadvantaged in some way.

■ *Emotional and physical reasons*: Apathy, depression, inability to pay attention to detail, or fatigue can hamper an individual's ability to perform the duties assigned to him. Under these circumstances, the quality of the work done while performing the control activity will be inferior.

When comparing risks and controls, there is always a need to find the appropriate equilibrium between the two. Internal auditors must be careful not to fall into the trap of thinking that whenever in doubt, they should recommend an increase in controls. Conversely, performing internal audits using checklists that have not been reevaluated for each review, or where the auditor performs the same procedures performed in previous audits without giving enough thought to currently prevailing conditions, will yield unsatisfactory results. An imbalance between risks and controls is problematic for the reasons shown in Table 5.5.

1. When defined, control activities are deployed through policies and procedures. Policies are principles, rules and guidelines designed to influence the behavior of workers so they act in ways that support the organization's mission and long-term goals. They influence thought

Table 5.5 The Result of Excessive Risks and Controls

Excessive Risks	*Excessive Controls*
Loss of assets	Bureaucracy
Loss of grants	Reduced productivity
Poor business decisions	Increased complexity
Noncompliance	Increased cycle time
Increased regulations	Increase in no-value activities
Public scandals	
Inability to achieve objectives	

and conduct at a high level. Procedures on the other hand are the specific methods and action steps used by workers to express the policies in their day-to-day actions. Procedures documentation provides detailed information about what should be done, how, when, how often, and by whom. A common misconception is that policies and procedures documents are controls and that having them in place is enough. The reality is that P&Ps are a means to communicate the control activities and to set expectations for their performance. So, while P&Ps are essential for effective internal controls, and are key to promote an effective internal control environment, it is people, systems, and equipment that actually perform the control activities.

Information and Communication

The fourth component in the COSO IC/IF model refers to the flow of information in an organization. Ideally, there are clear, consistent, timely, and purposeful directions emanating from the top of the organization providing direction and establishing the criteria to measure performance results.

There should also be information flowing up in the organization, providing feedback about results and any issues or unaddressed challenges employees are facing. This forms the foundation for management operating and financial reports.

Lastly, there should also be lateral flows of information between individuals and operating units to ensure cooperation and coordination among them. Effective, timely, and clear lateral communication can prevent confusion, duplication of efforts, and the purchase of assets already in place in the organization.

Communication is one of the most important activities in organizations. At the most basic level, relationships grow out of communication, and the effective functioning and even survival of organizations is based on having effective relationships. This applies to individuals and groups and it helps them coordinate activities to achieve goals. It is essential for socialization, decision-making, problem-solving, and change-management processes.

Internal communication also provides workers with important information about their jobs, the organization, the working environment and each other. Communication helps to improve motivation, builds trust, creates a shared identity and corporate culture, and engenders engagement.

Bruce Berger states that internal communication occurs on multiple levels.

1. Interpersonal or face-to-face (F-T-F) communication occurs between individuals. For many years organizations have worked diligently to develop the speaking, writing, and presentation skills of their leaders, managers, supervisors, and even lower-level workers.
2. Group-level communications occur within and among teams, units, and interest groups. The focus at this level is information sharing, discussing issues, coordinating tasks, solving problems, and gaining agreement through majority vote or consensus.
3. Organizational-level communications focus on company vision and mission, policies, new initiatives such as strategic plans, and organizational knowledge and performance. These communications typically follow a cascading approach where leaders communicate with their respective subordinates. Recently, however, social media is changing communications at this level.[14]

Information is also necessary for the organization to perform internal control activities that support achievement of objectives. Information constitutes the data that will be used during reconciliations. It is needed when reviewing supporting documents before authorizing a purchase. It is needed when performing inventory counts or verifying that a user is authorized to access certain records in a computer system. Consequently, without the requisite information many controls cannot be performed at all, and when the information is inadequate, this can also compromise the quality of internal controls.

Management is therefore required to obtain or produce relevant and quality information from internal and external sources. This information can then be used to support the performance of internal controls. Document retention is another key aspect of information and communication and the organization should implement clear document retention guidelines. Conversely, documents and data should be destroyed after the retention period as expired to reduce storage and handling costs. This is also important to reduce the amount of information an unauthorized individual could obtain if there were a data breach.

Communication should be a continuous, iterative process of obtaining and sharing necessary information. Information must be shared for its utility to be maximized. While there are always considerations related to appropriate use and need to know, many organizations are afflicted by the scarcity of information and its limited distribution among those who could benefit from it. Communication is the lifeblood of organizations as it allows stakeholders to know what happened, what is happening, and what is planned for the future. It also defines or clarifies performance details and the challenges employees encounter during their work-related activities that management should address.

The movement of information can follow multiple patterns. Sometimes it moves in a direct straight line fashion, while in other instances it could be back and forth, zig zag over time or circular, it could converge, radiate out, or even pulsate like particles as bits of information are sent out to others. As internal auditors and consultants, who both generate and use information, it is essential that we support management efforts to increase the production, analysis, dissemination, and use of information so better decisions can be made and the organization can be more effective in its activities.

Communications can be internal or external. Internal communications are disseminated throughout the organization, flow up, down, and across the organization, and enables personnel to receive clear message from senior management that controls must be taken seriously.

External communications enable inbound communication of relevant external information, and provide information to external parties in response to requirements and expectations. These may range from financial results information, to safety indicators, environmental impact, and inventory needs. While some may be subject to prescribed cyclical dates (e.g., publicly traded companies must disclose financial results quarterly), others may be required if a critical event takes place (e.g., the accidental leak of hazardous materials). Given the increasing number of regulatory and disclosure obligations, organizations should implement a mechanism to identify all applicable reporting requirements and identify who is responsible for making sure that these expectations are met.

Since the 1990s, the volume of information, especially raw data, has increased substantially. The access to this data, the ability to collect and analyze it, and its storage creates both opportunities and risks. Opportunities because with this data organizations can gain a better understanding of their customers' characteristics, new product ideas, and buying preferences and patterns. Risks because the storage of this information carries the risk that if it is accessed or lost due to hacking, insider sabotage, or accidental disclosure, it can be costly. Even the transmission of data during short periods of time, such as when clearing credit card transactions, can be compromised by someone intercepting the transmission. For many organizations, avoiding the risk during transmission is impossible, so controls are needed to make sure that the data have strong access controls, it is encrypted during transmission, and it is promptly deleted from all storage devices when it is no longer necessary.

The free flow of information is important to allow management and employees to understand new or changed events in their operating environment. When information is suppressed, there is an increased risk that management will operate in a vacuum. If there are complaints from customers that their payments are not being credited to their accounts, management may be unaware that fraud is underway by someone who is intercepting incoming payments. Similarly, if inventory stock outs are increasing, management may not know that forecasts are inaccurate and that revenues will likely decrease in the future. By receiving, monitoring, and responding to changing business dynamics, the organization can reevaluate its risks and modify the internal control system as needed.

Today, there are more diverse and complex sources of information for financial, operational, and other uses within the organization. Outsourced service providers support organizational processes through connected inventory management systems that may be designed to automatically resupply the client organization. Financial institutions provide foreign currency exchange rates to facilitate international trade or future contract prices for commodity derivatives. Other intermediaries may handle credit card transaction information to clear those transactions between merchants, debit and credit financial institutions. As shown in these examples, some transactions happen in real time, across geographies, and in multiple currencies and any disruption to these flows of information can significantly reduce the company's operations or halt it altogether until the services can be restored. Due to these intricate dependencies, it is important to evaluate the quality and verify the source of information.

In addition to the structured arrangement mentioned above, more internal and external networks have emerged that create unstructured and organic information-sharing mechanisms. Facebook, Twitter, LinkedIn, Instagram, and Pinterest did not exist in 1992 when the original COSO framework was released. Yet today, social media constitutes an essential aspect of most organizations' communications infrastructure, linking employees, customers, vendors, supporters, and detractors sharing news, providing feedback, announcing new product releases, and generating interest among those who may be interested in working for the organization. At the same time, anyone unhappy with the decisions and actions of an organization can organize boycotts, file petitions, gather signatures, and otherwise mobilize massive amounts of people to support their views. Organizations are increasingly aware of the power of social media and are using it to leverage their public relations functions and get their message out to their followers.

As the amount and type of information gathered, analyzed, and stored expands, organizations have also experienced an increased amount of regulation over these matters. Laws like HIPPAA have placed significant restrictions on the use of this data, requiring organizations to act responsibly. The EU's data protection regulations restrict where data are hosted, creating unique requirements and restrictions, and affecting cloud computing and backup storage arrangements. The result is the need to expand the analysis of the impact of these regulatory requirements on reliability and protection of information.

As data flows expand beyond pairs (e.g., company–customer, company–vendor, and company–bank) and incorporate intermediaries (e.g., company–credit card operator–customer and company–customer–shipping company) there is a constantly evolving need to ensure the compatibility, quality, speed, and reliability of all of this information. There are varied information and communication needs between organizations and third parties, and processes are needed to ensure the stability of these mechanisms.

These relationships and data flows mean that companies obtain information from and communicate with separate organizations; parties operating outside the company's legal and operational boundaries. However, it is still the company's responsibility to protect the customer's data and information. Quite often companies share demographic, personal, and otherwise PII and when this information is compromised, customers and employees can suffer financial losses and identity theft. Yet liability lines are sometimes blurred so efforts are required to make sure that expectations are clear and protocol, controls, and agreements are in place to verify compliance

Mark Stabelton states "the objectives of a business are not to perform internal human resource operations. Nor is the objective to perform fixed asset analysis, receivables collections, or information technology (IT) support operations. The objectives of a business are to perform its core competency, whether that is manufacturing, media production, software development, distribution, or any other activity."[15]

There are several benefits of third-party service providers, including the proficiency that they have in their service area, lower cost per transaction, and high quality. However, there are three broad types of risks that outsourcing creates:

> *Operational risks*: Often manifested as slippages of time, cost, and quality, usually due to breakdowns in the transfer of work processes or repetitive processes likely to succumb to human error. This usually occurs because the service provider does not fully understand the client's requirements or has the capability to achieve them.
> *Strategic risks*: Generally caused by deliberate and opportunistic behavior by service providers or their employees. Examples include intellectual property theft, understaffing, and significant price increases after some years of stable pricing because the client is locked in and will find it difficult to switch suppliers.
> *Composite risks*: This occurs when the client loses its ability to implement the process for itself because it has outsourced the process for a long time. After a lengthy

outsourcing arrangement, the client may not have any back-office operational capabilities, either material or intellectual.

Regardless of the type of risk, the outsourcing organization retains the responsibility to properly manage the risk related to the activities and for making sure that clients are protected and financial statements are correct, regardless of the origin of the information entered into those financial reports. Therefore, service providers must document their financial and operational processes, perform a risk assessment, and make sure that adequate controls over financial and operational reporting and related matters have been implemented and tested. Similarly, controls over outsourced information and transactions processing activities are equivalent to those implemented if the activity were conducted internally.[16]

To gain the proper amount of comfort that outsourced risk is at an acceptable level, the outsourcing organization can have its own internal or external auditor review the service provider. Conversely, or additionally, the service provider can have its own internal or external auditor provide reports to its clients. Since most service providers have multiple customers, accommodating every customer that wants to conduct an audit would disrupt the provider's ability to carry out its normal operations.

Organizations today have numerous third-party intermediaries that play an important role in their business operations and interactions with governments. This dynamic, combined with lengthy supply chains, has made it extremely important for organizations to monitor their third parties' activities. Companies need to conduct the necessary due diligence and investigate their third parties before they contract with them. Once the relationship is underway, they must understand who their third parties are, what they do, how they do it, and how they put the company at risk. For example

- Do they interact with foreign government officials?
- Do they have access to sensitive data?
- Do they perform critical activities?
- Do they present a cyber threat because they hold data that is desirable and could be vulnerable?

The hiring organization must also determine how to manage the process of monitoring their third parties and how technology can help them in this regard.

One of the most effective solutions currently is for the service provider to provide a standardized audit report for all its customers to use in their risk assessment. The Statement on Standards for Attestation Engagements (SSAE) No. 16, Reporting on Controls at a Service Organization, was finalized by the Auditing Standards Board of AICPA in January 2010. SSAE 16 replaced SAS 70 for reporting on service organizations. Service organizations that previously had a SAS 70 service auditor's examination ("SAS 70 audit") performed converted to the new standard in 2011 and subsequently used a SSAE 16 report instead. This is also referred to as a Service Organization Controls (SOC) 1 report.

SSAE No. 18 replaced SAS 70 and SSAE No. 16 as of May 2017. It addresses the importance of accurately disclosing the relationship between the service organization and the subservice organization. Under SSAE 18 a service organization should:

- Identify all subservice organizations (i.e. sub-contractors) used in providing the services.
- Include a description of any subservice organization controls (referred to as Complementary

Subservice Organization Controls) that the service organization relies on to provide the primary services to its customers.
■ Provide the service auditor with a risk assessment of the organization's key internal risks.

Under SSAE 18 a service organization should monitor the controls at subservice organizations as it is no longer sufficient for service organizations to vet their subservice organizations during the initial buying process and then never check on them again.

There are three types of SOC reports:

SOC 1—Report on Controls at a Service Organization Relevant to User Entities' Internal Control over Financial Reporting (ICFR): These reports are intended to meet the needs of the managements of user entities and the user entities' auditors. They evaluate the effect of the controls at the service organization on the user entities' financial statement assertions. These reports are important components of user entities' evaluation of their internal controls over financial reporting for purposes of complying with laws and regulations such as the Sarbanes-Oxley Act and the user entities' auditors as they plan and perform audits of the user entities' financial statements.

SOC 2—Report on Controls at a Service Organization Relevant to Security, Availability, Processing Integrity, Confidentiality, or Privacy: These reports are intended to meet the needs of a broad range of users that need to understand internal control at a service organization as it relates to security, availability, processing integrity, confidentiality, and privacy. These reports are performed using the AICPA Guide: Reporting on Controls at a Service Organization Relevant to Security, Availability, Processing Integrity, Confidentiality, or Privacy and are intended for use by stakeholders (e.g., customers, regulators, business partners, suppliers, and directors) of the service organization that have a thorough understanding of the service organization and its internal controls. These reports can form an important part of stakeholders who are interested in oversight of the organization, the vendor management program, internal corporate governance, risk management processes, and regulatory oversight.

For SOC 1 and 2 reports, there are two types of report for each: Type 1 is a report on management's description of a service organization's system and the suitability of the design of controls. Type 2 is a report on management's description of a service organization's system and the suitability of the design and operating effectiveness of controls. Note the words "operating effectiveness" as the differentiator for Type 2.

SOC 3—Trust Services Report for Service Organizations: SOC 3 reports are designed to meet the needs of users who want assurance on the controls at a service organization related to security, availability, processing integrity, confidentiality, or privacy but do not have the need for or the knowledge necessary to make effective use of a SOC 2 report. These reports are prepared using the AICPA/CPA Canada (formerly Canadian Institute of Chartered Accountants) Trust Services Principles and Criteria for Security, Availability, Processing Integrity, Confidentiality, and Privacy. SOC 3 reports are general use reports and can be distributed freely.[17]

It is to be expected that information will be sometimes restricted to those who need to know and also to protect the information from getting to others who can cause harm by misusing this information or profiting from it. It is important, however, to avoid situations where restricting access to information beyond what is necessary would stifle the ability to get work done and crimp productivity and speed.

Principles underlying the control activities are as follows:

Monitoring Activities

Monitoring activities consist of ongoing, separate or a combination of evaluations used to determine whether each of the five components of internal control is present and functioning. Ongoing evaluations are built into business processes at different levels of the organization and provide timely information on how well or poorly these activities are performing.

Separate or cyclical evaluations will vary in terms of scope and frequency based on the risk assessment performed and the results of previous evaluations. For example, if previous reviews indicate that certain components, systems, or activities are underperforming, it may be necessary to review these more frequently. If the susceptibility to loss or damage increases due to business growth, increased liquidity, new system introductions, and so on, then a more in-depth review may be warranted as well.

The review themselves and the criteria used during these reviews, will be based on internal requirements and other criteria established by external parties, such as regulators, recognized standard-setting bodies (e.g., ISO), management, and the board of directors. All deficiencies should be communicated to management and the board of directors as appropriate. In some instances, deficiencies should be communicated to regulators.

When applying the 1992 COSO Framework, users of the model often focused their monitoring efforts on control activities to the point where it could be described as being a model to identify and test controls. One of the goals of COSO 2013 is to reiterate the original intent of the framework and encourage us to consider a holistic view. With that in mind, monitoring should be viewed in a broader context relating to more than identifying and testing control activities. The following illustrates how monitoring applies to other components:

Control environment: The control environment is concerned with ethics in the organization, but what is the state of ethics in the organization? How can we find out and how can we monitor it? One approach is to conduct employee surveys. These are great tools to collect information and begin to assess the condition of ethics in the workplace. This entails, among other things, asking employees. Themes of interest are

- Their opinions and impressions about the tone at the top
- Management's efforts to promote ethics
- Asking whether there is employee agreement that ethics are important and are rewarded, while unethical behavior is punished promptly, fairly, consistently, and universally?

Then management can conduct annual surveys to perform trend analysis and monitor the results. This monitoring activity can indicate deterioration in employees' opinions about ethics, and prompt management to act more aggressively to correct this deterioration.

Risk assessment: The risk landscape is constantly changing, and as such, a risk assessment performed at one point in time may be inaccurate a few months, weeks, or even days later. This can be the case with inventory shrinkage. While cyclical counts are designed to compare the amount of inventory on accounting records to warehoused amounts, variances require monitoring as well. It is certainly possible that warehouse personnel are performing cycle counts, but the management team is not monitoring the size and frequency of deviations. By monitoring variances and inventory write offs, management can intervene promptly when the pattern begins to emerge and the theft, damage, misplacement, or short-shipment of merchandise begins to become evident.

Information and communication: Information flows are essential to keep employees and managers aware of business dynamics. If employees are filing complaints with the Human Resources department that a supervisor is unresponsive, displays favoritism toward selected individuals, and is abusive in the treatment of staff, management would be well served to research the matter right away. Otherwise, employee turnover will likely start to increase, employees will vent their frustrations on customers, or they will take matters in their own hands and either commit fraud or sabotage or become apathetic, driving operational performance down.

In general, the monitoring component serves as a very effective tool to assist management in understanding how all components of internal control are being applied and can enhance organizational effectiveness when applied as intended. Monitoring activities can be performed as ongoing or as separate evaluations.

IT and Its Impact on Organizational Success

IT increasingly plays a pivotal role in organizational success. Organizations should think of, or transform it if it isn't yet, to be a business service partner, instead of just a back-end support unit. It is important to align IT actions and expenses to business needs and revise them as the business grows or changes direction.

Following is an examination of several IT frameworks that expand on the previous discussion about IT in the COSO framework.

Global Technology Audit Guides (GTAGs)

Global Technology Audit Guides (GTAGs) are a collection of guides published by the Institute of Internal Auditors (IIA) that provide essential IT management, control, and security information. They are written in business language to facilitate the comprehension of technical topics and their implementation by practitioners. They focus on IT general computer controls, which apply to computer systems, processes, and data, and can be useful to auditors in virtually all organizations, regardless of type, industry, or size.

Internal auditors can use these guides to increase their knowledge, learn how to review and improve the related subject areas, and apply techniques to improve programs, data, and computer operations.

The IIA has released 18 GTAGs, which are as follows:

1. Assessing Cybersecurity Risk: The Three Lines Model
2. Auditing Application Controls (Formerly GTAG 8)
3. Auditing Insider Threat Programs
4. Auditing IT Governance (Formerly GTAG 17)
5. Auditing IT Projects (Formerly GRTAG 12)
6. Auditing Smart Devices: An Internal Auditor's Guide to Understanding and Auditing Smart Devices
7. Auditing User-Developed Applications (Formerly GTAG 14)
8. Business Continuity Management (Formerly GTAG 10)

9. Continuous Auditing: Coordinating Continuous Auditing and Monitoring to Provide Continuous Assurance, 2nd ed. (Formerly GTAG 3)
10. Data Analysis Technologies (Formerly GTAG 16)
11. Fraud Prevention and Detection in an Automated World (Formerly GTAG 13)
12. Identity and Access Management (Formerly GTAG 9)
13. Information Technology Outsourcing, 2nd ed. (Formerly GTAG 7)
14. Information Technology Risk and Controls, 2nd ed. (Formerly GTAG 1)
15. IT Change Management: Critical for Organizational Success, 3rd ed. (Formerly GTAG 2)
16. IT Essentials for Internal Auditors
17. Management of IT Auditing, 2nd ed. (Formerly GTAG 4)
18. Understanding and Auditing Big Data

COBIT

The 1992 COSO IC-IF and 2004 ERM Frameworks did not directly address IT considerations. That changed with the 2013 COSO Framework, which refers directly to IT General Computer Controls (GCCs) in Principle 11. This principle states that the organization selects and develops general control activities over technology to support the achievement of objectives. In this way, IT's pivotal role as essential for long-term success is manifested and recognized. Furthermore, it recognizes that there is an inherent dependency and linkage among IT GCCs, processes, and automated control activities.

While this is an improvement, more detailed coverage of IT considerations is necessary. This coverage gap has largely been addressed by the Information Systems Audit and Control Association (ISACA), which first published COBIT framework in 1996. The version currently in force is version 2019. The COBIT Framework addresses more than technical subjects, but also includes critical managerial and accounting/financial activities such as

Establishing IT direction: Today it is imperative that organizations establish and communicate their strategic direction, get all levels of management involved, and get employee buy-in so they support those initiatives. The IT direction should inform organizational priorities, the assignment of resources, and the identification of appropriate metrics to track performance and the achievement of those goals.

Project management: Since many activities within IT involve system development, and the acquisition and implementation of software and hardware solutions, project management has gained a great deal of attention. Many IT projects cost millions of dollars from concept to rollout, and when ongoing maintenance and support costs are factored in, the costs are even larger. Given the impact that these IT projects have on the strategic objectives of the organization, and the extensive project management elements that must be managed, it is not surprising that COBIT includes project management as one of its areas of focus.

Purchases: While project management often refers to the conversion of ideas into deliverables over a period of time, these activities often require the purchase of hardware, software, and the payment for technical knowhow. In addition, there are costs related to the rental of physical work space, tools, and transportation, among others. All of this must be paid for, so the subject of planning for, making payments, and accounting for these expenditures appropriately in financial reports is an ongoing priority in the IT environment.

Training end users: Since IT projects often have a hefty price tag, take a substantial amount of time to develop and implement, and their scope is often critical to the long-term success of the organization, it is essential for the organization to make sure that end users are trained thoroughly, promptly, and cost-effectively. In many instances organizations spend great sums of money, time, and effort to build a robust application to meet strategic and operational needs, only to provide limited or no training to end users. This is a deficiency that should not be taken lightly. In fact, many well-engineered systems may be underutilized or not used at all by employees who are uncomfortable with the system out of a lack of knowledge about its capabilities, features, and functionality.

Upon implementation, many auditors find that data fields are populated with incorrect data, that available reports are not being used, and that other tools, such as spreadsheets and desktop databases, are in use rather than the system that was built for company workers. Internal auditors are encouraged to look for these signs of failure as they indicate an erosion of future productivity, lower ROI, and in general a waste of company resources.

ISO

ISO is an independent, nongovernmental organization. Through its 162 national standards groups, it brings together experts to share knowledge and develop voluntary standards that support innovation and provide solutions to global and business challenges. The organization is based in Geneva, Switzerland.

International standards give world-class specifications for products, services and systems, to ensure quality, safety, and efficiency. They are also instrumental in facilitating international trade by providing standardized parameters and criteria and establishing expectations. The organization has published more than 19,000 international standards and related documents, covering almost every industry, from technology, to food safety, to agriculture and healthcare. Popular standards include

ISO 9000 Quality management
ISO 14000 Environmental management
ISO 3166 Country codes
ISO 26000 Social responsibility
ISO 50001 Energy management
ISO 31000 Risk management
ISO 22000 Food safety management
ISO 27001 Information security management
ISO 45001 Occupational health and safety
ISO 37001 Anti-bribery management systems

Internal auditors should become familiar with ISO standards as they drive the decisions, goals, and operational practices of the management team at many organizations. It also provides structure to common business initiatives that some organizations may be at various levels of development. For example, quality management is an important focus point for many organizations in developed and developing markets alike. It also constitutes an important Second Line of Defense function. ISO 9000—Quality Management and related standards address various aspects of quality management and provides guidance and tools for organizations that want to ensure that their products and services consistently meet customer's requirements, and that quality is improved continuously. It consists of the following:

- ISO 9001:2015—Requirements of a quality management system
- ISO 9000:2015—Basic concepts and language
- ISO 9004:2009—Guidance on how to make a quality management system more efficient and effective
- ISO 19011:2011—Guidance on internal and external audits of quality management systems

If we turn our attention to risk management, we see a similar pattern. In general, risks affect organizations in many ways and can cause damage in terms of business performance, reputation, environmental impact, and stakeholder safety, among others. As a result, it is imperative to identify, assess, and manage risks effectively.
ISO 31000 is comprised of

ISO 31000:2009—Principles and guidelines
ISO 31000:2009—Risk assessment techniques

ISO 17799 provides guidelines and general principles for identifying, initiating, deploying, and maintaining an organization's information security infrastructure. It provides guidance and best practices on commonly accepted information security objectives, such as security, asset management, human resources security, physical and environmental security, communications and operations management, IT asset acquisition and maintenance, incident response, and compliance and business continuity.
Since ISO facilitates communication and the setting of expectations between organizations, it also becomes important in the context of third-party services and other B2B services. This aspect of coordination and unification of industrial standards provides an appropriate compliment to COSO's components, such as information and communication. Lastly, they can help internal auditors supplement their audit programs by incorporating the wealth of knowledge that these standards contain.

ITIL

ITIL defines the organizational structure and skill requirements of an IT organization and standard management procedures and practices to manage an IT operation. The operational procedures and practices apply to all aspects within the IT Infrastructure. ITIL describes processes, procedures, tasks, and checklists which are not organization-specific, but can be applied by an organization for establishing integration with the organization's strategy, delivering value, and helping to maintain a minimum level of competency. It allows the organization to establish a baseline from which it can plan, implement, and measure its activities so it achieves predictable service levels. It is used to demonstrate compliance and to measure improvement.

ITIL contains templates, checklists, and downloads that can be used as is or be tailored to the organization where it is being implemented. Due to these ready-made tools, it can be implemented quickly. It also separates related, but distinct, administrative and technical roles, making it easier to define and assign resources to tasks. All of this makes it easier to reduce implementation and management costs. ITIL v3 was published in May 2007, and updated in July 2011 as ITIL 2011.

In general, the framework is quite comprehensive and addresses service strategy, design, transition, operation, event and incident management, request fulfillment, and continual service improvement. In terms of service, the five ITIL 2011 volumes provide the following guidance:

1. *ITIL service strategy*: Understanding organizational objectives and customer needs
2. *ITIL service design*: Turning the service strategy into a plan for delivering the business objectives
3. *ITIL service transition*: Developing and improving capabilities for introducing new services into supported environments
4. *ITIL service operation*: Managing services in supported environments
5. *ITIL continual service improvement*: Enhancing service delivery and making large-scale improvements.[18]

ITIL is a comprehensive set of best practices for IT service management that promote a quality approach to achieving business effectiveness and efficiency in the use of information systems. It was commissioned by the British Government's Central Computing and Telecommunications Agency to drive down IT costs and improve performance and efficiency. It began in the 1980s and its major goals and characteristics include

- Provides a process-driven approach
- Improves resource utilization
- Helps organizations become more competitive
- Decreases rework
- Eliminates redundant work
- Helps to improve project deliverable quality and turnaround time
- Improves availability, reliability, and security of mission critical IT services
- Justifies the cost of service quality
- Provides services that meet business, customer, and user demands
- Integrates central processes
- Documents and communicates roles and responsibilities while providing services
- Provides performance indicators[19]

The following are some companies that have implemented ITIL successfully.

Procter & Gamble: Started using ITIL in 1999 and has realized a 6%–8% reduction in operating costs. Another ITIL project has reduced help desk calls by 10%. In 4 years, the company reported overall savings of about $500 million.

Caterpillar: Embarked on a series of ITIL projects in 2000. After applying ITIL principles, the rate of achieving the target response time for incident management on web-related services jumped from 60% to more than 90%.

Nationwide Insurance: Implementing key ITIL processes in 2001 led to a 40% reduction of its systems outages. The company estimates a $4.3 million ROI over the next 3 years.

Capital One: An ITIL program that began in 2001 resulted in a 30% reduction in systems crashes and software-distribution errors, and a 92% reduction in "business-critical" incidents by 2003.

Some of the key goals, then, are to

- Streamline service delivery and support processes
- Develop repeatable procedures to help first-level support groups
- Reduce the number of service incidents and outages
- Implement standards to do things right the first time
- Perform proactive analysis to improve prevention and issue resolution
- Ensure future capacity through planning
- Define clear service targets
- Accurately allocate and recover costs
- Audit, manage, and improve IT processes

All of these objectives, when achieved, will reduce the cost of operations and improve service quality, customer satisfaction, and compliance.

CMMI

The CMMI is a process improvement appraisal program administered and marketed by Carnegie Mellon University. It is widely used in project management, software development, process assessment, and performance improvement within a project, division, or an entire organization. CMMI states that it can improve the key capabilities within project and work management, process management, support infrastructure, people management, product development, service delivery and management, supplier management, and data management. Over the years I have used it to assess and improve performance, speed, quality, and profitability.

There are five characteristic maturity levels as follows:

Level 1 —Initial: Unpredictable, undocumented, and poorly controlled, typically ad hoc, in a state of constant change with the reactive handling of activities and events

Level 2 —Repeatable: The process is understood sufficiently so that repeating the same steps may be attempted by workers. Activities are consistent and there may be consistent results

Level 3 —Defined: Process is sufficiently defined and confirmed through documentation so that it is the standard business process

Level 4 —Managed: Processes are measured and controlled quantitatively based on agreed-upon metrics. Management is typically able to control the process by adjusting and adapting the process based on the established metrics.

Level 5 —Optimized: The focus is on process improvement and the pursuit of best practices. The process is in a state of continuous performance improvement involving incremental and innovative process and technological changes (Figure 5.3).

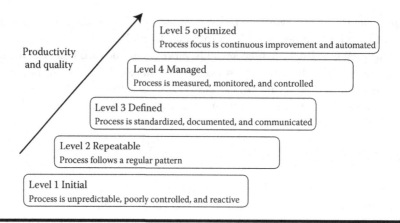

Figure 5.3   The five maturity levels.

Linking internal control frameworks to effective business management

Auditors have been the main consumers of internal control frameworks, using them to identify, map, and assess risks and internal controls. That was not the only audience COSO had in mind. In fact, it was conceived as a management tool. As such, it is important for auditors to help management appreciate the versatility of tools such as COSO's and others like the ones discussed in this chapter. These frameworks can be used for planning, analysis, decision-making, and monitoring. Let's examine this concept in more detail.

Planning is one of the Ps of classical management. It is defined as the process involving the formulation of one or more detailed plans to achieve the optimum balance between needs or demands and the available resources. The planning process identifies and defines the objectives to be achieved, the strategies to achieve them, and arranges or creates the means required to implement, direct, and monitor the established steps in their proper sequence.

In many organizations, and all too often, planning is insufficient and inadequate. The result is waste, inefficiency, unpleasant surprises, and confusion. The COSO and COBIT Frameworks can provide a roadmap to evaluate critical elements of business decision-making.

Decision-making is part of day to day organizational activities, since organizations operate with limited resources, tight deadlines, and varying stakeholder priorities. Decision-making is enhanced when the deciders must weigh the risks threatening their objectives, and must build communication and information networks to stay abreast of progress. Monitoring is essential to ascertain the success or failure of the execution on these plans.

COSO's intent was for its framework to be used as a management tool. The framework provides guidance and a roadmap to effectively structure and run organizations so that objectives are more likely than not to be achieved. Another key aspect of the framework is for internal controls to act as enablers minimizing risks and their negative impacts on organizations, programs, and processes.

Managers should be taught about these frameworks. In fact, internal auditors often state that managers "own the objectives, risks, and controls" of the organizations' programs and processes, but interestingly enough, many managers don't know that. This creates an unfortunate discrepancy where owners don't know they own these critical aspects of the organization and often don't act as owners, which should not be surprising.

It is interesting to observe how this dynamic originates. The only business students that routinely take auditing classes are accounting majors. Even then, these auditing classes often focus on external audit, not internal audit concepts and practices. Those business students majoring in marketing, management, and even finance often receive no instruction on internal controls, so there is a gap in the academic coverage and preparation that most business students receive. This knowledge gap is even more problematic when we consider that in many organizations, managers have other types of backgrounds. How then would the internal controls in these programs and processes fare given this situation?

If current and future managers are not prepared on internal controls, then it rests on internal auditors to provide some guidance regarding these matters and expose these individuals to these concepts. An important aspect of this awareness process, is that beyond orientation and training, managers should have their performance measured at least in part based on the quality of internal controls in their areas of responsibility. This would reinforce the importance of internal controls, reward them for making sure these are robust, and reduce their compensation when internal controls are missing or nonperforming under their watch.

Summary

As we discuss the increasingly important role of internal audit, and the various frameworks and tools available, we must remember that internal audit needs to be more proactive identifying and helping management determine how best to mitigate risk, not just assessing the controls already in place. The goal is to perform risk-based auditing, which means applying a timeline view of risk: past, present, and future.

Manager/leaders play a key role setting the formal systems in the organization, promoting the values and priorities of the organization, and supporting the dynamics that eventually create the culture of discipline, creativity, and high productivity we hope to promote.

Employee morale and engagement play a key role in the pursuit of excellence, because in their absence, apathy, and carelessness surface. We must remember that performance management and productivity enhancement models won't work if workers and their managers don't care. The tool won't work if the operator doesn't use it.

Employee surveys can be a great way to evaluate the opinions of employees and identify opportunities to improve morale, communication, and the effectiveness of values transfer. We should be careful not to only look at blended data (e.g., totals and averages) but to look for pockets, slices, and columns where the data may differ, indicating variation, and the need for intervention and corrective action.

These are some of the key processes that influence the organizational climate as follows:

1. The interview process and making sure it is fair and that we don't only focus on technical skills, but also on cultural and values alignment
2. Onboarding to make sure that expectations, rights, obligations, resources, and messaging is clear from the beginning
3. Background checks that are fair, consistently applied, and relevant to the job to avoid disparate impacts
4. Documenting and enforcing policies that provide sufficient guidance so employees know

what the expectations are and what to do/not do, a framework to navigate questionable situations and resources when in doubt

5. Performance evaluations that are timely, fair, and performed by knowledgeable managers
6. Training that is timely, content rich, and relevant to the participants
7. Communication that is constant, clear, and consistent

Control frameworks provide a roadmap to identify, assess, and manage objectives, risks and controls. Whether the organization uses COSO, ISACA, ISO or any other exclusively, or embraces a customized control framework that better suits its unique needs, having one in place is highly advisable. It is also important to note that control frameworks are updated periodically and these revisions give organizations an opportunity to further improve their internal control mechanisms.

In general, it is essential that we spend time identifying the characteristics of the formal and informal systems, while remaining aware of the culture and ethical climate because a key aspect of our job is to ensure alignment between these. Should there be dissonance between them, the likelihood of organizational issues increases.

Chapter 6 surveys 20 tools and techniques that can help internal auditors improve the procedures and systems in their organizations. They serve as a great toolbox to improve quality, reduce costs, accelerate deliverables, and increase yields. The goal of this book is continuous process improvement and these tools are a fundamental part of that effort.

QUESTIONS

1. What are the five components of the COSO IC-IF Model?
2. Describe each of the components of the COSO IC-IF Model.
3. Explain the benefits of the COBIT Model in the IT and the general business context.
4. Describe the implications of Principle 11 of the COSO 2013 IC-IF Framework.
5. Explain the relevance of IT GCCs for business auditors.
6. List five ISO standards and explain their relevance to internal auditors.
7. Explain how ISO 9000—Quality Management and related standards can help internal auditors improve business practices and strengthen the Three Lines of Defense framework.
8. Explain how ISO 31000—Risk Management and related standards can help internal auditors improve business practices and better identify and assess organizational risks.
9. What is ITIL and how can it help improve the practice of integrated auditing?
10. What are the five maturity levels in the CMMI Model?

Notes

1 For more information about the history of COSO, see http://www.coso.org/aboutus.htm/
2 Ibid.
3 For additional information related to this case, see https://www.sec.gov/news/press/2003-16.htm, https://www.sec.gov/news/press/2005-59.htm and https://en.wikipedia.org/wiki/Xerox#Accounting_irregularities
4 For more information about these cases, see http://www.delcotimes.com/article/DC/20140122/news/140129839
5 For additional information about the FCPA and companies penalized for non-compliance, see http://www.sec.gov/spotlight/fcpa/fcpa-cases.shtml and http://www.fcpablog.com/blog/2016/1/5/our-top-ten-list-didnt-change-in-2015-but-heres-when-it-did.html

6 For details about the scandal at the Veteran's Administration hospitals, see http://abcnews.go.com/Politics/veterans-adminstrationscandal/story?id=23914029

7 See COSO 2013 ICFR Executive Summary, p. 3.

8 A mnemonic is a learning technique to help memorize facts, often in the form of an acronym that is associated with a list of items.

9 See Hernan Murdock's book *10 Key Techniques to Improve Team Productivity*, published by the IIA Resource Foundation.

10 Ibid.

11 Details about the VA hospitals scandal are available at http://www.pbs.org/newshour/rundown/administration-moves-address-va-hospital-allegations/ and http://www.cbsnews.com/feature/va-hospitals-scandal/

12 Ibid.

13 Millenials, Generation Y, or the Net Generation are the demographic cohorts reaching young adulthood around the year 2000.

14 To read the full article, see http://www.instituteforpr.org/employee-organizational-communications/

15 See Governance, Risk and Compliance Handbook by Anthony Tarantino, p. 95.

16 Ibid.

17 For a more detailed review of SSAE 16 and SOC reports, see http://ssae16.com/SSAE16_overview.html and http://www.aicpa.org/InterestAreas/FRC/AssuranceAdvisoryServices/Pages/SORHome.aspx

18 For further information, see https://www.axelos.com/best-practice-solutions/itil/what-is-itil

19 See Source: Pink Elephant, "The Benefits of ITIL® White Paper," March 2006.

Chapter 6

Tools

> You cannot manage what you cannot control.
> You cannot control what you cannot measure.
> You cannot measure what you cannot define.

Introduction

Internal auditors have a very challenging job to do and over the last few years, it has become increasingly apparent that business dynamics, related risks, and the amounts of data that must be examined have increased much faster than the staff levels of internal audit departments. Even when the number of internal auditors has increased, the headcount is not enough to handle the expanding number of responsibilities. In this environment of demands exceeding the availability of resources, internal auditors must use new and innovative tools and techniques to meet their responsibilities.

Since the 1990s, when CAATTs joined the internal audit lexicon, auditors have been searching for ways to leverage these computer tools and techniques to broaden their reach. CAATTs refer to the collection of software tools that allow auditors to examine transactions using computer tools. These include Excel, Access, ACL, IDEA, and many others. In addition to these tools, internal auditors are also using other visual tools and techniques to collect, analyze, interpret, and present data and transform it into information that both auditors and management can use.

Over the years, I have found the tools described in this section very useful. They help to identify, analyze, and present facts and operational dynamics. They also help to apply a collaborative approach to internal auditing, which when used effectively yields many positive results. To be effective, internal auditors cannot remain in a closed room reviewing ledgers, spreadsheets, and company documents for the duration of the audit. They should engage process owners and use an interactive approach to evaluating the processes under review.

In this section, we examine 16 tools ranging from highly quantitative to qualitative ones. They provide diverse means of gathering information, analyzing it, presenting it, and serving as tools to persuade our clients that either conditions are satisfactory or that they need corrective actions. Those familiar with quality control tools and methodologies will recognize some of these because they have been proven effective by quality experts for many years. There is no reason internal auditors can't benefit from these tools as well. In fact, like me, many have found them effective when working with clients and routinely use them during their reviews.

These tools were developed by experts in the fields such as statistics, economics, mathematics, quality control, and management, and include Vilfredo Pareto, Joseph M. Juran, W. Edwards Deming, Walter Shewhart, Genichi Taguchi, Karl Pearson, Kaoru Ishikawa, and many others. It is important to remember that internal auditors are in the quality business too. We are interested in how programs and processes are designed, how consistently activities are performed, if they are in alignment with established procedures documentation, and if there are ways to get the work done by reducing costs. Consistency, predictability, and minimal variability are typical criteria elements. In other words, it is searching for ways to get the work done faster, cheaper, and better.

To help in this regard, quality assurance provides methodologies and tools to prevent mistakes or defects in products and services. While many of these tools have been proven time and time again in manufacturing environments, companies are increasingly finding that they are equally beneficial in service industries and functions where customer service, software development, payment processing, transportation, case handling, research and development, and other activities would be well served by flawless execution.

Quality assurance helps to avoid problems and can help auditors give management and the board reasonable assurance that activities will be performed as expected, requirements will be met, and resources will be used responsibly. There is another fundamental difference that is important to note; while internal auditors have traditionally placed their emphasis on quality control, which focuses on detecting defects and nonperformance on the process output, the profession is increasingly embracing the concept of quality assurance, which focuses on defect prevention.

Some may argue that this shift could compromise the independence and objectivity of the internal auditor. Not so, there will always be a need to inspect *a posteriori* and report on the results achieved. There will always be a need to investigate, discover, conclude, and opine on the degree of success achieved. The internal auditors' responsibility to perform assurance reviews is a fundamental aspect of our role.

Giving sufficient emphasis to preventive practices, helping management find effective ways to prevent defects and errors, avoiding fines and penalties, building customer goodwill, and reducing unnecessary waste are key aspects of the consulting role of auditors. This is also part of the definition of internal auditing. We should not forget that the definition also states that "internal auditing is … designed to add value and *improve an organization's operations*" (emphasis added).

This shift toward quality earlier in the process is an important development, because detecting problems and reporting on them is important and useful, but this highlights issues after the fact. By then, aspects of the process may have changed, employees may have moved on, customers could have abandoned the organization, regulatory fines and penalties may be forthcoming, and correction will often require rework—all costly.

By shifting the focus to error avoidance, issue prevention, and high quality, processes are more likely to avoid producing faulty products or delivering services poorly. Doing it once, and doing it right is a much better operating practice and in general, error avoidance is superior to error detection.

Histograms

Histograms are charts that show the frequency distribution of numerical data using rectangles, each of which represents intervals. They display the probability distribution of a continuous variable. The range of values of the continuous variable is divided into a series of intervals on the X-axis. Then, the count of how many values fall into each interval is shown as bars on the chart—the number of cases per unit of the variable on the horizontal. The intervals are consecutive, adjacent (i.e., there are no gaps between the bars), and of equal size.

In a histogram, the X-axis represents a dimension arranged over equal intervals and can represent hours of operation for a service center, prices, odometer readings, or similar variables. The Y-axis represents the quantity, frequency, or other metric being plotted against the interval, this could be the number of properties, visitors, vehicles, calls, etc. So, the histogram, when constructed, could plot the amount of sales revenues per hour, the number of vehicles serviced per hour during a workday, the number of calls received in half-hour increments per shift, the odometer readings of vehicles serviced in a garage, and so on.

To prepare a histogram, the following steps are used:

- Calculate the range of values (i.e., maximum and minimum)
- Divide the range into evenly spaced intervals
- Count the number of observations in each interval
- Create the bars where the height represents the count in each interval
- The Y-axis represents the number of items fitting into each category

At first glance, histograms resemble bar charts and casual observers, or chart preparers, may confuse the two. Histograms are used for continuous data, so the X-axis and the intervals shown on it represent a range of data and the bars are stacked next to each other. Bar charts on the other hand, plot categorical variables (i.e., categories of data points) and gaps or spaces between the bars differentiate one variable from each other.

Histograms are used to assess the distribution of data and help to identify how the data points are distributed. In so doing, the information is more than a picture of the data points, but instead shows a flow of the data. This can be very useful for the auditor and very helpful to understand the dynamics affecting the process under review. Rather than simply focusing on the total transactions during a period of time, histograms provide what I refer to as a fluid view of the transactions.

By observing the pattern of a histogram, internal auditors can get an enhanced understanding of the data plotted (Figure 6.1).

Control Chart

Process owners are responsible for setting the structure of their processes and programs, establishing goals and objectives, identifying the relevant risks to the achievement of those objectives, and designing controls to mitigate those risks. Controls, just like risks, must be monitored and the tracking of their performance will provide management with valuable information about the strengths and weaknesses of these controls and what should be done to strengthen them. Management is also responsible for establishing performance standards, which should be used to monitor the performance of processes and programs, and also to identify anomalies that require management intervention.

These performance standards are best when they are based on quantitative information that can be counted, sorted, analyzed, and reported periodically. It can also consist of qualitative information that can shed light regarding the characteristics of the underlying information. In either case, this information can be, and should be used, by internal auditors during the performance of their work. Errors, anomalies, and variations should be identified by management

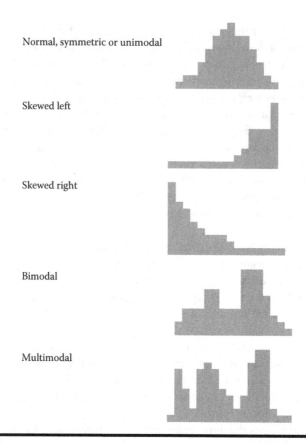

Normal, symmetric or unimodal

Skewed left

Skewed right

Bimodal

Multimodal

Figure 6.1 Histogram shapes.

during the course of their management activities. Among the tools available to document this monitoring are control charts. In fact, they are a particularly well-suited tool for this task.

A control chart is a graph used to plot and study how a process changes over time. Data are plotted in time order, in a similar fashion as run charts. A control chart has a central line for the average or target value for the process being plotted, an upper line for the upper control limit (i.e., maximum allowable value given the established performance specifications) and a lower line for the lower control limit. These upper and lower control lines are determined from historical data and in general, control charts help the analyst detect and show the causes of deviation for the transactions shown and help to answer the question: Is the process in a state of statistical control?

Control charts are one of the seven basic tools of quality and although it is widely used by quality control specialists, it is seldom known, and even less frequently used, by internal auditors. This is unfortunate because control charts can help auditors determine if the process is stable and under control. Furthermore, these charts can be used to predict the future performance of the process and if the process is not in control, an analysis of the chart can help to identify the source of the problem.

They are modified run charts and show the placement of data points so that patterns and deviations can be promptly identified. Their sophistication level can vary, but in general, they typically consist of the following:

1. Points representing the mean (i.e., average) ranges or expected value of measurements of a characteristic in samples taken from the process at different times. These data points are similar and related to the sample units internal auditors select for testing during audits.
2. The mean using all the samples is calculated (e.g., the mean of the means, mean of the ranges) and a center line is drawn at the value of the mean.
3. The standard deviation for the mean of the values is calculated using all the samples.
4. Upper and lower control limits, typically set at three standard deviations of the center line, are drawn to indicate the thresholds at which the output is considered statistically "unlikely" and out of bounds.
5. Additional lines may be drawn at one and two standard deviations above and below of the center line, creating bands around the mean to assess the frequency of observations or transactions in each zone. This division into zones provides a mechanism to formulate rules that can be translated into risk triggers or concern points.

If the process is in control, more than 99% of the transactions will fall within the control limits (i.e., three standard deviations of the mean). If there are observations outside these thresholds, or if there are patterns as explained below, this suggests there are sources of variation that will increase costs due to errors, omissions, or other process anomalies.

There are several rules that are applied to control charts to identify anomalies. While there are several sets of rules, the following are the most common ones. Table 6.1 describes the rules and the explanation.

The rules and the statistical analysis involved can be substantially more complex, but in practical terms, most internal auditors don't need to go to that level of detail. It is enough to say that by setting upper and lower control limits, and by observing the patterns as shown above, internal auditors can substantially increase the sophistication of their data analytics and support their findings with measurable data. They can identify patterns and trends and relate those to actual, suspicious anomalies, and research them before problems compound. This in and of itself can enable better data analytics and continued controls auditing for high-risk activities.

When the source of the variability suggests a better practice than the one currently in place, it possibly should become the new way of performing the work. When the source of the variability is unacceptable, it should be identified and removed.

Pareto Chart

The Pareto principle, also known as the 80/20 rule, posits that for many events approximately 80% of the effects are caused by 20% of the causes. This principle essentially means that there is a concentration of sources that internal auditors should identify for best results.

Pareto diagrams are designed to organize data and can be used to prioritize improvement effort by focusing on major root causes of the problems under review. The focus is to focus on the root causes, and look for cause and effect relationships. The grouping can derive from data analytics, where the analyst looks for concentrations of the data. For example

- By running a cumulative total, what are the categories that when added together add up to 80% of the total?
- Which items, based on the knowledge of process owners, accounts for the majority of the manifested problems?

Table 6.1 Rules for Detecting Out-of-Control Variables

Rule	Explanation	
A single point outside three standard deviation (SD) limit above or below the center line	Since the data point is outside the upper or lower control limits, this indicates the threshold has been breached and the sample is grossly out of control	 Rule 1: One point is more than 3 standard deviations from the mean
Two out of three consecutive points on same side of mean fall in Zone A or beyond	Zone A is the outermost band around the centerline and having two points there signal a near miss. Near misses should be analyzed to determine what happened to prevent a future point from being outside the upper or lower control limits	 Rule 5: Two (or three) out of three points in a row are more than 2 standard deviations from the mean in the same direction
Four out of five consecutive points on the same side of mean fall in Zone B or beyond	This indicates a shift in the process and a need to examine the reason for the drift	

(continued)

TABLE 6.1 (continued) Rules for Detecting Out-of-Control Variables

Rule	Explanation	
		Rule 3: Four out of five consecutive points fall Zone B or beyond UCL · A · B · C · X̄ · C · B · A · LCL
Six or more consecutive points increasing or decreasing	This indicates a trend	Rule 3: Six (or more) points in a row are continually increasing (or decreasing) UCL · X̄ · LCL · -3σ · -2σ · 1σ
Eight points in a row in Zone B, A, or beyond, on either side of the center line (without points in Zone C)	This indicates oscillation and may indicate that there are subprocesses within the process being reviewed. For example: all	

(continued)

TABLE 6.1 *(continued)* **Rules for Detecting Out-of-Control Variables**

Rule	Explanation	
	points above may correspond to one operator or machine, while those below, may correspond to another. One operator is performing his duties consistently, but differently from the other operator	Rule 8: Eight points in a row exist with none within 1 standard deviation of the mean and the points are in both directions from the mean
Nine consecutive points on the same side of mean fall in Zone C or beyond	May denote a shift or drift in the process. For example, the machine is out of calibration or the department or operator is slowing down	Rule 2: Nine (or more) points in a row are on the same side of the mean

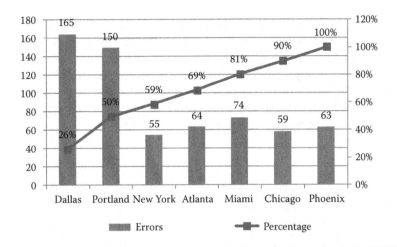

Figure 6.2 **An example of a Pareto chart constructed using Excel and its two vertical axis feature.**

When drawing the Pareto diagram, draw the diagram with the cause(s) on the horizontal axis. Then put points assigned on the vertical axis.

For each cause, construct a bar with two components:

1. Number of votes (or points) received for that component.
2. Number of people voting for that cause. When done, rank the items in order of importance.

Figure 6.2 is an example of a Pareto chart constructed using Excel and its two vertical axis feature. It shows the number of errors by location as bar charts, and the cumulative percentage as a line against the second *Y*-axis.

Cause and Effect (Fishbone, Ishikawa) Diagram

Identifying the root cause of problems is a constant challenge for internal auditors. One of the best tools I have found to help me identify contributing causes of an issue, and hone into the root cause most accurately, is the fishbone diagram. This tool is also called cause and effect diagram or Ishikawa diagram for the name of the person who invented it, Kaoru Ishikawa.

It is very important to remember that many organizational issues are the product of multiple causes or reasons. However, many internal auditors, especially those accustomed to performing compliance and financial audits, treat issues from a binary perspective. This means they use the following process:

1. Identify what should have been done
2. Verify that what was done is consistent with what should have been done
3. If yes, report no finding and close workpapers
4. If no, write up a finding and recommend that the practice in the future be consistent with the guidelines set in item 1 above

This approach is useful for compliance reviews where operators should do what the contract, law, regulation, or procedures documentation requires. This approach is also useful for financial reviews, where accountants and others involved in record keeping and preparing financial statements must adhere to applicable accounting standards. For virtually all accounting activity, there is guidance about what should be done, so if those involved are not doing what the rulebook states, they need to stop that practice, and do as the rulebook dictates. In other words, the auditee is either doing or not doing what the rulebook states. It is binary. And if they are not doing it, they need to comply.

For example

- When do you declare AR uncollectable and write them off?
- When do you declare a sale realized and book the revenue?
- When does ownership of that shipment transfer from the supplier to us?

The answer to these questions is fairly straight forward and there are specific guidelines to answer those questions, and if the accounting treatment is not followed, the accounting treatment is incorrect.

When confronted with operational issues, however, the answer may not be that simple. For example

- If the profit margin on a product line is dropping, why is that happening and how can that be reversed?
- If customers have to make multiple phone calls before the customer service agent gives them the correct answer, why is this happening and how can that be remedied?
- If drivers are unable to deliver packages by the promised time, why is that happening and how can they meet delivery deadlines?

- If customer retention is dropping, how can the organization slow and reverse that trend?

The resolution of these issues is not just a matter of "this or that."

Even in compliance, accounting, and financial reporting environments, there are often challenges that follow a similar pattern. For example

- Why are there so many errors when paying invoices?
- Why does it take so long to close the accounting books and publish the financial statement reports?
- Why are there so many credit adjustments issued to customers?

A large percentage of operational matters are caused by a combination of people, process, and technology issues, so beyond identifying the problem, internal auditors should attempt to identify the root causes of these conditions. Otherwise, they are likely to issue findings with very vague recommendations, or recommend remedies for symptoms which won't fix the underlying problem and will inevitably lead to the problem recurring in the future. Either approach will result in suboptimal results because management will be frustrated by the vague recommendations when the first approach is followed, and value won't be maximized if the second practice is employed.

When searching for the root cause of issues, auditors are effectively searching for the source of variation, which are often grouped into categories. The following six categories are often used:

1. *People.* Individuals involved in the process.
2. *Methods.* How the process is performed and the requirements for doing it. This may include policies, procedures, regulations, laws, and rules.
3. *Machines.* Any piece of machinery, computers, tools, or equipment required to perform the work.
4. *Materials.* Inputs used to produce the product. This may include raw materials, parts, semifinished goods, and paper.
5. *Measurements.* Data used to evaluate the quality of the process.
6. *Environment.* Conditions in which the process or activities are performed. This may include time, location, temperature, humidity, noise, and culture.

To facilitate remembering these six items, they are sometimes referred to as 6 M. In that case, people become manpower, and environment is mother nature.

The list of typical categories can be longer than six items, and in some cases, it is categorized based on the type of organization or environment where the effect is being analyzed. As shown in Table 6.2, the list is slightly different when the exercise is performed in an industrial versus a service organization.

These only represent major categories that cause variation and other categories can be used as well. When preparing a fishbone diagram, the items can be selected from either column.

The name fishbone diagram is due to its shape, which is similar to the side view of a fish skeleton (Figure 6.3).

To construct the fishbone diagram, the head of the fish represents the condition identified during the audit. The major categories of issues, as shown above, are placed around the periphery as arrows pointing to the backbone of the fish. Related items are then identified and placed as smaller arrows connecting the subcauses to the major causes in a drill-down fashion. These smaller bones are inputs, causes, and sources of variation. For example, let's consider people as the main category. The related inputs could be high employee turnover, insufficient number of skilled workers, lack of training, and poor motivation. For each of those, further details could be plotted, for example, shown in Table 6.3.

When done drawing the diagram, it becomes clearer why the presenting problem exists. In fact, repeating items may surface, showing how a number of root causes impact multiple

Table 6.2   Major Categories of Problem Causes

Service Environments	Industrial or Manufacturing Environments
■ Policies ■ Procedures ■ Training ■ System (IT) ■ Technology ■ Environment ■ Plant and equipment ■ Processes ■ Customer ■ Budget/funding/money ■ Management ■ Skills	■ Machinery/equipment/technology ■ Methods/process ■ Materials/money ■ Staffing/manpower ■ Measurement/inspection ■ Environment/mother nature ■ Maintenance ■ Suppliers

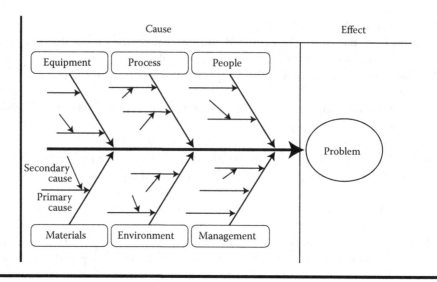

Figure 6.3 Fishbone diagram.

Table 6.3   Sample Breakdown of Problem Category: People

Category	Subcategories	Sub-Subcategories
People	High employee turnover	Poor compensation
		Poor management practices
		Excessive work volume
		Excessive travel requirements
	Insufficient number of skilled workers	High employee turnover
		Uncompetitive compensation
		Inadequate training
		Inadequate recruitment
		Remote location
	Lack of training	Underfunded training programs
		Workload limits time off
	Poor motivation	High employee turnover
		Uncompetitive compensation
		Limited training opportunities
		Inadequate recruitment

categories. When I am done preparing the fishbone diagram, I like to identify the top two or three items that have the biggest influence on the effect. This is similar to applying the 80/20 (Pareto) rule where we search for the most impactful variables. It is also a recognition that it is not always possible to fix all of the factors causing a problem due to time and monetary limitations, or due to organizational priorities. But if the main ones are corrected (the 20% of the causes), then the organization will be able to remedy close to 80% of the effects. This is a good way to achieve the highest cost benefit in a situation and maximize the impact of any efforts employed in the correction of the issue.

The next step I like to follow is to identify two or three corrective actions to correct each of the issues. This way the fishbone diagram is not merely a tool to identify the root cause of the problem, but also a tool to explore solutions to the problem. It helps to train our mind to get into solution mode by using the same tool, and not just enumerate problems. In fact, it is a formidable tool when used in conjunction with the CCCER model to document internal audit findings. The condition is placed on the fish head and the bones represent the cause(s). With this information, our recommendations would then be more precise and useful to our clients.

Fishbone diagrams are ideal for participative exercises, where instead of an auditor working in isolation, she can engage the team during the construction of the fishbone diagram or with the audit client. By combining the ideas of multiple people, internal auditors can obtain better information and get those affected by the corrective action to be involved in shaping their own destiny. It also helps to support the maxim: people support what they helped to create.

Force Field Analysis

Internal auditors are tasked with the identification of issues in organizations and often document these observations using the CCCER model. Unfortunately, the recommendation for corrective action doesn't always receive a positive reception. In fact, recommendations sometimes receive a significant amount of pushback by the client. While this can occur because the auditor did not perform sufficient testing, or did not communicate the attributes of the observation sufficiently, it can also be due to other reasons.

Some of these reasons may be legitimate, such as what happens when the auditor did not fully meet the requirements for effective audit evidence. Internal auditors must "*identify sufficient, reliable, relevant, and useful information to achieve the engagement's objectives*" (Standard 2310). If the auditor does not test sufficiently, obtain and review relevant information, or talk to the appropriate individuals, perform procedures that are relevant given the objectives of the review, or show that the work performed helps to support the organization's objectives, process owners have an understandable reason for pushing back.

Other instances of auditee pushback may be merely excuses not to do what should be done. In either case, the outcome is often the same: the auditor attempts to convince the client about the virtues of the recommendation, while the client raises objections. The auditor retorts by re-emphasizing the virtues of the idea, while the client continues to repeat and raise objections. Eventually, the parties reach an impasse and in the worst case scenario, the disagreement turns personal, the relationship is strained, and the report includes the recommendation, followed by the client's statement that they disagree with the recommendation or find it impractical. Sometimes there is an auditor comment stating something to the effect that despite the client's objection, internal audit remain steadfast in its belief that this is an issue worth addressing. In the end, the relationship is strained and the audit committee is forced to intervene to resolve the logjam and make a decision that supports one of the disagreeing parties or arrives at a compromise that the auditor and auditee could not reach on their own. This is not a desirable outcome.

To help prevent this scenario, auditors may want to consider using force field analysis. This is a great decision-making tool to identify the forces for and against a course of action. It is a technique to list, discuss, and evaluate the forces that support or hinder a decision. It can also help to strategize the best way to present the information by understanding the big picture and the pros and cons of the recommendation. Lastly, it forces the proposal advocate to "walk a mile in the auditees' shoes." By understanding the auditees' perspective, the auditor is more aware of the challenges that the client faces, and shows empathy during the process.

Force field analysis is useful to resolve conflict of opinions, comparing pros and cons of a decision and to evaluate the strength and weaknesses of an idea, product, or project.

The following are the necessary steps to do it:

1. Write a T at the top of a piece of paper, flipchart paper or whiteboard. The plan or proposal can be written above the T, then follow the steps below. An alternate approach is to write the plan or proposal in the middle, and place the items to the left and right of it.
2. Write driving forces/forces for/enabling forces that support the change initiative on one side of the diagram. For business initiates, examples may include
   a. Lower costs
   b. Faster speed
   c. Increased customer satisfaction
   d. Fewer errors
   e. Increased sales

3. On the other side, write factors and forces that prevent the achievement of the ideal state. These are called restraining forces/forces against/hindering forces. When considering business initiatives, examples may include
   a. Implementation costs
   b. Complexity
   c. Time to roll out
   d. Lack of knowledge/skill
   e. Conflicting priorities
   f. Past failure with similar initiative

4. Score each factor based on the influence it exerts on the recommended course of action and add up the scores for and against change. The scoring can be done using a five-point Likert scale, where 1 exerts the lowest influence and 5 represents the highest impact. The items can be prioritized through discussion, ranking, and multivoting techniques, and the result will show which side scores the highest.
5. Determine what strategy to employ. You can then decide whether or not to move forward with the change. If the decision is to proceed, the strategy could consist of strengthening the forces that support the change initiative, or managing/diffusing the forces against change.

Figure 6.4 is an example of a completed force field analysis diagram.

Some helpful questions to consider while preparing a force field analysis and related analyses are

■ What business benefit will the change deliver?

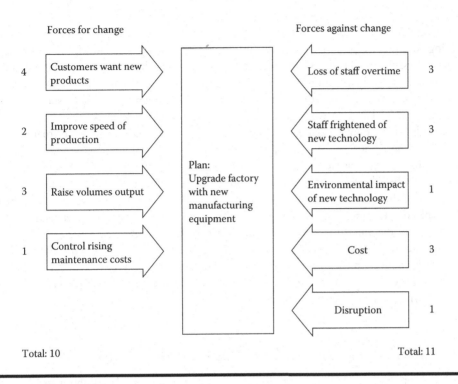

Figure 6.4 Force field analysis.

■ Who supports the change? Who is against it? Why?

■ How easy will it be to make the change? Do you have enough time and resources to make it work?
■ What costs are involved?
■ What other business processes will be affected by the change?
■ What are the risks to successful implementation?

It is important to identify as many of the factors that will influence the change as possible. Where appropriate, involve other people, such as team members and experts in the organization during this exercise.[1]

Force Field Analysis is a very effective tool to correct the approach most people use when advocating for change. The typical approach is to present the arguments supporting the change initiative and when confronted with objections and counter arguments, restate the position, include additional facts, and reiterate the perceived benefits. If this doesn't work, and the client continues to object, the tone, volume, speed, and general intensity increases. As this process of presenting and objecting repeat itself, it reaches a point where those involved may begin to argue.

Some resort to "pulling rank," which means they use their authority to force the other party to agree with their viewpoint. Some people, including auditors, may resort to "agreeing to disagree," where they make their claim, document the client's objection as part of management's response, then top it off by adding an auditor's comment. This essentially ends the immediate discussion, but escalates the issue to the audit committee, which must then decide what course of action should be followed.

A different approach can be followed by using Force Field Analysis. Since the process involves identifying the forces against change and ranking their intensity, the auditor can prepare arguments to address those objections. By systematically addressing these objections, the presenter will 1. demonstrate an understanding of the priorities, challenges, and concerns of the client and 2. eliminate the objections, which once removed, leave the arguments for change standing. Instead of repeating and insisting on the recommendation, the presenter disarms the objector.

Since auditees sometimes believe that internal auditors don't understand them, their challenges, resource limitations, priorities, and goals, this tool can be very helpful and give auditors an opportunity not only to make attempts to understand their clients, but also to demonstrate this understanding. Also, when this tool is used as a visual aid during presentations, it will become clearly evident to the client that the auditor has taken the time to research the client's point of view and if there is any disagreement, to at least meet them halfway. This should prompt the client to get engaged, and where necessary, inform the auditor if they truly believe there is some misunderstanding.

Internal auditors don't always have to present the completed diagram to the client. They can use it during their preparation, and incorporate the results as an input for their verbal presentation. In general, internal auditors discussing audit findings and presenting recommendations to process owners can benefit by using this tool.

Flowchart/Process Flow Map/Value Stream Map

Internal auditors review processes they don't have responsibility for, yet they must have a high-level of familiarity with them. They need to understand

- The objectives of the program or process
- How performance is measured
- How the activities are performed
- Who perform these activities
- Where the risks and controls are
- Where anomalies take place

Flowcharts are a very helpful and versatile tool to help auditors answer these questions.

A flowchart is a diagram that represents a workflow or process. It shows the steps in the form of boxes of different shapes and the order or sequence of events by connecting the items with arrows. Flowcharts are used to design, document, manage, and analyze a program or process in virtually any field by presenting the process flow in visual form.

By visualizing the flow of documents it is often easier to understand the process and find the defects affecting it. Common operational flaws include bottlenecks, rework, delays, excessive handoffs, and underutilized personnel. Compliance concerns include the performance of incompatible duties (i.e., lack of segregation of duties), circumventing controls by misclassifying transactions (e.g., by labeling transactions as emergency orders some review procedures are sometimes obviated), and misplaced or absent reviews and approvals.

The visual nature of flowcharts makes it easier to spot these deficiencies and note them prominently for others to see. This is fairly easy to do by putting visual markers that others can focus on, showing where the anomaly is. This in contrast with narratives, where the description of the process could require many pages of text and showing process weaknesses may be difficult to make prominent enough for others to notice.

While flowchart is arguably the most common name given to this tool, it is sometimes also called process flow diagram, process map, process model, and work flow diagram. Although some argue that there are differences between each of these, the only distinction I will make is to state that flowcharts merely show the activities performed, while process flow diagrams include details, such as who performs the activity, the amount of time involved in either performing activities or waiting for the next step to begin, data and information flows as well as bottlenecks, delays and rework. Otherwise, we will use the terms interchangeably and encourage auditors to prepare flowcharts with details.

So what are some of the more common features of process flow diagrams?

While there are hundreds of symbols that can be used when drawing flowcharts, the most common are

- Rectangular boxes: They show a processing step or activity
- Diamonds: Represent a decision
- Arrows: Show direction of the flow of each activity
- Ellipses: Indicate the start and stop of the diagram

Flowcharts are normally prepared horizontally indicating primarily the movement of documents from left to right, but they can also be drawn top-down. Every symbol should be connected to something else and collectively flow towards the end of the process. There should be no loose ends or endless loops.

A cross-functional flowchart, often called a flowchart with swimming lanes, shows the steps in the process, but also the units or individuals performing the activities (i.e., actors). Each actor then has its own lane and the symbols appearing in that lane are performed, and controlled, by that actor. This approach allows the auditor to identify, locate, and analyze the responsibility for performing each activity and making the necessary decision. It also shows the responsibility of each actor and the absence of needed segregation of duties, where applicable.

It is common for flowcharts to be complemented by process narratives, where more detailed information can be captured and important details noted for the reader. For example, a flowchart may contain information regarding activities, documents and data flows as they are created, modified, and transmitted among multiple actors. When the amount of detail involved could render a flowchart too confusing, it is best to supplement the diagram with a narrative that is cross-referenced to the diagram, so the reader can better understand and follow the dynamics shown, while noting flaws in the process.

Flowcharts indicate operations performed in detail, which can be very helpful to search for efficiencies. Since identifying areas of inefficiency, redundant activities, overprocessing, and rework is important as auditors incorporate efficiency in their assignments, flowcharts can be a great tool to identify these anomalies and easily show others where these flaws are occurring. A handoff is when transactions are passed from one actor to another to continue the process. While this is a natural aspect of most processes, internal auditors must be cautious as well at every handoff point. The following are some examples of potential process breakdowns due to handoffs:

- Not all transactions are handed over
- There are excessive delays during the handoff due to the preparation for the handoff, or the acceptance of the received items
- The handoff results in some degree of miscommunication, resulting in inaccuracy

■ When custody of the item(s) passes to another, others who may need information about the transaction may not know the exact whereabouts of the item, resulting in poor customer service

Another area of interest for internal auditors is the identification of control points. Flowcharts may be better than narratives in this regard. Control points are often hidden in the midst of multipage narratives, and efforts to make them more visible for readers have often led auditors to highlight them, use bold letters, color-code them and otherwise attempt to make them easier to identify in their lengthy documents. Flowcharts provide a flat surface on which control points can be shown more easily and prominently.

Microsoft Visio is one of the most widely used software packages to draw flowcharts. It is very user-friendly and contains numerous built-in symbols for drawing them. Other tools include SmartDraw, Flowcharter, Edraw, and RF Flow. More and more of these software solutions are being offered as online flowchart software that allow users to create and save projects in the cloud. This frees up PC or laptop storage and makes it easier to access the program remotely using a laptop, desktop, tablet, or other mobile devices.

When looking for flowcharting software, it is often a good idea to also look into its diagram features, which include automatic connection points, drag and drop features, snap-to tools, automatic spacing and alignment, grid lines, and premade chart templates. Since many flowcharts can be lengthy, the software application should make it easy to create the flowchart on multiple pages, collapse or expand sections of a diagram, and add hyperlinks to jump to another section within the flowchart.

Other useful features are the ability to change text font and size, insert graphics, use multiple colors, and text fields. Inserting pictures (e.g., employee or building pictures), setting backgrounds, and inserting titles and symbols can help the author personalize the flowchart. Lastly, even though flowcharts can be drawn using PowerPoint, Excel or Word, flowcharting software is an essential tool for creating professional-looking diagrams quickly and efficiently because they are specifically designed to create these diagrams easily and with fewer steps (Table 6.4).

Over the years I have trained, spoken with and heard from many auditors who tell me that their managers don't want them to draw flowcharts because "it takes too long to prepare them." While this may be so, this is a very narrow view of the value that flowcharts provide. Flowcharting may take a long time to draw when the auditor is unfamiliar with the way to do this and is still learning. It will also take longer when the auditor has not received sufficient training and coaching to avoid making mistakes. Over time, however, the process will be faster and auditors should be able to draw flowcharts more quickly and accurately. I see this as an investment in time and skill, rather than an expenditure of time and energy. The investment in skill development will pay off handsomely in the future.

Table 6.4   Benefits and Challenges of Flowcharts

Benefits of Flowcharts	*Challenges of Flowcharts*
■ A teaching tool ■ Managerial tool ■ Errors may pop out ■ Flexible ■ Worth a thousand words ■ Easy to review ■ Useful in discussions	■ May be too detailed if the area is complex ■ Can take a long time to prepare ■ User must learn symbols

When drawing flowcharts, internal auditors often show the As Is process. This is done to document the existing process, verify agreement between what the procedures documentation state and what workers describe, and to help the auditor understand the process before performing transaction tests. It is also helpful to identify control points and control weaknesses, such as a lack of segregation of duties.

The As Is diagram depicts the present or current state of the process and the auditor should document everything in the current state. In addition to the activities (i.e., boxes), decisions (i.e., diamonds) and arrows showing the flows, it is useful to show whenever possible:

Time. How long it takes activities to be performed. Time to execution can be a compliance requirement. Even when it is not, it is an operational risk in an environment where customers value speed as a measure of customer service. Unless there are few alternative options for customers, if the goods and services are not delivered promptly it is very likely that customers will buy from the competition rather than wait for the company to deliver. It will likely also impact customer satisfaction ratings and can potentially result in claims and complains against the company. I believe the speed of delivery is a risk that most internal auditors seldom consider, yet it represents a high risk to the success of the organization that should be recognized, explored, and discussed.

Bottlenecks. These represent a problem in processes because the limited capacity and performance of a process causes delays that impact cycle time. The resulting delays affect customer satisfaction, as mentioned above. This congestion or blockage can also trigger other operational anomalies as employees get frustrated, either on their own or by the actions of the unsatisfied customers whose calls, messages, e-mails, or visits become a source of stress. In these environments, employees may resort to shortcuts, workarounds, circumventing controls, ignoring procedures, labeling the transaction an emergency job, splitting transaction amounts to circumvent authorization limits, authorizing activities without having the authority to do so, or performing the activity without authorization and "dealing with it later." While none of these practices are desirable, and are much less encouraged, employees sometimes resort to these actions to alleviate the pressures caused by poorly designed or performing processes.

Production volume. Internal auditors examine the background of the program or process during the planning phase to understand the context of the review, how long the facility has been in operation, what systems are in use, how much revenue is generated by that unit, how many employees work there, and so on. What may be missing in some cases is an in-depth analysis of the volumes transacted and how they impact the process flows. In some cases there are alternate paths of production due to expedited processing, and exceptions made. Sometimes the volume processed by operator is not evaluated, so some employees, machines, locations, or shifts are disproportionately more productive than others and the process is uneven. So in general, it behooves auditors to obtain these measures of performance and evaluate the number of items per minute, operator, shift, day, week, month, and location as it relates to customer demand. This deeper understanding of the process can also help to identify higher risk areas within the process as well.

Delays. How long are the wait times? Quite often transactions are held up while additional information arrives, while a review and approval is underway, or while an employee batches transactions for processing later. Some waiting may be necessary and acceptable, but when the delay can be avoided, auditors should make a note of it. A situation I have noticed during several reviews is the wait for information from someone else. Upon closer analysis it was determined that the information could have been requested earlier, so while the transaction continued its path downstream, the outside party was obtaining the necessary information, then both the document and the information converged later on. This way a parallel path was created, one being the original path with the document itself, the second an information-gathering step performed simultaneously. Another case involved an employee (let's call her employee A) that sent a request to someone else (called employee B), who merely looked up the information in the computer system and relayed some facts and figures in response. It turns out that a major improvement in the process was achieved by giving read-only access to Employee A. This was a very simple change that relieved Employee B from the constant barrage of requests that took valuable time away from other tasks. This way, Employee B could work with fewer interruptions, Employee A was able to get her work done faster, the cycle time was reduced, and the overall cost per transaction decreased.

The As Is map serves as a great source of information to understand the process being reviewed, but also to establish a baseline for performance. Later, if anomalies are identified and corrective measures put in place, the internal auditors and management can compare before and after results to identify the improvements that internal audit has facilitated.

Some suggestions to effectively draw the As Is map:

■ *Determine the boundaries of the process.* Make sure to understand the scope of the review and where the process starts and where it ends. It was very common for auditors to audit the purchasing, warehousing and accounts payable activities as separate reviews. More recently, organizations are auditing the purchase to pay cycle, which would include all of the activities involved from the identification of the need and the purchase of the needed items, to the payment for those items after their arrival and subsequent storage.

■ *Identify the steps through consensus.* Operational audits are more effective when the auditor gets the employees in the audited unit involved. Engaging these individuals, hearing from them what works and what doesn't, how activities sometimes differ, and what issues they encounter, will help the auditor have a better appreciation for the process and its characteristics. By working with as many people simultaneously as possible, it is usually possible to collect more information faster, what one person says often triggers a comment or observation by another who supports, refutes, or clarifies another's comment, and in the aggregate helps the auditor better understand the dynamics involved. A common challenge is that individually each person only knows a portion of the process and is somewhat unaware of what happens upstream or downstream from them. This is another reason for getting enough people involved to make sure there is a comprehensive understanding of the process. The auditor needs to understand the flow of transactions and the related activities, including how the transactions are initiated, processed, authorized, and recorded, and the controls that management has implemented to prevent or detect anomalies in the process.

■ *Walk the process and arrange chronologically.* The flowchart should be constructed following the sequence of the activities performed. Quite often it helps to ask "what happens next?" and "are there other things that happen before moving to the next step?" A deeper understanding of the process can be obtained through walkthroughs and discussions with process owners. Auditors should seek the involvement of employees who are knowledgeable of the process, systems, and documents—this may require a cross-functional team.

- *Draw using appropriate symbols.* This step is subject to the requirements, expectations, and preferences of the organization. In some cases, there is an expectation that the most appropriate symbol will be used, resulting in very elaborate and complex flowcharts that use a wide variety of symbols to show the various activities performed. In other cases, the number of symbols may be limited to only a few. For example
  - Start/begin: an elliptical symbol
  - Activities: rectangles or squares (i.e., boxes)
  - Decisions: diamonds
  - Connectors: circles
- *Test for completeness.* After documenting the process and using the chosen symbols, it is important to verify that all loops are captured, dead ends avoided, arrows go to the right location, and the flow direction is accurate. A walkthrough of the process using relevant documents can be an effective and way to verify that the procedures and controls are identified and the way they function.
- *Look for problem areas as a team.* When done, it is important to discuss where there might be issues in the process that limit its ability to perform optimally. Some employees may be reluctant to have a candid discussion about this, or begin to blame others rather than approach this step objectively. The auditor can help to facilitate this process by reiterating that the objective is to improve the process and that data are essential to understand the magnitude of issues identified. Some employees believe a problem is pervasive, when that is rather their opinion and impression, but the data do not show that. Some employees may blame others without realizing that their actions also contribute to the problem. Yet others may not realize what others do with data, information, or documents, and how their act or omission affects others. I find it useful to reassure the group that the goal is to improve the process for everyone, eliminate as many sources of "headaches" for employees and customers alike, and lead the process to a "once and right" state. Using who, what, when, where, how, and why can often help to focus their attention and follow a systematic approach through this step.
- *Show details.* While many flowcharts only show "what" (e.g., boxes, diamonds, and circles), and others show "who" (e.g., individuals or units performing the activities), other useful add-ons include
  - Inputs, such as documents, data, and information
  - Outputs such as reports or updates to relevant records or accounts
  - Suppliers who provide inputs to the process
  - Metrics showing volumes and amounts transacted and moving through the various paths of the flowchart
  - Time: how long it takes from beginning to end, for each activity shown, and the interval from one activity to another. This can be very helpful to identify activities that take a disproportionate amount of time in relation to the total, or where wait times are customary and are accepted as natural parts of the process, but in reality represent an anomaly.

Preparing an As Is map is essential for the auditor to understand the current process and what is working or not working. Another step that auditors should do is explore what the process should be like. Recall that every program and process exists to accomplish objectives, so we should ask ourselves: "What is the desired output or outcome?" If the activity does not help to achieve those objectives, then why is it being performed?

Since those objectives are identified before performing the As Is map, we should use the insights gained during that work to brainstorm what the ideal process could or should look like. We have already assembled a team to examine the current process, and the discussions may have identified problems, so to add more value to the business it is recommended that internal auditors also prepare a flowchart showing the To-Be diagram.

The To-Be diagram should show the future state or desired condition. To accomplish this, we should think outside the box. Brainstorm different scenarios and possibilities, and think about "how else the activities and overall process could be performed." Some considerations are

- *Automation.* It can provide meaningful time and labor savings. So, what can be automated? Is there a way to program aspects of the process? This does not mean that we need to default to a multimillion dollar computer solution. Sometimes simple things like using Excel and Word features better, leveraging existing applications like SharePoint and IBM Notes (formerly Lotus Notes). Over the years, I have seen numerous instances where the work done using spreadsheets is very cumbersome, laborious, and error-prone. Similarly, SharePoint being used as a "barrel" where all sort of documents are saved, but it is difficult to say they are being "stored" and "managed" because there is little organization around documents saved, access control, and version control. The result is that employees are confused about which forms or templates to use, what information to put in them, where to store and retrieve them, etc.
- *Simplify.* What can be eliminated, combined, or simplified? In some of my work over the years, I have seen employees who are performing tasks that are no longer necessary, but they were not told to stop doing them. In other instances, if an activity stopped being performed, few people or anyone would actually notice or miss it. Some tasks that are still essential, are being done in a very cumbersome way. An example is the use of spreadsheets, where sometimes employees have multiple spreadsheets open simultaneously and manually copy information from one to another, unaware that spreadsheets can be linked so a value entered in one, can be systematically copied onto another.
- Who is involved? While the As Is diagram shows who is currently involved in the process and what their activities are, a question that is seldom asked is "why are these units/individuals involved in the process and do they have to be involved?" Sometimes there are too many actors in a process. Sometimes they are not the best actors in a process. Sometimes the process flow has transactions going back and forth among them, whereas it would be better to cluster activities to reduce the number of handoffs. Remember that with every handoff the likelihood of "things falling through the cracks" increases. This expression is used to denote a multitude of events, but what do we really mean? With every handoff there is a possibility that:
  - *Incomplete.* Not every item will be handed over.
  - *Inaccuracy.* Not every detail will be conveyed.
  - *Delay.* Transactions and documents may sit in a wait state until the next actor takes over. This can happen with physical documents that must travel via interoffice, or regular mail. It can also happen with electronic records, where the document sits

in a processing queue until the next actor takes the transaction and begins processing it

— *Damage/distortion.* Physical items may be damaged in transit.

■ What is expected? Performance standards help to shape priorities and provide a way to measure the success or failure of the process. A fundamental question should be "Is the process achieving the desired outputs and outcomes?" Outputs often refer to what is done, and are often measured in terms of volume as a measure of accomplishment and are often driven by objectives. Outcomes, on the other hand, refer to impact and the changes and benefits that happen as a result of what the process offers, and this can be measured in the short, medium, and long term. Program and process managers should establish metrics around customer satisfaction and retention, image, and in the end, delighting the customer. In the past, organizations focused a great deal on outputs, but in the twenty-first century, organizations need to focus more on outcomes.

Common Process Improvement Areas

When reviewing processes, it is often helpful to search for the following items to determine if the following areas present opportunities for improvement:

Backlogs. These represent an accumulation of work, often in the form of uncompleted work that needs to be done. This could consist of transactions to process and orders to execute. This can be problematic if there are deadlines that should be met either because there are rules or regulations requiring them, or customers depending on the completed work for them to perform tasks of their own.

Cycle time. Cycle time is the total time from the start to the end of a process. There may or may not be clear standards regarding transaction completion times, but in general, quick execution is a general expectation. With that in mind, delays and bottlenecks are anomalies worth correcting since they result in cost accumulation and possible customer dissatisfaction.

Rework. In many processes, transactions are returned because there are errors, missing or outdated information. This backflow is seldom accounted for quantitatively, even though when asked those performing the work often describe this as a recurring problem. Internal auditors should diagram rework in their flowcharts to show when this occurs, where items are returned from and to, how many transactions are re-presented, and how this impacts the total population flowing through the process. While this type of analysis is more often evident in manufacturing and otherwise industrial settings, it is less common in service and support operations. My work in this area has yielded some very interesting findings over the years that resulted in program and process improvements.

There are several components to total cycle time. It includes the process time specific to each activity, which is the time when the item is acted upon. This refers to the activities mentioned inside the flowchart boxes. It should also include the time when the item is waiting to take the next step, which is the time between the boxes. This time could be normal time or it could be extensive resulting in delays and even causing bottlenecks.

There are several ways to capture process cycle times:

1. *Stop watch.* The traditional approach is to use a stop watch. In this case, the auditor can document how long it takes to process the various steps in a flowchart and build a piece-by-piece schedule, with the sum being the total time for the corresponding transaction. By capturing the amount for several of them, we can obtain some reasonable data about cycle times within the process.

2. *Systems data.* Some information system can provide detailed cycle-time information through their reporting functionality. When that is not available, document flow management applications often capture user ID, date, and time every time a user accesses a transaction record. By collecting all of the transaction update information, a table can be built showing each step from the flowchart and the corresponding times. This way we can obtain detailed information for all transactions of interest for the scope period. With this information, we can build a data set showing detailed information for the entire population.

3. *Sample.* After selecting the sample of transactions to test, the auditor can expand the data capture during the review. Auditors often review individual files and test financial and compliance controls, checking for

   a. *Accuracy.* What the customer asked for is what the customer received.
   b. *Completeness.* All of the transactions that constitute a customer request, were executed.
   c. *Authorization*:
      i. Every transaction was business related
      ii. Every transaction was reviewed and approved as required

By expanding the data capture during the review, the auditor can test for speed of execution since delays and rework are a performance risk that impact customer satisfaction and eventually future sales, customer retention and reputation. When working with a sample, the auditor can capture evidence of each step being performed and note the operator, date, and time for each one of the steps. If the sample is random and representative of the population, the cycle time should provide some interesting insights about this (Table 6.5).

Takt Time

Takt time is the rate at which the production operation produces output. The term is derived from the German word "takzeit" that translates to "rhythm." It relates to the average amount of time, or

Table 6.5   Flowcharting Value-Adding Checklist

- Are the tasks necessary?
- What can be reduced or eliminated?
- Are activities in conflict with others?
- Can anything be simplified?
- Are all handoffs necessary?
- Can the sequence be changed?
- Are all checks, approvals, and decisions necessary?
- Are there loops or incompatible duties in the process?
- Are there dead ends anywhere?

pace, of activities. In this case, it relates to the amount of time to perform each activity. It has a deeper connotation than the word "rate" may suggest. It is the rhythm or heartbeat of the operation and it is the pace at which everyone in the process works to keep capacity aligned. Without takt time, there would be inventory between work stations and possibly shortages of material between others.

This metric can be used to determine the pace to keep a process flowing, so there are no bottlenecks in a process. In fact, a bottleneck results from the demand in a process, or number of transactions entering a process, exceeding the ability of the operators to do the work and make the transactions exit the process. It can also be used to set the performance expectations for the process, so operators know what their goal is so they can meet or surpass it.

The formula for takt time is

$$\text{Takt time} = \frac{\text{Total production time per period}}{\text{Customer demand per period}}$$

For example, consider a mortgage loan processing operation with a staff of 10 operators that receive an average of 180 loan applications per day. The unit spends 6 h actively processing these applications per day after deducting lunch, breaks, and required meetings. Takt time would be calculated as follows:

$$\text{Takt time} = \frac{10 \text{ operators} \times 6\text{h} \times 60 \text{ min per hour}}{180 \text{ applications per day}} = \frac{3600}{180}$$

$$\text{Takt time} = 20 \text{ min per application}$$

This means that operators should spend on average 20 min processing each loan application. Some applications may take less time, others may take more, but on average, they must keep a pace of 20 min per application. If it takes them longer, there will be delays.

Internal auditors can also combine procedures. They can calculate the average demand on the process and use this formula to calculate the required takt time. This would constitute the criteria to make sure there are no delays or bottlenecks in the process. Then through observation and time watch, note the pace and amount of time performing their duties. Lastly, calculate the actual takt time to determine what the pace of work is in the aggregate. This would then provide the condition. By relating these metrics, the auditor can document the expected and actual cycle times and determine if the process and performance are conducive to the success of the process.

Lead time. Lead time refers to the time from the initiation to the completion of a process. For example, if an item is needed in the production process, the lead time encompasses the time from the order being placed until the item arrives. Mismanaging lead times can result in stock out situations where production must halt until the needed items are received. To address this issue, many organizations must expedite merchandise delivery, resulting in excess costs. In more complex situations, the organization keeps extra inventory to compensate for the risk of stock out, resulting in extra costs built into inventory management.

To gauge process performance, management should have metrics in place. Some of the most commonly used ones include productivity measures such as units of production per employee, shift, week, or month; on time delivery record, uptime, or turnaround time.

The following are some suggested questions to explore opportunities to improve the process:

Operations
- How can the process be streamlined?
- Are any activities conflicting with each other?
- What can be reduced or simplified?
- Are there instances of excessive rework and where do they occur?

Documents
- Are all documents necessary?
- What are the documents used for?
- How is the information entered onto the document? If manual, can it be automated to minimize rekeying?
- Is there duplication?
- Who owns, needs, and uses these documents? For what?

Filing
- Is there a document retention and destruction policy? Is it followed?
- Is the storage and retrieval process efficient?
- Are there duplicate files?
- Are there multiple copies maintained?
- If manual/paper based, why is it not electronic/automated?

Delays
- What can be done to reduce or eliminate delays?
- Are there too many people involved?
- Are the delays necessary?
- Are there delays related to sending or returning documents for completion?
- Are there delays related to waiting for providers?
- Are there delays related to waiting for approvals?
- Are there delays related to inquiries and requests for information?
- Are there delays because the person is not available?

Transportation
- How can the process be streamlined?
- Are all transfers of work necessary?
- Is the sequence of the transportation and transfers optimal?
- Are vehicles loaded optimally?

Inspection
- Where are inspections happening? Are there too many? Are they too late?
- How much rework do the inspections detect?
- Where do errors get detected?
- Are all the approvals necessary?
- Are errors detected after the reviews and approvals?
- Are multiple people inspecting and checking the same things?

Decisions

- Is the process so complicated that excessive decisions must be made?
- Are alternatives sought and carefully examined first?
- Are repercussions examined before decisions are made?
- Are both quantitative and qualitative implications considered?
- Are decisions made at the right place?
- Do decisions slow the process unnecessarily or create other issues?

Eight Areas of Waste

Waste reduction is imperative to increase profitability and better utilize the limited resources that most organizations operate with. Waste occurs when more resources are consumed than necessary to produce the goods or services the customer actually wants. Taiichi Ohno, Toyota's chief engineer, developed the "seven wastes" as part of the Toyota Production System. Those were transportation, inventory, motion, waiting, overprocessing, overproduction, and defects. Under the Lean concept, there are eight: the seven wastes mentioned above plus underutilized employees:

1. *Transporting.* This relates to moving people, products, and information. While transporting items is essential in many processes so it gets to where it needs to be, we must remember that every time an item is moved there is a risk that it will be damaged, delayed, or lost. Also, transportation does not add value to the product, it only repositions it. Furthermore, if the transportation is unnecessary, it incurs a cost, such as fuel, packing, unpacking, and handling, that the customer will be unwilling to pay for. So all transport should be minimized, so the costs are minimal and the product is delivered to the end user as quickly as possible.

2. *Unnecessary inventory.* This relates to storing parts, pieces, and documentation ahead of requirements. Remember that the best inventory is zero inventory. While this goal is unachievable in many instances, the goal should be to maintain as little inventory as possible because inventory ties up the organization's capital, it raises the risk of theft, damage, and obsolescence, and it requires the expenditure of resources on storage space and preservation. All of this adds cost to the production activities and do not benefit the customer. Whether it is raw materials, work in progress (WIP), or finished goods, all of them require outlays often before income is generated since customers rarely prepay.

3. *Excess motion.* This should not be confused with transportation, which refers to the unnecessary movement of people or parts between processes. Motion refers to the unnecessary movement of people, parts, or machines within a process. There is a concern that this excess motion can damage or cause extra costs on the unit or person that creates the product or delivers the service over time. These include, for example, wear and tear of equipment and repetitive strain injuries for workers. Excess motion can also slow the process down as an activity takes more steps and more time. Examples of motion include bending, turning, reaching, and lifting.

4. *Waiting.* Goods can be in one of three states: being processed, transported, or waiting. In many processes, a large part of an item's life is spent waiting to be worked on or to be sold. Products and services, in addition to their suppliers and operators, often wait for parts, information, instructions, and equipment.

5. *Unnecessary processing or paperwork.* Overprocessing occurs any time, more work is done on an item other than what is required by the customer. This waste also includes using components that are more precise, complex, higher quality, or expensive than required.

6. *Defects.* In manufacturing environments, defects are often viewed as produced parts not manufactured as required or that don't work as intended. This can consist of appearance-based issues (e.g., paint quality, size, and shape) or performance based (e.g., fit, speed, smooth, and consistent operation). In service environments, defects are often a little more difficult to define because what service workers do doesn't fit easily into the description provided above. In this context, defects may consist of a service being delivered late, not providing the information the customer requested, or giving incorrect information verbally or in writing. This also includes reports and statements.

Whenever defects occur, extra costs are incurred reworking the part, rescheduling production, causing additional transportation and motion, requiring more time in the WIP stage, and creating the need for replacement shipments, all generating additional costs to the organization and hurting its reputation. Defects can double the cost of one single product. If this cost is passed on to the consumer, it will inflate production costs and could make the organization less competitive overall. It is a loss and should be treated as such. Examples include rework, scrap, longer lead times, rework loops, rescheduling, delivery failures, customer complaints, and incorrect documentation. In general, it is best to follow these three rules: don't accept, make, or pass a defect (Table 6.6).

Defects can arise from

- *Physical causes.* Material items fail in some way, like the brakes or the drive belts in a car.
- *Human causes.* Individuals did something wrong or failed to do something that was necessary. In many instances, human causes are the source of physical causes. For example, no one checked the brakes or the condition of the drive belts, which led to the car's mechanical problem.
- *Organizational causes.* There are weaknesses in a process, system, or policy used by workers to make decisions or perform their tasks. For example, no one was personally responsible for vehicle maintenance so everyone assumed that someone else had checked the vehicles' mechanical condition.[2]

7. *Overproduction.* Overproduction occurs when more goods are produced than is required by customers. Whereas JIT produces and delivers the amount needed at that time, just in case (JIC) produces in anticipation of a future demand. A common practice that leads to this waste is the production of large batches, as consumer needs may change during the long times large batches require for production and sale. Overproduction can hide or generate other wastes, so special care should be given to this practice. In fact, some argue that it is the worst of the seven wastes because it includes all others and was the main driving force for the development of the Toyota JIT system. Overproduction can be caused by various reasons, including poor forecasting.

Table 6.6   Three Rules

1. Don't accept a defect
2. Don't make a defect
3. Don't pass on a defect

Overproduction in a manufacturing environment is clear to the observer. Quantities stockpile and are held as inventory in warehouses, silos and liquids may be stored on tanks, tanker cars, and tanker ships. In service environments, this may take some unusual forms. Consider the marketing and sales unit of a financial services organization that prints mutual fund brochures for distribution to current and prospective customers. The brochures are date sensitive and perishable because mutual fund returns vary every quarter. The printer offers a volume discount for large print jobs, so the organization prints large quantities that are unfortunately not completely used, so they must be discarded periodically. After comparing the number of items typically used, the cost of printing the large batch, and getting the discount but throwing some out, with the cost of paying full price for the amount actually used, the analysis showed that it would have been cheaper to pay full price for the smaller lot, than pay for the larger quantity even with the discount.

In general, this waste refers to making more than is immediately required.

8. *Underutilized employees.* Organizations employ their staff for specific skills that these workers have. These employees have other skills too, so it is wasteful to not take advantage of these skills as well. As organizations become more sophisticated in their manufacturing activities, or become service providers, or both, their competitive advantage rests on their ability to capitalize on their employees' creativity to eliminate the other seven wastes, continuously improve their performance, and delight the customer. Examples include underutilizing the capabilities of the workforce, delegating tasks with inadequate training, and promoting individuals for reasons other than merit.

Affinity Diagram/KJ Analysis

Affinity diagrams, also called affinity charts or the Jiro Kawakita (KJ) method, are very useful tools that can help auditors organize ideas and large amounts of data. After a successful brainstorming exercise or analyzing large amounts of survey results, the facilitator may have a large number of items that need to be processed, analyzed, and summarized. This can be a daunting task if there is no method to organize this information, so in these situations, the affinity diagram can help to bring order and clarity.

Affinity diagrams are useful to gather large amounts of data, organizing the data into groupings or themes (i.e., creating clusters based on the affinity that some items have to others), when you need group consensus, and when issues seem too large and complex to organize.

Affinity diagrams require the following materials: sticky notes or cards (e.g., Post It® Notes) and a large work surface to work on (e.g., wall and table).

The first step is to place each idea on a separate sticky note or card. These items can be copied off flipchart paper if that is where the original items were written on. If the facilitator believes that the brainstorming exercise will be followed by an affinity diagram, the ideas can be written directly onto the sticky notes or cards. It is best to begin with a list of at least 20 items or issues.

Next, place all the notes randomly on the large work surface. The items should be visible to everyone involved in this exercise.

The following step should be done silently. Taking turns, each team member looks for ideas that appear to be related somehow and places them side by side. The process is repeated until all notes are grouped, then someone else takes a turn performing the same procedure and this is repeated for each member. It is OK to move a note that someone else moved already. In fact, a note can be moved multiple times. It is also OK to have single cards on their own. If a note appears to belong in two groups, a second note can be made. Don't rush through this step and make sure it is done in silence. This can be difficult for some people, but it is important so that other team members are not influenced by their colleagues.

After everyone has had a turn, team members can begin to talk and discuss the rationale for clustering several items together, for moving notes, and creating a duplicate note if that was done. When the movement of notes from one cluster to another stops and the team members are satisfied with the clusters formed, write a note that reflects the meaning or name of each group. This is similar to a heading or title that best describes the related notes. This title should be placed at the top of the group. To make this title more visible, you can use a note of a different color.

Affinity diagrams give groups an opportunity to exercise their creativity, break out of their habitual thinking, avoid jumping to conclusions, and avoid allowing preconceived notions drive their thinking. It also helps build consensus, as the clusters are created by the entire team.

Report writing is another task that I found to be improved by this tool. It can be difficult to decide in what order the findings and observations should appear on the report when an audit results in multiple findings and observations. An affinity diagram can be helpful to arrange the items so the findings flow logically.

Two common challenges auditors face are (1) making sure they are not reporting on symptoms, but rather on the root cause of problems and (2) reducing the length of the audit report. After preparing an affinity diagram, the reader may find like I have on several occasions that the number of findings is actually lower than it appeared originally, because some of the findings were in fact symptoms of a higher-level, global issue. In those cases, the items that I originally thought were findings, were actually symptoms of that higher-level issue and now the finding can be presented in its proper context, supported by the other information, and elevated for maximum attention as the global issue that it really is. By consolidating findings, the report is therefore shorter and more focused and the case for corrective action is made more effectively.

Internal auditors must remember that as the profession matures further and our role expands into one of change agent and facilitator, audit clients are looking for more than reports that state "the organization lacks KPIs." Audit reports that describe a problem are good. Audit reports that include pragmatic recommendations are better. Audit reports that describe a collaborative effort to cooperate with management and help them implement a solution that will help the organization well into the future are best. Consider an organization lacking performance indicators and an affinity diagram is used during a facilitated meeting with management to identify the appropriate metrics, determine what business units those metrics belong to, and which individuals will "own" those metrics. Rather than generating a long list of assorted items as a brainstorming session would, the affinity diagram can help to arrange those items for inclusion in the audit report, management operating reports, and monitoring activities.

Summary. Affinity diagrams work best when the team is small and you want to highlight similarities in ideas to build consensus and organize ideas or items into categories or themes.

Check Sheet

Check sheets are a common tool widely used by internal auditors, but seldom called by that name. A check sheet is a structured form or document used to collect and analyze data. This is often done real time where the data are generated or collected. The information collected can be either qualitative or quantitative and the form is sometimes called a tally sheet because the data are often used to track and count the number of instances of various phenomena associated with the review being performed. Check sheets provide a tool to consistently capture information about transactions examined.

Check sheets can be used when the data are observed and collected repeatedly and the intent is to document the frequency or pattern of problems, defects, defect causes, or events.

The challenge resides not only on the use or lack of use of this tool, since most auditors use it already. The challenge lies in how check sheets are designed. Since most auditors focus on documenting issues, their construction and use usually only shows the problems where those are present, but not the root cause or the concentration of sources of the problem. For example, if a process requires a review of transactions, issues associated with those items could include errors in the amount, the date when the transaction was recorded, transactions that were not reviewed and approved as required, and the lack of supporting documentation.

A check sheet could be constructed following these steps:

1. Identify and document the operational definitions and criteria that will be used when evaluating the selected transactions.
2. Decide what event or problem will be observed and documented.
3. Decide when the data will be collected, and for how long.
4. Design the form so that data can be recorded simply and clearly by making check marks (e.g., tickmarks or symbols) or entering numbers. It is best to select check marks or numbers than can be analyzed (e.g., added, multiplied) easily. Make sure the check sheet collects the appropriate data and is easy to use.
5. Label all rows and columns.
6. Select the transactions, items, or events that will be reviewed.
7. Record on the check sheet every time the event or problem occurs.

Figure 6.5 is an example of a check sheet that can be used to collect data on errors made while paying invoices.

Figure 6.6 shows an enhanced check sheet.

With the second (enhanced) approach shown, the source of the problem becomes clearer as it becomes evident that operator A accounts for a disproportionate amount of the errors. This approach provides insights into the source of the errors and facilitates the next step in the process:

	Monday	Tuesday	Wednesday	Thursday	Friday	Total
Processed without approval	4	3	1	2	2	12
No PO created for invoice	3	1	5	3	1	13
No PO referenced on invoice	2	3	3	1	0	9
Charged to wrong cost center	3	2	1	0	2	8
Goods not received	2	3	1	0	3	9
Calculation error	0	0	1	1	0	2
Total	14	12	12	7	8	53

Figure 6.5   Sample check sheet.

	Monday				Tuesday				Wednesday				Thursday				Friday				Total
Operator	1		2		1		2		1		2		1		2		1		2		
Shift	AM	PM	AM	PM	AM	PM	AM	PM	AM	PM	AM	PM	AM	PM	AM	PM	AM	PM	AM	PM	
Processed without approval	3	1	0	0	1	1	0	1	0	1	0	0	2	0	0	0	1	1	0	0	12
No PO created for invoice	2	0	0	1	1	0	0	0	3	1	0	0	3	0	0	0	0	1	0	0	13
No PO referenced on invoice	1	1	0	0	1	2	0	0	2	1	0	0	1	0	0	0	0	0	0	0	9
Charged to wrong cost center	2	1	0	0	1	0	1	0	0	1	0	0	0	0	0	0	2	0	0	0	8
Goods not received	2	0	0	0	1	1	0	1	1	0	1	0	0	0	0	0	3	0	0	0	9
Calculation error	0	0	0	0	0	0	0	0	0	0	0	1	0	1	0	0	0	2	0	0	2
Total	10	3	0	1	5	4	1	2	6	4	1	1	6	1	0	0	6	2	0	0	53
Total	13		1		9		3		10		2		7		0		8		0		53
Total	14				12				12				7				8				53

Figure 6.6 Sample enhanced check sheet.

investigating the cause of the problem. It is clear that with minimal extra work, and by simply modifying the layout of the tool used to capture the information, the auditor is now aware of a great deal of useful information.

Auditors should examine the design of their work templates to make sure that they are not missing the opportunity to hone in on the source of the issues they are identifying during the course of their audits. It only requires a minimal amount of additional work, but the results are very valuable.

Scatter Diagram

A scatter diagram is a visual tool for analyzing pairs of numerical data and showing the relationship between two variables. It is sometimes called a scatter plot or an *X–Y* graph, with one variable on each axis. One variable is plotted on the horizontal axis and the other is plotted on the vertical axis, and if the variables are correlated, the points will fall along a line or a curve.

Quite often, variables like error rates, accident rates, delays, or merchandise returns are examined as individual metrics to determine if the item is increasing or decreasing. Sometimes the analysis is done to determine if the item is oscillating or fluctuating in erratic ways, which may indicate that the underlying activities are unpredictable. Further, the analysis may be done to determine if a directional change or sudden spike occurred and when that happened. All of these procedures are useful and part of what auditors may want to check for.

There are, however, other analyses that auditors may want to perform. For example, to what degree does the accident rate increase as the number of work hours per shift increase? Does the number of merchandise returns increase as the delivery date promised to customers decrease?

When analyzing the plotted data, the objective is to determine if a correlation exists between two values. The correlation exists if a change in one value causes a change in another value. The relationship has two general key elements: direction and intensity.

Direction. If the two variables increase in tandem, there is a positive correlation between the two. This means that as one variable increases, the other variable increases as well. On the other hand, if one variable increases, while the other decreases, there is a negative, or inverse relationship between them.

Intensity. This has to do with how strong the relationship is or the correlation coefficient. The stronger the relationship, the higher the correlation between the two. The correlation coefficient ranges from +1: highly positive correlation to –1: highly negative correlation. When the data are plotted, the more the data points resemble a straight line, the stronger the relationship. If a line is not clear, statistics determine whether there is reasonable certainty that a relationship exists. If the statistics say that no relationship exists, the pattern could have occurred by random chance.

Table 6.7 summarizes the correlation coefficients and their interpretation.

This correlation analysis can be very effective when trying to determine whether the two variables are related, such as when trying to identify potential root causes of problems. For example, after brainstorming causes and effects using a fishbone diagram, a scatter plot can be used to determine objectively whether a particular cause and effect are related.

A note of caution. Even if the scatter diagram shows a relationship, we should not assume that one variable caused the other. Both may be influenced by a third variable, but in general, the correlation may be established while remembering that correlation is different from causation. Two variables may be correlated, but one may not necessarily cause the other. However, if a correlation exists, it can help both the auditor and the corresponding manager estimate what future values will be given to the relationship that exists between them. For example, it is generally assumed that there is a positive

Table 6.7 Interpretation of Correlation Coefficients

Correlation Coefficient	Meaning
0.0–0.3	Little to no correlation
0.3–0.5	Low correlation
0.5–0.7	Moderate correlation
0.7–0.9	High correlation
0.9–1.0	Very high correlation

correlation between the volume of transactions processed and the number of errors made. As the number of transactions processed increases, more errors will be made. This could happen because with the increased volume the workers make data entry mistakes and make calculation errors. While this is expected intuitively, the auditor may want to know how strong the correlation is. If we consider two organizations' processing units, their graphs may look as follows:

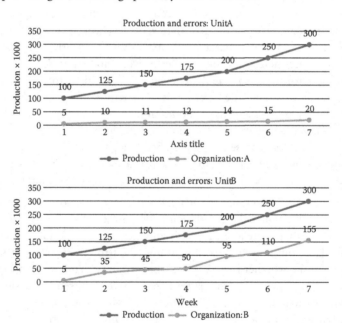

In both graphs shown, there is a positive correlation between the two, but A shows that there is only a slight increase in the error rate when the volume increases, while B shows that the number of errors increases substantially when the volume increases. By extrapolating the results and projecting it forward, it is reasonable to assume that if the volumes were to increase, the relationship would hold and the dynamics would repeat themselves.

This is a very important discovery, and helpful evidence to have available. If we further assume that each organization in its strategic plan has a goal to grow the business by 25% and expect transaction volumes to increase proportionately, then organization A is better prepared to handle that volume increase. All else being equal, it has a higher likelihood to maintain low error rates despite the upsurge.

Organization B, on the other hand, will likely face monumental problems as the processing volume increases. It fact, its ability to process the transactions and keep customers happy could very well collapse due to the significantly higher number of errors that are expected. The process lacks scalability.

As auditors provide advice to management and helps them identify risks that threaten the achievement of their objectives, some discussions are encouraged to show that unless the operating practices are examined and some changes are made that contain or drive the error rate down, their growth objective is not only difficult to achieve, but also it could be catastrophic to the organization.

In general, auditors should think creatively how to use scatter diagrams to discover root causes and support their findings with information about the relationship between multiple variables. This can enable them to provide management with useful forward-looking assistance when making decisions.

5S

5S is the name of a workplace method that uses a list of five Japanese words to describe how to clear, organize, and maintain the workspace for efficiency and effectiveness by identifying, storing, and maintaining the items used, maintaining the physical space and items, and sustaining the arrangement (Table 6.8). These Japanese words are seiri, seiton, seiso, seiketsu, and shitsuke. When transliterated into English, each starts with the letter "S."

Seiton

This word translates to "systematic arrangement," "set in order," "straighten" or "streamline," It calls for workers to arrange all necessary items, so they can be easily found and selected for use. By embracing Seiton, the workplace can prevent the loss of necessary items, avoid the waste of time from searching around for items needed, and make it easy to find and pick up necessary items. This concept generally relates to neatness and suggests that by maintaining the work environment tidily and in order, it will be clearer where items must go, where to find what is needed, and it will also reduce the likelihood of workplace accidents. It behooves workers to embrace this practice to avoid wasting time searching for items.

Seiri

This word is translated to "sort." It calls for workers to remove unnecessary items and dispose of them appropriately. This makes the work easier to be performed by eliminating obstacles,

Table 6.8 The 5S Methodology

Element	Meaning
Seiri	Organization
Seiton	Neatness
Seiso	Cleaning
Seiketsu	Standardization
Shitsuke	Discipline

reducing the likelihood of being disturbed with unnecessary items and it also prevents the accumulation of unnecessary items.

When sorting the items, it is necessary to evaluate the needed items with regard to cost and need, then removing all parts, tools, and equipment not in use. All other items should be removed or segregated away from the workplace. Since conditions may change over time, it may be necessary for area supervisors and workers to check periodically to make sure that the rule is still being applied and that previously needed items remain essential, otherwise they should be removed. In general, Seiri calls for organization and for all unnecessary items to be removed from the workplace and placed in a designated area.

This term is often related to organization and encourages optimizing the arrangement of parts and materials so that this better design will improve workplace efficiency.

Seiso

This is translated to "shine," "sweep," "sanitize," or "scrub." It can also be explained as "cleaning." This S admonishes cleaning the workplace completely and keeping it so. Seiso will help to prevent machinery and equipment from deteriorating, keep the workplace clean and safe, while making the entire work environment easy to work in.

The word is typically related to cleaning, and in many work environments, this can be achieved by dusting, scrubbing, vacuuming, and washing the workplace and surrounding areas.

Seiketsu

Seiketsu refers to "standardizing" the best design and operating practices in the work area. The key is to maintain high standards of workplace organization and housekeeping at all times. By ensuring everything, everywhere is in order the organization will be more likely to operate efficiently. Standards should be clear, communicated, and enforced for the design, storage, and operation of the workplace.

By standardizing workplace activities, we eliminate variability and unpredictability. Erratic processes are generally problematic because they make it more difficult to know what to expect as outputs. Employees may be confused and the difficulty to train others increases. Furthermore, it is more likely to make mistakes as employees forget what they should do, or think they are doing things correctly when in fact they may be mistaken.

A place for everything, and everything in its place.

Shitsuke

The translation of Shitsuke is "sustain." It means to keep in working order and "do without being told." In this regard, it suggests that the organization should thrive to create a culture of compliance. Remember that one of the characteristics of culture, whether in the organizational sense, or otherwise, is that behaviors become so ingrained that they are automatic. That's the case with Shitsuke.

Achieving this level of cultural unity requires management involvement and investment over time. This is enhanced by well thought-out training that teaches employees what is expected and shows them how to do it. Training is a goal-oriented process that provides knowledge, but should also be repeated periodically to provide refresher training and an opportunity to explore improvements. The resulting feedback on how to make programs and processes work better can then be escalated to those who can facilitate the implementation of these ideas.

The previous description may conjure images of discipline, and that is correct. Shitsuke also includes performing regular audits and reviews to verify compliance with the standards set.

The benefits of applying 5S are widespread. They include eliminating hidden inventory and unnecessary items, freeing up floor space, improving the flow of materials, reducing time and distance of walking and other means of transportation, and eliminating unnecessary items for reuse somewhere else.

RACI Diagram

In every organization, there is a hierarchy of responsibilities that facilitate the completion of work. In fact, one of the reasons organizations are created is to leverage the contributions of multiple individuals so that by their integrated work and collaboration, more can be accomplished. This integration creates synergies that boost performance. The total is greater than the sum of the parts.

In a well-functioning process involving multiple parties, there should be clarity around the tasks that will be formed, who will perform them, who will provide assistance, who will be informed about what is being done, and who approves the tasks. However, the presence of multiple parties in a process can also create a troublesome dynamic when the parties involved have not formally documented the segregation of activities and the related responsibilities. When this happens, there will likely be poor coordination, confusion, and redundancies. Another problem is the lack of accountability that will be manifested in finger pointing when those involved realize that an important activity was not performed as expected. The blaming that this can cause is frustrating, affects employee morale and can cause customer dissatisfaction.

The RACI diagram, also referred to as responsibility assignment matrix, and linear responsibility chart, is a very useful tool to help correct this deficiency. RACI is an acronym derived from the four roles and responsibilities that various parties play in a program or process. It describes the participation by various roles in completing tasks or deliverables and it is especially useful in clarifying roles and responsibilities in cross-functional or departmental projects and processes because it identifies who does what. The roles identified are responsible, accountable (or approver), consulted, and informed.

Let's examine each of them.

Responsible

This describes those responsible for performing the task and refers to those who do the work to achieve the task. So for every task identified, there needs to be at least one role participating as responsible, even though others can be delegated to assist in the required work.

It answers the question: Who does this?

Accountable (Also Approver)

This identifies the person that approves the completed activity. Since an approval should always include a review prior to the sign off, this person is accountable for the completion of the activity according to established standards. This person may also be the person who delegates the work to those responsible. In other words, an accountable must approve the work that the person(s) responsible provides. There must be only one accountable specified for each task or deliverable.

It answers the question: Who approves the activity after it is completed?

Consulted

Those whose knowledge is important for the successful completion of the task are identified as consulted. Their opinions and skills are sought, so they are team members or subject matter experts. There is a two-way communication between those responsible and those consulted.

It answers the question: Who will assist the people responsible?

Informed

This role refers to anyone that should be kept up to date about the activities being performed, the progress made on them or their completion. In many instances, the notice often only happens upon the completion of the task or deliverable. It consists of one-way communications to them.

It answers the question: Who should be kept up to date about the activities?

How to Construct a RACI Chart

The matrix is typically created with a vertical axis (left-hand column) listing of tasks. The items on the list can consist of the key activates from a Gantt chart or other list of activities or deliverables for the project. The horizontal axis on the top row shows the parties involved. It can be individuals, teams, or relevant units from an organizational chart.

At the intersecting point, the corresponding letter is entered based on the role each party plays in the accomplishment of the activities noted. Figure 6.7 is an illustration of a RACI diagram.

It may happen that the role that is accountable for a task is also the one responsible for completing it. This is indicated on the matrix in one of two ways

1. The task or deliverable has a role accountable for it, but no role responsible for its completion. In this case, it is implied.
2. The task or deliverable has a role of R/A: responsible/approver.

Beyond this exception, it is generally recommended that each task have one of the RACI participation types assigned to it. It is also helpful to make sure that everyone involved agrees to the roles being assigned to them, and that they have the necessary skills and resources to get the work done. Upon implementation, a communications matrix may be useful as well.

	Employee	Secretary	Manager	Accounting
Document expenses	AR			
Complete expense report	AR			C
Forward to manager	A	R		
Review	C		AR	
Approve	I		AR	
Forward to accounting		R	A	
Classify expenses	C			AR
Process payment				AR

Figure 6.7 Sample RACI chart for processing expense reports.

Communications Plan

A communications plan is very simple to prepare and very useful to make sure communications within and outside the team are effective. The means of communication can be formal or informal. However, it is usually best to make the majority of them formal to ensure consistency, provide the proper coverage, and make sure this happens promptly. Informal communications are also very important and serve as a great supplement to formal communication channels and activities.

A communications plan identifies the key elements to make sure the intended message is received, understood, and acted upon by the main stakeholders during the engagement, providing a schedule of key communications and defining what will be shared. It helps to make sure the messages get to the audience.

To decide what should be on a communications plan, it helps to think about these six simple questions: what, when, where, who, how, and why.

What. This refers to what will be included in the communications. This may include performance, progress, and status of the unit's activities. Examples include what tasks have been completed, which activities are in progress, a list and description of up-coming activities, a variance analysis from the budget and if working on a project, variance from the project plan. Also, issues that have surfaced, whether they were anticipated or not, and what was done or is being done to resolve them.

When. This refers to the timing of the communication activities, so here we are focusing on the timing. In terms of their frequency, meetings sometimes work very well early in the morning to prepare for the day ahead. In other cases, it is much better to meet at the end of the day to discuss what occurred and while events are still fresh on everyone's mind and begin planning for the next business day.

Where. The focus is on the location of the communications. Meetings can be held in the office, conference room, or open-space near the department's location. For teams or de-partments that are geographically dispersed, or where members travel often, the meetings and updates can be done via conference call, video conference, or online instant messaging.

Who. This relates to the decision of who should attend the meetings. Answering this question can be as important as deciding what is going to be discussed during the meeting. In most cases, it is best to have everyone present, because this helps to avoid miscommunication and eliminates the need to repeat what has already been discussed. However, sometimes everyone can't or doesn't need to be present. In some cases, some team members may attend, while others interested in the topic that can't be there can receive a brief update or the meeting minutes so they are up to date about the key items discussed. When answering the "who," it is as important to decide who does the communicating as well as who receives the communication.

Communications Matrix

While the communications plan provides a framework for communicating, the communications matrix is used to summarize and facilitate the communication plan by defining the details regarding the communications activities that are used during the team or department's activities during the course of the project.

The key components of a communications matrix are the communication type, description, delivery method, frequency, documents, participants, and those responsible for making sure each communication event takes place according to the plan. Table 6.9 is a sample communications matrix for a project.

A common challenge that teams encounter is that some people feel that they, or others, have been left out of important communications. With a communications plan and communications matrix, you can avoid these issues. By being proactive, you can minimize the disruption that complaints and confusion can create.

Suppliers, Inputs, Process, Outputs, and Customers Map

Auditors are expected to gain familiarity with the program or process they are going to review. Two areas of weaknesses that sometimes complicate the completion of the review is the limited knowledge of the parties involved and inadequate understanding of the process itself. Flowcharts with swimming lanes often help to ameliorate this issue, but even those flowcharts often fail to incorporate other critical components and participants in a process. As internal auditors apply risk-based auditing techniques to their reviews, and increase their focus on the needs of customers to achieve organizational aims, it is essential to gain a panoramic understanding of the program or process. A suppliers, inputs, process, outputs, and customers (SIPOC) diagram can be very helpful in that regard because it summarizes the participants, inputs and outputs of a process. An SIPOC diagram is a tool used by a team to identify all relevant elements of a process before work begins.

SIPOC is an acronym that stands for suppliers, inputs, process, outputs, and customers. All of these items form the columns of the matrix. It prompts the audit team to consider:

> Suppliers of the process
> Inputs to the process
> Process the team is reviewing
> Outputs of the process
> Customers that receive the process outputs

The SIPOC map is particularly useful when defining the scope of the review because it can give auditors a high-level overview of the program or process. All of the elements captured in the SIPOC

Table 6.9 Communications Matrix

Communication Type	Description and Purpose	Delivery Method	Frequency	Participants	Responsible	Deliverables
Opening meeting	Introduce the team and initiate the project. Review the project scope, objectives, and approach	Face to face	Once	Project team	PM	Agenda
						Presentation
				Process owners		Minutes
Project team meeting	Review status of the project	Face to face	Weekly	Project team	PM	Agenda
		Conference call				Minutes
Project status report	Report the status of the project, including activities, progress, and issues encountered	E-mail	Monthly	Project team	PM	Project status report
				Project sponsor		
				Division V.P.		
Team morale	Morale and team building exercises	Event (preferably offsite)	Quarterly	Project team	Business analyst	Team event

map are important to fully understand what the auditors are going to review. Failing to fully understand any of the elements of the matrix can limit the effectiveness of the auditor developing the scope during planning, or limit the team's ability to effectively understand the program or process during fieldwork. This diagram can also help to perform a stakeholder analysis, so the key participants in the program or process are identified. Lastly, the interactions among the parties involved can help to define risk exposures, the size of the operation and related audit coverage needed, and customer requirements. It helps to answer the following questions, among others:

- Who supplies inputs to the process?
- What is supplied and what material or informational inputs enter the process?
- How critical are these inputs to the effective functioning of the program or process?
- What does a high-level breakdown (or flowchart) of the process look like?
- What does the program or process produce?
- Who are the customers of the process?
- What are the requirements of the customers?

In addition to these questions, further analysis of each of the components can provide valuable assessment information too. For example, the location of the suppliers can provide some insights into the length of the supply chain, the risk of foreign currency conversion, and political risk. Suppliers and customers may be internal or external to the organization that performs the process so all of this is vital information that can inform the auditor about the size, spread, and complexity of the distribution network. Inputs and outputs may be materials, services, or information, so gaining an understanding about these can help to define roles during integrated audits.

It is also very important that internal auditors identify the relevant stakeholders during a review. Some stakeholders share in the benefits a company creates, while others bear the risks that are generated as a result of the organization's activities. Good decisions are made when the proper attention is given to the effects that corporate decisions have on all stakeholders, and the SIPOC map is a great tool to help in this regard.

Poka Yoke/Mistake Proofing

Poka Yoke is the term used to describe a mechanism in a process that helps operators avoid mistakes. Poka Yoke is a Japanese term that means "mistake-proofing" (Avoid: yokeru, mistakes: poka). The purpose of Poka Yoke is to eliminate defects in products by preventing or drawing attention to human errors that can occur. A common expression to describe this condition is trying to fit a square peg into a round hole—a frustrating and impractical action that is likely to yield unwanted results.

Examples from daily life abound:

Power plugs. Often they can only be plugged in one way because they don't fit into the power outlet upside down.

Ethernet and UBS cable plugs. Can only be plugged in one way and they have a minute latch to keep the cable from being pulled out of the device accidentally.

Garage door sensors. They prevent garage doors from closing accidentally when an object is in the door's path.

Microwave motors. The microwave oven stops operating when the door is opened.

Automobiles. The driver cannot change the gears from park to drive, unless the brake pedal is pressed.

Plumbing. Sink overflow outlet.

Automatic faucets. The water runs when the presence sensor detects an object and shuts off automatically after a predetermined amount of time.

Poka Yoke can be a phenomenal tool for internal auditors who are often called upon to examine the design of programs and processes, and make recommendations for improvement. The best Poka Yoke solutions are as simple as possible, use the lowest cost solutions, make the solution mandatory and intuitive, and avoid requiring the operator to make a decision to apply the solution or not (Table 6.10). In industrial settings, forcing parts to fit only one way by adding pins or other obstructions that makes it impossible to fit them any other way helps to avoid parts from being put in incorrectly.

The following lists some of the common ways of mistake-proofing processes:

Orientation. Part won't fit incorrectly.

Sequence. Process must be performed in a predetermined sequence.

Weights. Inaccurate weights forces the machine to stop.

Location/size/count. Requires the presence, absence, or different size of components.

System check. Machine stops operating when out of specification.

If we apply Poka Yoke in a service environment, it becomes evident that the principles are equally applicable. Note the following examples:

Spreadsheets. Color-code and password-protect the spreadsheet so data can only be entered on predetermined fields.

Reconciliation templates. Use formulas with check totals that indicate through color changes when the totals agree.

Data entry. Operator is required to reenter certain figures to make sure data entry is accurate.

Expense reports. System automatically displays a child window when the amount of the expense is above a given threshold.

Entry-log. Information is selected from a pull-down menu for company employees, or typed for visitors to eliminate penmanship issues—an often overlooked limitation of sign-in sheets where the security officer doesn't pay attention, or can't decipher, the names written on the entry–exit log.

Table 6.10 Poka Yoke Attributes

- Simple
- Inexpensive
- Fail-safe
- Mandatory
- Intuitive

Table 6.11   Poka Yoke Principles

Principle	Objective
1. Elimination	Eliminate the possibility of error
2. Replacement	Substitute for a more reliable process
3. Facilitation	Make the activity easier to perform
4. Detection	Detect the error before further processing occurs
5. Mitigation	Minimize the effect of the error

Source: Adapted from http://leanapplied.com/blog/wp-content/uploads/2012/11/126-300×226.png

As we examine the objectives of Poka Yoke's principles (Table 6.11), it is evident that those are applicable in both industrial and service environments. As internal auditors examine business issues and explore alternative solutions, it is helpful to consider the attributes and characteristics of Poka Yoke. After all, Poka Yoke's objectives are consistent with the effective recommendations for process improvement.

Benchmarking

> While they were saying among themselves it cannot be done, it was done.
>
> **Helen Keller**[3]

Benchmarking is the process of comparing statistical information. It consists of comparing at least one performance metric to a standard, or multiple performance metrics to each other. It is a great tool to determine if the item under examination is performing at an acceptable level. The results can show that the item is performing below the standard, or above it, in which case the item could become the new standard.

This is an important point to keep in mind, especially since internal auditors focus on exception-based reporting and have traditionally focused on what is missing the mark. They must be careful not to only identify poor performance, or only comment on poor performance. In fact, the *Standards* indicate that "internal auditors are encouraged to acknowledge satisfactory performance in engagement communications" (Standard 2410.A2). With this in mind, benchmarking can provide objective information showing when a process fails to measure up. Conversely, it can also show areas of excellence within the organization. I have found these communications to be well received in organizations, especially when audit clients had not had that experience before. It helps to soften their view about internal auditors and broaden their opinion away from the singular viewpoint of the auditor being "the corporate cop."

Typical metrics used in benchmarking are time, quality, and cost. In most cases, benchmarking consists of identifying the best performing organizations in the same or another industry where comparable processes exist and comparing one's results to those of the other organizations.

The result can be a better understanding of how well or poorly the process or overall organization compares, but also why organizations are successful. It is often best not to benchmark only once, but rather to make this a continuous process linked to one's continuous quality improvement initiatives, ERM, and audit planning.

Robert Camp, in his book *The Search for Industry Best Practices that Lead to Superior Performance,* states that benchmarking is "the search for those best practices that will lead to the superior performance" of a unit or organization. It is not only about gathering results and trying to match or outdo them. It is about studying the practices in others' processes recognized as leading organizations and finding out how to do what they do. The goal should always be to provide the level of customer satisfaction, quality, and efficiency that your organization wants.

Two common issues associated with benchmarking are (1) the information is often proprietary and organizations are reluctant to share it with other organizations, especially competitors and (2) the information is sometimes not comparable, because the organizations are of different sizes, maturity, or operate in different markets. To collect benchmarking information, it is not always necessary to have face-to-face contact with the other organization(s). In fact, a great deal of information is available in the news, trade publications and professional journals, annual reports, and online databases. If the information is being gathered personally, there must be an agreement regarding confidentiality of the information and as a professional courtesy, a plan to share the information collected with all of the benchmarking partners.

By performing benchmarking analyses within the organization, the information should be more readily available and it can serve as a great way to identify centers of excellence within the organization itself.

A third approach is to perform trend analysis where the unit being examined is compared to itself over time. This third approach raises the issue of "how long should be the time period of an operational audit?" If a metric is viewed during a 1-year cycle, the number may provide one perspective or even appear satisfactory, but if we examine multiple years, we may arrive at a different result. For example, a call center has been receiving a similar volume of daily phone calls over a 5-year period, and its average response time is as shown in Table 6.12.

Further, let us assume that the organization has a goal that its response time should be under 1 min, 30 s. If we only look at Year 5, we would conclude that the call center is operating within management's expectations and no further action is needed. However, if we inspect all 5 years, we notice that response times have been deteriorating. Whereas the average response time was only 33 s in Year 1, that same metric has now increased to 1 min, 12 s. The auditor may want to discuss this condition with management.

Table 6.12 Call Center Average Response Times

Year 1	Year 2	Year 3	Year 4	Year 5
Time: 33 s	45 s	57 s	1 min, 2 s	1 min, 12 s

Five Whys

> If you do not ask the right questions, you do not get the right answers. A question asked in the right way often points to its own answer. Asking questions is the A-B-C of diagnosis. Only the inquiring mind solves problems.
>
> **Edward Hodnett**[4]

The 5 Whys is a very powerful tool, useful to identify the root cause of issues. Many auditors are accustomed to treating situations using a binary approach. When performing financial audits in the United States, transactions are either compliant with US Generally Accepted Accounting Principles (GAAP) or they are not. If they are, there is no finding. If they are not, they must be corrected and recorded according to US GAAP. The situation is binary.

If the auditor is performing a compliance review, the situation is often similar. The criteria used during the evaluation may be a contract and the review may consist of verifying that practices are in agreement with the terms and conditions spelled out in said contract. If practices are consistent with the expectations, there is no finding. If there are deviations, the observation is noted and the recommendation is made to comply with the terms of the contract. The situation is binary.

However, when performing operational reviews, the situation is often far more complex. A problem could be caused by a variety of reasons, so auditors must search for the root cause. "Root cause analysis is defined as the identification of why an issue occurred (versus only identifying or reporting on the issue itself). In this context, an issue is defined as a problem, error, instance of noncompliance, or missed opportunity" (Practice Adv 2320-2). Internal auditors should deliver insight to their clients, and this means they must also determine when they need to facilitate, review, and conduct RCA.

The 5 Whys is a one of the simplest tools for RCA. It is easy to use and does not require statistical analysis. The approach consists of asking "why" multiple items, each of which probes further as to the source of the problem.

The 5 Whys is an iterative technique used to explore the cause-and-effect relationships underlying a problem. The primary goal of the technique is to determine the root cause of a defect or problem by repeating the question "why?" The process is sequential and each question forms the basis of the next question. The "5" in the name is the typical number of iterations typically needed to resolve the problem, but identifying the root cause may take fewer or more times than 5 whys.

Since not all problems have a single root cause, it may be necessary to repeat the process multiple times for each problem or issue. This technique does not provide specific rules about what types of questions to ask, which subjects to explore, or how long to repeat the process to search for additional root causes. As a result, even when the method is used and applied correctly, the result still depends on the knowledge of the people involved. It is also important to work through the process sufficiently and go to a lower-level root cause; otherwise, the tendency to stop at symptoms will yield an inadequate solution.

To illustrate the process, consider the example of the water on the floor.

Problem statement. The floor is wet.
Why 1: Water leaked from the ceiling
Initial answer/solution. Mop up the floor and dry the water. However, if water

continues to fall on the floor, mopping the water is an inadequate solution to the problem. We should ask "why?"

Why 2: Why is there water on the floor?

Answer: Because the pipe overhead is leaking. We can stop there and repair the pipe, but we should probably ask "why?" again.

Why 3: Why is the pipe leaking?

Answer: Because it has poor fittings.

Why 4: Why did the pipe have poor fittings?

Answer: Because the plumbing work was done by an unqualified plumber. We should ask "why?" again.

Why 5: Why did we use an unqualified plumber?

Answer: Because of poor procurement practices. The plumbing work was granted to this plumber through favoritism rather than skill and a proven history of good workmanship. So, now we know what caused the water on the floor!

With this knowledge, we can now move forward to address the vendor contracting process to eliminate favoritism and not allow this plumber to do any additional work for the organization. If we stop at any of the preceding steps, we would continue to experience water leakage because that was merely a symptom of inadequate vendor selection and poor workmanship.

Let's examine another example. Suppose the auditor notes that the processing unit is making mistakes when shipping goods to customers.

Why 1. Why are there so many mistakes? Because instructions are given verbally.

Why 2. Why are instructions given verbally? Because it takes longer to write orders and they want to make shipments as quickly as possible, so they call the orders in.

Why 3. Why does it take so long to write orders? There is no tool (e.g., form, template, and system) to record the information.

At this point, with three whys we can see that the absence of a consistent method of capturing orders and communicating them to the shipping department is causing the problem. The problem can be fixed in a number of different ways. If resources are sufficient, a new order taking system can be bought and implemented. That would be ideal, especially if it interfaces with the inventory and billing systems. If that is not feasible or possible, then having a standard form should clearly inform the shipping personnel what to send, how many units, and to what address.

Penmanship issues can create problems when the reader cannot decipher what was written by hand, so a printed form would work best. Such a form can be prepared using common software like Word and Excel, especially if they are used as a form.

The 5 Whys can be used individually or in conjunction with the fishbone diagram or other related tools. The fishbone diagram, also called cause and effect diagram and Ishikawa diagram, helps to explore all potential and real causes resulting in a single defect or failure. After identifying all of the inputs on the fishbone diagram, the 5 Whys technique can help to drill down to the root causes.

Work Breakdown Structure

According to the Project Management Institute (PMI), a Work Breakdown Structure (WBS) is a "deliverable-oriented grouping of project elements that organizes and defines the work scope of the project. Each descending level represents an increasingly detailed definition of the project work."[5] It includes the tasks that must be done to complete the project and these tasks are arranged in hierarchical order. This way, the larger jobs that must be done, followed by the smaller tasks needed to do the larger jobs, and so on in more and more detail until arriving at the most detailed tasks needed. This is called "de-composition" and it is done step by step with increasing detail. The stopping point is when there is enough detail to estimate staff, resource needs, costs of the task, and the risks associated with getting that task done.

Each item should be numbered to keep track of everything in the project. Since this creates strings or chains that resemble outlines, it provides an easy way for the project manager (PM) and team to trace tasks up and down the chain with increasing or decreasing detail.

A key benefit of creating and using a WBS during a project is that it forces the project planners to avoid high-level planning that focuses on core tasks only. By working at the summary or multitask level (the more visible to the management team and the client), they may fail to identify the many support tasks that are required to finish a project on budget and on time. These support tasks include preparatory work, lead time planning (e.g., training and document review) that are necessary to get the work done and consume time and resources as well. If these activities, which have to be paid for somehow, are not identified, it is likely that the team will have to pay for this through unpaid overtime.

A WBS is best prepared with the input from others who have done similar work in the past or the project team, who will be doing the actual work.

Summary

As we consider all of the tools covered in this section, it is important to remember that they serve as tools to help internal auditors identify the root cause of problems. RCA is a concept often mentioned by internal auditors, and for some, it is almost an elusive goal. It is perceived as a high value outcome because not identifying the root cause of a problem carries consequences to the auditor and the process under review. When the recommendation to correct a problem only addresses symptoms rather than the source of the problem, the problem recurs.

In everyday life, it is easy to understand the difference between treating the symptoms of a malady and curing the condition itself. A classic example is that of headaches. A person can treat the headache with a variety of pain medications, but unless that individual addresses the underlying source of the problem, the headaches will continue. Headache sources may include alcohol consumption, certain food additives, stress, changes in sleep patterns, eye strain, sinusitis, fatigue, and dehydration, so unless the underlying lifestyle practice or medical condition is addressed the headaches won't go away permanently.

A similar dynamic is present when examining business processes, like inventory stock outs. Quite often a stock out situation is attributed to the warehouse personnel, when in fact they are only shelving the items received. Some may suggest that the problem lies in the purchasing department, which is clearly ordering too few items. But we should be careful when placing the blame on them since the problem could be poor forecasting by the sales and marketing units. As a result of situations like this, some organizations are moving away from auditing inventory, purchasing, or accounts payable activities in isolation, and auditing the entire process instead: purchase to pay.

Internal auditors are encouraged to consider using the tools presented in this section to help them identify the problem's root cause.

QUESTIONS

1. How can internal auditors use histograms during internal audits?
2. How can management use control charts as part of their ongoing monitoring activities?
3. How can internal auditors use takt time during internal audits?
4. How can the 5S model be used during an operational audit?
5. How can management use RACI charts to improve accountability in operating units?
6. Describe the benefits of a communications plan and a communications matrix.
7. What are the elements of an SIPOC map and how can using it improve the understanding of a unit under review?
8. Explain how using the principles of Poka Yoke/mistake proofing can help further the goal of preventing errors, accidents, and operational breakdowns.
9. Describe how the 5 Whys can be used to identify the root cause of an operational issue.
10. What are the benefits of RCA?

Notes

1 See https://www.mindtools.com/pages/article/newTED_06.htm for more information about this tool.
2 For a more detailed description of root cause analysis, see https://www.mindtools.com/pages/article/newTMC_80.htm
3 See http://www.brainyquote.com/quotes/quotes/h/helenkelle120891.html
4 See http://izquotes.com/quote/344345
5 Project Management Institute. 2000. *A Guide to the Project Management Body of Knowledge.* Newtown Square, PA.

Chapter 7

Eight Areas of Waste

> Facts are stubborn things; and whatever may be our wishes, our inclinations, or the dictates of our passions, they cannot alter the state of facts and evidence.
>
> **John Adams**[1]

Introduction

An organization is the collection of structures, processes, and people working collaboratively to pursue a mission and achieve business goals. While organizations aim to pursue their missions and goals by adhering to principles of efficiency and effectiveness, many suffer various degrees of dysfunction during day-to-day operations. These issues can result in the erosion of stakeholder value up to the point of insolvency, but internal auditors can support management efforts and curtail these dynamics from taking hold by anticipating problems, reviewing current dynamics, and making recommendations for improvement.

Waste is anything done or acquired that is not required to successfully complete an activity or support a process. Waste manifests itself in many ways, often resulting in higher time consumption or underutilized financial resources. The Eight Areas of Waste Model provides a simple methodology to identify actions and items that reduce the value obtained from available resources. The model can be used as a diagnostic tool, as one of the elements used during the development of audit programs, and as a memory jogger when outlining the benefits expected from recommendations.

Eight Areas of Waste

One of the key objectives of organizations is to maximize the utility they extract from their resources. These inputs, whether financial, material, or human, are acquired to further the organization's mission, and great care is exerted to deploy and use them to achieve organizational objectives. This should be a key aspect of every organization's operating philosophy, whether it is a for-profit or nonprofit organization.

The Merriam-Webster dictionary defines waste as the

- "Loss of something valuable that occurs because too much of it is being used or because it is being used in a way that is not necessary or effective
- An action or use that results in the unnecessary loss of something valuable
- A situation in which something valuable is not being used or is being used in a way that is not appropriate or effective"[2]

All three segments of the definition show that waste occurs because more resources than necessary are being used, or the resources are not being used in the most appropriate and effective manner. This highlights the importance of

1. Proper planning: This involves the structure of the operating area, the step-by-step activities that will be performed to produce a product or deliver a service, the training of workers, setting expectations for performance, and deploying appropriate tools and machines.
2. Proper execution: There are two key aspects to effective execution: performance monitoring, which can be ongoing or periodic, and issue identification and remediation.

Effective performance is a continuous process that begins with the design of the process and the visioning required to plan for and anticipate the products or services to be delivered. Producing these expected outputs and outcomes involve monitoring during the production process to correct deviations. However, all too often organizations are plagued by performance issues due to wasteful practices.

Three words popularized by Toyota in The Toyota Production System (TPS) and The Toyota Way are muri (overburden), inconsistency (mura), and eliminate waste (muda). A key element of the TPS is making sure the process is predictable and adaptable without creating too much unwanted variability because this often results in waste. There are several types of muda (waste) that are addressed in the TPS that are a recurring problem in many organizations.

Overproduction

Overproduction refers to the production of a given output in excess of what is required. Avoiding overproduction can be a challenge in manufacturing operations, where items are often produced and stocked for sale later. This problem can occur for a variety of reasons.

Batch production is a common practice, often embraced as a best practice to take advantage of economies of scale. Economies of scale are the cost advantage obtained with the increased output of a product. It occurs due to the inverse relationship between the quantity produced and per-unit fixed costs. This happens because the greater the quantity of a product produced, the lower the per-unit fixed cost will be since the costs are shared over a larger number of goods. Economies of scale may also lower unit variable costs due to operational efficiencies and synergies.

This advantageous situation decreases when the production level reaches a point where the organization then has to incur additional expenses to warehouse, safeguard, and move this additional inventory. Also when the items are stored for later sale, there is an added risk of theft and damage. To address these risks, organizations perform cycle counts and physical counts, build/rent and use climate-controlled facilities, implement access controls, and in general build an infrastructure to address overproduction, thus incurring costs that would be absent if production matched demand.

In a service environment, some useful questions include

- Are making extra copies necessary?
- Are employees printing, faxing, or e-mailing more than what is needed to get the necessary work done?
- Is the concept of "FYI" (For Your Information) overdone?
- Is repetitive information being entered on multiple documents or forms?
- Is all the information requested on forms necessary?
- Are more tests or services being ordered than what the customer needs?
- Is the organization preparing reports that are not read and used?

Waiting

Speed has become a key differentiator among competing organizations. In government and nonprofit sectors alike, speed of execution is a desirable quality, if not a requirement. Customer complaints often center on errors and delays, so avoiding both would go a long way toward increasing customer satisfaction and maximizing the use of available resources.

In most cases, waiting is the delayed action that happens until some other productive action is done on the item produced. If we consider the step-by-step process of producing an item or delivering a service, each action adds value to the product or service and cumulatively produces what the customer is willing to pay for. Waiting is usually nonvalue added, as the goods await further action at a subsequent time.

While waiting is often a nonvalue-added period of time as described above, there are instances when it is required. For example, in a process where something needs to be painted, waiting until the primer dries before putting the paint on is a requirement. In a process where concrete is laid down, it must cure before additional work is done with it and this wait-state cannot be rushed. However, if the delay occurs because information is missing, we must ask ourselves

- Could the request be processed faster?
- Could the individual who needs it obtain it himself/herself?
- Could it be requested earlier in the process so it is available at the time and place where it is required to continue processing?

Waiting sometimes occurs because there is a lack of coordination and timing between complementary activities within an organization or a process. One part of the process produces on a certain schedule, and the subsequent operation is either not ready for the input, cannot keep pace with the number or timing of inputs, or needs additional information before proceeding.

Some useful questions are as follows:

- Are there excessive reviews, signatures, and approvals required?
- Are activities requiring the involvement of too many parties slowing down the process?
- Are there delays while waiting for needed information?
- Do differences in computer system versions cause delays while issues are addressed?
- Are other departments causing delays?

In all of these cases, the auditor can help the organization by examining what is happening, where, why, and by whom, then recommending improvements to the process that will allow production to occur more evenly.

Transporting

Transporting refers to the action of moving an item from one location to another. In a manufacturing environment, moving items from one location to another could be a requirement, but in other instances, it is the result of poor physical layout. By going back and forth, the operation incurs additional fuel and time costs, and it increases the likelihood of accidents and damage to merchandise.

In a service environment, the biggest challenge could be the time wasted on unnecessary transportation. In general, transportation waste is the unnecessary movement of parts, excessive handling of materials, or shuffling of inventory to get access to the correct components. Walking 200 feet to get parts 20 times a day adds up to more than 180 miles a year!

In hospital settings unnecessary transporting can cause additional fatigue, stress, and hinder alertness in nurses, while simultaneously increasing the unproductive use of nurses' time. What is better, walking back and forth or spending the time and energy at patients' bedside or other care tasks? In a 36-hospital time-motion study, a team from Ascension Health, Kaiser Permanente, and Purdue University found that nurses walked between 2.4 and 3.4 miles on a 10-h day shift, and 1.3 and 3.3 miles on a 10-h night shift. That means about 4 miles on a 12-h shift. These figures are consistent with other studies that found similar long walking time for nurses.[3]

UPS reported some great results when it leveraged GPS technology to minimize transportation time and cost through telematics. UPS piloted the technology on 1500 delivery trucks across the United States, testing the equipment in various geographies and climates. The company installed telematics in roughly 10,000 vehicles with plans to expand the program further. As part of the initiative, UPS installed GPS tracking equipment as well as sensors in key areas, such as brakes, seat belts, engine box, and on the exterior, and these devices helped UPS track the location of its delivery trucks as well as identify ways in which drivers could make adjustments and improve their performance based on collected data.

Two key areas the company focused on for improvement were idle time and route efficiency, including the use of left- versus right-hand turns. The problem with left-hand turns is that it forces drivers to stop and wait for oncoming traffic, it increases idle time resulting in more fuel, and it also increases the risk of head-on accidents. The study found savings of over a million gallons of fuel per year. When expanded, expectations are for even bigger savings in fuel, and also in terms of performance and safety.

In workplace settings, transportation waste is often caused by poor floor layout and large batch sizes. Parts need to be moved when processes are not close to each other. Batches usually come from large, multifunction machines that serve many product lines and these large machines are one of the causes of poor factory layout.

Shared machines can also cause transportation waste. This can often be observed in offices where printers, copiers, and fax machines are shared and people walk a long distance to retrieve documents and operate the machines. Having printers, copiers, and fax machines far from where the users are can create another problem because users may leave documents on one of these machines for long periods of time between the moment the document is printed and the time it is retrieved. If the documents printed contain proprietary or personal information, this can compromise the security of this information, and even put the organization in noncompliance with applicable laws and regulations.

HIPAA, the Health Insurance Portability and Accountability Act, provides regulations for the use and disclosure of an individual's health information. It defines how covered organizations can use individually identifiable health information or the PHI (Personal Health Information) and limits its use while requiring organizations to minimize the chance of its inappropriate disclosure. Best practices and other regulations are imposed by the Organization for Economic Cooperation and Development (OECD), the Federal Trade Commission (FTC) and the Privacy Act of 2005 in the United States, the Privacy Act of 1988 in Australia, the Personal Information Protection and Electronic Documents Act, in Canada, and many others around the world to protect Personally Identifiable Information (PII) or Sensitive Personal Information (SPI).[4]

Some useful questions include

- Are unnecessary documents being sent or received?
- Are unnecessary documents being printed or copied and filed?
- Are all approvals required and are these approvals performed by the most suitable person?
- Are documents that can be sent via interoffice mail or postal mail being hand delivered instead?

Eliminating transportation waste requires a focus on the flow of materials, machines, and people. When parts move directly from one process to an adjacent one, the distance traveled is minimal. Two ways to reduce transportation waste is to reduce batch sizes, focus on single-unit processing, and design work cells so they are product oriented.

Unnecessary Paperwork or Processing

The idea of the paperless workplace has been circulating since the 1970s. While the concept and vision of workplaces where paper is redundant for routine tasks like documentation, bookkeeping, and communication has a lot of merit, the reality is that we still use paper for a multitude of reasons. Even the widespread adoption of the personal computer did not eliminate the use of paper. However, improved computing tools, related software, and the demographic shift caused by younger people who are often less inclined to print out documents or use paper for record keeping are making this transition increasingly feasible and possible.

When we consider the use of paper in the workplace, we should aim for a work environment where the use of paper is eliminated or greatly reduced. This can be done by converting documents into digital form to save money by reducing the amount of paper and ink used, increase productivity, save space, and make documentation and information sharing easier. This can also help to keep personal information more secure because the information can be secured through access controls, and backups can protect the data from natural events, accidents, and other types of hazards that can damage physical records. Lastly, going paperless can also help the environment.

The concept can be applied to communications outside the office as well, since mailing documents back and forth causes delays and increases the risk of the information being lost or intercepted by others. Traditional offices have paper-based filing systems that may include folders, binders, filing cabinets, and shelves requiring maintenance, equipment, considerable space, and in general, are resource intensive. A paperless office, on the other hand, consists of a desk, chair, and computer or tablet using a relatively modest amount of digital storage and physical space. All of the information can be stored in digital form either directly or by initially scanning documents, then continuing any subsequent work electronically. Recent advances in speech recognition and synthesis facilitate the creation, storage, and use of information.

Paper records are expensive to create, maintain, and protect, but they are also difficult to sort, analyze, and inspect. They can be out of sync with electronic records due to version control gaps or lags, and if stored in multiple locations, they can be expensive to track, update, and retrieve. Some of the technologies available include

- E-forms (electronic form) to create, integrate, manage, and route forms and data with other processing systems
- Workflow applications to route information and documents
- Web servers to host the process, receive submitted data, store documents, and manage information

The proliferation of PDF to create, display, and share information has accelerated this transition for many organizations, while increasing storage capacity at an ever lower cost is also making this transition feasible and economical. Lastly, the increasingly widespread adoption of digital signatures allows users to digitally sign documents rather than relying exclusively on manual signatures on paper documents.

Unnecessary Inventory

Inventory consists of goods, parts, and materials on hand as input for other production items or sale to customers. The goal should always be to maintain a balance between the future demand and the inventory on hand. Excess products, materials, parts, and documentation not being processed immediately, or ahead of requirements, constitute unnecessary inventory. If the item, or information, is sitting idle, we should ask ourselves, why is it there?

All inventory requires the organization to incur carrying costs, and since parts and materials are purchased with organizational resources, it ties up needed capital until it is deemed needed again. If the items are never needed, damaged, or lost/stolen, they must be written off as excess and obsolete (E&O), only compounding the problem.

Some helpful questions include

- Are we purchasing items just in case they are needed?
- Do we have items stored in multiple locations creating duplication?
- Are items held as inventory for too long before they are actually used?

Excess Motion

Processes are designed to achieve a stated purpose and to deliver a product or service. Ideally, every process will require the minimum number of steps so that there are no superfluous activities performed since every action is paid for somehow, causes wear and tear on people and machines, and requires time to be completed. The combination of these elements means that additional steps are wasteful and should be eliminated whenever possible.

This waste of movement can occur because people or equipment is operating in a poorly designed work environment. In this case, the poor layout of the workspace is the culprit. Other causes are insufficient consideration of ergonomic issues and excess motion while searching for misplaced items during production.

This category often refers to individual motion, whereas the movement of products and materials is often captured under transportation above.

The waste attributed to individual motion can cause financial and time waste, but over long periods of time can also cause physical ailments such as soft-tissue injuries called repetitive motion disorders (RMDs). RMDs are muscular conditions resulting from repeated motions performed during normal work or daily activities, and include carpal tunnel syndrome, bursitis, tendonitis, and trigger finger, among others. These conditions are caused by too many uninterrupted repetitions of an activity or motion, unnatural or awkward motions such as twisting the arm or wrist, overexertion, incorrect posture, or muscle fatigue. These conditions are often characterized by numbness, tingling, weakness, visible swelling, and other problems in the affected area.[5]

Affected employees may need to take time off from work to reduce or stop the motions that cause symptoms, such as taking breaks to give the affected area time to rest, stretching and relaxation exercises, applying splints, and taking medications. In more severe cases, physical therapy, surgery, and disability time off of varying lengths may be necessary. Another potential cost is the increase in workers' compensation insurance premiums. Worker's compensation is a type of insurance providing wage replacement and medical benefits to employees who are injured while engaged in work activities.

All of this suggests that the costs can be substantial to the organization. Unfortunately, many processes are saturated with excess motion causing excessive costs, delays, and pain. In the long term, the impacts can be substantial. A common technique to show how damaging excess motion can be is spaghetti mapping. A spaghetti map, also known as spaghetti chart or spaghetti diagram, is a method of viewing data to visualize the flows through systems. The flows appear like noodles, which gives the method its name. It is a very effective tool to track routing through factories and other types of workplace to identify inefficiency within the flow of the system (Figure 7.1).

For example, note in Table 7.1 that while each individual activity does not represent a substantial distance in itself, collectively, the entire process requires 210 feet of transportation. Similarly, when looking at the time exerted, the amount is 2 h 40 min. By shortening the distance and/or time, we can calculate the efficiency gained.

Defects

Quality is a key differentiator among competing organizations. Even in the nonprofit sectors, stakeholders expect transactions to be performed without defects. Customers expect flawless products and services. Failure to do so has deleterious effect on the organization's reputation and

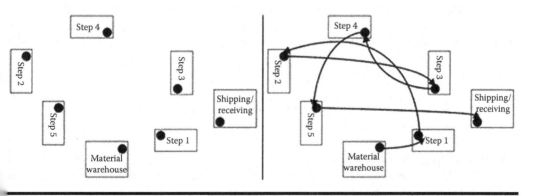

Figure 7.1   Spaghetti map.

Table 7.1 Distance and Time Analysis

Step Number	Distance (ft)	Time (min)
1	25	15
2	10	10
3	15	10
4	20	20
5	30	15
6	40	20
7	15	10
8	10	45
9	25	10
10	20	5
	210	160

has a negative impact on customers' propensity to buy. In general, customers are demanding higher quality while insisting on low prices.

The Merriam-Webster defines defects as "a physical problem that causes something to be less valuable, effective, healthy, etc., something that causes weakness or failure and an imperfection that impairs worth or utility."[6] When customers (whether individual or organizations, internal, or external) make a purchase, they expect the item(s) received to meet their expectations. When that is not the case, the almost immediate need to correct the deficiency is created instead.

Defects prompt the need to rework the item to correct the error made, so the organization must then spend additional resources to correct and deliver an acceptable product or service as initially expected.

The source or sources of defects vary. They can be caused by machine wear, human error due to lack of training, unclear specifications, or by more troublesome causes such as tampering or broken machines due to neglect or conflicting priorities. Defects are often considered to be related to the physical attributes of the product, and that is a reasonable assessment. But defects can be qualitative as well. The appearance, size, timeliness of delivery, and symmetry between the item and the price charged are considered defects when they don't match the customer's expectations.

Defects are caused by errors, often associated with making a mistake or producing something that has a flaw in it. Other definitions of error are

- An act or condition of ignorant or imprudent deviation from a code of behavior
- An act that through ignorance, deficiency, or accident departs from or fails to achieve what should be done
- Something produced by mistake
- The difference between an observed or calculated value and a true value, such as a variation in measurements, calculations, or observations of a quantity due to mistakes
- The amount of deviation from a standard or specification[7]

A consistent theme from the definition is that it is getting something different from what you expected. Given this set of cause and effect dynamics, it is incumbent on internal auditors to ascertain as best they can what the expectations are in the first place, then comparing the end result to that standard. In my experience, there are many workers in organizations who are not completely sure what exactly the customer wants, and only take the time to find out exactly what that is after it has been returned by the customer or there are repeated complaints. If the exact specifications are unknown or unclear, we should focus on finding that out first.

In some cases errors occur when an individual is distracted by something else or is confused about what should be done, how, and in what sequence. These are process specifications that internal auditors should also be attuned to and help organizations improve upon. A very important point, however, is the fact that customers usually don't care what the reason is for the discrepancy—they just want the product or service to be delivered error free, on time, and at a price they believe reflects the worth of the item. It is up to the organization to avoid defects in workmanship, delivery time, and value.

Some useful questions to help pinpoint the cause of the defect include

- Do we have any data entry errors?
- Do we have pricing, quoting, billing, or coding errors?
- Do we forward partial documentation?
- Do we ever lose files or records?
- Do we ever encounter incorrect information on a document?
- Is there a lack of standardized work?

Underutilized Employees

> Employees are a company's greatest asset—they're your competitive advantage. You want to attract and retain the best; provide them with encouragement, stimulus, and make them feel that they are an integral part of the company's mission.
>
> **Anne M. Mulcahy**[8]

"Our employees are our greatest asset" is a common expression made by organizations. Yet when the activities surrounding recruitment, selection, hiring, motivating, evaluating, training, developing, and promoting employees are put under the microscope, it becomes clearly evident that in most organizations there is a huge gap between that statement and management's actions.

Employees are a resource, yet they are not always treated as a resource, or even an asset. In some instances, employees are instructed to perform activities beneath their capabilities, or they are prevented from being employed in positions where their capabilities would be better utilized. Some managers do such a poor job with their employees, that they treat their workers as if they were a liability instead.

Glass ceilings and walls limit the placement of employees where they can maximize their contribution to the organization. Employees should be given every opportunity to work in, and get promoted to, the position where they can use their skills and talents to their full potential. This will increase satisfaction, engagement, and lead to satisfied customers who will return for repeat purchases while recommending the organization to others.

Business leaders should perform skill assessments in their organizations to identify the entity's present and future needs. Then collect information about the skills and competencies of their workers to perform a gap analysis. This information should inform their training and development programs, their hiring practices, outsourcing/cosourcing plans, and alignment of strategic plans with resource availability. Without such assessment, it is likely that the organization will be making uninformed decisions and raising the likelihood that their plans will fail.

Useful questions to assess the organization's optimization of their labor pool include

- Are employees in positions they were educated, trained, or certified to work in?
- Are employees hired for, placed in, and trained to perform the duties they are qualified for?
- Are employees developed so they can grow into future positions within the organization?
- Are employees having meetings without a clear agenda, objectives, or the necessary information to take action?
- Do employees help other areas when their work is slow or completed?
- Are employees trained to do more within the organization either on specific tasks or by serving on projects and committees?
- Are the business tools and equipment adequate for the job?
- Are delays in the implementation of computer systems delaying the employees' ability to get their work done?

Decreased productivity is also a byproduct of the decrease in employee morale caused by employees who feel that their skills are not being fully utilized. When employees' career prospects are hampered by subpar work that limits their skill development, or they feel that their efforts will not result in the rewards they expect, they are likely to lower their efforts. This waste of human potential within an organization is tragic, and organizations that allow this to happen are not only missing on the creativity, energy, and synergy that engaged workers can give their organizations, but they also waste some of the compensation given to these workers because they are not getting the maximum benefit in return.

When employees are fully engaged, both the employee and the organization gain. It is imperative that managers pay close attention to the morale level of their workforce and take consistent and assertive action to elevate it. Internal auditors should audit employee engagement as it influences productivity, retention, customer satisfaction, and the quality of internal controls.

Identifying, Assessing, and Preventing the Occurrence of Muda

The internal auditing cycle begins with the identification of the auditable universe in the organization. This audit universe consists of all auditable entities, accounts, programs, processes, and systems relevant to the organization. Western Economic Diversification Canada defines the audit universe as

> An audit universe represents the potential range of all audit activities and is comprised of a number of auditable entities. These entities generally include a range of programs, activities, functions, structures, and initiatives which collectively contribute to the achievement of the department's strategic objectives.[9]

This audit universe should be reviewed and updated periodically to assess the risk level of each of these items, which in turn informs the priority that should be given to each of them and to schedule the review. This review is often part of the annual risk assessment and internal auditors have traditionally done this as they develop their annual audit plans.

While these activities are widely accepted practice and carry many benefits, they also have some weaknesses. The main one is that by the time auditors perform the risk assessment, prepare the audit plan, and review processes, weaknesses may have already been present for a year or two, and losses or damages may have been accumulating for a long time. The realization that this sequence of events carries some inherent weaknesses can be explained by examining the dynamics associated with building computer systems.

Traditionally, internal auditors reviewed computer systems after their implementation. If the auditors identified issues and made recommendations for corrective action, the costs to make those corrections were significant. The estimated cost to fix defects postproduction is estimated to be at least 10 times the costs to detect and fix preproduction.[10] As a result, internal auditors have begun reviewing computer system development projects during their construction. This way, issues can be identified promptly and timelier recommendations are made for immediate correction.

However, this approach still has some weaknesses because the observations made by auditors, such as poor workmanship, lack of embedded controls, cost overruns, unqualified programmers, and excessive change orders and so on, occur after the organization has already entered into contractual agreements with vendors and consultants. At this point, it is difficult to correct these problems because the project is ongoing and the contracts are in effect. Obtaining needed documentation to perform the audit can be very difficult if the contract does not provide an avenue for these reviews. Declaring a breach of contract if the abuse is excessive, or if the workmanship is severely substandard, is often a complicated and expensive recourse, because litigation can be expensive and the entire project may stop. Furthermore, the relationship between the parties involved can be severely strained at that point. If the source of the problem is the poor selection of software consultants, they have already been hired. Another common issue is the usage of inadequate software for the job as a result of conflict of interest during the software selection.

As a result, internal auditors are now performing audits at the beginning of the entire cycle. This way auditors can check the system development life cycle, check the feasibility studies, planning documents, bidding and contracting process, vendor selection procedures, and the process to embed internal controls in the design. Other areas of focus include budget allocation and payment processing procedures, right to audit, and periodic reporting mechanisms.

This approach, which is now yielding great results in many organizations is illustrative of the approach more broadly being applied throughout the business. By identifying, assessing, and preventing the occurrence of business risks, internal auditors can add more value to the business and not only detect anomalies, but actually help management prevent them. This process is more in line with quality assurance (QA), which focuses on the ability of a process to produce or deliver a quality product or service. It attempts to prevent issues by identifying anomalies and improving a process until it can produce a quality deliverable. This approach is strategic. It looks at the entire system as a living organism, and focuses on building quality as an ongoing goal. The goal is to catch errors before they occur.

QA is different and an enhancement from the traditional approach embraced by auditors in the past. This after-the-fact traditionalist approach can be described as being more in line with quality control (QC). QC is designed to detect problems with a product or service through inspections. It is tactical and adds value by identifying problems before they get to the customers, but this approach identifies the problems a bit late in the cycle—after production.

In general, we can think of QA as occurring during production (i.e., real time), while QC takes place after the production of the goods or services. QA ensures that there will be quality during production while QC controls the execution to make sure that there was quality. One is future oriented and prospective. The other focuses on the past and is retrospective.

I believe there will always be a need for auditors to engage in postmortem reviews and assess activities after their performance, but the benefits of helping management design better processes and anticipate anomalies is unmistakable. Some may be concerned that this would impair the auditors' judgment and limit their independence and objectivity. This doesn't have to occur. Internal auditors need to clarify their role as advisors, issue communications identifying weaknesses in that context, and ensure management takes ownership for the recommendations, if any are made. It is management's prerogative to accept or decline adopting the recommendations made, but from a risk identification and management perspective, advising management to avoid potential pitfalls is consistent with the auditor's responsibilities.

The Institute of Internal Auditors' International Standards for the Professional Practice of Internal Auditing (*Standards*) does not specify if reviews should be prospective or retrospective. In fact, it states

The internal audit activity must evaluate risk exposures relating to the organization's governance, operations, and information systems regarding the

- Achievement of the organization's strategic objectives
- Reliability and integrity of financial and operational information
- Effectiveness and efficiency of operations and programs
- Safeguarding of assets
- Compliance with laws, regulations, policies, procedures, and contracts (Standard 2120.A1)

With this in mind, internal auditors can examine these Eight Areas of Waste from a prospective perspective and anticipate their occurrence and their impact on the organization. Table 7.2 provides an overview of how they can help auditors meet this standard.

Internal auditors can play an important role helping to avoid the Eight Areas of Waste by searching for their occurrence during audit and consulting projects. These areas of waste can occur prospectively due to the poor design of programs and processes, while activities are underway, or after the work has been performed and the auditor reviews the transactions, retrospectively. In any case, by searching for these problem areas, internal auditors can help the organization operate more efficiency and be more likely to achieve its financial and operational objectives.

Summary

Managers are responsible for maximizing stakeholder value and displaying prudence in the use of the resources provided to pursue the organization's mission. Waste represents the erosion of stakeholder value and both managers and employees should work diligently to minimize it.

The Eight Areas of Waste Model provides a simple, concise, and practical tool to identify common areas of waste, the practices that cause them, and the items that when present show that waste is being generated. This has financial implications. This has time utilization implications. This has ecological implications. This has health and safety implications.

Table 7.2   Using the Eight Areas of Waste during Internal Audits

Standard	Areas of Waste
Achievement of the organization's strategic objectives	Any of the Eight Areas of Waste occurring en masse over extended periods of time can limit the organization's ability to achieve its expansion goals, profitability objectives, and accomplishment of its mission.
Reliability and integrity of financial and operational information	Excessive waiting during the financial reporting cycle can delay the timely publication of financial reports. Defects in accounting transactions, or notes to the financial statements can result in costly restatements and significant decreases in stock price.
Effectiveness and efficiency of operations and programs	Any of the Eight Areas of Waste will limit the organization's effectiveness and efficiency. By eroding the efficiency of operations, they can collectively limit the ability to achieve organizational objectives.
Safeguarding of assets	Misusing limited financial resources and increasing the need for operating capital due to waste is contrary to the concept of safeguarding assets. Unskilled workers are more likely to be inefficient in their transportation planning, motion assessment, and inventory management, and cause more defects to occur. Furthermore, by not having the skills to perform their duties, they may engage in waiting as they try to figure out how to get the work done.
Compliance with laws, regulations, policies, procedures, and contracts	There are many ways that noncompliance can occur, based on specific laws, regulations and internal expectations. Environmental laws frown upon excessive waste, which is caused by overproduction and defects. Compliance with clean air regulations are hindered by idling vehicles, excessive transport, and vehicles carrying heavier loads due to overproduction and inventory accumulation. Workplace safety laws, and in-house ergonomics expectations would be compromised through excessive motion.

To the extent that these issues can be identified, resolved, and mechanisms put in place to prevent their recurrence, stakeholders within, and outside the organization will enjoy the benefits.

Chapter 8 provides an overview of QC concepts and practices, and shows how internal auditors can benefit from increasing their base of knowledge in this field. Whether it is reducing the number of errors, increasing consistency in existing processes, or reducing the variability in the results obtained, internal auditors can help organizations excel during their day to day operations by incorporating these principles, identifying weaknesses, and making useful and pragmatic recommendations.

QUESTIONS

1. How can overproduction be minimized?
2. Describe three reasons why waiting is damaging to organizations?
3. How is transporting a waste? Provide an example to support your answer.
4. How can organizations avoid, or at least minimize, unnecessary paperwork and processing?
5. If inventory is an asset, why is it considered a waste?
6. Explain how you can identify excess motion during an operational audit.
7. Describe the impact of defects on organizational success from an internal and external (e.g., competitive) perspective.
8. Provide three recommendations to minimize the presence of underutilized employees.
9. How can the Eight Areas of Waste be used to build an operational audit work program?
10. Show how a process can have more than one of the Eight Areas of Waste present simultaneously.

Notes

1 See http://www.brainyquote.com/quotes/quotes/j/johnadams134175.html?src=t_wishes
2 See http://www.merriam-webster.com/dictionary/waste
3 To read the full report, see http://www.healthcaredesignmagazine.com/article/designing-smart
4 For more information about HIPAA, other regulations and recommendations for protecting personal information, see http://whatishipaa.org/, http://www.oecd.org/sti/ieconomy/informationsecurityandprivacy.htm and https://www.ftc.gov/news-events/media-resources/protecting-consumer-privacy
5 For additional information about these conditions, see http://www.ninds.nih.gov/disorders/repetitive_motion/repetitive_motion.htm and http://www.webmd.com/pain-management/carpal-tunnel/carpal-tunnel-syndrome-topic-overview
6 See http://www.merriam-webster.com/dictionary/defect
7 See http://www.merriam-webster.com/dictionary/error
8 See http://www.brainyquote.com/quotes/quotes/a/annemmulc424886.html?src=t_greatest_asset
9 See http://www.wd.gc.ca/eng/12853.asp
10 Figure provided by Debra Mallette based on her study of writings of Gerald Weinberg, Tom DeMarco, Robert B. Grady, Lawrence Putnam and Capers Jones. See http://www.isaca.org/Groups/Professional-English/governance-of-enterprise-it/Pages/ViewDiscussion.aspx?PostID=18#comments

Chapter 8

Quality Control

Operating flawlessly is the key goal of quality improvement programs.

Introduction

Internal auditors are in the quality business. They evaluate the design of processes to determine if the structure is conducive to success. They also evaluate how processes are functioning to determine if they are operating as intended. In either case, the focus is the achievement of objectives, consistent execution with minimal errors, minimal use of input given production levels, and stability over time so the process is sustainable. With these objectives in mind, QC concepts and practices provide a solid foundation to build upon.

There are several methodologies in place, and some of their underlying tools, techniques, and methodologies were introduced in Chapters 6 and 7. In this chapter, we examine some of the methodologies that bring these elements together and facilitate the creation of high-quality, high-performing organizations.

By the time we close this chapter, the reader should be familiar with these principles, but more importantly, have a better sense about the next phase in QC. QA is arguably the desired destination. Upon arrival, an environment will be created that depends less on inspection and detection at the end of the production cycle, and more on building quality from the beginning through better design and immediate correction of deviations.

Understanding Assertions and Using Quality Improvement Methodologies

Internal auditors are in the quality business even though we don't talk about our role in those terms. When we take a close look at what we do, it becomes apparent that our focus for decades has centered on the examination of programs and processes to determine if transactions are executed according to certain parameters.

We can usually summarize our transaction testing by asking: Were all (i.e., completeness) transactions processed according to the requestor's instructions (i.e., accurately) and were these transactions consistent with necessary business purposes (i.e., approved)? We can add other criteria in the form of financial statement assertions commonly used for financial reporting. Assertions are affirmations or declarations; they are statements of fact regarding the financial activities of the organization. While these are often associated with financial audits, the concepts and goals of most of them are equally relevant during operational audits.

There are three main categories related to transactions, balances, and presentation assertions.

1. Transactions and events

   Occurrence: The business transactions recorded actually took place.

   Completeness: All business events and their related transactions that should have been recorded were recorded.

   Accuracy: The transactions were recorded in the corresponding ledgers at their full amounts without errors.

   Cutoff: The transactions were recorded in the appropriate accounting period; neither early nor late.

   Classification: The transactions were recorded in the appropriate general ledger accounts.

2. Accounts balances

   Existence: Assets, liabilities, and equity balances exist as shown.

   Rights and Obligations: The organization has rights to the assets it owns and is obligated as indicated in the outstanding liabilities reported.

   Completeness: All reported asset, liability, and equity balances that should have been recorded were recorded.

   Valuation: Asset, liability, and equity balances are valued and recorded at the proper valuation, and all adjustments were recorded appropriately.

3. Presentation and disclosure

   Occurrence: The reported transactions and disclosures occurred.

   Rights and Obligations: The transactions and disclosures are related to the organization.

   Completeness: All disclosures that should be disclosed were disclosed in the financial statements.

   Classification and Understandability: Financial statements are clear, understandable, and present all necessary information appropriately.

   Accuracy and valuation: All relevant information is disclosed at the appropriate amounts and reflects the proper value.[1]

While there is some duplication in the assertions across the three types, this occurs because each type is intended for a different financial statement or purpose. Transactions and events relate to the income statement, account balances relate to the balance sheet, and presentation and disclosure relate to the disclosures that accompany the financial statements.

The reader will notice that when performing an operational audit of a government or research program, a construction project or how an educational institution operates, most of these assertions apply. For example, occurrence, accuracy, completeness, classification, and valuation, to name a few, are very important considerations and many organizations have had serious problems by failing to meet these expectations. Government contracts, donor requirements, and foundations often dictate adherence to strict performance, effectiveness, and financial record-keeping guidelines. Companies that evaluate and rate charities, such as Charity Navigator, Charity Watch, and the BBB Wise Giving Alliance, also depend on the reliability of performance and financial information. So the assertions listed above are relevant beyond financial audits (Table 8.1).

When we broaden our viewpoint and perform operational reviews, the objectives and criteria tested to determine if the program or process is operating well also require an examination of the 8 Es: Economy, Efficiency, Effectiveness, Ethics, Equity, Ecology, Excellence, and Emotion.

Economy: The program or process obtains resources at the optimal value to the organization. This is accomplished through the display of care in the procurement of financial, human, or material inputs. Frugality and thrift are important in the acquisition and use of resources, but this should not be confused with being cheap and focusing disproportionately on price. Total value should be the goal, and for many items, that means looking beyond price and including consideration of quality, warranty protection, and return policy, among others. Organizations should reuse what they can, and when they must make purchases, only buy what they need according to the principles of JIT procurement, manufacturing, and production. This means purchasing items as close as possible to when the item will be placed in productive use.

Efficiency: The program or process operates in such a way that it achieves maximum productivity with the lowest possible wasted effort, expense, or time. Operating efficiently suggests that goods and services are produced without wasting time, energy, or materials. While this concept is sometimes deeply embedded in manufacturing activities showing a great deal of oversight and monitoring, that is usually less often observed in service environments. With the exception of call centers, it is quite common for support departments to operate with few scientific and quantitative measures in place to assess efficiency. Internal auditors can help management optimize processes and systems by eliminating all forms of waste (e.g., materials, time, and energy) and other resources above what is needed to generate value for the customer. By finding ways to do things better, organizations can improve their productivity and maximize the use of available resources.

Table 8.1 Management Assertions

Assertion	Meaning
Validity	The transaction exists and the amount is not overstated
Completeness	All transactions were recorded without omissions
Cutoff	Transactions were recorded in the corresponding period
Valuation	Balances are valued accurately and the amount is neither over nor short
Recording	Transactions are recorded at the proper amount
Presentation	Amounts are presented with the corresponding disclosures
Existence	Assets and liabilities exist

To achieve this optimization, the focus needs to be on the integrated systems of people, materials, machines, money, knowledge, energy, and information. When all of these elements are applied simultaneously, the process, system, or organization will maximize its production while minimizing its need for inputs.

A great deal of efficiency can be achieved by eliminating waste and rework. Sustainable efficiency gains are achieved through continuous assessment, monitoring and controlling of resources, modifying operating procedures, and when necessary, redesigning operations related to the production of goods and services. Furthermore, it also requires examining job design and workplace layout.

> *Effectiveness*: The program or process achieves or exceeds its objectives. Effectiveness pertains to the achievement of desired results, so if the program or process under review does not have clearly defined objectives, it is essentially impossible to assess effectiveness other than anecdotally. During the planning phase, internal auditors must consider the objectives of the activity being reviewed and the means by which the activity controls its performance (Standard 2201). Without clearly defined goals, it is very difficult, if not impossible, for the auditor to define the criteria that will be used as the basis for verifying the adequacy of the performance. So while this "E" relates to effectiveness and the basis for that assessment, the lack of clear objectives has wider implications for the entire audit and the possible lack of a clear sense of mission within the unit being reviewed.
>
> *Ethics*: The operation acts in accordance with acceptable moral principles that govern the organization's behavior. The rules of behavior must be outlined in policy documents and supported by the organization's culture and reinforcement mechanisms, such as performance reviews and compensation programs. The lack of clarity and enforcement of ethical standards within the organization can have a very detrimental impact on the organization and its effects can extend from low level skimming and theft, to payroll hours manipulation, expense report falsification, lying to customers and vendors, and financial reporting misstatements. Internal auditors must assess and make appropriate recommendations for improving the governance process in the promotion of "appropriate ethics and values within the organization" (Standard 2110), and "evaluate the design, implementation, and effectiveness of the organization's ethics-related objectives, programs, and activities" (Standard 2110.A1).
>
> *Equity*: The program or operation acts in ways consistent with expectations of equality, and fairness when dealing with individuals or other organizations. Internal auditors generally default to compliance considerations when examining matters related to equity. In terms of people, there are many laws protecting individuals against discrimination and avoiding both disparate treatments through overt discriminatory motives and behavior, as well as the adverse impacts caused by employer practices. US Federal laws exist protecting individuals against discrimination on the basis of race, color, religion, national origin, age, sex, pregnancy, citizenship, familial status, disability, veteran status, and genetic information. Individual states also create protected classes. At an organizational level, equity obliges the organization to treat vendors fairly during the selection process and while engaged in commercial activities.

So while key concerns here are the fines and penalties that can be levied against the organization, it can also be subject to individual or class action lawsuits. However, the problems can also have other implications. For example, if favoritism becomes a manner of selecting individuals for promotion rather than merit, the best candidates with the qualifications and skill will be disqualified. In this case, the organization is overpaying for the lower benefits that the poorly selected individual provides. In addition, there is a negative impact on employee motivation when it becomes apparent that merit is not the determining factor and the reward (i.e., promotions) is not awarded based on effort, contributions, and outcomes, so why bother working hard? Why stay here? This rationalization is the precursor to apathy, decrease in employee commitment, and eventually higher turnover.

A similar problem is evident when conflicts of interest result in the selection of unsuitable providers. Poor vendor selection due to favoritism and the pursuit of personal gain cause uneconomic cash flows such as kickbacks, bribes, and higher costs that are charged to the harmed organization.

> *Ecology*: The operation's activities protect and promote protection of the natural environment. The main driver for ecological stewardship tends to be compliance due to laws and regulations that limit the environmental impact of business activities, such as the Clean Air and Clean Water Acts, waste management and contaminant cleanup, chemical safety and resource utilization regulations. Similar to ethics considerations, for a large number of managers the assessment of their responsibilities begins and ends with compliance with laws and regulations. More recently, however, ecological considerations have in many ways been driven by economic opportunities where developing products that are made from environmentally responsible harvesting practices garner the interest of so motivated consumers. Lastly, altruism sometimes drives business decisions to emphasize and adhere to environmental practices. The 3Rs are a very helpful formula to improve organizational stewardship:
>
> *Reduce*: Use fewer resources in the first place. Reduce the amount of inputs by cutting back from what is being used presently. This has a direct relationship to the concept of economy discussed previously, so organizations can purchase energy efficient, durable items and consume less water, fuel, and electricity.
>
> *Reuse*: Before recycling or disposing of items, consider repurposing the item so its useful life can be extended. Upgrading computers, reselling, or donating vehicles and cellphones can help reduce costs or realize tax benefits. In addition to reducing the time and amount of new purchases, it avoids having old resources enter the waste stream and incurring the resulting disposal costs.
>
> *Recycle*: While this is the most recognizable of the 3Rs, it is the third in order of environmental protection because it requires the use of resources, such as water, electricity, fuel to collect, transport, process, and redistribute the reprocessed items.

Organizations can save energy to save money by reducing the temperature on thermostats in the winter and raising it a few degrees in the summer, installing low energy lights, installing motion-sensitive on–off switches, reducing the amount of water, and recycling the water used in maintenance facilities, installing faucet aerators, planting drought-tolerant vegetation in green spaces to minimize the need to water the plants, purchase locally grown produce for company cafeterias, give employees reusable water bottles, and use water filters for employees' water rather than bottled water.[2]

Companies can also build LEED (Leadership in Energy & Environmental Design) certified green buildings. These standards affect how buildings are designed, built, maintained, and operated. It addresses the materials used, water usage, energy generation, and consumption, as well as the location of the building in relation to transportation options. By using better materials and optimizing the use of natural heat, light, ventilation, and open space, occupants enjoy better working and living environments.[3]

Excellence: The program and related activities adhere to the highest possible degree of quality and seeks near-zero error rates as much as reasonably possible. A cultural attribute of high-performance companies is that they have an orientation toward excellence in what they do. This is influenced by setting performance expectations and having monitoring mechanisms in place. But excellence is more than that; it is a state of mind that compels workers to do things right the first time. It should be a core value of every individual and organization, supported by effective training and development. It is also the result of employees having high motivation and feeling personally invested in the organization's future (Table 8.2).

Financial statement assertions are made as of the last day of the organization's fiscal year, and are made retrospectively. This means that as of the last day of the fiscal year, the balance sheet shows the condition of the organization in all material respects and its status is reflected accurately as it pertains to assets, liabilities, and equity. All of these Es should be achieved consistently.

On that same last day of the fiscal year, the statement of cash flows and the income statement reflect in all material respects the transactions that took place during the entire fiscal year, and all relevant amounts are classified correctly as shown on the reports. All of these assertions related to the financial statements pertain to a date in the past.

Operational objectives (we don't refer to them as assertions, since that term is reserved for financial statements) are made with a broader, more balanced viewpoint: retrospectively as relates to past activities to report on past practices, and prospectively, related to the future implications of these practices. When these operational goals are seen from that perspective, it becomes apparent that the auditor is evaluating the program or process' ability to execute flawlessly in the future. Operating flawlessly is the key goal of quality improvement programs.

Table 8.2   The 8 Es

Economy
Efficiency
Effectiveness
Ethics
Equity
Ecology
Excellence
Emotion

The Link between Process Weaknesses and Internal Control

Many people think of internal controls as "getting in the way" and impeding work from getting done. The reality is quite the opposite. Unchecked risks can derail the achievement of objectives. So, by mitigating the likelihood and or impact of these negative events, objectives are actually more likely to be achieved.

Since there is such a strong link between operational results and financial health, internal auditors should remember that as per the definition of internal auditing, the objective is to help our clients achieve their objectives. This process, which is very similar to the process improvement process and consists of the following:

- Where do we want to go?
- Where are we now?
- How do we get to where we want to be?
- How do we know if we are making progress?

This process can be aligned with the organization's business activities as shown in Figure 8.1.

COSO states that "internal control is a process effected by an entity's board of directors, management, and other personnel, designed to provide reasonable assurance regarding the achievement of objectives relating to operations, reporting, and compliance."[4]

These internal controls are "geared to the achievement of objectives, it consists of tasks and activities, and adaptable to the entity structure, from the entire entity, to its operating units and business processes." Internal controls enable the achievement of operational objectives by helping to mitigate the risks that can jeopardize the achievement of those objectives. It is unfortunate, however, that many people think of internal controls as "getting in the way" and impeding work from getting done. The reality is quite the opposite. Unchecked risks can derail the achievement of objectives. So, by mitigating the likelihood and or impact of these negative events, objectives are actually more likely to be achieved.

Another important point is that processes are a series of actions taken toward a purpose. Without an end, processes don't have any meaning, they become "busy work" characterized by erratic actions that consume time, financial, and material resources, and wear out equipment unnecessarily. Employees should engage in activities within a process because the series of actions and steps will be orchestrated so as to achieve a goal.

Internal controls, then, support existing processes by helping to protect the organization against risks that threaten the achievement of objectives. Formally documenting, establishing responsibility and accountability to perform these activities, and ideally linking the performance of these controls to the organization's rewards mechanism, will go a long way toward making sure that negative events are held in check.

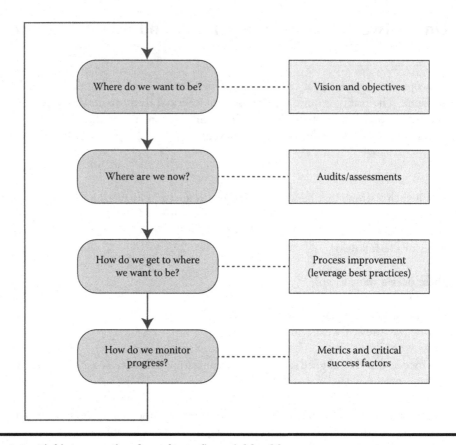

Figure 8.1 Linking operational results to financial health.

Six Sigma and Lean Six Sigma

Six Sigma is a process improvement methodology designed to make sure that a process will deliver its output within a prescribed tolerance range. It is a business and process improvement methodology used to improve processes by using statistical analysis to identify the sources of error and determine the best way to eliminate them. It is a collection of management tools and methodologies to reduce variation, errors, and increase the speed of execution, while focusing on eliminating mistakes, rework, and waste.

Bill Smith introduced Six Sigma at Motorola in 1986 and Jack Welch further cemented the program by introducing it, promoting it, and making it a key aspect of his business strategy at General Electric in 1995. De Feo and Barnard indicate that by the late 1990s about two-thirds of Fortune 500 companies had Six Sigma initiatives in place.

Mike Harry and Richard Schoeder define Six Sigma as

> ... a business process that allows companies to drastically improve their bottom line by designing and monitoring every day business activities in ways that minimize waste and resources while increasing satisfaction.

Table 8.3   Parts Per Million Out of Specification for Each Sigma Level

Sigma	PPM Out of Specification	%Out of Specification
1σ	690,000	69
2σ	308,537	30.8537
3σ	66,807	6.6807
4σ	6210	0.621
5σ	233	0.0233
6σ	3.4	0.00034

The term Six Sigma is based on statistical modeling, whereby the maturity, stability, and conformance with expected accuracy yields is described by a sigma rating (Table 8.3). This yield relates to the percentage of total production that is defect-free. The ratings are as follows.

PPM relates to the number of parts per million out of specification. In other words, it represents the number of defects per million opportunities (DPMO). Therefore, the table shows that at Six Sigma, a process has 3.4 DPMO or conversely, 99.99966% of all opportunities to produce are statistically expected to be free of defects.

To illustrate the high-quality Six Sigma represents, let's consider a process where the auditor selected a random sample of 50 transactions representative of the population for testing. Five of the 50 transactions tested are found to have a reportable condition, so there is a 10% error rate. By extrapolation that means we there to be 100,000 defects per million, which puts the sigma level between 2.7 and 2.8 sigma. Quite an underperforming process!

Based on this information, it is evident that a Six Sigma process is one where it is performing at near zero error rates. It is important to note, however, that given the limited resources available in many organizations that can be allocated to quality improvement, it could become prohibitively expensive to achieve precision at the Six Sigma level. Furthermore, is it really necessary? If the consequence of a slightly higher error rate is tolerable, cost-benefit considerations would make it unnecessary, or outright unwise to spend those limited resources in that way. This does not constitute a license to accept mediocrity. It simply means that organizations must allocate limited resources and this must be done judiciously based on cost-benefit considerations. Despite this, organizations should create a general culture and related operating practices where the pursuit of excellence and perfection is constant and efforts are made in the most cost-effective and pragmatic way possible to reduce error rates. So management should determine an appropriate sigma level for their most important processes and work toward achieving it.

It is important to note that Six Sigma is to be used to further the organization's goals and objectives and is a means to an end, not an end onto itself. The purpose is to increase the effectiveness of the organization, by identifying and removing the causes of defects. The result is better functioning processes that are more efficient and have near zero errors, so quality improves.

There is a widely held misconception that Six Sigma is only applicable to manufacturing organizations. That is incorrect. Over the years, Six Sigma has also been applied to service organizations with positive results. The reason is that the tools and techniques are applicable in any environment where processing activities are performed. Whether it is manufacturing or other business processes, both have characteristics that can be quantified, measured, analyzed, and improved upon. These characteristics can and should be controlled as well to improve consistency and predictability.

These attributes are consistent with the objectives of other QC methodologies such as total quality management, total quality control and continuous quality improvement (CQI). All of them embrace the concept of Kaizen, which is a Japanese business philosophy focused on continuous improvement of working practices.

Six Sigma relies heavily on statistical methods, but it also creates an infrastructure of subject matter experts who are experts on the methodology and tools. Each project follows a defined sequence of phases and steps that aim to reduce errors, improve customer satisfaction, reduce cycle time, reduce pollution, or minimize rework.

This is achieved through efficiency and near zero mistakes, based on some guiding principles:

- Good processes generate good results
- It is imperative to go see for yourself to fully understand the current situation
- Speak with data, manage by facts
- Take action to contain and correct the root cause of problems
- Work as a team
- Quality is everyone 's business[5]

An important feature of CQI is that excellence is the result of many small changes and improvements accumulated over time. Embedding and sustaining quality improvement requires strong and active commitment from top management to allocate needed resources for process improvement projects, to hire qualified personnel capable of conducting these projects, training as many people as possible and providing career opportunities for those certified in this methodology. Management leadership, support, and promotion are key to ensure the sustainability of the program and follow-through by company employees. The focus on data and verifiable results should form the basis for decision-making. This should replace mere intuition, guesswork, and assumptions as the basis for making decisions.

The most common methodology in Six Sigma is DMAIC (Table 8.4).

D—Define the current process, system, high-level project goals and capture details about customer requirements and expectations (i.e., the voice of the customer)
M—Measure key aspects of the current process, collect relevant data, and determine the capability of the process in its current state (i.e., the "as-is" process capability).

Table 8.4   DMAIC Project Methodology

D: Define
M: Measure
A: Analyze
I: Improve
C: Control

A—Analyze the data to investigate and verify cause-and-effect relationships. Determine what the relationships are. Search for the root cause of the defect under investigation.

I—Improve the current process based on the data analysis performed. Use techniques such as design of experiments, Poka Yoke (i.e., mistake proofing), training, update procedures documentation, and apply change management procedures to create an improved process. Consider the use of pilot programs during the rollout and to evaluate the new process capability.

C—Control the future state process to ensure that any deviations from the performance targets are corrected before they become defects. Implement control systems to monitor performance, such as statistical process control and continuous monitoring procedures. Note that in Six Sigma, the word "control" has a slightly different meaning. While internal auditors associate the word with practices that reduce the likelihood and/or impact of risks, in Six Sigma it relates to the activities that would indicate that the process is performing as defined, or not. The activities help to mitigate negative outcomes, but they go further because the entire phase is designed to prevent the process from reverting to the initial state where the Six Sigma team intervention was required in the first place.

In general, the DMAIC methodology is used for existing processes, while DMADV (DFSS) is used when building a new or highly modified process or product (Table 8.5).

D—Define design goals that are consistent with customer needs and wants and verify that these are aligned with the organization's strategy.

M—Measure and identify those characteristics that are critical to quality for the customer, measure product performance capabilities, measure production process capability, and identify and measure risks.

A—Analyze available information to develop and design alternatives.

D—Design an improved alternative to the existing product or process that is most appropriate given the analysis performed by optimizing the design. Plan for design verification and run simulations if possible.

V—Verify that the design meets customer and business requirements, set up pilot runs, implement the production process, and transition the process/product to process owners.

Table 8.5   DMADV Project Methodology—DFSS (Design for Six Sigma)

D: Define
M: Measure
A: Analyze
D: Design
V: Verify

A key objective of Six Sigma is minimizing variability. Variability refers to the degree to which results differ from what was expected. It has to do with how much results can vary or change. This is generally not a desirable outcome for a process, since predictability and consistency of results is better. In fact, identifying and communicating variability is the key concept driving the formulation of internal audit findings: The difference between the performance criteria of a program or process and the condition the auditors identified through audit techniques while performing a review. Hence, the goal of Six Sigma and the goal of internal auditors to report deviations from the expected practice are similar. At a consultative level, internal auditors are tasked with identifying opportunities to improve business processes, and here again, Six Sigma can help internal auditors.[6]

ISO 9000 and ISO 31000

According to the ISO, the ISO 9000 family of standards address various aspects of quality management. This is only one set of the more than 20,500 international standards the organization has published and that are widely embraced around the world. In fact, with members in 162 countries and 3368 technical bodies, ISO provides a great deal of guidance on almost all aspects of technology and manufacturing. The guidance and tools available are helpful for companies and organizations who want to ensure that their products and services meet customers' requirements, and that quality is improved consistently.

Standards in the ISO 9000 family include

- ISO 9001:2015—It sets the requirements of a quality management system
- ISO 9000:2015—Addresses the fundamental concepts and language
- ISO 9004:2009—Focuses on how to make a quality management system more efficient and effective
- ISO 19011:2011—Provides guidance on internal and external audits of quality management systems

ISO 9001:2015 establishes the criteria for a quality management system and it can be used by any organization regardless of its size or field of activity. According to the ISO website,[7] there are over a million organizations in over 170 countries that are ISO 9001 certified.

This standard is based on seven quality management principles (Table 8.6), namely:

1. *Customer focus*: The primary objective of any organizational activity should be to meet or exceed customer requirements and expectations. Organizations exist because of their customers, so they must identify, attract, retain, and please their customers. Organizations that understand this achieve higher levels of customer satisfaction, loyalty, repeat business, increased sales, and bigger market share.

   To accomplish this, organizations must link their objectives to their customers' expectations, communicate customer needs throughout the organization, make sure that their entire product or service life-cycles are aligned with these needs, and monitor customer satisfaction.

2. *Leadership*: Leaders establish unity of purpose, set the direction for the organization, create the conditions, and promote the practices that result in meeting the organization's quality objectives. Leaders align the organization's strategies with the organizational structure, establish policies, build processes, and assign resources effectively to achieve its mission.

Table 8.6 ISO Seven Quality Management Principles

1. Customer focus
2. Leadership
3. Engagement of people
4. Process approach
5. Improvement
6. Evidence-based decision-making
7. Relationship management

Effective leadership results in higher efficiency and effectiveness, better coordination of organizational activities, and better communications, and lead by example. This is achieved by issuing clear, constant, and consistent messages, promoting the adoption of shared values, establishing a trusting work environment and making sure that employees have the resources, authority, and training to get their work done.

3. *Engagement of people*: Knowledgeable, engaged, and empowered workers are essential for the creation and delivery of value to stakeholders. Competence is fundamental to the effective functioning of any organization. But beyond competence, employees at all levels must be involved and respected.

   It is not enough to establish quality objectives; employees must understand them and have the skills to work toward achieving them. This will release creativity, improve collaboration, encourage open communication and discussion, knowledge sharing, and facilitate self-evaluation.

4. *Process approach*: When activities are designed, understood, and managed as part of a coherent integrated system, it is more likely that the organization will achieve consistent, predictable results. The efficient allocation and use of resources, breaking down silos, and understanding process limitations will enable process owners and those working within the processes themselves to better anticipate problem areas, acquire and share critical information, and manage the risks that can hinder productivity. Well-developed, integrated and managed processes are better equipped to deliver according to established expectations and meet quality standards.

   Organizations must manage more than outputs. They must also focus on the process capacity, scalability, flexibility, and consistency. Too many organizations find out the hard way that error rates, employee turnover, and delivery times are severely hampered because processes cannot handle change.

5. *Improvement*: Winning organizations embrace the concept of continuous improvement. Inertia can be dangerous in today's world, so organizations must constantly examine how they are structured and operating, identify, and react promptly and effectively to both internal and external changes. In fact, by focusing on early identification of changes and applying root-cause analysis to understand the triggers of these changes, organizations can anticipate and react appropriately to changing conditions.

While learning is generally viewed as forward-looking, a keen understanding of past developments can help the organization avoid repeating past mistakes or those of others. Lastly, innovation is the key for sustained success, so a concerted effort is required to learn, train, monitor, and share lessons learned so that every day can be better than the previous one.

6. *Evidence-based decision-making*. Desired results are more likely to be achieved when decisions are data driven and based on the careful analysis of information. When cause and effect relationships are understood, the organization will be more likely to make better decisions. Excessive subjectivity and the inability to justify decision-making often results in opinion-based decisions, politicized practices, and a general inability to demonstrate the effectiveness of decisions.

   Organizations are increasingly moving toward metrics-driven performance evaluations, sharing needed information with a wider pool of relevant individuals, making sure that data is accurate, reliable, secure, and ensuring that employees have the knowledge and skill to collect, analyze, and interpret data.

7. *Relationship management*. For long-term success, organizations must manage their relationships with their stakeholders, especially suppliers. Organizations don't operate in a vacuum, and as such, they must manage the impact that their stakeholders have on them. Opportunities and threats may arise from the pool of stakeholders, quality-related risks may be caused by vendors, shipping companies, or distributors. In general, vendor problems can disrupt the organization's supply chain.

Organizations should identify their internal/external, economic/noneconomic stakeholders and make sure that the diverse interests, needs, and expectations of their investors, suppliers, lenders, employees, customers, governments, and others are addressed. Since sustainable success cannot be achieved by merely focusing on short-term results, organizations must balance both sets of priorities while building collaborative relationships to ensure the reliable supply of goods and services from source to final user.

Using ISO 9001:2015 helps ensure that customers get consistent, good-quality products and services, which are an area of focus for internal auditors as well.

So what are the implications for internal auditors? The definition of internal auditing states that internal auditing is "...designed to add value and improve an organization's operations. It helps an organization accomplish its objectives..."[8] Internal auditors do this by defining the scope of their review and developing a risk-based audit program during the planning phase. Later, during fieldwork, they test the structure of programs and processes, the transactions performed within those programs and processes, and interact with the operators working within those structures, programs, and processes.

The ISO Quality Management Principles provide a useful baseline to examine the structure, conditions, and practices within the designated scope area to determine if the criteria are sound and if the practices are conducive to successfully meeting the expectations of the organization's stakeholders. Internal auditors can use the principles, and the aspirational tenets within them to construct audit programs that probe for the presence and functioning of the mechanisms that will enable the program or process to achieve them. Table 8.7 provides some sample questions an internal auditor can use to enquire about them.

Table 8.7   Sample Questions to Evaluate ISO Quality Management Principles

Principle	Relevant Questions
Customer focus	■ Does the organization perform a stakeholder analysis? If yes, what does it do with the results? ■ How does the organization make sure that its strategic and operational objectives reflect the needs and wants of their customers? ■ How does the organization make sure that the requirements of all regulatory bodies are identified and complied with? ■ Does the organization capture, measure, and respond to customer (dis)satisfaction? ■ How does the organization capture customer needs and wants, and incorporate that knowledge in its research and development activities?
Leadership	■ Are the organization's vision, values, and ethical expectations communicated to all employees promptly upon hire and do they receive periodic reminders? ■ Do employees receive sufficient training to perform their present duties? ■ Do surveys show that employees share the organization's values? ■ Do employees feel that management walks the talk and leads by example? ■ Does management lead, inspire, encourage, and recognize employee contributions in terms of what was accomplished and how it was accomplished?
Engagement of people	■ Does management create, promote, and reward collaboration throughout the organization? ■ Do employees feel empowered to do their jobs and challenge people or ideas that threaten the organization's values and performance expectations? ■ Are employee surveys conducted that assess employee satisfaction levels, communicate the results of the surveys, and take appropriate corrective action where necessary? ■ Do employees have enough, reliable, and confidential mechanisms to share their grievances with management and does management take corrective action as necessary? ■ Are employee rewards commensurate with their contributions and achievements?
Process approach	■ Are process objectives clearly defined using a model such as SMARTER? ■ Is it clear what success looks like? Does it include objective measures of performance? ■ Are process narratives and flowcharts available that show the linkages upstream and downstream, as well as laterally? ■ Beyond production metrics, do processes also have adequate outcome measures of success (e.g., customer satisfaction, timely delivery, and error-free functioning)?

(Continued)

TABLE 8.7 (*Continued*) Sample Questions to Evaluate ISO Quality Management Principles

Principle	Relevant Questions
	■ Are risk assessments performed at the process level to identify, assess, and manage process-level deficiencies? ■ Are opportunities for process improvement identified and implemented, as applicable? ■ Are process capabilities identified to define the optimal production volume, work pace, and resource requirements to meet current and future demands?
Improvement	■ Does the organization encourage and reward submission of improvement ideas? ■ Are performance metrics results used to provide timely feedback to the related unit to correct the root-causes of issues and avoid their recurrence? ■ Is there a QA or similar unit within the organization that is sufficiently staffed, resourced, actively engaged, and respected? ■ Are improvement opportunities and ideas from sales, marketing, customer service, employees, and others channeled to the R&D unit for product/service development? ■ Are employees trained on tools and methodologies that will enable them successfully achieve improvement objectives?
Evidence-based decision-making	■ Are decisions primarily driven by data, facts, and information? ■ Are key performance indicators (KPIs) and key risk indicators (KRIs) widely used in the organization as an input for consideration during performance evaluation and decision-making? ■ Is information reliable and available to those who need it, when they need it? ■ Are decisions sufficiently balanced among data, facts, information, and intuition so subjectivity is neither the main nor only means of decision-making? ■ Is data in the organization's computer systems reliable?
Relationship management	■ Has the organization communicated, and expressed a requirement that its values and goals be embraced by its suppliers and made a part of its operating practices? ■ Are quality standards shared with suppliers and are there measures in place to make sure that those standards are met? ■ Has a stakeholder map and analysis been performed so the interests of key stakeholders are identified and managed? ■ Is there an appropriate balance between short-term and long-term goals? ■ Is there a process in place to ensure collaboration between the organization's management, workers, suppliers, and other relevant partners?

Summary

Financial assertions provide a solid foundation for financial audits. They remind the auditor to determine if elements of completeness, occurrence, accuracy, cutoff, classification, existence, and valuation are satisfactory. If business auditors conclude that these assertions are irrelevant for operational reviews that would be an incorrect conclusion.

During operational audits we still want to know if all transactions were executed as expected because hearing that something "fell through the cracks" is never a good thing. We also want to make sure that what was supposed to happen, did in fact happen, like the arrival of merchandise, the shipment of finished products, or the loading of materials on a ship. We also want to ensure accuracy by making sure that amounts, dates, recipient addresses, and shipping codes are what we agreed with the client, the insurance company, and the bank that issued the letter of credit. It becomes a matter of adapting these financial assertions to the operational realm and using them as needed to ensure everything done meets, or exceeds, the customer's expectations.

Six Sigma and Lean concepts continue to enhance stakeholder value by providing discipline in organizations. No longer considered a tool for manufacturing organizations, these methodologies have proven time and time again that companies in service industries, NGOs, and government organizations can also benefit from them. In fact, many internal auditors are pursuing Yellow, Green and Black Belt certifications to understand the principles, apply the concepts, incorporate the results in their work, and leverage this expertise to persuade their organizations to adopt the methodology.

Chapter 9 explains how to document findings using a model that systematically outlines the key components of these communications. In previous chapters we examined the objectives of operational audits, and discussed multiple frameworks, tools, and methodologies to identify weaknesses in either the design or operation of business processes. Internal auditors should follow the CCCER/5C Model when documenting those observations that represent an opportunity for improvement.

QUESTIONS

1. Use operational events as examples to show how internal auditors can use financial statement assertions in their operational audits.
2. Use operational events as examples to show how internal auditors can use the 8 Es to assess and improve operational success.
3. Explain the importance of focusing operational audits on management's business objectives. What should be done if business objectives have not been identified or are inadequate (e.g., unclear, unrealistic, and completion cannot be verified).
4. Prepare "an elevator pitch" to explain to someone that internal controls are not obstacles to business success, but rather enablers.
5. How are Lean and Six Sigma methodologies related to the work of internal auditors?
6. What is the error rate (DPMO) for a process operating at the Six Sigma level?
7. Should all processes operate at the Six Sigma level? Why or why not?
8. Give two examples to show how Six Sigma can be applied in a service organization.
9. What are the elements of the acronym DMAIC?
10. What are the seven quality management principles of ISO 9001?

Notes

1 For more information about financial statement assertions, see Auditing Standard No. 15 at http://pcaobus. org/standards/auditing/pages/auditing_standard_15.aspx#assertations

2 For additional tips, see http://ehs.columbia.edu/ReduceReuseRecycle.html

3 For more information about LEED green building certification program, certification, rating systems, and credits, see http://www.usgbc.org/LEED/

4 The COSO Internal Control Integrated Framework (IC-IF) Executive Summary is available at www.coso.org/documents/coso 2013 icfr executive_summary.pdf

5 See http://www.kaizen.com/about-us/definition-of-kaizen.html

6 I have found the following two websites very useful sources of information regarding Six Sigma: http://www.isixsigma.com/new-to-six-sigma/getting-started/what-six-sigma/ and http://asq.org/learn-about-quality/six-sigma/overview/overview.html

7 For additional information regarding ISO and its standards, visit http://www.iso.org/iso/home/about.htm

8 See https://na.theiia.org/standards-guidance/mandatory-guidance/Pages/Definition-of-Internal-Auditing.aspx

Chapter 9

Documenting Issues

Keep the client informed.
Keep the client involved.
Keep it simple and present it directly.

Introduction

One of the outcomes of operational reviews is the identification and communication of findings. If conditions and practices meet expectations, the internal auditor can notify the relevant stakeholders that performance was satisfactory. When there is a discrepancy between the criteria and existing conditions, the CCCER/5C model provides a structured, reliable, simple, yet effective framework to document these conditions. By following the model, internal auditors will organize their facts and be better prepared to deliver a compelling argument for management to adopt their recommendations.

Using the CCCER/5C Model to Document Findings

The vast majority of what internal auditors do is verify that conditions are consistent with relevant expectations. The expected performance is determined by company policies and procedures, laws, regulations, standards, SLAs, and similar guidelines. Internal auditors also examine the design of programs and processes to determine if the design is conducive to the achievement of company objectives.

Internal auditors must document relevant information to support their conclusions and the results of the work performed. So, when internal auditors find discrepancies between what is expected, and what is occurring, they prepare what is commonly referred to as a finding. A finding is the name given to the discrepancy between what is expected and what is actually in place, as discovered by auditors during the course of their work. A finding provides the details about the

Table 9.1   CCCER Model for Documenting Audit Findings

C: Criteria
C: Condition
C: Cause
E: Effect
R: Recommendation

anomaly and is determined as a result of the procedures performed by the auditor. When conditions meet the criteria, the auditor's communication can indicate that the performance was satisfactory.

In some organizations, the term "finding" has been replaced by other labels such as "opportunities for improvement" or "observations." In other organizations, the term is still being used, but it is reserved for the more serious items, while medium or lower risk observations are labeled "observations."

When preparing the finding, it is very helpful to follow a systematic framework and the CCCER/5C model (Table 9.1) is widely used. While some organizations add other elements, such as "risk" or impact rating, these are additions and seldom a replacement. But what do these letters mean and what are their implications to the practice of operational audits?

Criteria

The criteria are the performance standards or expectations set by relevant stakeholders. The criteria are used in making the evaluation or verification, and consist of the expected performance.

When performing financial reviews, the criteria would consist of relevant accounting and financial standards that dictate the recording of transactions for financial statement purposes. Criteria can also be established through external expectations like those encapsulated in government laws and regulations. Others are based on internal expectations such as those defined in the organization's policies and procedures that govern employee conduct, the use of company resources, and procedures describing how control activities or operational activities within a process should be performed. Lastly, the criteria can be a combination such as those reflected in contracts and SLAs.

Internal auditors may also use the organization's mission, values, and prevailing best practices as the basis for their review. For example, if a process being reviewed does not have cycle-time performance standards that set turnaround times, or escalation procedures are missing, the auditor can refer to the overarching corporate value statement indicating that stakeholders will receive prompt service and that the organization will protect its image by quickly responding to customer inquiries and requests.

The criteria consist of what should exist—the correct state.

Condition

The condition refers to what the auditor discovered as a result of applying auditing procedures. It is the factual evidence that the internal auditor found during the review. Internal audit procedures include gathering testimony, reviewing documents, observing the work conditions and dynamics, and performing calculations of important figures, where applicable.

Whereas the criteria are what *should* be in place, the condition is what *is* in place. The finding exists because there is a difference between the criteria and the condition. What is happening is not what should be happening, so this creates a deficiency that warrants reporting.

The condition is the current state.

Cause

The cause is the reason the condition exists. The cause explains why there is a difference between expected and actual conditions. Internal auditors should search for and identify the root causes of the condition. Failing to do so will result in the auditor working with the symptom(s) of the problem and in the end making inadequate recommendations that provide an insufficient solution.

Getting to the root cause of a problem is not always easy. In many cases, there may not be just one reason, but rather several factors creating the problem. Larger issues often follow this pattern and internal auditors should be cautious not to attempt to describe the root cause without exerting sufficient efforts to find it.

Another challenge with getting to the root cause is that it takes additional time and effort on the part of the auditor. Too many auditors develop overly ambitious work programs that attempt to cover a very broad selection of review areas, leaving little time for in-depth analysis of findings. This creates a dilemma for well-intentioned auditors, who then limit themselves to "skimming the surface" on issues, without spending enough time diving into the problem areas to fully understand the causes, triggers, impacts, and consequences of problems identified.

Some of the tools I have found particularly suited to help auditors get to the root cause of problems are

- *5 Whys.* Ask "why?" until you get to the root cause of the issue.
- *Cause and effect diagram (also known as fishbone diagram).* Create a diagram to show visually all the possible factors creating the issue to see where the problem may have started.
- *Drill down.* Break down the condition into smaller parts to gain a better understanding of the larger picture. This could also involve data analytics.

This is one of the most common reasons for recurring problems: misdiagnosing the cause of the problem and focusing on correcting symptoms instead.

Effect

The effect constitutes the consequence of the condition identified. It relates to the risk or exposure the organization, program, process, or others will face because the condition is not consistent with the criteria. The effect is the impact resulting from the problem itself. A helpful approach to document the appropriate effect, and to make sure that the auditor has in fact identified a finding worthy of being included in the report is to ask: "So what?" Why should anyone care about this condition?

If the auditor is unable to articulate the consequence of the finding, the auditor may also have difficulty convincing the auditee that there is in fact a problem that warrants their attention and correction. Furthermore, being unable to verbalize the consequence will often identify a preference on the part of the auditor, rather than a real problem.

Petty findings are often referred to as nitpicking, and these are also frowned upon by audit clients. This occurs when the auditor reports findings of low impact and consequence to the organization. Nitpicking is a nuisance to members of senior management and the board of directors who are the main readers of audit reports and are generally concerned about significant matters. As a result, nitpicking is a distraction that discredits the auditor who will be perceived as focusing on minutiae rather than substantive issues.

It is extremely helpful for the auditor to quantify as much as possible the effect of the finding. This will make the finding more compelling and convincing, and serve as a useful yardstick to determine if the finding has merit or not. This will also inform the reader about the importance of heeding the next item presented in the report: the recommendation.

Recommendation

The recommendation is the action, or collection of actions, that if successfully implemented, will neutralize the cause, stop the effect, and restore the condition to the desirable state (i.e., criteria). The effectiveness of the recommendation will depend on the auditor fully capturing the details about each of the components of the CCCER model. By elaborating sufficiently on each of the components, the finding will be convincing and compelling so that the reader comes to the same conclusion as the auditor who identified the deficiency.

Recommendations should be cost effective when correcting the problem. Care must be applied so the cost of correcting the deficiency does not exceed the exposure or loss the deficiency is identifying. It is also useful for the auditor to consider the principles of effective processes when making recommendations. For example, Poka Yoke focuses on mistake proofing a process or activity so an operation cannot be performed incorrectly. If the auditor's finding has to do with an operator making a mistake while performing a task, then the Poka Yoke principles can be particularly helpful. For example, Poka Yoke's is geared to

1. Eliminate the possibility of error by redesigning the process or product so the problematic task is no longer necessary. This is arguably the best course of action.
2. Replace or substitute the part, task, or process for a more reliable one. In an industrial environment, this can be done through robotics. In a service or support environment such as accounting, this can be accomplished by automating the activity. With spreadsheets, this could include more extensive use of formulas, linking spreadsheets, or password-protecting cells.
3. Detecting the error before further processing occurs. Preventive controls, such as those in computer applications that notify the operator when an incorrect input is made, can accomplish this. Checklists are another example, because they can prevent workers from investing time and effort processing a transaction that is incomplete or inaccurate. Similarly, before the completed work is passed on to someone else or is filed away, a checklist can also serve as a self-inspecting tool to identify the mistake immediately.
4. Minimizing the effect of the error, as is the case with circuit breakers that shut off when there is an electrical overload or a short circuit. In a service environment, authorization limits provide similar protection.
5. Make the work easier to perform by color-coding items, combining steps, and so on. I have witnessed cases where forms were so lengthy and confusing that I was not surprised there were errors on them and when the information was entered into a computer system. Simplifying the forms, clarifying the instructions, automating date entry, and choosing from preselected values, all of these changes improved accuracy and speed, and were gladly accepted by those using them.

Making Findings and Recommendations Persuasive

Internal auditors should remember that the purpose of the review is to determine if conditions are conducive to the achievement of business objectives. Audit reports communicate the status of conditions. If the structure and practices are deemed effective, communications should say so. If conditions are not, the auditor's role goes beyond that of reporting on the problems, but also working with management to formulate the best recommendations for corrective action. The report must provide enough evidence to convince management and the board that action must be taken. This is the purpose of writing recommendations. In other words, the recommendation is a means to an end.

Findings and recommendations will be persuasive to the extent that they convince the reader that there is a real problem that requires correction. This can be achieved through a number of actions:

1. *Quantify as much as possible.* When internal auditors write reports and fail to provide data that support their arguments, the reader is left wondering whether there is really a problem. The auditor should tell the reader, as much as possible, how big the problem is in monetary terms, number of units, percentage of transactions affected, how many people are impacted, and how long the problem has been occurring. Abundant and reliable data will compel the reader that a problem exists.

2. *Make sure findings are significant.* Since organizational management is increasingly dealing with complex and worrisome risks, managing large volumes of transactions and monetary amounts, and faces constant time limitations, they should not receive audit findings pertaining to minutiae.

3. *Consider the cost/benefit involved.* Every activity carries some risk, and organizational leaders understand there are some costs of doing business. These risks can't be excessive because they come in conflict with the principle of prudence and fiduciary responsibility to protect the interests of their stakeholders, especially owners. Remember that costs can be monetary, but also reputational or precedent setting, in that they can create an opportunity for the same action to be replicated at other times, at other locations, or limit the effectiveness of control activities in the future. With this in mind, internal auditors should evaluate quantitative and qualitative costs and benefits in an effort to refrain from presenting problems that are not particularly significant and require a higher cost to correct.

4. *Use appropriate language.* Traditionally internal audit reports were lengthy, contained numerous acronyms and jargon, and used obscure and complex language that made it difficult for some report readers to comprehend. It has become apparent that this practice is counterproductive, since the purpose of writing a report is to communicate the conditions noted during the audit and convince management to take corrective action when necessary. Internal auditors should know who their readers are and make the language appropriate for the audience. Some readers may be familiar with the topic and language involved, such as the name of systems, methodologies, and regulations, while others may not and require a simplified presentation of the material. This dynamic can be represented using Figure 9.1.

This can be accomplished by limiting the use of excessively technical language, including full names rather than acronyms, including footnotes and endnotes, adding a glossary, and using terminology that is used within the business and more likely to be familiar to the audit report readers:

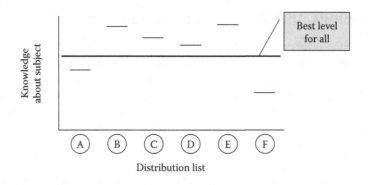

Figure 9.1 Comprehension level of audit report recipients.

1. *Use a readable report format.* Audit report formats have changed and many organizations are now submitting one to three-page reports. Since audit report recipients typically don't have a lot of time available, they cannot read lengthy reports. Furthermore, by making the format simple, using color, bullets, graphs, and diagrams, it can make it easier and faster for readers to follow. Another benefit is that some of these simplified formats reduce the amount of time auditors must spend writing the report itself.

2. *Order of importance.* Internal auditors should carefully examine the totality of the findings presented in the report and make sure they are presented in order of importance. More significant findings should be presented first and the remaining issues in descending order. An audit manager told me early in my audit career to put findings in descending order because if the reader runs out of time and can't read the entire report, you want that person to at least read the most important points, which would be at the beginning. Very good advice.

3. *Compressing findings.* Audit reports are getting shorter. One of the ways to accomplish this is to compress the findings. This means consolidating some findings so there are fewer in total. This practice does not eliminate the findings, it merely groups them. In fact, I have found that sometimes what I thought was a finding was actually the symptom of something else. So, compressing them results in the real problem being presented, the previous findings becoming examples or manifestations of the larger issue, and the recommendation gets to the root cause of the problem itself. One way to do this is to use an affinity diagram.

4. *Too lengthy.* Similar to the observation related to the length of the audit report, sometimes the length of the finding itself is excessive. Findings should be succinct without losing any necessary details. Internal auditors should be careful not to elaborate excessively on the issue, or provide unnecessary details.

5. *Proper tone.* Some internal auditors forget that the purpose of most internal audit reports is to convince the reader to take action, not to be accusatory or demeaning to those whose actions failed to meet performance expectations. Except for reports describing egregious conditions, where the tone must be commensurate to the severity of the problems, reports should balance the nature and magnitude of the problem with the tone used when presenting it. In general, it is best to be constructive, positive, and factual in the report, and present any opinion on the matter in a level-headed manner. This also includes avoiding excessive negative expressions.

Using Quantitative Methods to Improve the Quality and Impact of Audit Findings

Few things beat facts when the objective is to argue for a particular course of action. When the internal auditor collects reliable data, performs appropriate analysis, and formulates conclusions based on these related facts, it is difficult for others to contradict or ignore the communication.

Auditees may dislike the results or the implications, but a reasonable person cannot negate the truth.

The veracity of the auditors' work is based on quantitative information anchored in reliable data. This quantitative approach to documenting results will improve the impact of the audit findings.

More qualitative elements can be included as well, but they may not carry as much weight and could be subject to auditee challenges. To address this, internal auditors are encouraged to collect objective information to support subjective matters. For example, if motivation is a concern and this is known either anecdotally by observing the mood of workers or the diligence with which they perform their duties, internal auditors may want to consider interviewing multiple workers, documenting the results of those meetings, and using this information as the basis for any mention of employee morale of dissatisfaction. A survey, conducted by internal audit, human resources or a third party provider, can also add quantitative elements to this topic.

Another situation that illustrates this dynamic is what occurs when employees explain that the number of phone calls, e-mails, and window customers rob them of too much of their time and that is the reason for their inability to keep up with the work volume. While this complaint may be true, care is needed before attempting to put this as a finding or the root cause of the condition. Creating a check sheet, and asking workers to log the number and type of calls, e-mails, customer visits, and other distractions over a reasonable amount of time would be very helpful to document the incidence of this. The result is the conversion of workers' opinions into facts and figures that can support the workers' assertion.

The illustrations provided above refer to persuasion on the basis of fact or reason. This is derived from the Greek logos or logic. When this is used, the process is based on the fact that people believe they are logical and reasonable, so if we appeal to this through data, we expect them to respond accordingly and be persuaded by the strength of the evidence. But this is only one of multiple approaches.

Persuasion can also be achieved by appealing to the character of the presenter. Derived from the Greek word for ethos, this approach is based on the character of the presenter, who must be trustworthy, honest, intelligent, or otherwise credible. For internal auditors, this is a desirable objective as well. In organizations where internal audit has a record of professionalism, accuracy, consistently delivering outstanding results, being helpful to the organization through the depth and appropriateness of its findings and recommendations, and displaying leadership, internal audit is likely to reach this level of credibility. When this is achieved, the reaction from auditees will be "if the auditor said it, it must be true."

There is a third approach based on emotion (i.e., pathos). In this case, persuasion is based on expressing feelings on a subject, getting an emotional reaction, or both. This may consist of engendering good or bad feelings, using scare tactics, showing pity or through flattery. In general, internal auditors should rely the least on this approach. It may be effective when the goal is to connect with auditees and to let them know that we identify with their challenges. Sometimes auditees have the opinion that internal auditors lack an appreciation for the difficulties they are experiencing, they don't understand the resource limitations and other constraints limiting their ability to do their work. Some individuals believe that internal auditors only want to find problems to put in their reports. Given this backdrop, using emotion strategically may help if it is done with sincerity. And, this is very important. If the auditor comes across as being disingenuous, the approach will backfire and the auditor will be seen as hypocritical.

Persuasion and Diversion

As much as internal auditors should know how to increase their ability to be persuasive, they should also remember that sometimes audit clients want to persuade the auditor as well. This could be done to argue a point of view, educate the auditor, decrease the severity of the rating on a finding, to convince the auditor to review or not review certain items, and so on. Auditors should know about some of the techniques used to persuade, distract, and divert their attention. For example

> *Repetition.* By repeating an argument often enough, the perpetrator hopes that the frequent repetition creates legitimacy. Some do this with distorted and untrue statements. Because someone says it many times, that doesn't make it true.
>
> *Will of the majority.* Another approach is by representing one's argument as if it were the will of the majority. This gives the person's argument the aura of legitimacy. If that were so, then the mere fact that many people share the same knowledge or opinion would lend it credence. But if that is fabricated, then it is done with the intent of deception.
>
> *Generalization.* Making unwarranted generalizations that represents one's behavior as that of the whole is another way to distort the truth. This consists of what is commonly stated as "everyone is doing it." While this may be so, it does not make the behavior acceptable.
>
> *Creating information.* Some individuals attempt to present a different version of the truth. This can be done by choosing to exclude some information that if known would have resulted in a different opinion. Internal auditors must be careful not to do this themselves and by looking at situations, problems, and even choosing recommendations from a biased perspective, the auditor could also introduce bias into the analysis and be guilty of this as much as auditees can be.

When presenting information to auditees, management, and the board of directors, it is very important for internal auditors to focus on getting their audience's attention, being sincere and personal in their presentation, showing concern, and engaging the audience. While the facts, in the form of data, tables, charts, pictures, and so on are quite compelling, it is equally important for internal auditors to show auditees that they care about the organization. This will lend additional strength to the information presented and create an amicable working environment where peers and colleagues can work together to arrive at desirable outcomes, rather than trying to force them into agreement through the sheer weight of facts and figures.

The facts and figures that the auditors will use when presenting their findings will likely constitute the preeminent source of information to persuade auditees. All of these items constitute evidence that should be part of the finding and the related communication with the client. Internal auditors should remember that the evidence should meet certain criteria:

Verifiable. All results should be based on reliable facts, figures, and documents that others can inspect independently, and by applying the care and judgment of a reasonable person, arrive at the same conclusion.

Transparency. When there is a legitimate need and authority to do so, the facts, figures, and documents should be available for review by others.

Sufficiency. The facts, figures, and documents used during the review should be enough to convince an equally qualified, prudent, and unbiased person.

Reliability. The facts, figures, and documents used should be free from tampering, or significant and unexplainable quality variances, prepared by a suitably qualified individual or system and provided timely for review and analysis.

Relevancy. The facts, figures, and documents used during the review should be applicable based on the scope of the review and the objectives of the organization, program, or process.

Usefulness. The facts, figures, and documents used should help the organization, program, or process improve its operations, and enhance its ability to achieve its objectives.

Developing Useful, Pragmatic, and Effective Recommendations for Corrective Action

The Standards state that "Internal auditors must communicate the results of engagements" (Standard 2410). Reporting audit observations are a key requirement for internal auditors, and the board and management expect internal auditors to be their "eyes and ears" about what is happening in their organizations. They trust the accuracy, completeness, and timeliness of the information.

Beyond identifying and providing a laundry list of problems, however, audit clients expect internal auditors to provide timely, useful, relevant, and feasible recommendations. These recommendations should help the organization restore the deficiency so it meets the performance expectations. It can, however, help the organization go beyond the minimum performance requirements and propel it into the territory of leading practices. By going one step further, competitiveness is enhanced and the organization perceives that internal audit is adding value beyond its baseline expectations.

Summary

A key aspect of operational reviews is to determine if management has designed, deployed, and managed business processes in a way that provides reasonable assurance that the organization's risks have been managed effectively and that the organization's goals and objectives will be achieved efficiently and economically. This is the definition of adequate control and facts are key to reach this determination. However, merely putting figures, charts, graphs, and tables in front of management and the board is not enough. Internal auditors must organize that information, arrange the items in a logical sequence, and by providing a beginning, middle, and conclusion, persuade decision makers that the recommendation is worthy of their consideration. Better yet, be so convincing through fact and presentation that any reasonable and prudent individual would arrive at the same conclusion—implementing the recommendation is in everyone's best interest.

Chapter 10 examines the practice of continuous auditing and how it can be used to improve the evaluation and monitoring of business processes. There are inherent limitations to intermittent, sample-based, paper-focused reviews. As our world becomes increasingly digitized, internal auditors must search for opportunities to leverage technology to perform risk-based reviews that provide a deeper understanding of process dynamics, zoom into problem areas and pinpoint the what, when, where, how, who, and why of process issues.

QUESTIONS

1. Explain the elements of the CCCER/5C model.
2. What constitutes criteria and how can operational auditors identify it?
3. What constitutes the condition and how can operational auditors define it?
4. What constitutes the cause and how can operational auditors find it?
5. What constitutes the effect and how can operational auditors calculate it?
6. What constitutes the recommendation and how can operational auditors formulate it?
7. Explain three methodologies that can help operational auditors find the root cause of operational deficiencies.
8. List three actions that can help to make findings and recommendations more persuasive.
9. Explain the use of logic, character of the presenter, and emotion as tools for persuasion.
10. Explain three tactics used to persuade, distract, and divert the attention of others. How should operational auditors use this knowledge to prevent being manipulated themselves?

Chapter 10

Continuous Monitoring

> Internal auditors have been using software to test transactions for decades, and new technology continues to improve their ability to test both transactions and controls. The same software that a bank's compliance department uses to monitor transactions for possible money laundering also could be used to test whether they were approved by the correct individuals, identify potential duplicate or over-payment of vendors, or detect unusual transactions such as large inventory adjustments.[1]
>
> **Norman Marks**

Introduction

The internal audit profession has undergone tremendous changes over the years and expectations have never been higher. As business dynamics become more complex, as organizations grow and expand worldwide, and as the intricacies of the risk environment multiply, internal auditors must find new, faster, better, and more accurate ways of getting the work done. Paper-based, cyclical reviews that rely on sampling are being challenged by fast developments that can't wait months, much less years, to be detected. Clever employees, vendors, and customers defraud organizations through unique trickery that may not appear in a sample, and attempting to test every control related to the process in question would demand having an army of auditors with virtually no time constraints to go through it all.

Instead, data analysis tools and the capture of digital information provide a unique combination that internal auditors would be remiss in their duties not to capitalize upon. In this chapter, we examine those and provide suggestions that business auditors should consider implementing.

Continuous Auditing of High-Risk Activities

The internal audit profession has been undergoing significant changes since I first became an internal auditor in the late 1990s. At the time, change was imminent and evident, propelled by a

241

number of factors. Among them was the fast adoption of computer technologies that created vast amounts of data in organizations. Simultaneously, this allowed auditors to review not just paper records, but also computer records.

Over time, it became evident that performing audits periodically presented some limitations. Among these was the fact that if the auditor reviewed an area every 2 years, by the time the auditor identified anomalies the issue might have been going on for over a year. If the problem had a cumulative cost or financial loss effect, the amount could be quite high by the time it was detected. If the issue straddled accounting or compliance periods, the problem could have magnified penalties from regulatory bodies, and if the impact had tax or financial statement implications, it may require reissuing tax records and paying fines and penalties, or restating financial results.

Years ago, internal auditors made sample selections to evaluate attributes of a population of transactions and the testing procedures were traditionally based on a sampling approach that included activities such as reviews of policies, procedures, approvals, and reconciliations. Sometimes this selection was made statistically, sometimes randomly, and sometimes through judgment. The objective was to have a representative sample so that a valid conclusion could be made about the population. As new software tools became available in the market and organizations stored more data, internal auditors queried and analyzed the transactions with the goal of finding attributes or trends that might indicate if errors occurred during processing or if the reliability of internal and external information and reports was faulty.

With this data, tools, and objectives, it became evident there was less need to test transactions that were processed correctly. Internal auditors could focus instead on those transactions with at-risk attributes or characteristics. Another benefit to this approach was that the entire population could be examined, not just a sample.

Internal auditors also realized they could run queries and analyze at-risk transactions, so there really was no need to wait months for a traditional audit to be declared, planned, performed, and reported upon. Instead, reviews could be done continuously as the transactions were being processed, and at-risk transactions could be flagged when they occurred and not only during this intermittent audit cycle. This changed the traditional approach which gave internal auditors a narrow scope of evaluation that is often too late to be of real value to business performance or regulatory compliance since it identified problems after they occurred.

This continuous audit approach is one that many internal audit departments are just now starting to adopt. Many are still at the exploration stage and others are at the wish-list level. Some may argue that an annual cycle is enough. Depending on the risk characteristics of the attributes being evaluated, an annual cycle may be the right choice. In other situations, a real-time evaluation may be more appropriate, especially given the rapid developments affecting organizations and some of the existing regulations in place. In the cases of food contamination, fraud, and corruption, customer complaints about product safety, payments to or from specially designated nationals (e.g., Office of Foreign Assets Control's [OFAC] Specially Designated Nationals [SDN] list), audit clients cannot afford to wait a full year, or two, or three, to identify and report anomalies.

The goal of continuous auditing is twofold. First, deploy limited internal audit and management resources more efficiently in search of problematic activities and transactions. The objective is to identify what is not working well, and less on validating what is working well. Second, identify at-risk transactions as soon as possible for early intervention, keeping problems to a minimum. Problems should not be allowed to fester because there is typically a cumulative effect

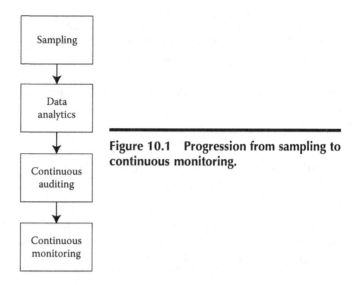

Figure 10.1   Progression from sampling to continuous monitoring.

involved. In some cases, there is a compounding effect and for others, grounds for accusation of neglect that could result in more severe fines, penalties, and judgments.

The last stage of evolution in this cycle (Figure 10.1) is continuous controls monitoring (CCM) and continuous controls auditing (CCA), which results in information that identifies potential anomalies, risk exposures, and control breakdowns. This information should prompt immediate attention, further investigation, and remediation.

Organizations should recognize, and remember, that the ownership of internal control belongs to management. Continuous monitoring takes continuous auditing and puts the at-risk transactions at the fingertips of management. It is done through enabling technology that can scour large volumes of data, or evaluate individual ones in real time or near real time, and identify anomalies using a variety of reporting mechanisms.

The report of deviations can be done via traditional electronic or printed reports in typical charts and tables, but notifications can be sent via e-mail using visual reporting and dynamic reporting interfaces as well. Previously, management waited for the audit results to know that they had a problem, and then reacted to audit findings with corrective actions. The evolution of technology is such that, today, internal auditors can provide management the at-risk transactions in real time for ownership, response, and resolution.

The fix was to reduce the review process and do so as close to real time as possible. The data available, and the computer technology available, created a fertile environment for what was called CAATTs (computer assisted audit tools and techniques). Furthermore, the ability to write scripts, macros, and other forms of programs to replicate testing procedures, made it possible to embark on continuous auditing of high-risk activities, where delays in reviewing could have a significantly damaging effect on the organization.

Continuous auditing changes the audit process from periodic reviews of a sample of transactions to ongoing audit testing of 100% of transactions. It becomes an integral part of modern auditing at many levels and should be closely tied to management activities such as performance monitoring, balanced scorecard, and ERM. With automated, frequent analyses of data, auditors are able to perform control and risk assessments in real time or near real time.

Care must be applied to this concept, however, because internal auditors are not supposed to engage in comanagement activities. Management is responsible for making sure that processes have adequate controls and that these controls are operating as expected. Auditors, on the other hand, are responsible for staying abreast of risk profile changes that warrant faster intervention. Table 10.1 shows some examples of continuous auditing examples and procedures.

Data Analysis Software Applications

Data analytics has been facilitated by the development and adoption of various tools (Table 10.2). Among these, the most widely known one is Microsoft Excel. The days when Excel had a capacity of 56,000 records are long gone. Current (e.g., 2013 and 2016) worksheet capacity is over a million rows and more than 16,000 columns; this is more than enough to meet most auditors' needs. Simple, but very useful formulas include: AVERAGE, CONCATENATE, CORREL, COUNT, COUNTA, COUNTBLANK, COUNTIF, IF, LEN, MAX, MIN, RIGHT, LEFT, SUM, SUMIF, TRIM, and VLOOKUP. Another set of very useful functionality is the TEXT TO COLUMNS, REMOVE DUPLICATES, and DATA VALIDATION in the Data tab.

Auditors can also work with more complex functions, pivot tables, and array formulas taking advantage of Excel's analytical functionality and improved visualizations and business logic capabilities. Additional formulas are available in the Add-Ins, which include the Analysis ToolPak, Analysis ToolPak—Visual Basic for Application, and Solver Add-in. In general, there are many useful financial, logical, lookup and reference, statistical, and information formulas available, but their usage, of course, depends on the nature of the audit.

A widely regarded tool, and a favorite of many auditors is ACL. Originally called Audit Command Language, it has a built-in functionality that auditors generally find helpful to identify gaps, duplication, and other anomalous transactions. It can also facilitate the extraction and analysis of data by making data conversion easy. ACL includes many formulas that are geared for the type of analysis that many auditors perform, so rather than developing a complex formula or a macro to perform certain functions, ACL has functionality already preloaded. But the gap is narrowing, for example, as Excel's increased ability to import files of diverse formats has reduced some of the advantage that ACL had in this regard, and a similar dynamic is emerging regarding analytics.

A very useful feature in ACL is that it works with a copy of the data, so the original information is never compromised and errors are minimized. The benefits of data integrity cannot be overstated. ACL also documents each step or procedure applied to the data, which can be advantageous when it comes to documenting the work done. In the event of a dispute where questions are asked about the integrity of the data and the analysis performed, having it done by the tool itself is a very valuable feature.

With ACL, auditors can access files of unlimited size (as opposed to the 1 million records of Excel). Users can work in the server directly, allowing the auditor to link directly to the production machine. Furthermore, when ACL operates on a server as well, the speed and power of the server makes data processing faster because the work is not dependent on the auditors' laptop or desktop.

Although auditor software generally come preloaded with a library of tests designed to help auditors perform traditional testing, the new generation of analytics software is easy to use and has the ability to perform complex analyses of millions of transactions quickly. Most modern

Table 10.1   Sample Data Analysis Procedures and Their Purpose

Type of Analysis	Objective
Review of requisition, POs, expense, and adjustment limits	To make sure transactions are authorized and in compliance with company-set limits
Split transactions (e.g., POs, requisitions, expenses, and payments)	To make sure there were no transactions processed in an effort to circumvent authorization limits
Overdue requisitions, POs, and expenses	To makes sure transactions are processed promptly
Unauthorized requisitions and approvals	To make sure only authorized individuals create and approve requisitions
Critical data	To make sure expected values and formats exist and are followed
Duplicate payment	To make sure liabilities are only paid once
Segregation of duties	To make sure transactions are valid and authorized
Retroactive transactions (e.g., PO vs. invoice)	To make sure POs are not created after invoice date
Invoice sequence	To identify suspicious number sequencing
Prohibited vendors, customers, and personnel	To make sure vendors, customers, and personnel (e.g., employees, contractors, and consultants) are authorized (e.g., not on OFAC SDN list)
Employee and vendor match	To identify suspicious demographics and transactions between employees and vendors
Expense posting	To make sure that expenses are posted accurately, to the corresponding cost center, and in the appropriate period
Invalid purchase and travel cards	To make sure that all cards are issued to existing and authorized personnel
Invalid purchases	To make sure that P-card and travel card activity is for legitimate business purposes and from authorized merchants
Excessive cards	To make sure personnel don't have more P-cards and travel cards than authorized
Unusual activity	To identify suspicious purchases including payments, journal entries, adjustments, physical and logical access based on time of day, day of the week, time of the month or amount (e.g., even amounts, small value, and below threshold)
Authorized payroll: individuals, amounts, and periods	To make sure employees are only paid as required

(Continued)

TABLE 10.1 (*Continued*) **Sample Data Analysis Procedures and Their Purpose**

Type of Analysis	Objective
Excessive inventory	To identify slow moving, perishable, or expiring inventory to limit obsolescence
Duplicate claims	To make sure T&E, benefit, or similar activities are accurate and are accounted for only once
Contract terms	To make sure key contract demographics and terms (e.g., prices, dates, sales amounts, and discounts) critical data elements are valid and authorized
Sales	To identify discrepancies among shipping, billing, prices, amounts, and terms (e.g., INCO terms, destination, charges, and freight operator)

Table 10.2 Commonly Used Data Analytics Software

Microsoft Access
Arbutus
Microsoft Excel
ACL
IDEA
IBM Business Analytics
IBM Cognos
IBM SPSS
Lavastorm
Picalo
SAP Business Objects (BOBJ)
SAS
SQL
Tableau
WizSoft (e.g., WizRule, WizWhy)

tools can be used from anywhere in the world and are also portable, available not just on desktops and laptops, but on tablets and even smartphones. With their more robust accessibility, extensive functionality, and capability, internal auditors can develop data extraction and mining routines, run them, analyze the results, and share the information with their colleagues anywhere in the world, at any time.

The past barriers to continuous auditing are dissipating as the software becomes more versatile, powerful, and easy to use through drag and drop and hyperlink enabled functionality. Furthermore, by using software already available in the organization, or that can be used by others, such as the accounting, finance, quality control, operations management, logistics, and other units, the cost can be reduced. By leveraging the tools that were purchased by others for other purposes in the organization, the cost can be lowered and its usage increased since it is more widely used and shared by others. Lastly, some applications can be integrated into the company's GRC solutions and electronic workpapers, thus making it easier to share information, and direct exceptions to process owners and others for further review and investigation.

The recipients of internal audit reports have limited time, and often lengthy reports and the abundance of detail in them makes it virtually impossible for them to read the entire document. As a result, there has been a trend where organizations are moving away from traditional text-heavy reports and replacing them with shorter, easier to read formats. In many cases, audit reports are prepared using PowerPoint. This limits the amount of text that will be used to communicate the results, graphs and charts are easily included, and it provides a more versatile and conversation-friendly format that encourages discussion.

When deciding to use data analytics, a good first step is to understand the current state of the organization's information governance, management process, and the requirements for defining how data are created, stored, accessed, used, and transmitted. Internal auditors need to determine what information is critical for the program or process, how and where it resides, and who has access to it. This information can be obtained by performing a risk assessment, which should identify the critical information. Another approach is to leverage the existing business continuity and disaster recovery documentation (if it exists) because the impact analysis that precedes such documentation should have identified that critical information. A third approach is to leverage the organization's data inventory that identifies what information is available.

The next step is to determine where the data are stored. Since these data reside in databases, the IT department may need to help identify the relevant systems and how the data are stored. Increasingly, due to the increasing use of outsourcing, the information could be hosted outside the organization's IT environment by a third party, including the cloud. The capture, movement, and storage of the data present multiple risks, so internal auditors should work with the person most familiar with the database architecture to understand the data dictionary, data models, and where the data resides. If the information is hosted by third parties, then the auditor should review the third-party contract and any other agreement in place.

The extraction of the data can be done by the auditor or by requesting the informant from the IT department or process owner. While a common objective is to review the data to determine if the related controls are present and functioning as intended, a common objective is to analyze the information to determine how well or poorly the process is working compared to what is possible (or against the competition). Since operational audits focus on the effectiveness and efficiency of programs and processes, data should be analyzed with these types of goals in mind.

When evaluating the organization's risk and compliance conditions and readiness for data analytics, it is helpful to begin with a gap analysis. By documenting the current state of the organization, and comparing that with the organization's plans for the future, the auditor can identify areas of improvement (Table 10.3). The following questions can help internal auditors determine the condition of their organization's risk and compliance functions whether they are performing an assessment or acting in an advisory capacity:

1. Assess the current state:
    a. How would you define the current approach to managing risks and compliance issues?
        i. Centralized or silo-based
        ii. Coordinated or uncoordinated
        iii. Proactive or reactive
        iv. Strategic or tactical

    b. How mature is the process?

With this information, a plan can then be created that addresses strategic, process, people, and technological impact, and defines who will be doing what and when.[2]

Using CAATTs to Achieve Operational Excellence

Internal auditors have traditionally performed audits using a cyclical approach. That is to say that they review areas intermittently to verify that the infrastructure of the area under review was established effectively and to verify that the controls in place are operating as expected. While this approach has been quite effective for decades, it presents some challenges because problems could lurk in the background for months before the auditors arrive for their review. CAATTs offer a way to avoid the time lapse that cyclical reviews create.

CAATTs can also help to enhance risk identification by leveraging the power of metrics. By establishing KRIs, and monitoring their behavior over time, internal auditors can get an early indication when the underlying risk profile is starting to drift. KRIs are similar to KPIs, which are quantifiable measures that an organization or industry uses to gauge and compare performance in terms of their operational and strategic goals. For example, sales, production figures, number of employees, and number of customers are all examples of KPIs. KRIs, on the other hand, are also metrics, and a subset of KPIs, but they provide a slightly different view of operational results.

KRIs shed light on the underlying risk. For example: whereas sales are an important KPI, AR balances and aging is a KRI because while it is important to sell, if you are unable to collect promptly, there is a significant financial risk to the sales process.

Production figures, as indicated previously, are a KPI, but the number of accidents suffered and errors caused during the production process are KRIs because they show underlying risks. The affected risks impact health and safety, compliance with regulations, and adherence with internal procedures and values. Errors are also KRIs because they affect the quality of goods and services causing decreases in customer satisfaction, increasing warranty claims, and returns handling, they waste company physical and human resources and can result in fines, penalties, recalls, and lawsuits.

Table 10.3   Organizational Readiness Levels for Data Analytics

Level	Characteristics
Initial	Ad hoc processes developed over time
	No specific plan in place
	Limited use of technology, primarily based on spreadsheets and shared folders
	Multiple responsibilities with little coordination and overall leadership
	Inconsistent ranking of risks
	Difficult to achieve a reliable overview of the status of organizational risk
Evolving	A plan is in place
	There is at least a basic business case developed for resource and technology requirements
	Various roles are collaborating to achieve a coordinated approach
	There is an increasing alignment around the three lines of defense model
	A consistent approaches to risk ranking exists across functions
	Risk and compliance issues are linked to strategic objectives
	There is an increasing use of technologies designed for audit, governance, risk, and compliance
	Senior management gets a consistent overview of the status of organizational risks
Functional	A plan is well managed
	Progress is measured against business case criteria
	Clear and effective leadership is in place
	Roles and activities are coordinated across functions
	Risk and compliance issues are clearly linked to strategic organizational objectives
	There is a high degree of consistency among risk ranking across the organization
	A widespread awareness exists among senior management of governance, risk, and compliance issues, including risk appetite
	The use of specialized technologies, including data analysis, is integrated into normal business operations
	A high degree of automation, such as continuous risk assessment and monitoring, and CCM, are in place
	Strategic and operational performance reporting systems are integrated into enterprise risk and compliance initiatives

The number of employees is another KPI, but the morale level of these workers is a KRI. Unmotivated workers are less productive, typically have higher absenteeism and turnover rates, and provide lower customer service to customers. So, the sheer number of workers is one thing, but demotivated or apathetic workers is quite another.

General KPIs include sales growth, sales by product or service, profit margin, sales by customer, inventory turnover, number of orders, number of calls received, and number of customers. In addition, internal auditors should be familiar with their industry's KPIs. Same store sales, point of purchase, incremental sales, and sales per square foot are common KPIs in the retail sector.

CCM and CCA

For many years, internal auditors depended on single-transaction testing to determine if controls were operating as intended. The idea was to apply audit procedures such as observation and document inspection to individual transactions. This practice resulted in a tedious and time-consuming approach to auditing that resulted in testing samples of populations. By leveraging the power of KRIs, internal auditors can use data to get a more objective understanding of risk dynamics and identify changes in the risk profile within the organization for more timely intervention and review.

The *Standards* require internal auditors to remain independent and objective in performing their work (Standard 1100). Due to this requirement, internal auditors must not perform control activities, which means that while engaging in CCA, caution is required to refrain from engaging in day-to-day management activities within processes that may constitute performance of controls. This can be a thin gray line and the role of the auditor should be explained to management, so they understand the different roles involved. When designing the continuous auditing and monitoring procedures, auditors and management must think through what the metrics are, and what thresholds would trigger the auditors' desire to gain a better understanding of operational issues. The following are two examples to illustrate this concept.

Consider an organizational procedure consisting of payment receipt and processing, where the payment received must be credited to the corresponding customer account. The control has two components: (1) the generation of an exception report when the customer cannot be identified and (2) the items on the exception report must be corrected within 2 days to ensure the prompt handling of the payments.

If on first day, a payment beneficiary is unknown, that night the system generates an exception report showing the funds received, but no corresponding customer credit, so the amount is placed in a suspense account. If the beneficiary is identified the next day, the payment is credited to the corresponding customer and this shows that the control worked as intended.

If the correction is not made that second day, the exception report should show the unapplied payment on the second day's exception report as well. If the payment is cleared that third day (2 days after the payment was received), the control has worked and there is no need to escalate the situation.

At the end of the third day, however, if the payments are still pending resolution, it means that the control was not performed as planned. The question then becomes, should the internal auditor be notified about this situation now? For a routine payment processing activity, the risk may not warrant such notification. It may, however, warrant escalation of the situation within management ranks, so they are aware of the control failure.

In traditional payment processing environments, the auditor could be notified after payments have remained unprocessed for 25 days because at this point, it is clear that the control failed to work after 2 days, and 23 days later, the problem has not been addressed yet. What is likely to happen in this scenario, is that when invoices are produced again, the unapplied payment won't be reflected on the invoice and this will trigger customer calls, letters, e-mails, visits, and complaints. This way the auditor can remain independent, yet become aware of the problem and contact management to make sure the matter is being researched. At this point, the auditor could find out what caused the control to fail as it did.

Another metric related to the example described above would show the total number of customers that had their payment processed one or more days after the funds were received, and an adjustment was made to the customer's account to credit those funds. Essentially, the aggregation of the independent instances described above. The frequency of such a report would depend on the risk, but let's consider it being produced every 2 or 3 months. The benefit of such a report would be to alert management if there is a trend that shows an increase in pending payment processing. Possible cause includes

- A lack of training for new payment processors
- Changes made to the billing system or related data feeds resulting in invoice numbers or customer IDs no longer being printed on the bills

Let's consider a third example. By monitoring the number of mild, medium, and severe accidents, internal auditors can get an early warning indicator that production workers are rushed, poorly trained, or that safety practices are not being followed. By identifying the problem early on, corrective actions can be mandated and directive controls enabled to (1) prevent the overall number of accidents from increasing, (2) prevent minor accidents from becoming more severe ones, and (3) preventing the collective intervention by regulators or employees who may seek recourse when the pattern becomes evident to all. Increasing production and generating more accidents is a dangerous combination since it will undoubtedly raise the risk of government regulation, lawsuits, and in general a breakdown of ethical operating practices.

Robotic Process Automation, Artificial Intelligence, and Machine Learning

Technologies continue to facilitate the continuous monitoring and auditing of activities in programs and processes. Much of this is driven by robotic process automation (RPA), artificial intelligence (AI), and machine learning (ML).

1. Robotic Process Automation (RPA): These consist of systems that use action lists generated by recording, or "watching," the user performs tasks and then repeating them through scripts or "bots." Examples include software that:
   a. Opens e-mail containing invoices, extracts key data elements, and then types necessary information into the accounting system to prepare for payment
   b. Reads multiple forms and their contents, and then enters the information into another system or a template

    c. Reviews insurance claims information, compares that information to the policyholders' policy coverage details, post acceptable transactions for payment, then generates exception reports for any anomalies or discrepancies identified

    d. Performs complicated calculations, searches for red flags, and identifies outliers based on established algorithms

2. Artificial Intelligence (AI): It consists of any device that perceives its environment and takes actions that maximize its chance of successfully achieving its goals. They emulate human cognitive functions such as thinking and problem solving. Examples include:

    a. Analyze healthcare claims data for gaps in patient treatment, then make recommendations, schedule appointments, and prepare payment-processing information

    b. Examine payment information in search of anomalous transactions and patterns pertaining to high-risk individuals

    c. Mobile security robots that search for spills and other hazards, identify misplaced items, and conduct inventory counts

    d. Self-deployed vacuum and cleaning robots that scan room sizes, identify, and avoid obstacles, and remember the best routes for cleaning

3. Machine Learning (ML): These are computer algorithms that improve through experience. They analyze sample or training data, and then make predictions and decisions. For example:

    a. Speech recognition software that converts audio to text files, voice-command-activated dialing and call routing, voice-activated appliance, and machine control

    b. Extracting structured information from unstructured data files, such as e-mail, web pages, articles, and reports

    c. Tracking spending patterns and identify trends and outliers

Automation generally improves operational efficiencies and reduces errors, which may be caused by human intervention during data input and calculation errors, among others. Automation can also improve monitoring by performing extensive and complex calculations, searching for errors in large data sets, and identifying information that does not conform to expected parameters. This monitoring can be performed periodically, but even more value may be derived by performing the analysis real or near real time, and doing so continuously. The benefits include the early identification of anomalies and helping management, audit, and compliance professionals provide faster, cheaper, timely, and more comprehensive assurance.

Summary

Continuous auditing provides unparalleled opportunities for today's operational auditors. Whereas the review of one fiscal year at a time was the norm for decades, that legacy from financial reviews should not be a constraint anymore. As long as the data are reliable and complete, it is possible to extract, merge, parse, analyze, organize, and opine on virtually any type or amount of data. Sampling and manual records often provide a limited view of operational dynamics, and may provide an incomplete telescope through which to examine the process under review. Furthermore, if the data are incomplete, unreliable, defective, or otherwise unusable, auditors should make that an observation anyway, because it raises questions about the ROI from existing systems, the value of efforts to capture what is evidently suboptimal information, and management's ability to make well-informed decisions given the limitations of available data.

Since it is management's responsibility to establish the processes that support business objectives and monitor the performance of those processes, they should also implement continuous monitoring activities. By focusing on KPIs and KRIs, management can identify anomalies promptly, and take corrective action before they become larger problems or are identified by other parties. It is preferable for management to identify problems as part of the first line of defense. Most people would argue that it is also acceptable for problems to be identified by the second line of defense. Operational problems being identified by internal auditors, the third line of defense, is clearly less desirable. Together, first, second, and third lines of defense should find ways to make sure it is they, and not external auditors, regulators, or journalists, who discover significant operational problems.

Chapter 11 examines change management and ways that internal auditors can become more effective change agents. There are several methodologies in place, but their success depends on previous knowledge gained about common pitfalls during change initiatives, why others are reluctant to embrace change, and how the transition process can be made more effective.

QUESTIONS

1. What are some of the limitations of periodic, manual, and sample-based audits?
2. Explain why auditing every transaction may be a requirement in today's risk environment.
3. Is auditing all transactions feasible? Why or why not?
4. Explain how auditing all transactions may in fact enable risk-based auditing and sample-based auditing perpetuate control-based auditing. Support your answer with examples.
5. Describe five continuous analysis routines and how they support the efforts of internal auditors.
6. Explain the concept and use of KPIs and KRIs for management review and operational auditors.
7. List five continuous monitoring/auditing routines you would recommend to a client for a payment processing operation. Specify what data would be collected, how it would be analyzed, the reporting mechanism, and frequency of its preparation.
8. List five continuous monitoring/auditing routines you would recommend to a client for a customer call center facility. Specify what data would be collected, how it would be analyzed, the reporting mechanism, and frequency of its preparation.
9. List five continuous monitoring/auditing routines you would recommend to a client for an IT service enter. Specify what data would be collected, how it would be analyzed, the reporting mechanism, and frequency of its preparation.
10. List five continuous monitoring/auditing routines you would recommend to an environmental health and safety manager. Specify what data would be collected, how it would be analyzed, the reporting mechanism, and frequency of its preparation.

Notes

1 Internal Auditor magazine, August 2013, p. 33.
2 John Verver, Strategic Advisor to ACL elaborates on these themes on an ACL article, see http://www.acl.com/2016/01/whats-your-plan-for-risk-and-compliance-in-2016/

Chapter 11

Change Management

> The rate of change is not going to slow down anytime soon. If anything, competition in most industries will probably speed up even more in the next few decades.
>
> **John P. Kotter in Leading Change[1]**

Introduction

We often hear the expression "change is the new normal." Business strategists advise their clients to encourage and push change within, and be adaptable to embrace change from outside the organization. Countless authors describe a world where old paradigms are being replaced by new ones. Brick and mortar business are replaced by online enterprises. Traditional practices that focused on stable, predictable patterns are replaced by dynamic, flexible, and unpredictable ones. Business disruption is the new buzz word and a sense of navigating in unchartered waters appears to describe the state of affairs.

In this environment, internal auditors are encouraged to become change agents. The professionals that many considered the guardians of the status quo are now expected to help their organizations identify opportunities to change, make sure they do so smartly, and check their strategic business models to make sure they are going to avoid unexpected surprises during these change initiatives.

This chapter provides the operational auditor with the fundamental concepts to understand the field of change management, the keys to success during change initiatives, common pitfalls to avoid, and the practices and conditions to look for during a review of the organization's change initiatives.

Identifying and Introducing Adaptive and Innovative Changes

The Association of Change Management Professionals defines change management as a deliberate set of activities that facilitate and support the success of individual and organizational change and the realization of its intended business results. In general, change management refers to any approach to transition individuals, teams, and organizations using methods intended to redirect the use of resources, business process, budget allocations, or other modes of operation that significantly reshape a company or organization. The general goal of change initiatives is to fundamentally change how business is conducted to help it cope with the challenging market environment. While internal auditors are often not tasked with implementing change initiatives themselves in their organizations, their recommendations often do. Furthermore, if the goal of today's internal auditor is to encourage action to bring about the needed changes, then success must be measured in part by the degree to which these change recommendations are implemented successfully.

Eight-Step Model

There are several methods of change management. One of the most widely regarded is the 8-Step Process for Leading Change developed by John Kotter. These stages should be worked through in sequence as skipping steps to try to accelerate the process causes problems. Since the success of a given stage depends on the work done in prior stages, a critical mistake in any of the stages can have a significant if not devastating impact (Table 11.1).

The eight stages are

1. *Establish a sense of urgency.* According to Dr. Kotter, half of all change efforts fail at the start. Without motivation for change, and getting people out of their comfort zones, employees won't help and the effort will go nowhere.
2. *Create the guiding coalition.* In successful transformation efforts, the chairman, president, or general manager, plus another 5 to 50 others, including many of the most influential people in the unit, develop a shared commitment to change. A group with enough power to lead the change effort must be assembled and encouraged to work together as a team. It is also advisable that there be a good mix of people from different departments and different levels within the organization.
3. *Develop a vision and strategy.* Without a coherent and sensible vision, a change effort dissolves into a list of confusing and incompatible projects. The guiding coalition must

Table 11.1 Kotter's 8-Step Model to Transforming an Organization

1. Establish a sense of urgency
2. Form a powerful guiding coalition
3. Create a vision
4. Communicate the vision
5. Empower others to act on the vision
6. Plan for and create short-term wins
7. Consolidate improvements and produce more change
8. Institutionalize new approaches

develop a picture of the future that is relatively easy to communicate and appeals to others.

4. *Communicate the change vision.* Management must use every existing communication vehicle to get the vision out. They must incorporate the vision into routine discussions about business problems and do so clearly and often. When the leaders keep the vision fresh on everyone's minds, they'll remember it and respond to it. Management should openly and honestly address the workers' concerns and anxieties, so employees believe that useful change is possible. To reinforce this process, apply the vision to all aspects of operations: from training to performance reviews. Everything must tie back to the vision.

5. *Empower others to work on the vision.* Renewal requires the removal of systemic and human obstacles from the vision. Transformation efforts sometimes fail because the executives in charge don't change their own behavior, don't reward the ideas called for in the vision even when they have requested unconventional ones, and leave the human resource systems intact even though they were incompatible with the new ideals. We must also look at the organizational structure, job descriptions, and performance and compensation systems to ensure they are in line with the vision. Leaders are advised to recognize and reward people for making change happen, identify those who are resisting the change, and help them see what is needed. In general, everyone must take action to remove human and other barriers.

6. *Plan and create short-term wins.* Clearly recognizable victories within the first year or two of a change effort help convince doubters that the change effort is going to be worth all the trouble. Thoroughly analyze the potential pros and cons of the wins and remember that if an early goal doesn't succeed, it can hurt the entire change initiative. Organizations must reward the people who help meet the targets.

7. *Consolidate improvements and produce more change.* After every win, management must analyze what went right and what needs improving. It is important to set goals to continue building on the momentum achieved and apply the principles of kaizen: continuous improvement. New change agents and leaders help keep ideas fresh. It is a good idea to celebrate short-term wins, but the work isn't done yet.

8. *Institutionalize new approaches in the culture.* If they are to stick, new behaviors must be embedded in the organizational culture. New behaviors must be rooted in the social norms, mores, and shared values of the organization. To do this, management must show people that the new behaviors and approaches have improved performance. It also helps to document the new approaches through policies and procedures, training programs, coaching, and mentoring initiatives. Also, the next generation of top management must embrace, embody, and live the new approach. Dr. Kotter suggests that leaders must talk about progress often and tell success stories about the change process. They must include the change ideals and values when hiring and training new staff, while publicly recognizing key members of the original change coalition, and making sure the rest of the staff, both new and old, remembers their contributions. It also helps to create plans to replace key leaders of change as they move on. This will help to ensure that their legacy is not lost or forgotten.

Unfreeze, Change, and Refreeze

Kurt Lewin developed a three-step change model: unfreeze, change, and refreeze. The model represents a very simple and practical model for understanding and enabling change. Essentially, the process entails creating the perception that change is needed, then moving toward the desired level of behavior and finally, setting that new behavior as the norm.

> *Unfreeze.* Before change can be implemented, the process or organization must go through the initial step of unfreezing. Since many people will naturally resist change, the goal during this stage is to create awareness of how current conditions are limiting the organization in some way. Past attitudes, ways of thinking, behaviors, practices, processes, systems, people, and organizational structures must be examined carefully to show employees how change is necessary for the organization to create or maintain a competitive advantage in the marketplace, or to protect itself against a risk. It involves overcoming inertia and breaking down the existing mindset. Defense mechanisms that want to preserve the status quo have to be overcome.

Communication is very important to inform employees about the coming change, the logic behind it and how it will benefit them. In general, the more workers know about a change and the more they feel it is necessary and urgent, the more motivated they will be, the more they will accept and also embrace it.

> *Change.* After workers and the organization have unfrozen, they can begin to move. Lewin recognized that change is a process where the organization must transition or move into this new state of being. This changing step, sometimes also referred to as "transitioning" or "moving," is characterized by the implementation of the change. This is when the change happens. It is also the time when most people struggle with the new reality. It is a time of uncertainty, confusion, and fear that make it the hardest step to overcome. Employees are aware that the old ways are being challenged and changed, but they do not know or experience yet what the new state will be like.

During this phase, employees begin to learn the new behaviors, processes, and ways of thinking. The more prepared they are for this step, the easier it is to complete. Therefore, it is essential for employees to receive education, communication, support, and time to adapt. Employees should be reminded of the reasons for the change and how it will benefit them once it has been implemented fully.

> *Refreeze.* During this phase, the new approach is frozen into place. The name of this phase symbolizes the act of stabilizing and solidifying the new state after the change. The changes made to processes, systems, structures, products, services, and people are accepted and refrozen as the new norm. During this step, the new mindset is formed and workers' comfort level returns.

This step is essential because management must make sure that people do not regress to the old ways of thinking or acting that were present before the implementation of the change. Management must make sure the change is not lost, but instead solidified into the organization's culture and maintained as the acceptable way of thinking and operating. Positive rewards, acknowledgment and recognition of individual, and team efforts are needed to reinforce the new status. Positive reinforcement and rewards will result in the desirable actions being repeated.

Some have the opinion that refreezing is outdated in today's business environment because we live in a world of constant change. Consequently, they argue, it is unnecessary to spend time freezing a new state when it is very likely that it will have to be reevaluated and changed again in the future. The problem with that viewpoint is that it ignores the fact that without refreezing the changes into the organization's modus operandi, it is likely people will revert back to the way they used to do things.

Plan-Do-Check-Act

W. Edwards Deming's model Plan-Do-Check-Act (PDCA) is also considered a simple, yet very effective model for change management. It is an iterative four-step management method used for the control and improvement of processes and products:

1. *Plan.* Establish objectives and processes. It consists of defining the requirements, objectives, expectations, and approach to deliver results according to the expected outcome and outputs. During this phase, improvements are planned for the process by looking for problems that affect the quality of the product or service. During this phase, management should
   a. Select the solution
   b. Recommend system changes
   c. State what change is expected
   d. Identify who is responsible for the action plan
   e. Identify staff members assigned to carry out portions of the plan
   f. Identify who is responsible for educating others
   g. Identify, select, and develop tools for monitoring the expected change[2]

2. *Do.* Implement the plan, execute the process, or make the product. Management should collect data for analysis that informs them of the progress made and to identify any anomalies along the way. When possible, and to mitigate the risk of large-scale failure, it is advisable to start on a small-scale to test, or pilot, possible effects. This also makes it possible to minimize disruptions to the targeted process. Management should implement the plan and state what the target completion date is.

3. *Check.* This involves studying the results that were collected in the do phase, and to compare those with the expected goals, targets, and results expected from the plan phase. A variance or gap analysis will determine if improvements were actually made. The aim is to search for deviation in the implementation from the plan. During this phase, management should
   a. Analyze data and determine the percentage of compliance met
   b. Monitor the effect of the change
   c. Identify staff members responsible for monitoring and data managers
   d. Identify desired compliance and other goals
   e. Identify monitoring dates
   f. Determine if the plan was a success
   g. Identify people, structure, and system issues that hinder the success of the plan[3]
      The results will influence the last phase, act.

4. *Act.* Enact new standards. Ideally, the check phase will show that the plan implemented in the do phase is an improvement over the original condition. If that is so, then that becomes the new standard for how the organization should operate (i.e., act) going forward. If the check phase shows that the plan implemented during the do phase is not an improvement, then the existing standard remains in place.

I agree with Ruth Jacks, who stated in her isixsigma.com post that "the people side of any process improvement requires as much work as the technical side, and sometimes more." Success depends in many ways on making sure that the impacted business area agrees on the recommended solutions. Appropriate tools must be implemented to monitor progress and sustain the changes because this will ensure sustainability.[4]

Project Risk Assessment and the Risk of Failure

Organizations often undertake large projects as part of their strategic plans. The risks of such initiatives can be substantial, since the success of these initiatives could propel the organization forward into new markets, introduce new products that enhance its image as an innovative organization, increase its profile, and raise its stock price. Failure, on the other hand, can be quite damaging in the short and long terms affecting its presence psychologically and financially. Examples of both cases abound.

In many organizations, project management plays a pivotal role in its ability to remain competitive. Projects drive the introduction of new products and services, development of new computer systems, acquisition of a new organization, or entry into a new market. Given the large risk that strategic projects represent to the organization, it is no wonder that a risk assessment should be performed to identify and manage the risk of project failure.

The Project Management Institute (PMI) is the leading organization setting standards for the professional practice of project management. It advocates, for the performance of a risk assessment, to identify and manage the numerous risks that can jeopardize an organization's ability to lead a project to its successful conclusion. In fact, it is in their standards. These "global standards provide guidelines, rules, and characteristics of project, program, and portfolio management."[5]

Assessing and managing project risk should be a fundamental part of project planning, execution, and control. Risks should be managed proactively by the PM and risk management techniques should be employed to prevent and manage them. Key activities include identifying, anticipating, and planning for the occurrence of risk, performing quantitative and qualitative analysis, and planning responses to prevent their occurrence and reducing their impact should they occur. This entails implementing both controls and contingencies.

Unfortunately, all too often PMs fail to take the necessary time to perform effective risk management. This can happen if the PM is consumed with other administrative duties, if this is not required as part of the organization's project management framework and is therefore ignored, or due to a lack of skill. Sometimes it occurs because there is such a rush to begin the project work that thorough planning is neglected. This oversight, regardless of the reason, often results in cost overruns, delays, and scope limitations.

Projects represent a great risk, especially given some of the statistics related to project management and the rate of project failure. Poor project management is extremely costly. Some estimates indicate that organizations have a project failure rate of 70%, meaning that only 30% deliver the agreed upon scope within budget and on time (including approved changes).[6] A study of 10,640 projects from 200 companies in 30 countries conducted by PricewaterhouseCoopers, found that only 2.5% of companies completed 100% of their projects successfully. Another study involving 1471 IT projects, published in the Harvard Business Review, found that the average cost overrun was 27%, but approximately 15% of project had a cost overrun of 200% on average and a schedule overrun of almost 70%.[7]

Gallup reports that when projects fail, it is due to one of the following reasons:

- *Technical.* Technology developed or employed and project management techniques.

- *Individual.* Project leadership, scope management, internal and external communications.
- *Stakeholder management.* User involvement, executive buy-in, goal clarity, and specificity.

Interestingly enough, project management techniques such as quality control, budgeting, scheduling, and critical path analysis, which are commonly used by a large number of PMs, are great tools to solve technical problems, the first type. These tools are not as effective addressing the other two types of problems. That is because individual and stakeholder issues relate to human, social, and emotional factors.[8]

A study conducted by Spikes Cavell found the following as the major causes of project failure:

- Communications breakdown—57%
- Lack of planning—39%
- Poor quality control—35%[9]

Communication involves interactions among team members but also with other stakeholders throughout the life cycle of the project. PMs play a key role in making sure there are accurate and timely communications, but it is important to also remember that these communications must involve and reach out to everyone who should receive these communications. Leaving people out of the loop can be a very damaging practice, whether it is intentional or not.

A Gartner survey shows that excessive project costs account for one-quarter of project failures for projects with budgets greater than $350,000. The failure rate of large IT projects with budgets exceeding $1 million was almost 50% higher than for projects with budgets below $350,000. Given these statistics, PMs should limit the size, complexity, and duration of projects, while making sure that the necessary funding has been committed before the work begins.

It is imperative that PMs plan carefully and monitor constantly their project costs, especially for the largest projects. There should be appropriate mechanisms in place to identify budget variances and/or overruns early. Examples include progress reports and budget variance analysis. PMs should regularly review initial cost estimates and compare those with actual figures to determine how effective the approaches used are and how to improve the accuracy rate in the future. The Project Management Office (PMO) should also help in this regard. The PMO is a department within an organization that helps the organization to effectively select and deliver projects. They define and maintain standards for project management such as documentation requirements, provide support services, and facilitate strategy implementation through guidance and metrics on project execution. In fact, the KPMG Project Management Survey 2013 reports that it is increasingly recognized that high performing PMOs are causing a positive impact on project management performance, and are boosting organizational performance as a whole.

The report also shows that organizations that have a PMO reported that the main benefits are that PMs consistently apply a risk management methodology while the project is in progress. Project time and cost variations are reported in timely manner. In addition, high performing PMOs often choose metrics that communicate to executives how well the activities, and the related projects, serve the organization's strategic goals. Some of these metrics and measures include

- Alignment with strategic goals
- ROI
- Cycle time
- Cost of quality

- Customer satisfaction
- Cost and schedule performance
- Resource utilization
- Requirements performance
- Employee satisfaction

These practices are strongly associated with project success.

To be effective, PMOs must have sufficient authority and resources to do their jobs. PMOs are created to improve project performance; however, not every organization gives the PMO the amount of resources and authority it needs to do its job. Whether the PMO acts in a supportive or consultative role, or directing and controlling the work by enforcing compliance with policies and procedures and managing the projects themselves, the PMO needs to have the authority, resources, and competence to facilitate the successful completion of projects within the organization.

Poor scheduling is another common problem area, and large projects can fail because business conditions change after the project scope was set, and often continue to change throughout project execution. If mismanaged, this can result in a significant divide among the scope, budget, and timeline initially agreed upon, and what the organization will expect and pay for when the project is completed and delivered. Since dynamics can and do change, PMs should make sure there are frequent project status and review meetings that include confirmation of the project's alignment with the organization's strategy. This will help to identify and correct deviations, and in the worst case, cancel hopeless projects as soon as it is evident that they no longer meet the needs of the organization.

PMs must identify and manage unfavorable conditions that threaten the successful completion of the project; uncertainty emanating from a lack of knowledge about events, and opportunities that can be leveraged to lead the project to success. To accomplish this, it is imperative that open communication, being proactive in matters of risk, and breaking down silos so PMs can learn from each other. Effective PMOs can facilitate this process and make sure that lessons learned are captured promptly, analyzed within the correct context, disseminated among all PMs, and incorporated into the organization's monitoring and future project planning practices. This update to the internal project management framework and performance monitoring mechanism can help to create a culture of constant learning and effective oversight.

The risk assessment then, must identify and analyze the risks to the successful completion of its projects. Risk categories should be tailored to the organization, industry, and location. A list of some risk categories is shown in Table 11.2.

The risk assessment process involves gathering information and assessing the risks identified. Techniques to do this include are shown in Table 11.3.

Controlling quality, risk, budget, scope, and schedule are essential for project success, but given the poor success record project management suffers from, it is essential that organizations use a balanced scorecard and assess quantitative and qualitative factors across technical and nontechnical areas. Employee and other stakeholder engagement, motivation, and satisfaction must also be addressed if we wish to see project success rates to improve.

The importance of effective project management cannot be overstated. Millions of dollars could be at risk of being lost, business improvements can be delayed, and customer service could be compromised. Over time, this could result in the lack of competitiveness, reputational risk, lower sales, and a decrease in market share. This represents a massive waste of money and threatens organizations' ability to achieve their strategic objectives, especially since the success, or sometimes even the mere viability of many organizations depends on the success of large-scale, high-impact projects.

Table 11.2   Sample Risk Categories

Customer Satisfaction	Resources
Quality	External versus internal
Performance	Technical and technology
Scope	Customer
Project management	Knowledge
Suppliers	Communication and cultural
Resistance to change	Political
	Environmental

Table 11.3   Risk Assessment Techniques

Technique	What It Involves
Brainstorming	This is normally done in a meeting where one idea helps generate another
Delphi technique	This is an information gathering technique used to reach a consensus by experts on the subject
Expert interviewing	This technique consists of the team or PM interviewing project participants, stakeholders, or experts to identify project risks
Root cause analysis	This is done to identify the underlying source of a problem, and then to determine preventive actions
Strengths, weaknesses, opportunities, and threats analysis (SWOT)	SWOT analysis looks at the project to identify these four areas and their related risks[a]

Note
[a] See more at: http://www.pm-primer.com/pmbok-risk/

As we discuss project risks, one of the challenges is workers who don't do what they are supposed to do. So, a need is identified and a solution found, a vision is set, plans are drafted, people are hired or reassigned to do certain work, yet the people don't do what they are supposed to do. A similar problem may occur in recurring work environments where people are engaged in process activities. So, why is it that people don't do what they are supposed to do?[10] (See Table 11.4).

Understanding and Managing Resistance to Change

People will do what is measured, repeat what is rewarded, and stop doing what is punished.

Table 11.4   Why Workers Don't Do What They Are Supposed to Do

Why They Don't Do It	What You Should Do
1. They don't know what to do	■ Provide accurate job descriptions ■ Ask involvement questions ■ Describe observable behaviors
2. They don't know how to do it	■ Training ■ Develop manuals, P&Ps, and scripts ■ Seek and give constant feedback
3. They don't know why to do it	■ Communicate constantly ■ Show the benefits to the organization ■ Show the benefits to the individual
4. They believe something else is more important	■ Assign and prioritize assignments ■ Update priorities as conditions change ■ Don't label everything as urgent
5. They think they are doing it	■ Provide immediate praise or reprimand ■ Provide a variety of contacts (e.g., verbal and print)
6. They believe your way won't work	■ Seek opinions upfront ■ Provide examples ■ Sell the benefits
7. They believe their way is better	■ Show causes and effects ■ Show them ■ Ask "can you think of anything you would do differently?"
8. There Is no punishment for not doing it	■ Monitor accountability ■ Reward positive behavior and punish negative behavior ■ Implement a progressive disciplinary system
9. There are problems beyond their control	■ Identify and eliminate ■ Help them develop problem-solving skills ■ Avoid roadblocks and similar situations in the future
10. There are personal issues	■ Be flexible and cross-train ■ Show empathy
11. There is no positive outcome to them for doing it	■ Clarify rewards ■ Discuss what's in it for me with them
12. They are rewarded for not doing it	■ Review rewards measures for congruence ■ Identify diverging rewards and address
13. They are punished for doing it or anticipate negative consequences	■ Realign performance measures ■ Communicate desired results

Crave change and innovation. Cope well with uncertainty	Gatekeepers of new ideas into a system. Opinion leaders	Will adopt new ideas after deliberation	Might adopt as a result of increased pressure from peers Skeptical of change	Isolated from social network. Last to change. Suspicious of change agents
Innovators 2.5%	Early adopters 13.5%	Early majority 34.0%	Late majority 34.0%	Laggards 16.0%

Figure 11.1   People's predisposition for change.

Many important change initiatives have been vetted through financial analysis including ROI, payback period analysis, internal rate of return (IRR), and feasibility analysis. In many instances, the approved project has been identified as being key to the organization's long-term sustainability and success, so the need for the project to succeed is understood.

Resistance to change is a constant threat affecting the viability of projects. While some individuals embrace change and can be called pioneers, others may be what is often referred to as settlers because they accept change later in the process. Lastly, a third group, the laggards, are the last ones to embrace change initiatives and support them. Figure 11.1 illustrates this distribution.

The level of acceptance of the change initiative, whether it originated in an auditors' recommendation or a business decision, may encounter different degrees of acceptance. This can range from acceptance, characterized by enthusiasm and cooperation to active resistance, characterized by doing as little as possible, taking excessive time off from work, and outright and deliberate sabotage. This range of reactions and behaviors is illustrated in Figure 11.2.

In general, however, individuals resist change for the following reasons:

1. *Fear.* Many individuals fear change because it takes them outside of their comfort zone. They know their current process and related systems. They know what works and doesn't work. They have grown accustomed to it. A new process or system, however, is new to them. They don't know it and they fear that they will make mistakes, that they will have to struggle to navigate the new environment and that they will appear to lack knowledge.
   What to do: Provide information regarding what will change and what will not change. Explain who will be affected and how.
2. *Loss of power.* After some time, employees learn to control processes, activities, information, and resources. People must contact certain individuals for information and this provides them with power and control. Many change initiatives involve breaking down communication barriers and facilitating the flow of information to speed up processing. If the employees fear a loss of power due to democratization of the process, or reduction of approval levels, it may generate resistance.
   What to do: Examine job descriptions and workplace duties and responsibilities. Identify new tasks the employees must perform and how these workers will be needed, employed, and relevant in the new environment.

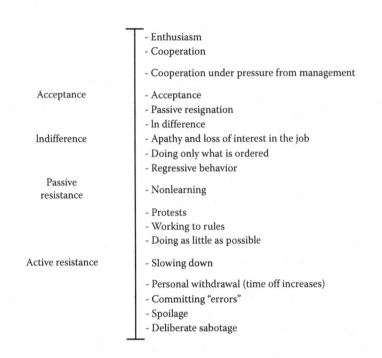

	- Enthusiasm
	- Cooperation
	- Cooperation under pressure from management
Acceptance	- Acceptance
	- Passive resignation
	- In difference
Indifference	- Apathy and loss of interest in the job
	- Doing only what is ordered
	- Regressive behavior
Passive resistance	- Nonlearning
	- Protests
	- Working to rules
	- Doing as little as possible
Active resistance	- Slowing down
	- Personal withdrawal (time off increases)
	- Committing "errors"
	- Spoilage
	- Deliberate sabotage

Figure 11.2 People's acceptance of change.

3. *Mistrust.* Quite often mistrust is the result of years of experiences showing management saying one thing and doing another, making promises that are not followed up, stating they support initiatives only to watch management move onto other priorities, and pulling the plug on previous commitments. The repetition of such patterns will eventually lead employees to question management in the future and when a new change initiative is announced, they are likely to be suspicious and avoid getting too deeply invested in its requirements and actions.

   What to do: Reassure employees that management is committed for the duration of the project. Secondly, be careful not to engage in the practices shown above!

4. *Apathy.* Employee engagement plays a pivotal in the quality of internal controls and the productivity of workers. When engagement levels are high, employees are committed, resourceful, supportive, productive, and deliver high quality services to customers. Employees who have been poorly supervised in the past, and whose performance evaluation process is deficient, generally care less about their work and what is happening within the organization. As a result of poor engagement, motivation levels are not sustained without constant intervention by manager–leaders.

   What to do: Management must act quickly and decisively to correct morale deficiencies and not allow problems to fester. When low morale and dysfunctional work environments are left unaddressed for long periods of time, employees will become apathetic. For example, if promotions appear to be arbitrary, or decoupled from performance, it will soon lead employees to the conclusion that their performance doesn't matter and other considerations are more indicative of future success: favoritism and nepotism in hiring, compensation decisions, and promotion decisions will lead everyone else to question the value of hard work, dedication, and sacrifice.

Constant communication, some element of cheerleading, setting clear performance standards and linking goals, and objectives to the performance evaluation process, are all effective actions to ensure motivation levels are retained and problems are corrected promptly.

5. *Threats to expertise.* I have observed on several occasions how employees have learned to use, navigate, and otherwise work with an antiquated and complex system. They know the quirks of the system. They have memorized hot key shortcuts to navigate and do their work faster. They know how to correct numerous problems caused by the faulty system and are in general proud of their prowess. They proudly embrace the label of "guru" when it comes to the troublesome system and related processes. When a new system is presented, some of these same individuals oppose the idea of deploying a newer, better functioning system because it threatens their expertise on the old system and they may no longer be perceived as the go-to person. They also perceive a threat to their job security because they may no longer be considered essential to the operation.

    I can't deny there are some merits to the concerns and some logic in their reaction. However, it must be remembered that all employees are temporary servants in their organizations, joining the firm to help it accomplish its mission and its objectives. Our personal desires cannot and should not be surrendered completely, but they cannot supersede the need of the organization to act efficiently and effectively either. If there is a better way of getting the work done, it should be considered. As far as job security and laying people off from their jobs, this is a delicate matter that involves people's livelihoods. My viewpoint is that organizations should first consider redeploying those that have needed skills and they should retrain those that have the needed capability and motivation. As for the rest, we cannot ignore the fact that job security is increasingly dependent on the individual and organizations have for decades sent the message that they should not be expected to provide lifetime job security.

    What to do: Employees must take ownership for their training and development, and make themselves essential to their organizations through skill development and consistent superior results. They must also make themselves marketable by acquiring skills that are in demand in the marketplace so they can find suitable employment if conditions change. When individuals become redundant or otherwise unnecessary in their immediate work unit, it is also important for organizations to exert every reasonable effort to redeploy these employees within their organizations before laying them off. The practice of laying workers excessively or without serious attempts to retain and retrain them carries long-term implications for organizations. This should be handled with care, considering the short- and longer-term implications.

It is always useful to remember the words of Peter Senge, "People don't resist change. They resist being changed!"[11]

The Big Three: People, Process, and Technology

When evaluating organizations and programs, it is important to remember the following: they are all organized to achieve a mission. While not all organizations take the time to fully develop, communicate, and ensure that their organizational structure, procedures, and personnel are effectively aligned, organizations are initiated to pursue a mission.

The mission should be supported by goals and objectives that provide a roadmap to take the organization from its current state to the desired one. There are three key components that require alignment, resource allocation, and constant management to ensure effectiveness and efficiency. Processes are developed to achieve the mission, goals, and objectives of the organization, and these will ideally be designed in such a way that they ensure efficiency and effectiveness. Next, people are hired to work within the processes put in place. Lastly, these people and processes are supported by needed machines and technology.

Let's examine each in turn:

> *Process.* They should be designed to accomplish the stated mission and objectives with the lowest use of resources (i.e., efficiency). In many organizations, processes are developed organically as needs arise to satisfy customers, liaise with suppliers, and provide the needed internal support activities such as handling payroll, processing incoming payments, and paying bills to suppliers. When organizations begin operations, their processes are established with limited analysis and scientific planning, they often meet needed requirements but as the organization evolves, these processes become increasingly cumbersome or outright inefficient.

Over time, workers add steps to processes and the cumulative effect is typically an aggregation of unnecessary steps, forms, and procedures. The gradual increase is imperceptible and workers grow into the process. Eventually, processes require in-depth analysis to weed out inefficiencies such as duplication of effort, unnecessary handoffs and reviews, and an over reliance on paper that exacerbates filing requirements.

Internal auditors can be very helpful identifying inefficiencies through careful review, performing walkthroughs, drawing process flow maps, and verifying the purpose of every step in the process. Streamlining activities can help reduce redundancies, rework, excess motion, unnecessary transportation, and waste.

> *People.* People are hired to complement processes. They should be hired based on a combination of technical skill and attitude so they have both the ability and the willingness to do the required work. Deficiencies in either of these attributes will result in quantity or quality problems.

Southwest Airlines states that they hire for attitude and train for skill. This is an interesting and somewhat counterintuitive approach, yet it has resulted in the airline receiving numerous awards over the years. Staffing organizations with people who share the mission and vision, values and goals, and who also possess the needed skills will increase the likelihood of being able to form a cohesive unit that can achieve superior results.

The number of people working within a process also requires careful consideration since labor costs can also jeopardize the financial stability and success of the enterprise. Understaffing and overstaffing create problems. The former by overworking employees who will likely make mistakes, rush while servicing customers, take shortcuts, suffer excessive stress, and eventually suffer burn out. The latter by causing boredom as employees are not consistently busy. Most people recognize that excessive workloads can result in employees making more mistakes than reasonably expected, but a similar problem can occur with underworked employees, whose lack of focus and concentration can result in them not performing their duties as expected.

Recruitment efforts must be aligned with present and future organizational needs so there is a suitable number of individuals with the required skills to perform their duties. The recruitment process should be examined with the elements of efficiency (e.g., speed and accuracy), effectiveness (i.e., meeting objectives and targets), and economy (i.e., paying what is required for maximum returns, and no more) in mind. The recruitment process can be dissected as shown in Table 11.5.

The performance evaluation process plays a key role reinforcing the expectations that management has set for its workers. In general, this process should make sure that staff performance is monitored and regularly evaluated so that employee contributions are maximized, since people will do what is measured, repeat what is rewarded, and stop doing what is punished. Goals should be established using the SMARTER model (see Chapter 5 for a full description of the model). With this in mind, the achievement of personal goals and objectives must be monitored, formal and informal feedback provided frequently, their achievement rewarded, and reasons for nonachievement identified, reviewed, and corrected. In general, the individual and collective performance and achievement must be linked to the reward structure.

Table 11.5   Breakdown of the Hiring Process

Phase	Key Activities
Position request	Determine the budget and amount that will be paid to the employee and authorization for that expenditure
Job description	If one is already in place, verify that it is up to date and reflects the responsibilities for the position. Job descriptions should not be so vague that they fail to properly describe the duties for the position and establish accountabilities. Conversely, they should not be so restrictive that the manager is restrained from asking the employee to perform other needed and related tasks. Job descriptions should describe the position, state the education requirements, skills, and required experience
Recruitment	This entails selecting the recruitment channel (e.g., LinkedIn, Facebook, recruiters, and job fairs), posting the position, and monitoring responses
Interviewing	To avoid nepotism and favoritism, I like the 3×3×3 formula. It requires at a minimum of three candidates per vacancy, three interviewers per candidate, and three individuals who vote to offer the position to the individual
Selection	Input should be obtained from the HR department and the hiring manager. Increasingly, colleagues of the ideal candidate will also provide input into the candidate and provide feedback
Offer	This involves determining the amount of the salary, the start date, what perks (if any) the individual will receive, benefits, perform background checks and tests (e.g., drug, medical, and physical)
Start	Workplace set-up, tour of the workplace, meet coworkers, and other onboarding activities like document signatures, orientation, and training

Many organizations have implemented a 360 degree review process to make sure that employee performance includes feedback from subordinates and colleagues, not only their immediate supervisor. To make this process work effectively, it is imperative that the organization establishes and promotes a no-retaliation policy and that the results are used to improve performance. Some organizations have implemented the 360 degree program as a mandatory and universal mechanism, while others make it optional. This can be done upon request or when an employee is concerned that the manager may not provide a fair evaluation of their performance.

During their reviews, auditors should verify that all employees receive a performance evaluation annually. Another useful analytical procedure is to calculate the average score for employees and determine if it represents "grade inflation," where everyone gets a high score, regardless of their real performance and accomplishments. Data confirming this anomaly can then be compared to the unit's achievement of their collective goals as the basis for discussion with management: How can the workers get such high evaluation scores, if the unit itself is not meeting its objectives? Conversely, if workers are getting low evaluation scores, but the unit is exceeding its objectives, does this indicate a punitive evaluation process that aims to undermine their accomplishments and delink any possibility of pay increases?

> *Technology.* While many people naturally think about computer hardware and software, the overarching category is actually machines. In some environments, this involves wrenches, drills, saws, and presses. In high-tech industries, support functions, and service environments, it is often related to IT. In others, it is a combination such as computer-aided design/computer-aided manufacturing, where computers assist in the design and manufacture of goods. Important considerations include the appropriateness of the hardware and software (machines), calibration, maintenance, capacity, and skill to operate effectively and efficiently.

As organizations increase the use of machines in their processes, automation reduces the role of individuals. Robotics are transforming how organizations design and perform their activities and the implications are profound. As auditors, this change cannot go unnoticed, not only because the skillset of workers is changing, but also because the number of workers changes, the capital investments made are substantial, and the data capture, analytics, and reporting mechanism must be adapted accordingly. Whether the organization is manually intensive, or highly automated, internal auditors must note the implications and identify the relevant risks so controls can be adapted accordingly.

Dysfunctions

Over the years, I have witnessed a wide variety of ways that problems emerge and evolve in organizations. A common misconception is that if you have operating problems, you can solve them by implementing a new computer system. A broken process cannot be fixed by buying a new computer system. If you try anyway, the result will be that you will have a very expensive system and problems will either continue or new problems will emerge. If there is an operational problem, the process should be fixed first, then the need for a new computer system can be examined. If that proves to be the case, then the new system can be installed.

If business goals point to the need to implement a new system, as is the case when the existing one lacks the capacity, speed, or scalability needed to support the business, the process can be fixed as the new system is being configured and deployed. But not a system in lieu of a process overall

Regarding people, I have also observed how the lack of skill, motivation, supervision, and monitoring can create or exacerbate operational problems. If the people issues are not addressed, changing the process or buying new computer systems won't fix the problem either. That weakness has to be addressed first or simultaneously. In this case, not addressing the people issues first often explains why new systems languish due to underuse or misuse because workers find other ways of getting the work done, circumventing the system in place, or only using it partially. Some readers may have experienced instances when they search for and review system data and discover that fields are left empty or contain placeholders. By placeholders, I mean phony or arbitrary data to trick required field controls during data entry.

This practice can be quite damaging because if management generates reports that rely on this information, or when the auditor attempts to verify the quality of information captured and used, they may discover that the information is unreliable. For example, if instead of using the serial number as the fixed assets' unique identifier, the operator enters the model number, it could be near impossible to identify the location of the asset. Similarly, if a control is in place requiring that a physical address and phone number be entered in the vendor file record, it is troublesome if employees copy the P.O. Box mailing address in the physical address field, or enter a single number or string of numbers (e.g., 9s) to trick the system.

Summary

Everybody has accepted by now that change is unavoidable. But that still implies that change is like death and taxes—it should be postponed as long as possible and no change would be vastly preferable. But in a period of upheaval, such as the one we are living in, change is the norm.

Peter Drucker, 1999

The PMI's Pulse of the Profession: The High Cost of Low Performance 2014 states: "Organizations that are highly agile, nimble and able to respond quickly to changing market dynamics complete more of their strategic initiatives successfully than slower, less agile organizations (69% versus 45%). But only 15% of organizations report high organizational agility."

As these two quotes show, change is an expected element of modern management, yet many organizations still struggle to drive and manage change effectively. Although there are several models for effective change management, many organizations still suffer due to their inability to adapt to change. This is a major constraint to success and the repercussions can be substantial.

Even when some stakeholders want change, others may resist it. This disagreement can have profound impacts on business success, so in addition to developing a great idea and plan for change, the change sponsors and agents should determine who may oppose it and with how much vigor. Countermeasures may be necessary to prevent great ideas from failing to gain traction due to an inability to anticipate resistance.

Managers perform a crucial role in organizations because they interpret company policy, execute corporate directives, fulfill all of the people-management needs in their particular area of responsibility, cascade senior management messages down the chain of command, and communicate employee feedback up to chain. If they fail to consider the amount, speed, and significance of change while doing these things they could manage the organization into serious problems. Internal auditors must help managers avoid this outcome.

QUESTIONS

1. Describe Kotter's 8-Step Process for Leading Change and the implications for operational auditors.
2. How does Kotter's Step 5—Empower Others to Act on the Vision impact internal controls in organizations?
3. Provide three examples that demonstrate the organization has implemented Step 8—Institutionalize New Approaches.
4. Describe Kurt Lewin's three-step change model.
5. What are the implications of Kurt Lewin's Step 3: Refreeze for operational auditors and how can they verify that management has effectively implemented this step?
6. Describe W. Edwards Deming's PDCA model.
7. How does W. Edwards Deming's Plan step relate to project management and how can operational auditors verify that management has effectively implemented this step?
8. List three reasons project planning should include a risk assessment.
9. Describe five key steps that an operational auditor should perform when auditing an organization's PMO.
10. Describe three reasons individuals resist change and indicate what should be done to correct them.

Notes

1 See http://www.leadershipnow.com/changequotes.html
2 See http://www.isixsigma.com/methodology/plan-do-check-act/six-sigma-pdca steroids/
3 Ibid.
4 Ibid.
5 See http://www.pmi.org/PMBOK-Guide-and-Standards.aspx
6 See http://4pm.com/project-failure/
7 http://www.gallup.com/businessjournal/152429/cost-bad-project-management.aspx, retrieved November 15, 2015.
8 Ibid.
9 Retrieved from http://www.it-cortex.com/Stat_Failure_Cause.htm on November 15, 2015.
10 See Ferdinand Fournies, *Why Employees Don't Do What They're Supposed To Do and What To Do About It* (New York: McGraw-Hill), 1999.
11 See http://www.leadershipnow.com/changequotes.html

Chapter 12

Project Management

> All things are created twice: first mentally, then physically. The key to creativity is to begin with the end in mind, with a vision and a blueprint of the desired result.
>
> **Stephen Covey**

Introduction

Project management consists of the process of defining, performing, and monitoring specific work, bounded by a timeline, a defined scope, and goals. It is often performed by a team and given a budget to work with.

Organizations often define, authorize, fund, and monitor projects because they are part of the strategic plan. As such, their success can result in the rollout of new products or services, introduction of systems that facilitate work and communication among stakeholders, or construction of a new building or power plant. With such a large scale and prominence, their budgets can be substantial. This presents a double exposure to the organization: the commitment of large sums of money to fund the work, and the opportunity cost if the project is not successful. The former represents a financial loss. The latter represents the delay or abandonment of benefits had the project delivered its outcomes as expected.

Internal auditors can add value to their organizations by helping management set the requirements for project planning, execution, and monitoring. This includes minimum required documents, procedures for obtaining and documenting key attributes and practices, and defines how performance will be monitored. The discipline and consistency can help to avoid problems later.

Project Management

The PMI defines a project as a temporary endeavor undertaken to create a unique product, service, or result. The two characteristics that define a project are that they are unique and

274 **■** *Operational Auditing*

temporary, as opposed to typical business operations where activities are performed within the confines of a process that is assumed to be permanent.

Unique

Projects are unique because they produce unique outcomes, ranging from highways, buildings, weapons, and computer systems, machines, new products, and the like. While some projects are one-of-a-kind from one perspective, many share commonalities as you find during construction projects. Although the buildings may have different shapes and sizes in the end, there are some common activities to most construction projects: preparing the foundation, framing, plumbing, electrical and communications wiring, roofing, etc. A similar pattern emerges regarding IT systems development; the system itself may be different, but most system development projects include a feasibility analysis, writing business rules, writing of the code, testing, and deployment.

In addition, each project is going to have different stakeholders, resources, staffing, deadlines, communications requirements, and other characteristics. Constraints are often unique to each project. So, although there are some similarities, each project is unique in the details of the outcome and the way it is conducted.

Temporary

Projects have a life cycle that affects their dynamics, structure, and operations, so project management is heavily influenced by this life cycle. Projects have a start that can be a discrete date or they could begin to emerge as business leaders identify a need, begin discussing its characteristics, hold meetings, and ask someone to put together a proposal. Projects also have an end date when agreed upon deliverables should be handed over.

This temporary characteristic is in contrast with business as usual, where activities are recurring in an indefinite cycle. Since projects are not permanent and repetitive only within a defined timeline, it means that controls and activities often require different skills and management practices. This also means that constraints may be unique to each project, with time limits and potentially significant repercussions if timelines are not adhered to.

Project Phases

Project life cycles are generally described as following these five phases: initiation, planning, executing, and closing. The fifth phase, monitoring and controlling, I prefer not to list as part of a sequence because it could be misunderstood as implying that it only occurs at a certain point during the progression. Monitoring and controlling applies to all phases.

Projects undergo various phases as the objective morphs from concept to reality. The approaches endorsed by PMI and the IIA are compatible. Internal auditors usually divide their audits and special projects in three phases: planning, fieldwork, and reporting and the five project phases fit into this model as well. While internal auditors don't explicitly mention monitoring and controlling, that would be covered in the requirement stating: "Engagements must be properly supervised to ensure objectives are achieved, quality is assured, and staff is developed" (Standard 2340). Otherwise, initiation and planning would fit into planning. Executing fits into fieldwork and closing entails reporting on one level, but also supervision and documentation closeout classic activities performed by auditors.

In general, project management is the process of combining systems, techniques, and people to complete a project's scope within established time, budget, and quality goals. All projects have a defined beginning and end, and are done to achieve unique goals and objectives. The five phases provide structure from concept, through execution, to delivery and closure. By following these phases, PMs and other stakeholders can improve the odds of bringing projects to their successful conclusion.

Initiation

This is the first stage of the project. One of the key tasks performed during this phase is defining the overall project goal. Defining the goals(s) may seem simple and obvious, but it is not as easy as it sounds.

Over the years, I have encountered numerous instances where answering the question "what should the project accomplish?" results in different people giving different answers. What people have in mind doesn't always get reflected in project documents. And what they mean may not be captured accurately in project specifications either. Part of the challenge is that the expectations of customers, management, and other relevant stakeholders are not always captured effectively at the beginning of the project. I make special mention of the word "beginning" because sometimes when the discrepancies are noted later in the project life, adjustments are made and there is a search for a better alignment between expectations and what designers are working on. Unfortunately, at this point stakeholder relationships may be strained due to misunderstandings and frustration. In addition, costs may escalate due to already built-in inefficiencies or the need to take corrective actions.

It is imperative that the expectations of every key stakeholder be identified, documented, understood, and communicated to other relevant stakeholders, and reflected in the project documentation. These are often captured in the business requirements. Some degree of failure, or even catastrophic failure, is likely to occur if the client expectations are unclear or unrealistic, especially if the gap is left unaddressed and the project moves into subsequent phases. Many projects fail to meet the expectations of the clients, and those numbers are staggering. Not assessing the time and resource requirements to accomplish those objectives only raises the risk that the project will disappoint in the end. If this phase is not performed well, it is unlikely that the project will successfully meet the business' needs.

The allocation of resources is also determined during the planning phase, so the lack of clear, reliable, and accurate feasibility and market studies, among others, will result in the organization committing resources and embarking on a journey under false or faulty assumptions and decisions.

The initiation phase includes defining the scope of the project, an analysis of the needs and requirements in measurable terms, a review of current operations to perform a gap analysis that highlights the transition from the current to the future state, a financial analysis showing the budget, and the costs and benefits expected from the project. It also includes a stakeholder analysis that identifies users and support personnel for the project, and a charter that defines the activity's purpose, authority, responsibility, and resources. The charter should help to clarify the objective of the project, formally establish the financial, human, and other types of support for the project, and gain the necessary commitment from key stakeholders.

An important aspect of effective project planning and launch is effective communications. Communications must be multidirectional. They must flow up because sometimes stakeholders may not realize that what they need and are asking for can be improved upon to increase customer satisfaction. Communications must also flow down because some expectations may be too high, given the resources, time, and technology/materials available.

These expectations are then used to define the scope, which is one of the three major parameters of projects: scope, cost, and time. In Leading Project Teams, Anthony Cobb defines scope as the sum total of all work to be done to produce the project's deliverables—the products and services to be delivered to the customer. Schedule, the second element, refers to the amount of time given to complete the projects, while cost is the total cost to do the project work.

These three elements are closely linked and must remain in equilibrium for the project to be successful. If the scope of the project changes to accommodate changing deliverables, the project's cost and time are affected and must be changed accordingly. This scope change, which can be gradual and is sometimes referred to as scope creep, may occur because minor additions are made to the project without adjusting the small increments in time and cost. The scope can also increase in large increments when "while you're doing that, can you also include …," or "oh, we forgot to include that, yes, we need that too" happen. So, if the scope increases, the project timeline must be extended and/or the cost must be increased.

If the timeline is reduced, which I have seen occur due to changing business conditions that require accelerating project deliverables, it is imperative that the other two elements be adjusted accordingly. With a reduction in the timeline, the costs will generally increase due to overtime or additional staff hired to get the work done. Otherwise, the scope will need to be reduced.

If business conditions or management decisions limit the available resources allocated to the project, the timeline or the scope will need to be adjusted. Lower budgets will result in fewer resources (e.g., fewer staff, purchasing less powerful computers and servers) available. When that occurs, it will take longer to get the work done, so the timelines must be extended. Conversely, the scope must be reduced because in the end, the resources, financial and otherwise, are buying deliverables. So with fewer resources, the scope will shrink.

The equilibrium being discussed here assumes that with the adjustments being made, the quality of the work done is never compromised. This is an important clarification, and a factor that some individuals forget when they make decisions and state that although the budget was reduced, the original scope and timeline must be adhered to. When asked "with the reduction in the timeline, are you prepared to increase the budget or reduce the scope?," some respond "no, the budget and scope must remain the same." In doing so, they are effectively asking for something that is virtually impossible and only a matter of time before they realize the flaw in their expectations.

What happens when this unrealistic approach is attempted? One of the outcomes is that the quality of the deliverable is lower, either by substituting materials, less sophisticated workmanship, fewer features, and in the case of computer applications, the release of the system with "bugs" in it. Over the years, I have encountered numerous instances when systems are rolled out with what developers label "known bugs," and it puzzled me from the early stages of my career, because it is an unfortunate compromise made that affects end users, affecting their productivity, lowering their morale and satisfaction with the application, and sometimes even affecting client relations. While one goal (i.e., delivering on an agreed upon schedule) is accomplished, the system fails in terms of scope and quality. This also diminishes the ROI expected from the system developed.

The triple constraint and the equilibrium that it engenders can be represented in Figure 12.1.

It is essential that close attention be given to each of these elements from the beginning (i.e. initiation phase) of a project, through the execution phase until its close. When effective planning updates, and monitoring take place, projects are less likely to suffer from surprising cost overruns scope limitations, delays, or quality problems.

Figure 12.1 The triple constraints.

During the initiation phase, an overview of the project and the strategy that will be used to achieve the desired results is defined. Having clear goals and developing a realistic strategy with the related steps is a key aspect of what should happen during this phase. Without a clear idea of where you want to go, it is virtually impossible to define a good roadmap and identify what resources are required to get you there.

With an understanding of the goals and scope of the project, another key aspect of the initiation phase involves the selection of the PM and the members of the project team. Choosing the wrong PM can derail the entire project. I have seen many instances where the project begins to fail as soon as the PM is selected because it was not the best person for the job. The PM is expected to clarify the project's mission, objectives, organize and structure the work, coordinate the flow of resources and outputs while controlling the operational side of the work. In addition, PMs must manage one-on-one relationships and group dynamics, staff, motivate, develop, and ensure the commitment from their project teams and other stakeholders. Negotiation skills, time management, and conflict resolution, in addition to the ability to serve as a liaison between these diverse constituencies are all key aspects of the job as well. With this in mind, the assignment to serve as the PM should be based on a combination of attributes, including technical, emotional, and experiential factors.

There are many skills and competencies that a PM must possess to be effective. To be successful, a PM must be a

Leader. The PM should motivate, establish the direction for the team, show initiative, and produce change. This individual must also be innovative, serve as a role model for everyone, and influence others through words, actions, and directives while inspiring everyone to put in their best performance. The leader must be fair and compassionate while directing the team to meet its objectives. Effective leaders are also impartial, not engaging in nepotism or favoritism, but selecting, rewarding, and promoting workers based on merit. Leadership is a very important attribute of effective auditors, because it is not enough to manage budgets, delegate tasks, and review workpapers, the leader must respond to the many needs that each stakeholder has.

Initiator. The PM should realize that their role goes far beyond administrative duties, and relies heavily on the application of effective management and human resource skills. This individual must be a self-starter that turns ideas and plans into action. When a problem emerges, the PM should address the issue immediately and fairly for everyone involved. Failing to anticipate issues, and respond promptly to them will damage the project's prospects for success.

Role model. The PM must walk the talk. Not only that, but also act appropriately even beyond the words spoken. With expressions such as "actions speak louder than words" and "what you do speaks so loudly that I cannot hear what you say," it is evident that

PMs set the tone among team members. They also set the expectations, and if their actions or behaviors differ from the expected practices, others are likely to emulate their behavior. PMs must act consistently in ways that support these written and verbal communications.

Negotiator. Effective PMs must be able to navigate the diverse agendas of the stakeholders and find agreement among them. This requires patience, effective communication skills, but also the ability to discern their needs, wants, and motivations. By showing strength of character, fairness and a willingness to compromise when necessary, the PM can help everyone involved feel appreciated, respected, and cared for. Labeling others "difficult to work with" is not a solution, and blaming people and events is not effective either.

Listener. Too many leaders believe that "might is right" and that the effective leader is the one that can force others to do as told. Being decisive and assertive are important, but effective leaders understand others and whenever possible get input from others before, during, and after making decisions. Before to determine the best course of action. During to take corrective action when necessary. And after as a way to learn from the past and as an input into future actions.

Coach. The administrative responsibilities of the PM are many. From managing the budget, to authorizing and managing the staff's time off, meeting deadlines, managing the scope, and similar matters, some managers have no time left for coaching others. This is a troublesome situation whenever it happens because junior staff members miss the opportunity to receive guidance from those who are more experienced. When the PM shares these life and professional lessons, it helps others grow personally, but collectively it can do wonders to build capacity within the ranks of the next generation of leaders and PMs. When the PM displays a willingness to do so, and takes the time to coach, guide, and mentor others, the practice will be adopted by others, and the result will be a culture of sharing that will make it easier for everyone to work together, share their talent and resources effectively, and resolve any conflict before it erodes team cohesion and productivity.

Working member. There is often enough work to go around when a project is underway, and it is important for the PM to get involved and help out. By being part of the group and working alongside the staff, the PM will demonstrate the concept of camaraderie and team spirit, but also that the success and failure of the endeavor depends on the results of the work done collectively. It will support the practice of mutual assistance and that no task is menial if it contributes to the successful completion of the work required.

Having said this, a word of caution is important here. If the PM is constantly distracted doing other people's work, or bails the staff continuously, it may create another problem that is best avoided. Everyone has a role that carries responsibilities and should do their job. Helping others is a natural extension of one's responsibilities and provides a boost to the sense of belonging to a group effort but no one should believe that they can shift their responsibilities onto others with impunity.

Facilitator. PMs are often required to speak publicly and make presentations to various stakeholders. Whether it is to communicate the project's goals, describe the product features, or give others status updates, the PM should be an effective communicator in the presence of small and larger groups. Facilitation, however, is a bit different. This involves listening to others while speaking, obtaining input while providing facts and figures, sharing the stage with others, encouraging the sharing of ideas, and providing a forum for concerns to be expressed when appropriate. This carries some additional risk, but the results can boost the quantity and quality of results significantly.

Employer. Since this team will be tasked with turning the project concept into reality, the composition is essential for success since their skill, experience, and motivation will drive the work that needs to be performed. Sometimes team composition changes as the project progresses due to employee rotations, business, and personal needs, so business requirements and the work done to date must be documented clearly for all to understand and use.

The initial project team should be selected carefully to ensure inclusion of the necessary skills and motivation. Selection of the initial team membership is also essential because it is easier to manage qualified and motivated workers, than it is to contend with untrained and apathetic ones.

Effective hiring will get the entire project started on the right footing, make it easier for the PM to work with a qualified team, and team members will have strong colleagues to work with.

If the organization recruits talented workers, as it should, then it should also get the workers' input as often as it can. The best idea can come from the PM (the boss) as much as it may come from the junior staff member who just finished an academic certification or training program and learned a new technique that can be applied in the situation at hand. The number of people who follow the traditional approach of leaving it up to the boss to come up with all the ideas, solve all the problems, and make all the decisions is shrinking. Organizations where the practice is for junior workers to wait for specific instructions before taking any action are less productive, act more slowly, and are less inventive in their work.

Planning

The second phase of project management involves the actions necessary to think and organize the activities necessary to achieve the goals of the project. During this phase, a plan is created that defines more clearly the precise tasks required to produce the project's products and services, establishes estimates of resource needs and related costs, and the amount of time required to perform the necessary work. Another important aspect of this phase is the arrangement of the tasks during the life cycle so they can form a project schedule.

During this phase, the scope is sharpened. This means that the project goes from a wide view and broadly described as aspirational—defined, to more tactical and detailed—refined.

Lacking plans is a surefire way to fail. Plans need to be reviewed and approved by significant stakeholders before major project work begins. Project launch is also important and should happen after the planning is complete and resources are committed. Starting the major work before this happens is often a recipe for trouble.

Planning is essential for success because it translates the "what" of the project into the "how." It defines not only the activities that provide the steps to achieve the goals, but should also be accompanied by the identification of the resources required to make the concept a reality. These resources, which are used to pay for the time people spend and the materials used, involves costs. Estimating those costs under normal circumstances, and incorporating some contingencies for unexpected costs, overtime, expedited shipments, and repairs, is also important during the planning phase. In addition, plans allow all involved to know what to expect from each person and collectively, providing clarity of purpose, accountability, and transparency.

Planning involves the creation of a list of required tasks and activities. This defines what must be done to get the work done that will accomplish the goals and objectives. Beyond listing the required tasks and activities, planners must also establish the most efficient sequence of activities. This is key because poorly sequencing activities result in inefficient execution and extensive stop-and-go situations where the realization comes later that an activity cannot be performed because a required step was not completed. This often results in backtracking to correct these issues, delaying the project, or increasing costs.

Estimating the duration of the activities identified in the planning phase can be difficult. A common mistake is to underestimate how long it will take for a task or activity to be completed, resulting in delays when the time goes by and the work is not yet completed despite the hard work of those involved. Underestimating can be caused by the limited knowledge and experience of the PM. This can also occur when the activity has never been performed before and there is no basis in experience to estimate it. Lastly, taking longer than the original estimate can be the result of unexpected developments during the performance of the work, such as delays by third parties.

The Critical Path Method and the Program Evaluation and Review Technique (PERT)

While planning projects, the manager must identify the activities necessary to achieve the project goals, and the sequence of these activities as well because there are often dependencies between them, so some activities cannot be performed unless preceding ones have been completed. Both tools show the critical path for a project, but while the Critical Path Method (CPM) shows one time estimate for each task, Program Evaluation and Review Technique (PERT) considers optimistic, most likely, and pessimistic timeframes. This way, PERT includes an element of probability to the time estimate calculated for the project.

Both techniques use a network of arrows and nodes to show the project's activities. The arrows show the task dependencies, while the nodes show where the tasks interconnect. The arrows show the relationship and sequence of the activities, while the nodes typically have information in them, such as the activity number, the name of the task, and the amount of time needed to complete it.

Metrics such as the earliest start, the earliest finish, the latest start, and latest finish for each activity provide clarity to what and when activities must be performed. With the time estimates, the CPM shows the project's critical path and where there is slack time. The sequence of tasks on a project that will take longer than any other set of tasks to get the project completed and have zero slack constitute the critical path.

Since the project cannot be completed any earlier than shown on the critical path, it determines the earliest completion date. Due to this, this path should receive a great deal of attention because any delays on the critical path delays the completion date for the entire project unless future timeframes can be shortened. This is an essential concept to minimize delays and work with a sense of urgency and clear direction.

It is fairly common for the duration of an activity to have a range of values due to multiple estimates, so managers may want to establish:

- *An optimistic estimate.* Assuming that everything works according to the plan and gets completed without unexpected circumstances.
- *A pessimistic estimate.* This is based on the assumption that things go wrong and the activity takes a long time to be completed.
- *A most likely scenario.* Based on a reasonable assumption that the activity is performed according to normal circumstances and the completion time lies between the optimistic and the pessimistic estimates.

Since these estimates range from the worst to the best possible scenario, managers should take the weighted average instead of relying on a single estimate. To avoid putting too much emphasis on either extreme of the values, the pessimistic and optimistic values are compared to four times the most likely duration. For example, if the amount of time required to perform data analytics has estimates of 2 (optimistic), 4 (most likely), and 8 (pessimistic) days, we can calculate the time to address the customer's needs using the following formula:

$$t_e = (t_o + 4t_m + t_p)/6$$

where

t_o = optimistic time estimate
t_m = most likely time estimate
t_p = pessimistic time estimate

By substituting the values, the expected duration for the auditor to perform the data analytics in our example is: $T = (2 + 4(4) + 8)/6 = 4.3$ days.

Internal auditors should review the preparation, use, and monitoring of the WBS, Gantt Chart, and CPM/PERT during project management reviews. These are very useful tools for project management, but sometimes underused reflecting a need for better planning. Likewise, internal auditors should consider using them during the planning and work on audits and consulting projects.[1]

Another critical aspect of project planning that when neglected causes many problems and often results in cost overruns is the failure to link tasks and activities in the schedule with the related costs and resource needs. Everything done during a project has a cost related to it. Even inaction is costly since employees are being paid, work space is being occupied, and even idle machinery is often leased or require monthly payments be made on them. With this in mind, effectively assigning costs to every activity is key.

Sometimes the costs are under-calculated intentionally to make the project appear cheaper than it is in reality, to get its approval, or secure its continued funding in smaller increments with the intent of prolonging its life. This is unacceptable and auditors should check for this. Sometimes the costs are over calculated to give the PM "wiggle room" later on. By coming in under budget later, some managers may get a bonus. Auditors should check for this too. So, accuracy throughout is key.

Another essential deliverable during the planning phase is the plan approval. I recall a situation at an organization where internal disputes were creating strain among the project stakeholders. Progress reports showed that the project was tracking well and consistent with its projections, but after closer examination and speaking with project members, it was discovered that the due dates for several deliverables had been changed numerous times and the reality was that the project was behind schedule. Further research showed that there was no conclusive project approval and "project plan freeze."

The project plan freeze is the sign off on the project's scope, timeline, and resources. This is critical because progress reports and the related variance analyses should relate back to these parameters as the project baseline. If changes are made to any of these three attributes, that should be noted and tracked, and upon approval, establish a new baseline. When this is not done, as in the example above, anomalies can occur.

The absence of an official planning freeze may occur out of neglect or if no one was designated to drive that action, but another reason for that is due to slow progress reaching agreement. Consider the case of an organization where key stakeholders are discussing the parameters of the project and delay making final decisions, while others involved in the project are hiring people, buying/leasing equipment, and are ready to get started on the project. Since time is money and these individuals can't wait anymore due to mounting costs and commitments, they start working. After a while, and as the work continues to progress, the formal approval and design freeze are forgotten because the work has now begun and progress reports start showing up. At this point, a formal approval seems unnecessary anymore and the project work continues without this vital step being performed.

Executing

This phase is when the actual doing takes place. The major objective is to keep the project on track after it has been launched and do what the plan calls for. Leaders work with the project team and need to make sure they are meeting the quality requirements and deadlines within the timeline agreed upon, while judiciously using the resources allocated to the project.

The concept and plan are acted on and some of the most important activities during this phase include

- Leading and managing the team
- Meeting with the team members
- Communicating with stakeholders

Communication is key and one of the key reasons projects fail. Effective communications must occur with all stakeholders, including project sponsors, vendors, users, and financial units. Making sure that supplies are received on time is essential, but quality issues must be communicated and corrected immediately as well. Another common issue involves delays communicating future needs, so lead times are insufficient and what is needed arrives late, causing delays or additional costs as expediting fees are assessed and added.

While often undesirable, conflict is to be expected during project management. It is best to avoid any kind of dysfunctional conflict that can derail the successful work of the project, but when it occurs, it must be resolved promptly and effectively. Unresolved conflict generates resentment and can lead to poor performance, lack of cooperation among those involved, and absenteeism and excessive turnover. The PM is the person responsible for managing project team dynamics and resolving them. It must be remembered, however, that dysfunctional conflict is often the result of poor planning and expectations setting, and delays addressing the early signs of disagreements. When problems are left unresolved, the problems seldom go away. In fact, they usually fester, grow larger, and costlier.

Another element of effective project management is obtaining necessary resources when needed. Delays or inadequate substitution can be very damaging to the successful completion of the project and often occur when conditions are unexpected and there is a rush to address them. Performing a project risk assessment, identifying control points, and contingencies will go a long way toward avoiding or properly addressing these issues. Progress reports that include relevant KPIs are a great tool to identify issues promptly and monitor their remediation.

Closing

During this phase, the final products, services, and other outcomes are delivered to the client. Ties to other organizations, such as the host and suppliers, are ended and the project team is disbanded.

It is common for a final report to be prepared that summarizes the project's accomplishment, future actions required, if any, and ongoing maintenance arrangements. Accounting adjustments may be made and unnecessary assets may need to be disposed of as well.

Workers are often reassigned at this point so having effective performance evaluations done during the execution phase will enable the organization to reassign workers in the most productive way.

Monitoring and Controlling

Team leaders, and especially the PM, need to control what is being done, how it is done, and by whom. The pace of project work, its costs, performance quality, and meeting the expectations of relevant stakeholders are also key concerns and key areas for project management oversight during the execution of the project. What is required, but not getting done, should also be determined because they will become the unmet deliverables and scope limitations that will haunt the project later.

While some focus their monitoring and control activities on the executing phase, that is not the only phase where that should occur. During the initiating phase, stakeholders must determine what the project should accomplish and define the overall project goal. If these goals and objectives are not aligned with corporate strategic, operational, and financial goals and objectives, the lack of alignment will result in confusion, the misuse of company resources, and potentially undermine the mission of the organization. The organization should have a project management methodology and defined tools to oversee this endeavor before the project begins, in addition to guidelines for progress reporting.

During the planning phase, the tasks and activities are defined, along with detailed plans and the sequence of events, often documented in Gantt and CPM diagrams, WBS and Communication Matrices. There are also contracts that should be written and agreed upon with workers and vendors. Preparing these documents poorly, having them reviewed and approved by the wrong parties, or not defining communication and reporting protocols are likely to cause problems.

The execution phase requires oversight of time consumption, resource usage, and work performance. Variance analysis and remediation of deviations on the triple constraint elements, minimizing the number and impact of change orders, and making sure that invoice payments are legitimate and accurate are essential for the successful execution of the project.

The closing phase requires verification that the ROI was achieved, that maintenance obligations will be kept, and that asset disposal is done appropriately.

Monitoring and controlling then is clearly something that should happen throughout the entire life cycle of the project and not something that happens "during phase four of a project." It should happen throughout the entire lifecycle and internal auditors are encouraged to get involved not only as auditors, but also as advisors early on in the process.

The traditional approach of reviewing outcomes after the project concludes is deficient because it happens too late. The building or system has been built, moneys have been spent, and some of the key individuals have most likely left. Recovering overpayments requires extra effort and the likelihood of getting that money back decreases with time. If we move back in time and only audit during the executing phase, that also carries its limitations because the organization has already entered into contractual agreements with vendors and contractors, prices have been agreed upon, and some of the money has been spent. It is difficult, and cumbersome to make corrections at this point. So, internal auditors should try to get a seat at the table earlier in the cycle, get information, and provide advice to management during the initiation and planning phases when internal and external negotiations are taking place to make sure that, among other things:

- A project management methodology is in place
- Feasibility studies are competent and comprehensive
- The right stakeholders are summoned to provide input into the process
- The right stakeholders are approving decisions
- Projects are aligned with strategic and other priorities and there is a sound business case on file
- Business requirements are identified and agreed upon
- A risk assessment is performed
- A comprehensive contract or similar binding agreement is in place

Getting involved at this point as an advisor does not preclude the auditors' responsibility to maintain independence. I am not advocating that the auditors make the decision regarding these matters. It is management who should be establishing the requirements for proper planning and reporting. Controls should be put in place for each of the project phases, so the role of the auditor is to identify weaknesses in the design of the process, reporting requirements, approvals, and providing knowledge inputs into the project process, to make sure that it has a greater likelihood of succeeding.

The PMI's Pulse of the Profession report The High Cost of Low Performance 2014 states that only 56% of strategic initiatives meet their original goals and business intent. This poor performance results in organizations losing $109 million for every $1 billion invested in projects.

Keys to Success and Reasons IT Projects Fail

Many organizations spend millions of dollars a year on IT projects, only to suffer various degrees of failure. IT projects represent a strategic and operational enabler for organizational success, but they also represent a large risk. Except for organizations that build and sell hardware or software IT represents the backbone of organizations allowing the flow of data within and increasingly outside the organization, it enables the provision of updates, instructions, and performance reports, and management of people, materials, and costs.

So, why do IT projects fail? There are many reasons. The following is a list that while being quite comprehensive, it is not exhaustive, but I have found these to encapsulate the vast majority of reasons IT projects fail:

1. Working backwards from a drop-dead completion date

   During the planning phase, many projects have a completion date defined, then the planning for the project begins. By working backwards, many projects contain artificial lists of activities and related due dates, all developed in such a way as to make them fit into the completion date, rather than based on realistic estimates. I am not suggesting that completion dates be stretched out into the future with little regard to other organizational priorities and needs. Those are clearly important and since many projects form part of the organization's strategic plans, aggressive dates are to be expected. But if the completion date and related activity dates are arbitrary, something is likely to fail along the way and quite often it is a combination of poor quality, scope limitations, or eventually realizing that the completion date is impossible so there will be delays.

   It is best to work from a realistic timeline, than to create artificial dates and unachievable expectations, and have to correct those later while dealing with the damaged relationships.

2. Inexperienced technical lead

   Having an inexperienced or unqualified individual at the helm of the project can result in poor planning, lack of coordination, poor monitoring and controls, failure to deliver with high quality, low worker morale, high worker turnover, and a number of other adverse results.

3. Buying off-the-shelf package and over-customizing it

   Most software tools today contain robust built-in controls and functionality. Unfortunately, many software buyers tinker with the software's code to adapt it to the organization's circumstances and remove or disable software features. These changes often degrade the functionality by suppressing safeguards. Over the years, I have seen problems with segregation of duties, record creation and editing, limited interfacing, and in general various transactions being allowed that caused adverse effects.

4. Poor data modeling

   This could involve not building an effective data model or not using the one built effectively. A data model organizes data elements and standardizes how the data elements relate to one another by determining the structure of the data. Data models define and format the data and facilitate system performance and compatibility when standardized.

5. Not using a specific methodology

   A system development methodology is the framework used to structure, plan, and control the development of an information system. Many methodologies exist and each has its own characteristics, strengths, weaknesses, and adherents. Any one of these system development methodologies is not necessarily suitable or recommended for all types of projects. Examples include

   a. *Waterfall.* Characterized by the project being divided into sequential phases. The emphasis is on planning, time schedules, target dates, budgets, and implementation of an entire system at a given time with intervening milestones. There are tight controls over the life of the project through extensive written documentation, formal reviews, and sign offs at the end of most phases before the project transitions to the next phase.

   b. *Prototyping.* The focus is on reducing project risk by breaking a project into smaller segments. It follows an iterative approach building mock-ups of the system until the prototype meets the users' requirements. Since the user is involved throughout the process, it makes it more likely that the user will accept the final product.

   c. *Rapid application development (RAD)*. It breaks a project into smaller segments making it easier to make changes during the development process. It is an iterative prototyping methodology with active user involvement. The Manifesto for Agile Software Development states the importance of developing software by valuing individuals and interactions over processes and tools, working software over comprehensive and extensive documentation, customer collaboration over lengthy contract negotiations, and responding to change over following a predetermined plan. Agile and Scrum use development teams that define problems and needs, and work off those rather than detailed designs. Smaller components are developed in "sprints" that last 1–2 weeks. At the end of each sprint, stakeholders and team members meet to see a demonstrated product that is potentially shippable and plan their next steps. The team is self-organized and technical decisions are made collaboratively. An example of this is the meetings held: backlog refinement, sprint planning, daily scrum, sprint review, and sprint retrospective meeting.

6. Using an inappropriate software tool

   The software chosen plays a pivotal role in the ability of the system to deliver what the customer expects. The selection should not be based only on familiarity or price, but should also consider priorities and features (e.g., remote access, compatibility), mission or business criticality, vendor credibility, reliability, integration with existing systems and processes, technical support, and scalability for future growth.

7. Poor data migration

   When an older system is being replaced by a newer one, it is common for the client to ask for the old data to be migrated into the new system. Since data from older systems tend to have quality and reliability issues, the process of migrating data often requires some form of cleanup to remove or correct poor information. Unfortunately, I have witnessed numerous occasions where the data were copied over without thoroughly cleaning it, so bad data are moved into the new system, data were not saved properly in the new system or some of it is missing because it was poorly mapped, and in the worst case scenario, no data were copied over, so old information remains in the old system, new information is found on the new system and queries require manual adjustments, manual entries, or running multiple
reports, and aggregating the data through some type of tedious process.

8. Poor or insufficient testing

   Testing is an essential aspect of effective system development projects. It makes it possible to determine if the system meets the requirements or not. In fact, testing can be further defined by the specific type of attributes or performance being examined, for example:

   a. *Graphical user interface (GUI) testing*. It evaluates the system's graphical use interface, such as the location, appearance, and functionality of buttons, menus, and dialog boxes.

   b. *Usability testing*. Focuses on testing a product's ease of use with real users to determine if it meets its intended purpose.

   c. *Performance testing*. Done to determine how a system performs in terms of responsiveness and stability under various workloads, including scalability and reliability. Load testing examines how the system performs (e.g., number of transactions or operations processed) under a given number of concurrent users, which can be defined as normal and peak load conditions. It may also include finding the maximum capacity (i.e., stress testing), sustained continuous expected load (i.e., soak testing), and sudden increase testing (i.e., spike testing)

d. *Compatibility testing.* This is done to determine if the system is compatible within the computing environment, such as working effective with different peripherals, operating systems, databases, emulators, and browsers.

e. *Security testing.* Designed to identify flaws in the security mechanism that protects the data and functionality as expected. Critical elements include integrity (i.e., only authorized parties can modify protected information), confidentiality (i.e., protected information is only disclosed to the intended recipients), authentication (i.e., verifying the identity of the person or that a computer program or device is a trusted one), and authorization (i.e., confirming that a requester is allowed to perform an operation, or receive information or a service).

f. *Penetration testing.* Involves simulating an attack by a malicious party by exploiting found vulnerabilities in the security infrastructure to gain access, highlighting the potential for a real attacker to gain access to confidential information, affect data integrity, or limit the availability of a service.

g. *Availability testing.* Tests designed to make sure that information, communication, and services are available and ready for use to requesters when expected or needed.

h. *Regression testing.* It involves verifying that software previously developed and tested continues to perform as intended after it was changed.

i. *Nonrepudiation testing.* As e-commerce continues to grow in volume and importance, nonrepudiation testing has also become increasingly important. This involves making sure that a transferred message or transaction that was sent or received cannot be denied by the sender or the recipient.

9. Scope creep
Business requirements that define the scope of the project should be identified during the planning phase. If the PM does not regulate additions to the scope definition, and allows additional deliverables to be included, the project will expand excessively. This can occur when the scope of a project is not properly defined, documented, or controlled. Other reasons include poor change control, lack of proper identification of what is required to achieve the project objectives, and poor communication between parties.

10. Lack of user involvement
All projects should be conducted to meet client (i.e., user) requirements. Failing to incorporate their needs and wants will lead to company resources being misused or under-utilized resulting in deliverables that fail to meet the expectations of the users. The best antidote to this problem is soliciting and getting early and abundant user involvement that is accurately documented and interpreted, as necessary. If the user fails to get sufficiently involved, it is the responsibility of the PM to communicate the associated risks to the relevant stakeholders. Failure to get involved, take responsibility, and participate appropriately should not be tolerated and in turn result in the fundamental question being asked: If the users are not invested in the project, should we still conduct it?

11. Poorly defined, unclear, or no requirements
If the users are sufficiently invested and involved in the project, the project team must make sure that business requirements are properly defined, documented, and shared with everyone who needs to know. Any confusion, questions, or concerns about these requirements should be documented, clarified, and recommunicated to the relevant stakeholders promptly. Communication is key to make sure everyone is "on the same page" regarding the project and there is a shared understanding of what needs to be done, who will do it, and when it must be delivered.

Over the years, I have found that discussing "why" certain requirements exist and how they will be used can help team members tremendously. Sometimes users want a certain functionality, reporting features, information displayed, or similar attributes, and this understanding helps team members to recommend innovative and cost-efficient ways of achieving them above and beyond what the user was hoping for.

12. Long-time schedules

When activities have long deadlines, procrastination becomes a bigger risk. In addition, long deadlines often mean that the activity contains multiple underlying tasks, so there are naturally multiple points where an action may not be performed, an input may not arrive on time, or an item may be unacceptable, and rework will impede the completion of the activity. It is best to have activities with deliverable dates that occur within a couple of periodic report cycles.

13. Stakeholder conflicts

Conflicts often occur when different stakeholders have different priorities and these are not balanced effectively. As the needs of one stakeholder compromises the expectations of another, and the PM and sponsor are unable to reconcile these to everyone's satisfaction, the result could be the withdrawal of funding, poor technical support, lowered engagement, lack of attendance of project meetings, delaying tactics, and failure to sign off.

14. Poor cost and schedule estimation

Poor cost planning can result in the early depletion of the project's budget. Likewise, poor scheduling can lead to over ambitious deadlines that are unrealistic and result in missed deliverables. These often lead to other maladies, like demotivated workers, quality issues, higher turnover, funding removal, and project termination.

15. Communication breakdowns

Communication makes it possible to perform the basic activities of planning, organizing, leading, and controlling. Key information must be communicated to the PM, the team, and other relevant stakeholders. It is essential to organize job tasks, request resources, correct misunderstandings, and clarify doubts. It is also important to control the project by defining reporting protocols and documenting the result of the work done. It facilitates decision making by helping to explain elements of importance. It improves interpersonal relationships and helps to socialize team members.

16. Poor failure warning signals

An important aspect of project management is making sure the project is moving along its predicted path. So, progress monitoring is essential and identifying scope, timeline, budget, and quality deviations must occur often enough to take corrective action. When failure warning signals are missing, not examined, or neglected, the project is likely to become dysfunctional. Over time, it may be very difficult or impossible to recover from the deficiencies and the project could eventually fail unless there is substantial intervention.

17. Lack of top management commitment

Senior management plays a key role helping to make sure projects run smoothly by making resources available. Also, quite often, business partners retain their regular jobs and allocate a portion of their total time to the project. Without senior management support, business partners may not make the necessary commitments or follow-through on them. Top management can also help in the following ways:

a. Setting and communicating policies and objectives throughout the organization to raise awareness and secure involvement by those whose contributions are needed on the project

b. Making sure there is a focus on customer and business requirements

    c. Making resources available because without needed resources, assets, and the means of production cannot be secured

    d. Making sure a credible and effective reporting mechanism is in place that includes an issues remediation process

18. Unrealistic expectations

When expectations are unachievable, they fail to abide by one of the components of the SMARTER framework. Objectives, which define expectations, must be specific, measurable, achievable, realistic, time bound, extend capabilities, and be relevant. When these objectives are not realistic, they demotivate those involved and can result in fraudulent results being published. Not much will be delivered if the expectations are unrealistic given technical capabilities, available resources, agreed upon timeline, and other relevant constraints. Net present value, ROI, payback period, and similar cost-benefit analysis will be for naught if the underlying assumptions and variables are outside the realm of reality.

19. Inadequate training

Many organizations spend a great deal of money, time, and effort conceptualizing, documenting requirements, building the system, and testing it prior to its deployment only to skip training end users. This is a terrible flaw in project management that often results in the limited use of the system, garbage in, garbage out, errors and omissions as users enter inappropriate data in the system, frustration, and excessive demands on technical support personnel. Organizations should be careful not to undermine the success of their system development projects by neglecting to train the very users for whom the system was built.

20. Failure to implement a PMO

A PMO can help improve project success rates by up to 65%,[2] boost efficiency, cut costs, and improve delivery in terms of time, budget, and scope. It helps to establish expectations and instill discipline in IT departments through better planning and monitoring to boost productivity. PMOs can provide project support, guidance, project management methodology, implement and enforce standard operating practices, provide training, mentoring, share best practices, portfolio management, and provide project management software tools.

21. Employee turnover

Lack of staff continuity, whether it is the PM, team members, business partners, or sponsors can derail the best planned and funded projects. While turnover is difficult to prevent as individuals' priorities and ambitions change, management should adopt healthy practices that encourage camaraderie, cooperation, personal and professional growth, and overall satisfaction to thwart voluntary turnover. Effective recruiting practices, performance evaluation and monitoring, and training can help minimize the need to terminate those who underperform and are terminated. The disruption and costs associated with employee turnover should be a key concern to the PM.

Project Selection

First of all, why was that particular project selected? That decision could have been made for a variety of reasons, including

- *Strategic plan.* The organization's strategic plan often defines large, impactful projects that the organization will undertake as it pursues its medium- and long-term goals. These projects often have multimillion dollar budgets and their failure could have a significant monetary, reputational, or competitive impact on the organization. In some cases, failure can be catastrophic to the ability of the organization's survival.

■ *Vision/mission.* Organizations exist to pursue a mission, and the project could be a critical component of their future vision. Some investors and regulators could end their support of some of these mission-critical projects if they are unsuccessful, and other stakeholders, such as clients and vendors, could be disillusioned as well as limiting business opportunities for failing to serve potential customers.

■ *Market analysis.* An analysis of market conditions could indicate that the organization needs to embark on a project in order to meet market demands. There are many types of projects. For example as shown in Table 12.1.

■ *Prioritizing projects.* The decision could be made after the organization performs a detailed analysis of the pros and cons of each project it has deemed of interest. Since organizations operate with limited resources, and have to manage multiple priorities, the selection of the project can be done several ways.

■ *Effort-impact analysis.* The effort-impact analysis or effort-impact matrix is done to decide which of several suggested projects or solutions to implement. It answers the question of which project or solution seems most productive (or easier) to achieve with the highest impact. The maximization of the intended result is the key driver.

Use the following steps to construct the effort-impact matrix:

1. Assemble the list of projects or solutions from previous discussions.
2. Draw a diagram with the effort required to implement the project or solution on the horizontal (x) axis. The impact of the solution will be charted on the vertical (y) axis. Divide the diagram into four quadrants.
3. Assess the amount of effort and impact for each solution. Typical variables include
   a. *Effort.* Amount of time, monetary cost, investment requirement
   b. *Impact.* Monetary gain, increase in users/clients' satisfaction of legal requirement
4. Place the solutions in the diagram according to these assessments. Use a symbol, color, coordinates, or label to identify each project or solution.
5. Results:
   a. Projects or solutions falling into the upper left-hand quadrant will yield the best ROIs and should be considered first. These are often considered important to the organization because they have a high impact and are often called quick wins because they require a low effort.

Table 12.1   Types of Projects

Type of Project	Product
Construction	Artifacts or processes
Research	Knowledge
Reengineering	Change
Procurement	Relationships

b. Items falling into the upper right-hand quadrant are major projects or desirable solutions. These are important because although they require a substantial amount of effort, they provide a high impact.

c. Items in the lower left quadrant, are fill-in projects because they are noncritical and produce low impacts, but since they require low effort, they are conducted as resources become available.

d. Items in the lower right-hand quadrant should be avoided if possible. They require a high amount of effort, but return only low impacts, so they are considered thankless (Figure 12.2).

Use the following steps to construct the prioritization matrix:

1. List the criteria horizontally at the top of the matrix.
2. List the projects or solutions from previous discussions on the left column.
3. Define a rating scale (e.g., 1 through 5 with 1 being lowest and 5 the highest). It is usually helpful to not only decide on a scale, but also define the value for each as well, so there is an understanding and agreement on the values. As you define the scale, pay attention to the direction of the values, so that 1 is always the low or less desirable rating and 5 is the highest or most desirable rating. For example:

a. *Ease of use.* Since ease of use is a positive attribute, 1 would define a difficult to use (or lesser ease of use) product and the scale would move incrementally to 5, which would denote a very easy to use item. In other words, as the numbers increase, the ease of use increases.

b. *Cost.* Since cost is a negative attribute, the scale would be reversed, so 5 would mean a low cost, and you can define what range of monetary values would define low. 4 would consist of a range of values that is lower than the previous, implying that the cost is decreasing. Continue the process to 1, where the cost would be highest, but the rating would be the lowest.

c. *Criticality.* Since criticality refers to a quality or condition where the item is of high importance, as the rating increases, the criticality increases as well. So, 1 would be of the

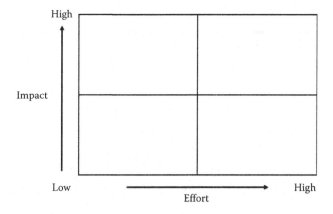

Figure 12.2 Effort-impact diagram.

lowest importance or criticality, while 5 would mean that it is of the utmost importance.

4. Using this L-shaped matrix, read across from the vertical axis and compare each criterion to each item (i.e., project or solution) on the horizontal axis. Enter the corresponding value.
   a. A modified approach is to assign a weight to each criterion since not all criteria are of equal importance. The weights should add to 100%.
   b. Each time a value is assigned, multiply that value by its corresponding weight and record the result.
   c. Total each horizontal row and select the project or solution with the highest score.

Note: This is a modified prioritization matrix that is much easier to construct than traditional prioritization matrices, which require criterion versus criterion comparisons, followed by options versus criterion comparisons using a scale that includes whole numbers and fractions (reciprocal values). For example (Figures 12.3 and 12.4):

1. 1 = equal cost
2. 5 = less expensive
3. 10 = much less expensive
4. 1/5 = more expensive
5. 1/10 = much more expensive

Other variables common to most projects are size, length of time (duration), industry, location, number of workers involved, cost, complexity, and urgency.

	Price	Maintenance cost	Ease of use	Ease of implementation	Performance	Scalability	Total
Project 1	5	3	4	2	1	1	16
Project 2	5	5	2	3	4	5	24
Project 3	3	4	4	5	3	2	21
Project 4	4	1	3	2	5	4	19
Project 5	5	2	5	2	4	4	22

Figure 12.3 Project prioritization matrix (1).

	Price		Maintenance cost		Ease of use		Ease of implementation		Performance		Scalability		Total
		30%		10%		10%		15%		25%		10%	100%
Project 1	5.00	1.50	3.00	0.30	4.00	0.40	2.00	0.30	1.00	0.25	1.00	0.10	2.85
Project 2	5.00	1.50	5.00	0.50	2.00	0.20	3.00	0.45	4.00	1.00	5.00	0.50	4.15
Project 3	3.00	0.90	4.00	0.40	4.00	0.40	5.00	0.75	3.00	0.75	2.00	0.20	3.40
Project 4	4.00	1.20	1.00	0.10	3.00	0.30	2.00	0.30	5.00	1.25	4.00	0.40	3.55
Project 5	5.00	1.50	2.00	0.20	5.00	0.50	2.00	0.30	4.00	1.00	4.00	0.40	3.90

Figure 12.4 Project prioritization matrix (2).

Project Metrics

A performance metric measures the activities and performance of an organization, program, or process. Metrics should support stakeholder needs, which can be external (e.g., customers, shareholders, and regulators), or internal (e.g., managers and employees). Although metrics traditionally focused on financial results, in this chapter we expand the discussion to include operational, strategic, and compliance ones as well.

Project management performance metrics may include safety, time, cost, resources, scope, quality, and activities.

Call center performance metrics may include calls answered, calls abandoned, maximum/minimum/average wait time, and maximum/minimum/average call time.

When it comes to metrics, they shouldn't collect data simply because the data are available. Capturing and reporting on metrics should serve a purpose. The following are some key considerations: CE: Better to use the singular form here ... as in "information is" rather than "facts are"? Cannot say "but not so often that they are overly burdensome"

- Data is easy to collect.
- Everyone involved understands the measurement process and uses consistent units of measurement.
- Data are collected frequently but not so often that it is overly burdensome.
- Data collected makes a difference because it will be used to make decisions, improve activities, and increase the likelihood of success and satisfaction of the relevant stakeholders.
- Pursue a balance between the metrics so that achieving one does not undermine another. For example, production speed and safety could work against each other because production volume and number of accidents could increase simultaneously. In isolation, some of the metrics can be counterproductive to the project.
- Factors that can allow or lead individuals to game the system should be eliminated. This could be the result of establishing goals that cannot be achieved reasonably. If the goals are perceived as being impossible, it could result in workers falsifying the metrics in an effort to appear to meet their targets.

Project Software

Over the years, many software packages have come to market providing project leaders and their teams many options to facilitate their work and related documentation. The following are some key features and characteristics that should be kept in mind when selecting project software:

- *Collaborative.* Software should make it easy for users to work together, sharing documents, and cooperating with each other to accomplish project goals.
- *Issue tracking.* Having the ability to capture, track, manage, and resolve issues during project work will increase the likelihood of achieving project objectives.
- *Scheduling.* Since most projects involve team efforts, having the ability to schedule tasks, track the progress made toward their accomplishment, and managing their accomplishment will facilitate the performance of the work required.
- *Resource management.* Project resources must be managed efficiently for project success. Resource management allows PMs to anticipate needs, distribute resources according to performance needs, monitor the consumption of these resources, and reassign them as needed.

■ *Document management.* Scope, timeline, and resource elements should be documented for tracking, to serve as justification for decisions made, and to address the needs of others who require justification for the assignment, use, and disposal of related items. Document creation, editing and deletion, document retention, access control, referencing, and archiving are also important considerations in addition to the ease of preparation.

■ *Platform.* As technological developments improve, standalone applications have been replaced by client–server, web-based applications that allow team members to access the system and use it 24/7 from anywhere in the world.

Summary

What people have in mind doesn't always get captured in project requirement documents. What gets captured in the requirements documentation doesn't always get built. The difference can be very costly to organizations. There is also a difference between needs and wants and that distinction is not always noted during project planning. As a result, deliverables are often below expectations.

An important aspect of project management is identifying and managing the expectations of stakeholders. Even if the project builds what people expected, data show that it is often delivered late and at a cost that is higher than what was originally projected. These failures highlight the importance of managing scope, timeline, and resources while making sure that quality standards are adhered to. Internal auditors can provide a very valuable service by helping their organizations maximize the benefits from the investments made.

Chapter 13 returns to the analysis of operational performance and provides objectives, risks, and controls for multiple business processes. It provides a primer on what to look for in these functional areas and applies many of the concepts covered in previous chapters. This practical dimension can help operational auditors begin preparing their risk matrices in anticipation of an audit of those units or processes.

QUESTIONS

1. Describe the difference between a process and a project. List three risks that are similar to and three risks that are unique from each other.
2. What are the five phases of projects? List three operational audit steps for each of them.
3. Explain the triple constraints model and its implications for effective project management.
4. Describe three audit procedures related to each of the three triple constraints model elements.
5. What is the CPM and why should PMs use one during their projects?
6. List five reasons IT projects often fail. Describe two controls for each reason that could help to mitigate their occurrence and the audit procedures to test them.
7. Describe RAD and how it differs from traditional waterfall methods.
8. Describe three types of systems testing and their importance for project success.
9. List five key metrics that are useful to manage project progress.
10. List three features that the software used to manage large projects should contain.

Notes

1 For a more detailed review of these tools, see Cobb (2006) and Avison and Torkzadeh (2009).
2 For more information about the benefits of PMOs, see http://www.cio.com/article/2441862/project-management/why-you-need-a-project-management-office—pmo-.html

Chapter 13

Auditing Business Functions and Activities

Controls are actions established by policies and procedures, not the policies and procedures themselves.

COSO 2013

Introduction

It is important to relate concepts and practices. Throughout this book I have provided tips, tools, and techniques to perform operational audits, and I have also given you examples to illustrate and support their adoption. This chapter consists of illustrations of objectives, risks, and controls to give the auditor a starting point when performing operational reviews. These lists are not all-inclusive and they should be used with caution since every audit has its own objectives and scope.

Project Management

Overview

When reviewing the organizations' project management processes, internal auditors should verify that the organization has in place

- Project management framework and methodology that clearly define how the project should be conducted, and the required documentation and key metrics for performance monitoring.
- Project evaluation and approval indicating what the scope is, deliverable due dates, resources available for use, and quality parameters.

Important Documents

- Project charter
- Budget
- Feasibility studies (e.g., Market analysis)
- Schedule (e.g., Gantt chart and CPM)
- Staff list and organizational chart
- Contract
- List of key suppliers
- List of change orders
- List of contractors and subcontractors
- Recent progress reports
- Concept and feasibility analysis

Key Objectives

- Projects are coordinated and aligned with organizational objectives.
- Projects are completed within budget, the timeframe agreed upon, and meet the scope requirements with high quality.
- Staff with the necessary skills are obtained and retained.

Key Risks

- Lack of formal expectations regarding project deliverables, documentation, hiring, communication, budgeting, and reporting requirements
- Lack of support from senior management
- Poor coordination with other projects and organizational priorities
- Project does not support strategic plans
- Excessive timeline, scope, or budget changes cause the project to fall short of plans
- Project does not achieve the stated objectives
- Human, technological, and financial resources are not allocated optimally among competing projects
- Project risks are not identified, assessed, managed, and results are not communicated
- The organization hires and/or retains unsuitable project management personnel
- Turnover is excessive
- External contractors and suppliers are not authorized, perform substandard work, and charge excessively
- Project success is hindered by outdated, inefficient, and ineffective management practices
- The project's financial resources are mismanaged
- Excessively costly sources of funding are employed
- Required documentation is not maintained as required
- Project managers and team members are unsuitable for the job
- Changing or unclear customer requirements
- Missing, conflicting, or inconsistent specifications
- Incomplete or poorly defined acceptance criteria
- Component defects
- Language or communications difficulties that limit productivity
- Changes in regulatory or user requirements

Key Actions by Phase

Initiation

- Obtain and review the project's key project objectives, scope, budget, and deliverables milestones and timeline
- Obtain and review the quality requirements
- Examine resource requirements (e.g., human, material, financial, equipment, and facilities)
- Determine through analysis and discussions with team members if the timeline, budget, and scope are realistic
- Identify the stakeholders of the project and verify their interests are being captured and addressed
- Review the project charter and determine if it provides sufficient clarity about scope, objectives, stakeholders, roles, responsibilities, resources, deliverables, and authority for the project
- Verify that the charter has been approved and accepted by the relevant stakeholders
- Determine if there is strong sponsorship for the project
- Determine if the planning process incorporates the input from subject matter experts (SMEs) and senior management
- Verify there is detailed project scope and plan/schedule documentation, detailing tasks/activities, and assignments
- Obtain and review the project risk assessment to make sure it is comprehensive and updated periodically to ensure its continued relevance
- Obtain and review the project's contract(s) to make sure it is in force, it was reviewed by the legal department before signature, and its terms and conditions provide reasonable safeguards to protect the organization's interests

Planning

- Review the Gantt, CPM, and financial analysis (e.g., payback, ROI, and IRR calculations)
- Review business requirement documentation
- Review time and cost projections and actuals
- Verify that system functionality and features have been signed off by the relevant stakeholders
- Verify that application controls (e.g., edits, validations, exception reporting, and control totals) are included in the design
- Determine if reporting functionality (internal/external, canned/ad hoc) is included in the design
- Determine if data migration is included in the project plan, and if the data will be cleaned before being migrated into the new system
- Determine if necessary interfacing/compatibility/integration is included in the design and being built according to plan
- Determine if access controls are included in the design and being built according to plan with necessary consideration given to segregation of duties
- Verify data quality receives appropriate attention to address accuracy, integrity, consistency, completeness, and existence expectations
- Confirm input, output, processing, backup, recovery, and security controls are part of the original design

Executing

- Review progress reports to determine if the work is advancing as planned by verifying that their content provides sufficient and relevant detail, they are generated with adequate frequency, are distributed to the necessary stakeholders, and variances are addressed promptly
- Review time, cost, and scope variance analysis
- Review change orders and search for excessive number or monetary amounts, concentration by vendor, and unauthorized or missing approvals
- Verify robust controls are in place for vendor selection and relationship monitoring
- Review purchases/procurement activities to verify they are for legitimate purchases, were budgeted, approved, executed, and recorded by authorized individuals
- Enquire with project stakeholders if meetings and other communications occur with sufficient frequency and detail to facilitate project work and address issues effectively
- Enquire with project stakeholders if conflict identification and management are effective
- Verify that risk monitoring and reporting mechanisms are identifying issues and correcting them promptly and effectively
- Determine if change management procedures are in place and being implemented consistently, effectively, and followed by everyone
- Review progress reports to make sure that metrics are being captured, analyzed, and appropriate responses applied to correct deviations in the project's progress
- Examine testing procedures, the issues log, and user acceptance records to make sure they are comprehensive and issues identified are being corrected promptly and appropriately
- Review relevant metrics. For example
  - Schedule metrics
    - Critical path slippage
    - Cumulative project slippage
    - Number of activities added
    - Number of activities completed early
    - Ratio of activities closed to date to number expected (i.e., activity closure index)

  - Resource metrics
    - Budget to actual variance
    - Excess consumption of funds
    - Unplanned overtime and activities
    - Staff turnover

Closing

- Review plan and process to transition the system to operations
- Verify training plans are in place, verify they are sufficiently detailed and will target all necessary system users
- Verify maintenance arrangements and service level agreements (i.e., SLAs) provide adequate safeguards to ensure the continuing operation of the system
- Examine impact analysis documentation
- Examine the following measures of effectiveness to verify the organization will maximize its benefits from the system:
  - Achievement of the established objectives
  - User satisfaction

- Usage
- Usability
- Compliance with required design and performance standards
- Flexibility

Contracts and Contracting

Overview

Contracts are written agreements that are enforceable by law. They provide a mechanism to document the roles, responsibilities, and agreements made between two or more parties. Contracts are also a great safeguard to protect all involved against misunderstandings. As such, managers are highly encouraged to avoid verbal legal agreements, and instead enter into written agreements whenever possible.

Some organizations have few contracts in place and have been working with suppliers and customers for years at times based on long standing verbal agreements or "a hand shake deal." Over the last few decades, business cultures have changed in many countries and the recommended practice is to have these agreements reviewed by corporate legal departments and signed by authorized business representatives.

Internal auditors should examine the following general topics within the contracting, record-keeping, and performance management processes:

- Policies and procedures are in place defining how company employees can enter into contractual agreements and the issuance of contracts
- Guidelines related to vendor hiring, performance monitoring, and payment terms
- Guidance related to the assessment of the viability and competence of contractors and consultants
- Provisions for engaging, monitoring, and paying consultants
- Provisions allowing or forbidding the use of subcontractors
- Procedures for receiving, processing, protecting, and evaluating vendor bids
- Procedures for handling sole vendor situations
- Requirements for obtaining insurance, bonding, and liability protections

Key Objectives

- The organization has all significant agreements ratified through contracts
- All relevant requirements are documented clearly in the contract.
- Contracts are in force and protect the organization appropriately.
- Management information and reporting requirements are clearly defined.
- Performance monitoring provisions are in place to ensure that continued timely, high quality, and appropriate goods and services are received.
- Guidelines are in place for handling materials, plant, and project assets.
- There is a methodology for valuing percentage of work completion and authorization for interim payments.
- A process for calculating and handling price fluctuations is in place.

- Performance monitoring and progress reporting guidelines are in place.
- Provisions exist for properly handling extensions of time and scope changes.
- Guidelines exist for handling final project accounting.

Key Risks

I don't include a list of suggested risks because to some extent, a contract serves as a control protecting the organization from performance, liability, and financial damage. With that in mind, internal auditors should focus on the following general aspects of risk surrounding contracts:

- The organization operates without contracts.
- Contracts are outdated.
- Contracts are signed by unauthorized individuals.
- Contracts do not protect the organization sufficiently and are missing key provisions (see list of suggested items above).

Typical Controls

- An authorization matrix defines who can enter into a contractual obligation on behalf of the organization
- All contracts are reviewed and authorized by competent individuals in the legal department
- Boilerplate language is in place ensuring consistency
- Contracts are retained in a database allowing updates, expiration date reminders, and the easy retrieval of terms and conditions
- Orientation and training programs are in place to educate employees about contracting procedures
- There is standard boilerplate contract language in place that includes, among other things
  - Terms, conditions, and scope of work
  - Dispute resolution, such as litigation and mediation provisions
  - The right to audit records and inspect sites, where applicable
  - Billing and payment provisions, late payment penalties, and recourse in the event of nonpayment
  - Limitation of liability
  - Workplace safety provisions, where applicable
  - Termination clause
  - Third-party claims and beneficiaries

Purchasing, Vendor Selection, and Management

Overview

Purchasing is a key function that consists of obtaining the goods and services needed to accomplish the goals of the organization. It takes many forms and includes

- Sourcing supplies required to keep production or service processes in operation
- Buying the items required for everyday business needs
- Engaging in contracting activities, which involve the bidding process and the selection of suitable suppliers

The major objectives are to ensure the appropriate number and quality of products, minimize the accumulation of inventory, and maintain the appropriate flow between inputs and outputs so there are no unnecessary delays or bottlenecks.

There are several interfaces between forecasting and the purchasing function, since forecasting typically informs the purchasing unit what needs to be bought, when it is needed, and where it should be delivered for use. There are also interfaces with accounts payable, since the invoices for the amounts purchased must be paid for. Quality control and manufacturing are also impacted, especially when items must be inspected to make sure they meet the organization's quality requirements before the items are entered into the manufacturing cycle. Lastly, warehousing and inventory control are also impacted, since the items received must be stored temporarily if they are not being used immediately, protected from loss or damage, and released to authorized parties when needed.

When evaluating purchasing risks, internal auditors should consider:

Operational needs requirements: This pertains to the process of deciding what is needed, when it must arrive and be ready for use, where it must arrive, and where it will be stored. In a JIT environment, order quantities are typically very small, as the amount purchased equals what is needed. In some organizations where this process is optimized, supplies may arrive more than once a day to minimize the amount of inventory carried. Otherwise, internal auditors should examine the forecasting process to make sure that amounts purchased are appropriate and excess inventory is not being kept.

Strategic alliances: These alliances help ensure the stable and reliable supply of parts and materials and it is accomplished by entering into agreements with suppliers who understand the organization's needs, meet specified requirements, make sure the supply chain is not disrupted, and that prices are predictable to provide stability to the organization's revenue and cost projections. These alliances can also ensure stable supplies in the long term, while guaranteeing quality standards are met. Furthermore, strategic alliances can also help protect the company's intellectual property by establishing confidentiality agreements. Lastly, many of these arrangements can also be described as partnerships where companies provide assistance during financial difficulties.

Information systems: Making the many purchases, sometimes daily, and factoring in multiple lead times from multiple suppliers can be a daunting process. Information systems make managing this very complex process easier. At the same time, access controls are essential to make sure there is data integrity and any adjustments, when needed, are only made by authorized individuals. Additionally, buyers and sellers are increasingly sharing information through EDI and other mechanisms to streamline the process. So, making sure there are no interruptions or mistakes in the data flows is also essential for success.

Personnel: Organizations need the right amount of employees and to make sure they are competent in their duties. It seems like a simple matter, but over the years I have seen this problem in many functions where the department is so severely understaffed that those attempting to do the work make mistakes or circumvent procedures and controls in their attempts to keep up with the volume of work required. Another common issue is the lack of competence by employees. This can occur because some workers were hired without the requisite skills, while others may not have been trained appropriately after system or procedural changes. It is essential for management to examine the skills of its staff and make sure they know how to perform their duties. Similarly, internal auditors should be attuned to this matter, as having documented policies and procedures and sophisticated systems in place do not guarantee that the work will be done as required.

Legal and regulatory compliance: While most of the commercial activities involved in purchasing are defined by internal procedures and partner agreements, in some cases it is also restricted by laws and regulations. For some government organizations, they must purchase a certain percentage of their goods, or allocate a predetermined amount of work, to minority-owned organizations. In other cases there is a maximum monetary amount that can be paid for specified parts, materials, and wages. In some instances there are restrictions related to export/import activities, and trade guidelines limiting or precluding purchases from certain countries. OFAC, which is part of the US Department of the Treasury administers and enforces economic and trade sanctions based on US foreign policy and national security goals against targeted foreign countries and regimes, terrorists, international narcotics traffickers, those engaged in activities related to the proliferation of weapons of mass destruction, and other threats to the national security, foreign policy, or economy of the United States. It imposes controls on transactions and places sanctions based on United Nations and other international mandates, that are multilateral in scope, and involve close cooperation with allied governments. This office also manages the specially designated nationals (SDN) list, which lists people and organizations with whom United States citizens and permanent residents are prohibited from doing business with. It is imperative that organizations establish controls to make sure there are no commercial activities with parties on the list.[1]

Control environment: Internal auditors should evaluate the control environment of the purchasing activities of the organization. The control environment plays an important role defining the culture and practices within the purchasing function and can create an environment where purchasing agents overlook and circumvent policies and procedures for illegitimate gain. Practices such as conflicts of interest, ignoring the code of ethics, steering business to others to the detriment of the organization, are examples of reasons this is an important aspect of any audit of the purchasing function.

Key Objectives

- Purchasing activities are performed promptly and accurately.
- Goods and services are obtained at the optimum price, within the required quality levels and are received when needed.
- The purchasing function supports the strategic and operational objectives of the organization.
- Accurate, complete, detailed, and timely information is available for financial and operational reporting.
- Purchases are valid, necessary, authorized, and within prescribed budgets.
- Suppliers are reliable, financially stable, and able to meet the organization's purchasing demands.

- Supplier performance is monitored.
- Trading terms and conditions are appropriate and fair.
- Purchasing activities comply with all prevailing laws and regulations and meet stakeholder expectations.
- Coordination across the organization prevents waste and maximizes buying power.

Key Risks

- The organization overpays for items purchased.
- There are excessive, overdue, poor quality, and late deliveries.
- Vendors are selected inappropriately (e.g., favoritism and poor quality).
- The organization buys more than it needs.
- Unqualified or illegal vendors are used (e.g., on SDN list).

Typical Controls

- Purchasing activities are supported by documented, up to date, and authorized policies and procedures.
- Authority limits and access controls restrict which employees can create and approve purchase orders and purchase requisitions.
- All purchases require documentation justifying the need for the items purchased and related budgets to be charged for the expenses.
- Vendor assessment and selection criteria are in place, detailing required documentation such as minimum number of price quotes, quality standards, financial condition, etc.
- Terms of the relationship are documented in purchase orders and/or contracts.
- Vendor records are reviewed periodically to make sure terms of the relationship are appropriate and up to date.
- The organization obtains audited financial statements and declaration of insurance before engaging in purchasing activities from significant vendors, and obtains updated documents periodically.
- Appropriate demand requirements (e.g., forecasts and replenishment thresholds) reduce the likelihood that excess items are purchased at any location, while there are excess supplies at another location.
- All POs are supported with sufficient details, descriptions, specifications, prices, delivery dates, delivery locations, and terms.
- All changes to purchase orders are valid, correctly applied, and authorized.
- A robust process ensures all vendors are screened when they are first contracted with, and performance monitoring mechanisms are in place subsequently.
- Purchasing decisions are based on highest value (e.g., combination of price, quality, service, and delivery), not merely lowest price.
- A preferred vendor list is in place and purchases from other vendors are restricted and monitored.
- Vendor records are reviewed periodically to make sure the information (e.g., addresses, contacts, and terms) are up to date and suppliers meet quality and delivery requirements.
- Approval decisions include a review of payment terms to make sure the organization takes advantage of all applicable discounts available.
- Employees have received, and agree to abide by a conflict of interest statement.

- An ethics hotline is in place and ways to contact that resource are prominently advertised within and outside the organization. Note: Sharing the contact information for the ethics hotline outside the organization is important because it makes it easier for others to contact an appropriate party in the event unethical activities exist.
- The activities of ordering, accounting, and receiving goods are separated to prevent inappropriate activities.

Bidding

Overview

The selection of a vendor is a critical step in many processes, and finding the most qualified and reliable provider is a key concern. Organizations must make purchasing decisions based on highest overall value, not only lowest price. Furthermore, if the vendor is technically unable to meet the buyer's requirements, cannot produce, manufacture, and deliver the number of items needed, or fails to meet ethical criteria, the contracting company may suffer operational, financial, regulatory, and reputational damage.

Bidding is a common process to obtain information from organizations that are vying for the work. It typically begins with the definition of requirements and the distribution of a request for bids, request for proposals, or request for tenders. This is a formal and structured invitation to suppliers. Interested organizations then respond by submitting their details as proposals, which are then reviewed by the hiring organization, and often after some final negotiations, a contract is signed and the relationship formalized resulting in the purchase and delivery of goods and services.

Since a common concern is the safeguarding of received bids for purchasing, bidding, contracting, vendor registration, and payment, many organizations are replacing their paper-based process with an electronic supplier or bidding portal. Suppliers interested in responding to request for proposals (RFPs) submit their credentials and information to participate in the bidding process electronically. The result is that suppliers can enter and update vendor information, elect to receive POs by e-mail, register, view, download, and respond to bid opportunities and in some cases even sign contracts.

Key Objectives

- The bidding process is competitive and prevents fraud and collusion.
- The bidding process is fair and the work is awarded to the vendor providing the best value for money.
- The bidding process is free from bias or undue influence.
- An adequate bidding timetable is used.
- Bids are correctly identified, recorded, accounted for, and protected from tampering.

Key Risks

- Bidders provide false information that result in selecting an inappropriate vendor.
- Nepotism, favoritism, or bribery results in inappropriate organizations being selected because individuals within the hiring organization steer business to preferred suppliers for personal gain.

- The hiring company hires a provider that is unable to meet its requirements.
- The organization suffers from internal and/or external fraud.

Typical Controls

- Bidding instructions are accurate, complete, and unambiguous.
- Appropriate internal procedures are in place to protect the recording, handling, storage, and assessment of submitted bids, including the prevention of unauthorized access, opening, amendment, or tampering/alteration.
- Management has established minimum competition criteria for the bidding process; generally a minimum of three bids, except in sole-provider situations, where detailed documentation is required to demonstrate there are no other eligible vendors in the marketplace.
- Documented and up-to-date policies and procedures for bidding on tenders are in place.
- The organization protects submitted tenders from alteration, information leakage, or destruction by using an electronic bid or supplier portal, or by retaining them in a sealed condition by an impartial party.
- All bids are opened simultaneously in the presence of an independent observer.
- Late or incomplete bids are disqualified.
- A scoring scheme is in place to make sure evaluation criteria are applied consistently, the evaluation process is transparent, and performed by independent parties.
- Management obtains reliable documentations to verify that potential bidders are financially stable, reliable, and technically competent, such as audited financial statements, certificates of insurance, reliable and recent references, and certificates showing quality standards are met (e.g., ISO 9000).
- Procedures are in place to make sure that any additional information or amendments to the original RFP are fairly circulated to all bidding vendors.
- The bid review committee or team is balanced, unbiased, and suitably qualified.

Pricing

With the exception of those organizations that provide goods and services free of charge to their customers, most organizations must establish and manage some type of pricing mechanism. This constitutes the primary revenue-generating mechanism for most organizations and as such, it represents a very important process that has implications for the subsequent invoicing/billing to customers and collection through the accounts receivable function.

There are many aspects to pricing and the determination of what price should be charged to customers. One of the key elements includes costs, since the price must be higher than the fixed and variable costs to generate a profit. Since cost accounting is beyond the scope of this book, I merely advise internal auditors to review the procedures related to capturing the total cost of the goods and services involved.

Pricing should be driven by the organization's strategic and operational goals, and is influenced by market share, competition, prevailing economic conditions, estimates of the quantity demanded by consumers, and price elasticity of demand. Inelastic demand indicates that price increases may be feasible, but the perception of value also plays a key role in that analysis.

Pricing also has implications for the company's marketing strategy, including segmentation, targeting, and positioning. It also affects promotional tactics and service, warranty considerations. Also of importance is the setting of objectives, as the pricing may drive the strategy to maximize profit, or market share. Lastly, pricing can also affect the organization's discount policies, since a low margin, high volume, high-market share approach would limit the ability to provide generous service warranties and discounting. The implications are that pricing goes beyond the mathematical and accounting requirements, but has operational and strategic implications that internal auditors should be aware of as well.

The price level method can vary based on the objective pursued. Pricing can be

- *Cost plus*: The price equals the production cost plus a predetermined profit margin.
- *Value based*: The price is determined by the value the customer perceives in relation to alternative products/services.
- *Target*: The price is set to achieve a desired return on investment.
- *Psychological*: The price is based on attributes the customer considers to be fair, the quality, positioning, and similar factors. The above discussion has focused on the list price of the product or service. In reality, customers often pay a different price due to discounts, such as
- *Quantity and cumulative quantity discount*: Offered to clients who purchase large quantities and which may increase as the cumulative order quantity increases.
- *Seasonal discount*: These discounts are offered based on the time the purchase is made. It is done to reduce or profit from seasonal variations in sales. This variation can be driven by the month of the year, the week of the month, the day of the week, or even the time of the day.
- *Cash discount*: These discounts are offered to customers when the bill is paid immediately in cash or within a certain time.
- *Promotional discount*: These are short-term discounts to stimulate sales.

Key Objectives

- Pricing and discount structures are documented, authorized, and followed.
- Pricing levels are competitive, profitable, and adequately cover the underlying costs.
- Market trends, competitor pricing, and legal restrictions, if any, enable the appropriate organizational response.
- Authorized prices and discounts are correctly applied to invoices.
- Accurate cost records are maintained to support the pricing policy.
- Costing information is captured and analyzed to identify potential cost savings.
- Costing information is captured, appropriately analyzed, and disclosed correctly and timely in financial and operational reports.
- The effects of taxes are taken into account when setting prices.
- Geographic differentials and cyclical sales patterns are considered when determining changes to the pricing policy.
- Local, national, and international restrictions are considered, as applicable.

Key Risks

- Prices and discounts make products/services uncompetitive or unprofitable.
- Prices, and related sales projections, are unrealistic.

- Prices and discounts are applied incorrectly.
- Excessive and unauthorized prices and discounts are applied.
- Individuals and organizations use proprietary information inappropriately.

Typical Controls

- Pricing and discount policies are documented, authorized, and implemented consistently.
- Management maintains an accurate awareness of market trends and competitor prices as determinants of pricing policy.
- Required price, profit, and quantity of returns are determined with the input of SMEs, market information, and accurate company data.
- Value-ranges, access, and data transfer controls make sure that price and discount amounts are within acceptable limits, authorized by appropriate individuals and are captured accurately in financial and operational reports.
- Process controls ensure the mathematical accuracy of cost, pricing, and billing information.
- System interfaces make sure that data input and output from other systems (e.g., product costing) are accurate.
- Segregation of duties is in place to protect sensitive pricing information from unauthorized access.

Product Receipt (Quality)

Overview

Quality is a critical differentiator for most organizations, and those in the manufacturing sector in particular, face an additional risk factor—suppliers who provide defective parts. Organizations must develop robust procedures to ensure production processes adhere to high-quality standards and that goods are shipped according to client expectations. Defective inputs, however, can diminish the effectiveness of such procedures.

Key Objectives

- Incoming materials meet company specifications and delivery requirements.
- Materials are protected from loss or damage.
- Materials are processed right away so they move promptly within the production cycle.

Key Risks

- Incoming materials are defective, arrive too early or past the due date.
- Inspection reports are inaccurate and prepared past their due date.
- Relevant quality and inspection reports are not retained as required.
- Supplier performance deteriorates without management knowledge and appropriate corrective action.
- Employees in the receiving department do not know how to inspect materials received.
- Materials are issued to production without, or before, being inspected.

Typical Controls

- Incoming materials are inspected upon receipt by a qualified individual.
- Inspection reports are reviewed by a designated individual who is objective and competent.
- Inspection reports are retained according to the company's document retention policy.
- Performance reports are prepared and distributed promptly for review.
- Corrective action is taken promptly if anomalies (e.g., packaging, quality, and delivery time) are identified.
- Materials are segregated upon receipt and are not entered into production/manufacturing cycle until after they have been properly inspected.

Human Resources

Overview

Management is responsible for making sure that adequate numbers of suitably experienced and trained workers are available to support the organization's objectives. In many organizations, however, HR is dedicated to obtaining and retaining employee files, and pays scant attention to the other aspects of the HR function, such as motivation, training, development, and succession planning to ensure organizational continuity.

When reviewing HR, internal auditors should be careful not to replicate the practice of many auditors in the past whose scope was limited to verifying that employee files were complete and accurate, that employee payroll was accurate and met labor law compliance requirements for minimum wage, overtime pay, record-keeping, and youth employment standards. While these are certainly important topics, the HR function is also key to having a motivated, creative, disciplined, engaged, productive, and punctual workforce. Senior management sets the specific work-related standards, but the overall guidance, and the support through rewards and disciplinary action are either driven by or reinforced by HR.

Since labor costs often represent the largest operating costs for an organization, especially those operating in service environments, internal auditors should examine how those costs are authorized, captured, managed, and reported.

In terms of organizational continuity, succession planning has long been regarded as a key mechanism to minimize the disruptive effects of the inability of senior-level employees to perform their duties. Customers, employees, and even stockholders can succumb to panic if the organization's president, board chairperson, or renowned sales leader is incapacitated or abandons the organization abruptly. As organizations become more risk conscious, succession plans have been upgraded to view the workforce and its leadership through the lens of risk and in so doing have increasingly identified individuals whose title may sometimes not draw much attention, but whose role could be critical to the organization's success. Such is the case with the person whom I often refer to in my seminars as "Barry in IT," who is the only person who knows how that obscure, yet critical, computer system works. If "Barry" can't come to work because he wins the lottery or retires, the organization will be hard pressed to find someone else who can keep that system running. That is the approach that should be adopted: identify key activities within the organization and make sure there is a backup or substitute available.

Consequently, internal auditors should consider broadening their scope when reviewing personnel matters and also include employee motivation, retention, training, absenteeism, and development.

Managers can be the inspiration for someone to stay with an organization or the impetus for someone to leave.[2]

Linda K. Trevino and Katherine A. Nelson

Key Objectives

- Sufficient, trained, and motivated personnel are available to pursue the organization's mission and objectives.
- All prevailing employment and employee laws and regulations are complied with.
- Staff is trained to perform their duties effectively and efficiently.
- The best employees are hired to fill available vacancies.
- Employee compensation is commensurate with the individual's credentials, role, and accomplishments.
- Turnover and absenteeism are maintained at an acceptable level.
- Disciplinary issues are minimized, and dealt appropriately and promptly.
- A healthy and productive relationship exists between the workforce and management.

Key Risks

- The organization is understaffed, and those workers present are unqualified, unmotivated, and unproductive.
- Poor labor relations impede productivity.
- Excessive turnover hampers business continuity and the ability to meet customer expectations.
- The organization fails to comply with applicable regulations.
- There is a lack of clarity regarding objectives, procedures, roles, and responsibilities for positions within the organization.
- Current and future staffing levels and skills are not aligned with the strategic and operational needs and plans of the organization.
- The organization is negatively impacted by overstaffing.
- The organization is understaffed and workers are unqualified for their jobs.
- The organization hires individuals who misrepresent their credentials or qualifications.
- The organization hires individuals not legally allowed to work in their country of employment.
- Excessive turnover affects the organization's ability to seamlessly provide needed goods and services to its customers.
- The organization's compensation program is above/below market levels, negatively affecting turnover, satisfaction levels, or exceeding needed compensation cost levels.

Typical Controls

- Policies and procedures that support the recruitment, retention, training and development, performance appraisal, motivation, compensation, disciplining, and termination of personnel are developed, implemented, communicated, and kept up to date.

- Employee records are kept electronically and subject to access controls to protect them from unauthorized access.
- The organization's compensation and benefits are competitive relative to industry standards.
- Personnel are adequately trained to perform their duties.
- Personnel skills and abilities are developed, maintained, and aligned with the organization's current and future requirements through professional development, coaching, and mentoring programs.
- Personnel turnover and absenteeism are monitored, maintained at acceptable levels, and problems are addressed promptly.
- Staff recruitment is suitably authorized according to the operational demands of the organization and is conducted cost effectively.
- Staff performance is monitored and accountabilities are clear so necessary remedial action is taken when necessary.
- Adequate personnel records are maintained and protected from unauthorized access.
- Accurate and timely information is provided to internal and external parties cost effectively as required.
- There is an effective formal complaint and disciplinary mechanism in place that includes escalation procedures to address employee concerns and grievances.
- All jobs have accurate and up-to-date job descriptions.
- There is a formal onboarding and orientation program for new employees.
- A comprehensive training and mentoring program is in place.
- The performance evaluation program is linked to employee performance metrics and the training and development programs.
- Management has multiple reporting mechanisms in place for employees to bring their concerns and grievances to their attention.
- Personal data are safeguarded through access controls and segregation of duties.
- Managers are trained on interviewing, anti-discrimination, cultural awareness, performance evaluation, documentation, and general management concepts.
- Employee absenteeism and turnover are monitored for prompt corrective action.
- All job applicants are screened centrally or locally by knowledgeable HR personnel.
- The HR department has clearly defined goals and objectives related to employee well-being (e.g., excessive overtime and disregard for vacation time) in addition to traditional staffing metrics (e.g., full time equivalents [FTEs], labor rates and length of time of open vacancies).
- The organization has established and supports a requirement for continuing training/education for all employees.
- Personnel policies and employee manual are current and reevaluated annually.
- Job descriptions are available for all positions in the organization.
- There is a formal and credible employee evaluation program.
- The pay, promotion, and transfer systems are based on candidate merit.

Recruitment

Key Objectives

- Appropriately experienced and stable staff is recruited to meet the organization's objectives.

- A structured, targeted, fast, and cost-effective approach to recruitment is in place.
- All recruitment activities and appointments are authorized.
- Recruitment activities comply with prevailing laws and regulations.
- New employees are hired in compliance with prevailing compensation policies and immigration regulations.
- All candidates are evaluated against the job description and screened to confirm their previous employment and educational history.
- Personnel records are established and maintained according to internal and regulatory requirements.
- Personnel records are protected from unauthorized access.
- Vacancies are filled promptly.

Key Risks

- Recruitment activities are inconsistent or too slow.
- Unfair discrepancies exist in compensation ranges and amounts.
- Excessive or misplaced staffing situations are in place.
- Phantom employees are recorded in the organization's payroll and/or benefit systems.
- Personnel records are incomplete, inaccurate, or missing.
- Information generated from the personnel and employment records are inaccurate, unreliable, and late.
- The organization employs individuals lacking proper immigration permission to work.
- Position roles, qualifications, and performance expectations are unclear or missing.
- Ineffective selection efforts are underway, resulting in unsuitable candidates and hires.
- Irregularities (e.g., errors, waste, and fraud) occur in matters of paying traveling expenses.
- Medical, drug, physical, and psychological tests performed do not comply with applicable regulations or ethical standards.
- The organization overpays in its selection process (e.g., poor hires that leave too soon, use recruitment agencies whose cost is excessive in relation to grade, compensation, or retention of workers).
- New employees are unaware of the organization's values, goals, and principles of conduct.

Typical Controls

- Recruiting policies and procedures are formally documented, communicated, and adhered to.
- Recruitment efforts are targeted (e.g., social media, recruiters, web portal, and career fairs).
- The organization has a proactive approach to presenting the organization in a positive way (e.g., web portal and public relations efforts).
- Budgets are reviewed and authorized.
- Performance metrics related to the effectiveness of recruitment efforts are collected, reviewed, and acted upon.
- A skills inventory and staffing needs assessment is performed with the input of operations managers.
- Employees involved in the recruitment process receive training and guidance on legal requirements/restrictions and best practices.

Training and Development

Key Objectives

- Training and staff development resources are targeted in order to maximize their effects and avoid wasteful activity.
- Employees are trained to enable them to discharge their responsibilities effectively.
- Workforce skills are maintained at the appropriate level and in line with the objectives of the organization.
- Motivate staff and increase their commitment by providing personal and skill development opportunities.
- Anticipate the future skill needs of the business and verify that relevant training is planned for.
- Provide adequate training facilities and related resources cost effectively.
- Consider the use of training and staff development as a means to gain a competitive advantage.

Key Risks

- New employees are unaware of the organization's values, mission, and goals because induction training is deficient.
- Employees lack skills or other development attributes.
- There is a gap between the present skills and personal attributes (e.g., leadership, willingness to change, and creativity) of the workforce and future skill needs.
- Overall training and development activities are ineffective.

Typical Controls

- The organization has established a T&D budget based on corporate needs and prevailing training costs.
- A policy is in place establishing annual training requirements (e.g., required courses and number of hours of instruction).
- The organization invests in physical and computer-based training.
- Training expenses are reviewed prior to approval.
- A central unit oversees the training program to ensure consistency, follow through, and alignment with organization needs.
- Qualified employees are hired to staff the T&D function.

Employee Benefits

Key Objectives

- Benefits are calculated and recorded accurately.
- Only bona fide individuals receive company benefits.
- All benefits are granted in compliance with federal/national, state, and local requirements.

Key Risks

- Inaccurate calculations result in financial and operational reporting errors.

- Unqualified individuals receive benefits (e.g., unqualified individuals are signed on or terminated individuals continue to receive benefits).
- Failure to comply with mandated employee benefit programs result in fines, penalties, and reputation damage to the organization.

Typical Controls

- The HR and legal departments are aware of compliance requirements and provide guidance for continued compliance.
- Beneficiaries of company benefits are verified before enrollment.
- Relevant employee benefits are terminated upon separation from the organization.
- Periodic recertification and reconciliations are performed.

Employee Termination
Key Objectives

- Prevailing employment termination requirements are complied with.
- Employee terminations are performed timely.
- Adequate personnel records are maintained as required.
- All terminations are dealt with appropriately (e.g., compensation terminated, company assets recovered, and removal from payroll).

Key Risks

- Noncompliance with employment termination procedures (e.g., timely notification and severance payments) result in fines, penalties, lawsuits, and negative publicity.
- Poor practices (e.g., age and gender discrimination) result in lawsuits, fines, penalties, and other sanctions.
- Terminated employees continue on the payroll, receive benefits, have physical access to company facilities, continue to have logical (i.e., system) access, and retain company assets.

Typical Controls

- HR and legal department receive timely regulatory requirement updates and implement those requirements throughout the organization through notifications and training.
- Document retention policies are in place.
- Checklists are in place to make sure that termination procedures are consistently and promptly applied in all instances.
- Reconciliation procedures are performed to confirm compliance with prevailing requirements and identify discrepancies.

Employee Evaluations
Key Objectives

- Staff is aware of their responsibilities and have SMARTER goals.
- Employee contributions are maximized.

- The staff performance evaluation system is effective and provides a valuable mechanism to incentivize workers, select the best individuals for advancement, and develop future organizational leaders.
- Performance and personal achievement are linked to the reward structure.
- The evaluation process is fair and unbiased.
- Employees with consistently poor performance records are dealt with appropriately.

Key Risks

- Poor productivity and confusion occur because employees are unaware of their responsibilities and the scope of their positions.
- Performance evaluations are ineffective because managers lack the skills to perform them effectively.
- Managers conducting performance evaluations fail to comply with prevailing labor laws.
- Performance evaluations are not done promptly, universally, and competently (e.g., consistently, fairly, based on actual and documented performance).
- The organization fails to maximize the value from the performance evaluation process (e.g., not linked to training and development, not the basis for promotions or advancement opportunities, incompetent managers, subjective process, and divorced from disciplinary procedures).
- The discipline policy is unknown, unenforced, inconsistent, arbitrary, and overly punitive.
- There is inflation in employee evaluation scores.
- Employees are unfairly punished by managers during the evaluation process.

Typical Controls

- Managers receive training on how to conduct performance evaluations.
- Analytics are performed on employee evaluations to identify anomalies.
- A performance improvement program is in place and there is a process to evaluate usage and results.
- All employees are required to receive a performance evaluation at least once a year.
- Performance evaluation forms are clear and contain clear guidelines on how they should be conducted.

Accounting, Finance, and Treasury Operations

Overview

This function aggregates several activities within the general accounting, finance, and financial reporting function. These units are concerned with the receipt, documentation, accounting, and reporting of accounting transactions and underlying activities such as cash collections, accounts payable, payroll, capital investments, and treasury operations. They often overlap or are the continuation of the work that occurs in other departments within the organization. For example, payroll is the process of paying employees for the work done, but preceding these activities HR hires the employee and defines hourly wages or salary amounts. During regular work cycles timesheets may be completed for nonexempt workers (those paid hourly), while the process result in equal payments for exempt workers (those on salary); both require approval by the employee's direct supervisor.

The primary concern within the treasury unit is the adequacy of funding, cash flow, and the accountability of transactions. Treasury also impacts, and is impacted by, payroll—the initial set-up of new employees, changes to employee compensation, payroll runs, payment arrangements, accounting for various taxes, and the discontinuation of payments upon employee termination.

Another example of the broader linkages in place is accounts payable, which is linked to the purchasing process, the confirmation of the receipt of goods and services (sometimes within warehousing and inventory management), verifying the accuracy and validity of invoices, and the maintenance of vendor records.

Treasury

Key Objectives

- The organization's funds are appropriately managed and provide adequate levels of working capital.
- The organization engages in suitable and secure investments to support operational and strategic goals.

Key Risks

- Company resources are misused because unauthorized personnel initiate and process treasury transactions.
- Company resources are stolen through fraud.
- The organization suffers liquidity challenges because working capital requirements are unknown or inaccurate.
- The organization is affected by financial losses due to unexpected market fluctuations.
- The organization is affected by speculative activities.

Typical Controls

- All treasury activities are defined by up-to-date policies, procedures, laws, and regulations.
- A treasury policy and procedures document exists that is formally documented, regularly reviewed, and kept up to date and it defines allowed transactions to avoid speculation and other risky transactions.
- Treasury staff operate with the oversight of an engaged treasurer, who enforces transaction limits established by policy and prudent practices.
- An authorization and escalation matrix is in place that defines allowable transaction types and amounts for treasury staff, the treasurer, other C-level individuals (e.g., CEO and CFO), and board members to preclude speculation and delineate appropriate hedging activities.
- All treasury transactions are supported and authorized according to established procedures.
- Monthly reconciliations verify that all income is recorded, the accuracy of financial transactions and exposures, and identify any changes in the value of investments and debt obligations.
- Covenant and other requirements/obligations are maintained centrally.

- A risk assessment and management methodology is in place to assess the risk of sensitive transactions (e.g., derivatives) and apply the existing authorization matrix.
- Market trends and key economic indicators are monitored through the organization's ERM function to manage organizational exposures.
- Application and access controls regulate the type and amount of treasury transactions.
- Bank and financial institution callback and confirmation controls limit exposures.

Payroll
Key Objectives

- Only valid employees are paid and at the correct and authorized rate.
- The calculation of all payments and deductions are correct and in accordance with the relevant taxation and other regulations.
- Deductions are disbursed correctly, in time, and to the appropriate entity.
- Payroll transactions are accurately reflected in the accounting system.
- Management and statutory information is produced and reported accurately and in time.

Key Risks

- Unauthorized individuals create, modify, or otherwise access the records of employees for inappropriate gain to the detriment of the organization or the employees (e.g., identity theft).
- Fictitious employees are created to extract a rent from the organization.
- Payroll payments continue to former employees who have left the organization or transferred departments.
- Payroll rates or pay-scales are modified inappropriately in the payroll system.
- Payroll, tax, and other voluntary and involuntary deductions are inaccurately calculated and paid or disbursed past the due date.
- Discrepancies exist between payroll and other deduction amounts and what is reported on financial, tax, and legal reports.

Typical Controls

- Specific roles, responsibilities, and authorization elements have been defined for payroll personnel in terms of record creation, edit, removal, and transaction processing.
- Payroll system controls prevent unauthorized access to the payroll system and related data.
- A monthly reconciliation of timesheets and worker activity confirms that only bona fide employees are paid wages, salaries, benefits, sick vacation, and authorized leave.
- Termination procedures and manager training requires timely reporting to HR and IT to remove system and payroll access.
- System tables automate the calculation of pay rates, tax rates, and all other forms of voluntary and involuntary deductions.
- All compensation (e.g., overtime, bonuses, and salary increases) are authorized before their entry into the accounting system.
- Reconciliations verify the accuracy of deductions and amounts reported in financial, operational, tax, and other reports.

- All payroll runs require prior review and approval.
- The organization actively enlists employees in electronic payment arrangements.

Accounts Payable

Key Objectives

- Payments are only made to valid and approved vendors.
- Payments are for goods and services received in acceptable condition.
- Payments are correct and reflected accurately in the accounting records.
- Prevailing sales taxes regulations are complied with.
- Positive working relationships are maintained with key suppliers.
- Financial statements reflect all liabilities outstanding and paid.

Key Risks

- The organization pays for goods and services not received.
- The organization pays multiple times for the same items.
- The organization suffers employee, contractor, and supplier fraud.
- Employees make purchases not previously budgeted and approved.
- Invoice payments are made to invalid, unapproved, or unauthorized vendors.
- Invoice pricing, amounts, deductions, or other terms are paid incorrectly.
- Financial statements are inaccurate.

Typical Controls

- All invoices are authorized at the appropriate level before payment and this is documented electronically in the company's payment processing system.
- A monthly reconciliation confirms the accuracy of financial reporting.
- There is adequate segregation between those originating purchase orders and those authorizing the related invoice for payment.
- System controls make sure all invoices are correctly coded and reflected in the financial records.
- All checks, electronic funds transfers (EFTs), or other forms of payment, are confirmed as correct and authorized by an appropriate manager before release.
- Vendor records are reviewed annually for accuracy.
- Credit notes and other adjustments (e.g., balance write-offs) are confirmed as correct and authorized before processing.
- Outstanding liabilities are accrued accurately and entered in the accounting system and financial statements during the preparation of financial reports.

Accounts Receivable

Key Objectives

- All amounts due to the company undergo collection efforts.

- Transactions are posted accurately and in time in financial statements.
- Credit is granted based on the buyer's risk profile.

Key Risks

- The posting of sales transactions is inaccurate.
- Collection efforts are inefficient, ineffective, inconsistent, or unlawful.
- Deposit of customer payments is delayed.
- Bills (i.e., invoices) are inaccurate or not sent to customers promptly.
- Customers with poor credit worthiness and lacking financial stability are granted credit.
- Unidentified payments are not processed promptly.
- Credit limits are excessive.
- Unauthorized individuals modify customer accounts or obtain customer information inappropriately.
- Fraud is perpetrated against the organization (e.g., embezzlement, skimming, kiting, write-offs, or credits for kickbacks).
- Excessive and inappropriate credits are issued to customers.
- Excessive account adjustments and write-offs are issued.

Typical Controls

- Procedures are in place for the authorization and setting of realistic customer credit limits and to make sure they are not exceeded.
- Credit limits are based on credit worthiness.
- Access controls prevent unauthorized employees from accessing and manipulating the accounts receivable system and data.
- Customer credits and bad debt write-offs are monitored and issued by authorized individuals and require management approval.
- All customer complaints are researched and appropriately acted on.
- Delinquent and uncollectable balances are researched and appropriately acted on.

Fixed Assets

Key Objectives

- Assets are reflected correctly and accurately in the accounting records.
- Capital expenses are justified and approved.
- Fixed assets are recorded and their existence and condition verified regularly.
- Depreciation is calculated and posted in accordance with company policy and prevailing accounting standards and regulations.
- Assets are appropriately protected from loss and damage.
- Asset disposals and write-offs are valid, authorized, and correctly accounted for on the accounting records.

Key Risks

- Depreciation charges are inaccurate.

- Excess and obsolete assets remain on the accounting registers with economic value.
- Assets are stolen, lost, and damaged.
- Asset valuation is inaccurate.
- Asset malfunction impairs productive capacity.

Typical Controls

- Up-to-date policies and procedures are available for all aspects of asset acquisition, accounting treatment, depreciation, and disposal.
- All asset purchases require prior approval.
- Automated controls in the system calculate asset depreciation.
- Periodic reconciliations identify the loss, misplacement or obsolescence of assets, resulting, in management approval and adjustment.
- Key assets are adequately insured and management verifies that insurance coverage is maintained at the appropriate level.
- All asset disposals are subject to authorization and the sale proceeds are accounted for and posted to the appropriate account.
- Assets are subject to periodic inspection to ensure their operating continuity.
- Key assets are identified and there are plans for their replacement.
- Assets are adequately protected from theft, loss, and damage.

Inventory

Key Objectives

- All inventory values and quantities are accurate in inventory accounts.
- Inventory is safe from damage and theft.
- Inventory quantities are sufficient to meet operating needs (i.e., without excess or shortages).
- All income from inventory disposals and scrap sales is maximized and fully accounted for.

Key Risks

- Inventory account amounts and quantities are inaccurate.
- Inventory is stolen, damaged, or misplaced.
- Excessive or insufficient inventory levels exist.
- The location or condition of inventory items is unknown causing excess purchases, confusion, delays, and unnecessary storage space.
- Inventory value is inaccurate.

Typical Controls

- All inventories are priced correctly and inventory values and quantities are periodically verified as correct.
- Adjustments to inventory valuations are investigated and authorized.
- Inventory write-offs due to excess purchases, scrap, or obsolescence are documented, reviewed, and approved by authorized individuals before posting.
- Inventory prices are set in computer database tables with access restrictions in place.

- The organization conducts periodic cycle counts and physical counts that are verified for accuracy by independent employees.
- Periodic reconciliations are done to verify the accuracy of the amounts reflected on financial and operational reports, adjustments are reviewed before approval, management monitors deviations, and applies appropriate corrective actions if there are variations from expected values.
- Appropriate segregation of duties exists between merchandise receipt, quality inspection, storage, cycle/physical count, removal, and account/variance adjustment.
- Write-offs and disposals of inventory items require authorization.
- Inventory movements are tracked with scanners and trackers.

Information Technology

Overview

Organizations are increasingly relying on IT to support their business operations. In most cases, this reliance is not incidental but constitutes a vital enabler of organizational success as it provides the information workers use within their processes to carry out their duties. Technology is the third peg in the people–process–technology triad. As such, it should interface with organizational processes, which are populated by individuals who pursue the organization's mission, vision, and objectives.

In this section, we describe the most important IT general computer activities and their objectives, relevant risks, and typical controls. A full exploration of IT is beyond the scope of this book and arguably beyond the scope of any one book, since this topic has increased significantly in size and complexity over the past three decades. Consequently, our focus here is on the ways systems support organizational processes and objectives, how it has impacted control activities and some of the key areas internal auditors should focus on when examining general technology controls.

Some of the key operational risks include system access, data/information storage, backup, protection, and retrieval, computer room conditions, access to freestanding or networked computers, and batch processing activities. Other risks being considered relate to data accuracy, validity, authorization, and completeness. Business continuity and disaster recovery are also a key concern to organizations today. During times of constant change, relentless competition, and pressure on for-profit and nonprofit organizations alike to accomplish more with limited resources, an assessment of the adequacy of the organization's technological infrastructure and quality of data have also received a significant amount of attention.

It is also important that the chosen data structure and the database management system used to contain and manipulate information are secure, reliable, and provide accurate information to support business needs. System development, whether in-house or outsourced, carries significant risks that should be examined. The related costs often represent a considerable investment and organizations expect the timely release of all scoped features. These activities bear much in common with project management, so the reader should refer to that section within this book for useful guidance in that regard.

Strategically, management must understand and determine the dependency and linkage between business processes, automated control activities, and technology general controls. The repercussions impact business success factors internally and externally. This also carries day-to-day operational implications as workers are sometimes overwhelmed by information systems that fail to support their needs appropriately. So management must select, develop, and promote control activities over the technology infrastructure to help ensure the completeness, accuracy, and availability of technology processing.

There is also a linkage between IT and finance activities, because oversight is needed over the selection, acquisition, development, and maintenance of IT and its infrastructure to achieve management's objectives.

There is also a strong relationship between automated controls and general controls over technology. Automation typically reduces operating costs, accelerates workflows, standardizes results, and provides remote oversight of business activities. However, poorly developed, deployed, or monitored activities and controls can spell disaster.

IT Processing Operations

Key Objectives

- All IT processing activities are valid, authorized, and accurate.
- Data and operating systems are reliable.
- The required service levels are achieved in support of business objectives with minimal downtime.
- Stable and reliable application programs are used that meet internal and external quality standards.
- Only accurate, complete, and timely data are provided to users.
- IT processing facilities operate at optimum performance without jeopardizing system integrity and reliability.
- Only authorized and reliable systems and operating software are used.
- The operating system prevents unauthorized access to systems and data.
- Appropriately skilled staff is available to maintain computer systems.

Key Risks

- Processing activity is valid, accurate, and authorized.
- Confidential and sensitive information is reliable and secure.
- Staff lacks the skills to perform their duties and support the IT infrastructure and activities.
- Hardware and software fail to support business needs.
- Unauthorized individuals have access to data, information, and resources.
- System performance is below operating needs.
- Unstable applications are rolled out to users (i.e., into production).
- Unlicensed software is in use.

Typical Controls

- Management has developed and implemented operational policies and procedures.
- Redundant systems and contingency plans are in place to recover from major systems failure and these are tested periodically.
- All configuration changes or software amendments applied to the operating software are valid and fully tested prior to implementation.

- Operating systems are configured for maximum performance and integrity.
- Operating systems are protected from tampering.
- The use of utility and diagnostic software is controlled and monitored to prevent disruption of services or corruption of data and systems.
- Data and operating systems are protected from unauthorized access and use.
- Only authorized and tested application programs are used.
- Key hardware is maintained regularly and key software is up to date in terms of the version in use.
- The data in computers and personal handheld devices are protected from tampering and access through passwords, screensaver lockouts, encryption, and can be deleted remotely.
- Software and data are removed from all computing devices (e.g., desktops, laptops, tablets, smart phones, and printers) taken off service (e.g., donated, sold, and discarded) before disposal.
- There is a review and approval process in place to prevent the loading and use of unauthorized and untested programs.
- Contingency measures are in place to promptly restore disrupted services.
- Staff is adequately trained and their actions are identified and tracked.
- Activity logs are monitored and routinely reviewed to detect unauthorized activities.
- The performance of the operating system is monitored.
- Access to utility and diagnostic applications, servers, and computer processing areas are restricted and monitored.
- A review and sign-off process is in place to make sure that all programs are tested before being introduced to the live/production environment.
- Upgrades and patches are promptly identified, tested, and distributed.

Backups and Storage

Key Objectives

- The organization's data are protected from loss, damage, and theft.
- Organizational data retained remain in a usable and accessible form.
- Critical systems and data are adequately and frequently backed up to protect business operations and ensure continuity.
- A mechanism is in place to promptly and accurately recover from a system failure or invalid processing situations (e.g., malware infection or hacker's data destruction).
- The organization is capable of complying with prevailing data retention laws and regulations.
- Data storage facilities provide the appropriate conditions to prevent data deterioration or damage.
- Data are not disposed of or destroyed prematurely.

Key Risks

- Data loss (e.g., organizational, customer, and vendor) disrupts business activities.
- The organization is penalized for not protecting, storing, backing-up, or disposing of data according to prevailing laws and regulations.

- Necessary data are disposed of prematurely or inappropriately.
- Infected media are transferred.
- Key hardware and software are damaged or stolen.

Typical Controls

- Workers are trained upon hire and annually after that to make sure they are aware of their responsibilities with regard to the use, backup, and protection of company data and equipment.
- Staff is skilled through hiring requirements and training in media handling techniques and relevant technologies.
- All media and data are accurately identified, tracked, and accounted for.
- Media and systems are prevented from virus and other types of malware infection through anti-virus, firewalls, and other utilities.
- A policy is in place that defines backup frequency, number of copies, and the retention period for company data.
- Annual tests are conducted to verify that systems and data can be recovered from backup copies.
- Utilities conduct frequent and automatic routines to make sure end-user data from servers, desktop, and portable devices are backed up.
- Antivirus screening utilities screen incoming and outgoing transmissions to prevent the transfer of virus-infected media.
- Physical and logical access to computing facilities is limited.

IT Access

Key Objectives

- Systems and data are secure from unauthorized access and usage.
- Management selects and develops policies and control activities designed and implemented to restrict access rights to authorized users commensurate with their job responsibilities and to protect the organization's assets from external threats.

Key Risks

- User behavior endangers organizational data.
- Unauthorized individuals have access to organizational hardware, software, and data.

Typical Controls

- Corporate standards have been established for passwords, including minimum length, complexity (e.g., upper/lower case and alphanumeric), changing frequency, avoidance of obvious, or previously used words.
- Access passwords are confidential, initial passwords are communicated to the relevant user through secure means and must be reset upon first login.
- Access rights and associated records for all employees are kept up to date to ensure safety and segregation of duties.

- Few and known individuals have super-user access rights, which is monitored and temporarily used when necessary.
- Complex passwords meeting corporate standards, and/or biometrics, with required authentication are used for all computers and personal handheld devices to protect them from tampering and access by unauthorized individuals.
- Periodic reviews (e.g., reconcile HR–IT–Operations) are conducted to verify access rights are accurate and relevant.
- A corporate policy outlining system access rights and obligations is in place, and employees are trained annually on it outlining the appropriate use of computing facilities and devices.
- A process is in place to make sure access rights are changed appropriately when users are terminated or transferred.
- Access credentials are protected from unauthorized access (e.g., change and theft).
- All system usage is recorded and potential breaches of access security are promptly detected and reacted to.

Personal Devices

Key Objectives

- Personal devices (e.g., laptops, desktops, smartphones, and tablets) are used consistently and securely.
- The use of all personal devices is justified and authorized.
- All personal devices and accessories are protected from loss, theft, and damage.
- Only authorized and licensed versions of software are used throughout the organization.
- Only authorized users receive company-issued devices and in authorized quantities.

Key Risks

- Unauthorized individuals receive company-issued equipment.
- Devices are lost containing substandard safety protocols in place.
- Individuals use personal devices with unsatisfactory safety protocols in place.
- Personal devices are lost, stolen, misused, or disposed off inappropriately.
- The organization pays excessively for equipment, software, and licenses.
- Substandard equipment is in use limiting the staff's ability to perform their duties efficiently and effectively (e.g., outdated and under-powered hardware/software).

Typical Controls

- A policy is in place outlining employees' rights and obligations, including the use of computer equipment for business purposes only.
- A purchasing policy defines the procedures to acquire and replace personal devices.
- Utilities regularly back up and securely store user data.
- Selectively assigned administrative rights limit the opportunity to install licensed and prevent the installation of unlicensed or pirated software.
- All hardware and software upgrades are applied by appropriately trained and authorized personnel.

- Virus infections are promptly identified and dealt with effectively.
- All computers and relevant peripheral equipment are covered by a maintenance service agreement that includes technical support.
- Periodic reviews verify that only the required amounts and types of licenses are purchased and are in force.

Systems Development

Key Objectives

- System development projects are authorized and support the organization's strategic objectives.
- All system developments are assessed and justified in terms of costs and benefits.
- Systems are developed to a stable and recognized standard.
- Development projects are effectively managed and are delivered on time, as planned in the scoping documents and within budget.

Key Risks

- System development efforts result in failed projects (e.g., late, over-budget, less than agreed-upon scope).
- Poor change management and rollout practices limit the use of systems.
- Poor quality systems are developed and deployed.
- Third-party developers infringe on the organization's intellectual property and/or data.
- Third-party developers overcharge for services provided.
- Poor or missing documentation limits the organization's ability to maximize the use of systems developed.

Typical Controls

- Sufficient and skilled development staff is retained to support the creation and maintenance of computer systems.
- All systems are fully and satisfactorily tested before going live.
- System documentation standards have been adopted and enforced to ensure consistency, clarity, and as a resource for developers and users.
- Internal and/or external recruitment efforts make sure skilled development staff is obtained, fully utilized, developed, and retained.
- Progress reports inform management of the progress made during system development and alerts them of project delays, financial shortfalls, scope limitations, and quality issues promptly.
- Company procedures are in place and are enforced to verify that all new systems are fully tested to the satisfaction of users prior to rollout.
- Where outsourcing is used, contracts, business requirements, and other procedures are in place to verify that all required quality and performance requirements are met.
- A system development life-cycle methodology and procedures are in place and enforced by PMO.
- Business analysts document business requirements and verify that system specifications are included in the design and testing.

- The corporate steering committee makes sure that all system development efforts support the organization's strategic direction.
- A secure and stable development environment is in place.
- Systems developed are compatible (e.g., interface) with existing applications and business needs.
- Data is mapped, cleaned, and migrated prior to new system rollouts.
- Human factors (e.g., change management and training) are considered during system rollouts.
- Appropriate documentation exists to support ongoing system maintenance.
- The acquisition of new hardware, software, and licenses is subject to appropriate prior assessment and authorization.
- All system developments are subject to formal feasibility studies, financial assessments, and authorization by senior management.

Foundations

Overview

Many organizations have established foundations as part of their efforts to continue or expand the legacy of the organization's founders, provide assistance to constituents of interest, support local communities, enhance the organization's image, coordinate their charitable giving, enjoy tax benefits and in general focus, track, and promote their philanthropic efforts.

Standalone, unaffiliated foundations may have their dedicated operational auditors review processes and business units like any other organization. Foundations under the umbrella of a parent company are often audited by corporate auditors, who review the foundation as a program. The perspective presented here focuses on corporate auditors reviewing the parent company's affiliated foundation.

Key Objectives

- Smooth gift giving during profitable and lean years while deriving tax benefits
- Increase organizational influence and reputation
- Make sure funds are used as intended
- Provide a positive image of the foundation and its parent organization

Key Risks

- Funds are misused
- The organization acts unethically and damages its reputation
- The organization is unable to achieve its objectives
- Funds are curtailed

Typical Controls

- The organization has a clearly defined mission, vision, and operating standards that are incorporated into daily business activities.
- Segregation of duties, access controls, reconciliations, and approval levels limit the ability to use funds inappropriately.
- Employees are trained on the importance of effective controls.

- The organization communicates its ethical principles and business objectives to internal and external stakeholders.
- Cash balances, other assets, and endowment funds, if any, are reconciled monthly to ensure the accuracy of reported figures and appropriate business use.

Auditing Management

Overview

When we consider the role of internal auditors, a large percentage of the work effectively focuses on auditing management. After all, management owns the objectives of the organization, builds the structures necessary to deploy needed resources, establishes needed processes, finds the staff for those processes, positions needed technology to support the staff and processes, and monitors performance. Management is required to implement control activities that are built into business processes and employees' day-to-day activities through policies, communicating what is expected, and defining relevant procedures that specify the required actions. They must periodically review process design and the allocation of resources to determine their continued relevance, and re-organize these when necessary.

Management is also responsible for establishing responsibility and accountability for control activities with designated personnel within the unit or function where the relevant risks reside. Responsible and competent personnel are then expected to perform control activities as defined by the policies and procedures and exercise diligence and continuing focus.

An area of interest for internal auditors should be the impact of values, integrity, proper conduct, and ethics when reviewing management decisions and actions. Another area of interest should be the link between the organization's strategic plans (long term), their operating plans (short and medium term), the allocation of resources, and performance monitoring. These plans should provide clear operational and financial objectives, benchmarking within and outside the organization, quality objectives and metrics, appropriate communication with stakeholders, and a feedback mechanism to identify and address feedback.

Lastly, internal auditors should leverage their knowledge about entity-level controls, as they provide a good baseline to begin the review of management activities.

General Objectives

- The enterprise, business unit, departments, managers, and staff have clear business objectives
- Authority and accountability are clearly defined
- Management provides timely performance feedback to all employees
- Management holds everyone, including themselves, accountable for the quality and integrity of their work
- Management establishes clear expectations and leads by example
- Business activities are conducted, goods are produced, and services provided with high quality
- All conflicts of interest and incompatible duties in appearance or in fact are identified and addressed
- Follow up procedures exist to address errors, negative variances and otherwise poor or unexpected operating results
- The organization protects individual rights through data and information confidentiality

- The organization responds quickly to customer needs and concerns
- The organization responds quickly to competitor and market changes
- Management emphasizes the importance of addressing customer needs and a commitment to quality
- Surveys are conducted and results concerning internal relationships and customer needs identified, addressed, and implemented where appropriate
- An active customer feedback mechanism is in place and important information is shared as needed
- A culture that requires ongoing feedback and accountability is created and procedures are in place to support this management philosophy
- Management reviews and monitors the prevailing business environment, including
  - The competitive position of the organization within its industry (e.g., market share, luxury versus low-end product placement)
  - Performance benchmarks and how often these are updated
  - The organization's strategic plan to determine if it is consistent with trends in the industry and the overall marketplace

Key Risks

- Reduction in sales leading to a drop in profits, market share, or insolvency
- Reputation damage
- Failure to achieve its mission, vision, and its operational, compliance, and financial goals
- Loss of contract, license, or funding to operate
- Inability to recruit or retain needed staff
- Insufficient operational and technical capacity to grow the organization

Typical Controls

- Given the entity-level subject mentioned in this segment, typical controls would be entity-level controls primarily. For example:
  - Training programs
  - Organizational structure
  - Code of ethics
  - Conflict of interest statement
  - Monthly operating and financial reporting
  - Performance management programs
  - System access and authorization levels
  - Authority, funding, and scope of work of second and third lines of defense

Ethics Hotlines

Overview

Among the remedies against unethical behavior are regulatory requirements like the ones imposed by the Securities and Exchange Commission and the Sarbanes-Oxley Act of 2002. The Sarbanes-Oxley Act requires, among other provisions, the establishment of whistleblowing programs for the anonymous and confidential disclosure of activities that may have an adverse effect on the organization' financial statements. Whistleblowing programs are an important tool to disclose inappropriate activities within organizations beyond financial reporting, as they can also serve to capture allegations of sexual harassment, unsafe working conditions, management abuse, and theft, among others.

ACFE reports in its 2014 Report to the Nations on Occupational Fraud and Abuse that 42% of frauds are detected through tips. That number has remained relatively unchanged for years: 43% in 2012 and 40% in 2010. The ACFE also found that having a reporting hotline had a significant impact on the initial fraud detection. For organizations with a hotline, 51% of frauds were detected through that mechanism, while that figure drops to 33% when the organization does not have a hotline. Some of the other and less effective means of detection include by accident, notification by law enforcement, and external audit.

It is important for organizations to implement whistleblowing programs and make sure they are credible and effective. It is also a good practice for organizations to make this mechanism known to outside stakeholders (e.g., customers and suppliers) in the event these parties know of inappropriate actions.

General Objectives

- The ethics hotline is a key component of the organization's ethics program
- The organization protects whistleblowers
- The ethics hotline is widely known, highly regarded, and accessible to employees and others

Key Risks

- Employees do not know or forget how to contact the hotline
- Employees are uncomfortable or afraid of communicating issues
- Individuals who file sincere allegations are ostracized, retaliated upon, harassed, and in general suffer negative consequences from using the hotline
- Allegations remain without resolution longer than necessary

Typical Controls

- The organization posts hotline program information prominently within and outside the organization.
- The organization provides annual reminders.
- The program is accessible easily and freely to all employees through multiple channels.
- There is clear cross-functional investigation protocol, including an escalation mechanism.
- Dual reporting is in place to make sure there are checks and balances for all allegations received.
- Performance reports are generated, reviewed, and acted upon.
- The program is referenced in the employee manual and code of ethics.
- Annual surveys are conducted to assess employee opinions regarding the hotline.

Production

Key Objectives

- Production lines are effective, efficient, operate economically and safely, and deliver with high quality.

- Product lines do not become obsolete prematurely.
- Production lines operate consistently (i.e., without unintended interruptions).
- The production process has a good safety record.

Key Risks

- Strategic business objectives fail to meet organizational objectives (e.g., deadlines, profitability, and market share)
- Intellectual properties are abused by others
- Product launch is ill-timed or otherwise ineffective
- Delays, miscommunication, and inefficiencies surface due to a lack of coordination with other affected functions (e.g., manufacturing, inventory, sales, marketing, and customer service)
- Employees are inconsistent when performing their duties or take longer than necessary to do so
- Useful suggestions from the quality control department (or other stakeholders) are not heeded
- Present manufacturing methods are outdated, inefficient, or otherwise ineffective
- Equipment breakdown is excessive
- Production facilities are uncomfortable or unsafe for workers (e.g., too hot/cold/humid/noisy, poor ventilation, inadequate emergency exits, risk of bodily harm due to fire, explosion, and contamination)
- The unit focuses on short-term goals at the expense of longer term priorities
- Cost considerations are not fully explored (e.g., size of production runs are inefficient)
- New facilities and equipment are purchased when production issues are related to the process or the people
- Production scheduling is informal and inefficient
- The layout of work facilities does not fit the normal flow of work
- Materials are unavailable when needed
- Materials awaiting processing are stolen, damaged, or impaired
- Production methods result in excessive waste, delays, bottlenecks, and emergency jobs
- Spoiled materials are not reused, recycled, or disposed of in the most efficient manner
- Workers get hurt while working
- Waste disposal is inconsistent with prevailing laws and regulations

Typical Controls

- Sales forecasts and performance are monitored closely and inform production decisions.
- The activities of all the affected functions are coordinated to achieve the objectives defined
- All intellectual properties and assets are protected from exploitation by others.
- Maintenance schedules have been implemented and followed, and preventive action is taken when needed.
- Metrics are captured, analyzed, and used to monitor and improve production practices.
- Production procedures and training are provided to workers.
- Floor layout, production flows, and materials used are examined periodically to identify improvement opportunities.
- Safety protocols and instructional materials are in place (e.g., material safety data sheets and use of safety equipment).

Notes

1 For further details about the regulations and to see the list of SDN, see https://www.treasury.gov/about/organizational-structure/offices/Pages/Office-of-Foreign-Assets-Control.aspx
2 Quote from Linda K. Trevino and Katherine A. Nelson in *Managing Business Ethics: Straight Talk about How to Do It Right*, 6th edition, John Wiley & Sons, 2014.

Chapter 14

The Toyota Production System

> We place the highest value on actual implementation and taking action. There are many things one doesn't understand and therefore, we ask them why don't you just go ahead and take action; try to do something? You realize how little you know and you face your own failures and you simply can correct those failures and redo it again and at the second trial you realize another mistake or another thing you didn't like so you can redo it once again. So by constant improvement, or, should I say, the improvement based upon action, one can rise to the higher level of practice and knowledge.
>
> **Fujio Cho, President, Toyota Motor Corporation**

Introduction

The TPS, often referred to as The Toyota Way, is an integrated social, management, process, and technical system, developed by Toyota reflecting and providing a framework showcasing its management philosophy and practices. The TPS incorporates elements related to manufacturing and logistics, and it goes beyond what is done within Toyota by including the interaction with suppliers and customers. It is a framework for conserving resources, eliminating waste, improving relationships, and building trust and teamwork.

The TPS popularized the concept of JIT or lean manufacturing system, which means only making what is needed, when it is needed, in the amount required. Another common practice is the replacement of inspection at the end of the production cycle, and instead building quality into the process itself. As such, when a problem occurs, the equipment or process stops immediately, preventing defective products from being produced. The result is that only products meeting quality standards continue to move down the production line. The TPS also popularized the concept of Kaizen, which entails continuous improvement, pursuing excellence, and driving innovation. This constant evolution of the production processes keep all involved searching for ways to make the process work better.

The 14 Principles

The TPS is arranged around four main themes and 14 principles.

   I. Long-term philosophy—the basis for management decisions
       1. Base your management decisions on a long-term philosophy, even at the expense of short-term goals.

  II. The right process will produce the right results
       2. Create a continuous process flow to bring problems to the surface
       3. Use "pull" systems to avoid overproduction
       4. Level out the workload (Heijunka): Work like the tortoise, not the hare
       5. Build a culture of stopping to fix problems, to get quality right the first time
       6. Standardized tasks and processes are the foundation for continuous improvement and employee empowerment
       7. Use visual control so no problems are hidden
       8. Use only reliable, thoroughly tested technology that serves your people and processes

 III. Add value to the organization by developing your people and partners
       9. Grow leaders who thoroughly understand the work, live the philosophy, and teach it to others
      10. Develop exceptional people and teams who follow your company's philosophy
      11. Respect your extended network of partners and suppliers by challenging them and helping them improve

  IV. Continuously solving root problems drives organizational learning
      12. Go and see for yourself to thoroughly understand the situation (Genchi Genbutsu)
      13. Make decisions slowly by consensus, thoroughly considering the options, then implementing decisions rapidly (Nemawashi)
      14. Become a learning organization through relentless reflection (Hansei) and continuous improvement (Kaizen)

The TPS includes many interrelated concepts and practices, and has been embraced by many organizations both in and outside the auto industry since its development in the 1960s. It is a framework with norms, philosophies, and tools with a common denominator: teamwork.

David Jacoby states that the TPS has four principles:

1. Continuous improvement—Kaizen: The system aims to provide a learning environment where each mistake turns into an opportunity for improvement. The goal: No error should be repeated twice.
2. The systematic elimination of muda (waste in Japanese): There is a drive to ensure that every decision and every action drives toward adding value for the end-customer.
3. People-centeredness: The TPS only works if people believe in it and act in accordance with it

It cannot be mandated and it cannot be managed virtually through information technology. People must internalize the norms and the values making it part of the culture. Then they must act on it daily whenever they encounter problems.

4. Simplicity: This means fewer breakdowns and more reliability than in a complex system.

The TPS is responsible for the creation of many of the tools that are associated with lean management, including

- *The pull-based demand trigger*: It eliminates waste by focusing all effort on satisfying customer needs rather than a forecast, which is inevitably erroneous.
- *JIT production*: This minimizes the waste that may occur when customer demands change by eliminating buffer inventories throughout the pipeline.
- *Jidoka*: It is a concept that highlights the causes of problems because work stops immediately when a problem first occurs. This leads to improvements in the processes that can be applied immediately as it builds in quality. It prevents problems before they occur and some refer to it as "automation with a human touch," because rather than a machine that runs on its own, with Jidoka, the machine stops when there is a problem. This allows an operator to monitor multiple machines simultaneously. Jidoka improves system stability and reduces the need for problem diagnosis and remediation.
- *Visual controls*: An example is Kanban cards, which are physical cards that are placed at the end of a batch of inventoried items. The card itself triggers replenishment rather than an information system. It ensures universal, real time, and easy to update access to information about the pace of production (takt time).
- *Capacity balancing and level loading*: This makes sure the work revolves around small lot sizes, which consequently generates minimum waste from changes in demand.
- *Root cause problem solving*: It includes diagnostic tools such as PDCA and the Ishikawa fishbone diagram, which makes it possible for the team to diagnose and resolve errors and restore normal operation following disruptions.

An important practice to identify operational issues is based on the Japanese word genba (sometimes referred to as gemba). It is often translated as "the real place," "the place where value is created," or the "scene of the crime." In a business setting it refers to the factory floor, construction site, where the service is delivered or the sales floor. In general, it refers to the place where value is created for the customer.

The concepts is built on the principle that problems are visible, and if a problem occurs, the full impact of the problem can only be understood and appreciated by going to the place where it is happening (TPS Principle 12). It forms the basis for another common process improvement practice called management by walking around. Genba walks describe the process of going to where the process is performed, understanding it, talking to those involved in the process, and learning the details about it. It is the personal observation of the work.

It can be done by the staff or management and during the genba walk, those involved note existing design or operating deficiencies, observe how machines and tools are arranged and used, note their condition, and become aware of waste, inefficiencies, unsafe conditions or practices, and other improvement opportunities.

Another key benefit of the genba walk is that it allows leaders and workers to build better relationships. It speaks loudly to workers when they see their leaders genuinely interested in the work being done and the conditions in which it is performed. It also reinforces the concept of "walking the talk" as it provides that direct interaction between workers and managers and a way for workers to see their managers display care, teamwork, attention to detail, curiosity, and discipline—conditions that many workplaces lack. It also provides an immediate forum for workers to describe and show problems they are encountering and for management to take action to fix issues.

This concept is then expanded to include genba kaizen, where continuous improvement is made to the workplace by reducing waste and searching for ways to improve efficiency. The adoption of constant change for the better is also important to build a culture that is relentless in is search for better ways to get the work done.

During operational audits, genba means worksite and the objective is that if there is a problem, the auditor must go there to understand the full scale and impact of the problem, gather data from all available sources, and talk to those directly involved to get first-hand knowledge of the issue. This is different from focus groups, surveys, or document reviews (e.g., operating and financial reports) because it involves unscripted face-to-face interactions.[1]

Conclusion

The TPS provides a formidable roadmap for internal auditors engaged in assurance or consulting engagements focusing on strategic, compliance, operational, IT, or other areas. It provides a framework for evaluating structural, staffing, operational, training and development of individuals, and the organization in the short and longer terms. In fact, it can serve as an audit program by merely turning each principle into a question and asking to what degree each of these principles is being applied and searching for the evidence to support that rating.

Toyota is the largest car company in the world and has been among the top ten for decades. It has gained widespread acclaim for the quality, durability, and reliability of its vehicles, which have become enormously complex computers on wheels that blend digital, analog, and mechanical components. Toyota provides great lessons on how to bring people, processes, and technologies together and internal auditors are advised to learn from this impressive company.

QUESTIONS

1. Explain how an organization can demonstrate its adherence with the principle that management decisions are based on a long-term philosophy (principle 1).
2. Provide three examples of how organizations can create continuous process flows to bring problems to the surface (principle 2).
3. Explain the difference between a pull and a push system, and the pros and cons of each model (principle 3).
4. What evidence would you ask to examine to determine if an organization is leveling the workload (principle 4)?
5. Give three examples of how organizations can build a culture of stopping to fix problems so quality is right the first time (principle 5).
6. Use three tools to describe how a process can be improved to standardize its tasks and processes in pursuit of continuous improvement and employee empowerment (principle 6).

7. Provide three examples of effective visual controls that make sure that problems come to the surface (principle 7).
8. What specific recommendations would you make to an organization that wants to grow leaders who understand the work and live the philosophy (principle 9) and develops exceptional people and teams (principle 10)?
9. How do organizations show that they respect their extended network of partners and suppliers (principle 11) and what evidence would you evaluate?
10. Describe genba walks and explain how managers can use them to thoroughly understand situations (principle 12).

Note

For additional information about genba, its uses and benefits, see http://www.isixsigma.com/methodology/lean-methodology/many-sides-gemba-walk/

Chapter 15

Organizational Structure

> Every company has two organizational structures: The formal one is written on the charts; the other is the everyday relationship of the men and women in the organization.
>
> **Harold S. Geneen**

Introduction

Organizational structures vary to accommodate the needs of the enterprise. There are different types and some work better than others to facilitate the flow of resources, information, to establish accountability, and to provide the goods and services that customers require. The form and function of the structure play an important role in determining the effectiveness of the enterprise and the achievement of its goals. Conversely, misalignment often leads to confusion, waste, and poor management of operational risks.

Instructions, guidance, and resources are authorized and assigned at the top and flow downward throughout the organization. Results, reports, requests, and questions generally flow upward. Coordination, communication, and collaboration often occur laterally, crossing horizontally to facilitate operational execution. An essential component of effective operational audits is to determine if the structure and the related flows are productive.

Internal auditors should understand the structures of the organizations, programs, or processes they review and use this information to better assess existing conditions and the likelihood of achieving established objectives. This knowledge can also help identify risks and the best placement of controls. In addition, many operational breakdowns can be better understood, explained, and corrected when the characteristics of the organizational structure are understood.

Organizational Hierarchies and Structures

Organizations are formed for a particular purpose: they may be for-profit or non-profit, and they come in many sizes. They sometimes have only a few or thousands of workers, have a minuscule or gargantuan budget, and operate in a small neighborhood or a global enterprise. Although there are many ways to describe organizations, one thing remains constant and that is they must have a certain structure.

If there are more than one individual involved, a hierarchy begins to emerge immediately. This placement of roles, from the head, through a senior management team, down through a middle management layer all the way to individual employees, all engaged in various activities that support the organization's goals, constitutes an essential element in establishing order, predictability, improving efficiency and effectiveness, and ensuring accountability.

Managers are responsible for organizing the enterprise, dividing the work into achievable activities, and deciding who does what. Organizations can be structured in many ways based on their objectives and resources. In the end, however, the structure determines to a large extent how the organization operates, how efficiently and effectively it performs, how decisions are made and by whom. Although there are different types of organizational structures, there are three that reflect the majority of structures in use. Essential to this definition of the structure is having clear roles and responsibilities.

Tall or Vertical

In a tall or vertical organizational structure, there are many levels of management from executives at the top, to middle managers, on down to supervisors, team leaders, and individual workers closer to the bottom. A hierarchical or bureaucratic structure, as it is sometimes referred to, is one where every unit in the organization is a subordinate to a single other unit. There is either an individual or a group at the top with the most power, controlling resources and setting the overall direction, and there are subsequent levels of power providing oversight below them.

This structure is the most common in organizations and employees typically communicate with their immediate manager and their immediate colleagues. People are arranged in order of rank or grade and it typically requires that decision-making goes through several layers for approval. In bureaucratic organizations, decisions tend to follow an organized and documented process by what is often referred to as command and control structure because the commanding authority that controls resources and issues instructions is at the top, and the information and instructions they produce flow from the top down.

While bureaucratic organizations tend to be more predictable, they are also often rigid, relying on policies and established procedures, and are often slow to adapt and change as internal and external circumstances change. The standardized way of operating and relatively high amounts of formalization can slow down decision-making processes, making the organization slow and inflexible.

This can be a liability in a fast-changing economic, political, and social environment where the ability to change, adapt, and respond to external influences could make a difference between staying in operation or going out of business. In today's complex world, it is becoming increasingly difficult for decision-making to be concentrated at the top of the pyramid. Instead, it is becoming more common for decisions to be pushed down to the middle managers and in many cases, even further down to front-line workers.

Functional

To address the fact that highly bureaucratic organizations tend to be inflexible, slow and sometimes decisions are made by people who don't have all the information needed to make them, modern organizations are increasingly focusing on a functional approach that facilitate dialogue and consensus instead of a strict command and control structure.

Functional organizations contain specialized units, called functional units or areas, that report to a single authority in top management. These specialized units have staff with related skills that handle one aspect of the product or service provided, for example, accounting, marketing, human resources, or information technology. The functional organization structure clusters personnel with similar knowledge and skills. Since employees develop within their field of expertise, this approach facilitates training and coaching and leads to the development of specialists.

This approach tends to improve performance because it facilitates the sharing of important expertise by superiors with their subordinates and makes it easier for managers to identify high performing employees and place them where they can be most effective. Senior management is responsible for coordinating the work of each unit and bringing them together as a cohesive organization because, since units are not accountable to each other, they tend to suffer from poor communication and synchronization with each other. Another key disadvantage is that employees tend to neglect the larger view of the organization and its overall objectives, instead of working in a vertical and disconnected manner in what has commonly been referred to as "silos."

This structure works best for organizations that produce standardized goods and services in large volumes at low costs. It is most effective for organizations operating in relatively stable environments where there is a low rate of change.

For this approach to work, the organization must encourage participation and empower employees more, so they share information and coordinate with other units. This has led to a recent trend where organizations use teams that cross departmental lines.

Matrix

A matrix structure usually groups employees in teams to create and take advantage of a combination of functional alignment and decentralization. It is more dynamic and makes it easier for employees to share information, thus improving communication. It is a more responsive arrangement for organizations operating in changing and dynamic environments, making it possible for employees to address changing conditions rapidly. This is done by tapping into their knowledge and that of others, without the limitations that strict hierarchical requirements often impose. Another advantage is that it provides opportunities for workers to learn from each other and facilitates the transfer of knowledge laterally in the organization. It also makes it easier to assign specialized resources to projects when these are needed.

In this arrangement, employees are grouped by function and product, and the organizational structure is very flat. Each worker reports to a functional head, but generally do not work under that person's direct supervision. In many cases, the worker belongs to a project and works under the supervision of a project manager.

In a matrix structure, each worker could have two managers, who together make sure the program or project progress as needed. Roles and responsibilities are often defined by the project manager keeping track of deadlines and costs, whereas the functional manager focuses on developing goods and services that reflect customer needs. When the work is finished, the team may be dissolved, and workers may be reassigned to other programs, projects, and activities.

In terms of challenges, it can be difficult for employees to know what to do if they are getting instructions from multiple individuals at the same time. In some cases, employees may have multiple bosses, each with potentially different priorities and objectives. This drawback can often be remedied through open, honest, and constant communication to make adjustments and prioritize activities as needed. Another important competence is the ability to influence others without clear authority. This means that all employees in a knowledge-based work environment, especially those using a matrix structure, must learn to be leaders.

In most cases, an organization's structure is neither predetermined nor fixed permanently. Instead, it evolves over time to match changes in the firm's strategy. As the organization's operations grow, spread, and become more complex, the structure typically comes under stress. As the strain grows and threatens the existing structure, the organization is usually compelled to consider and experiment with alternate organizational structures. Eventually, the organization must choose a structure that is consistent with its strategy and circumstances and that can handle the present and future needs.

Organizational Charts

Organizational, or org, charts are visual representations of the relations between people and units within organizations, so they show the organizational structure in the form of a diagram. These diagrams show the reporting lines that might include managers and their staff, directors and senior management, C-level executives (such as the CEO, CFO, and COO), and various departments.

These charts can be very helpful to clarify authority and reporting lines to avoid ambiguity in the workplace. However, we must remember that the org chart does not show informal relationships, can be outdated if the organization changes quickly, and they say nothing about the managerial style used by managers (e.g., autocratic, democratic).

Managing an organization and the many dynamics involved requires careful handling of the following elements:

- *Setting and Communicating Plans*: This involves defining the mission and vision, establishing the structure, defining goals, and hiring the people who have the right skills, background, and motivation. Manager-leaders must assess the environment in which the work will be done and develop the best course of action given the objectives and resources available to calculate the likelihood and best approach to succeed.
- *Facing Challenges*: Running an organization is challenging, so it requires understanding the dynamics inside and outside the organization, and dealing with matters of economy, efficiency, and effectiveness.
- *Execute through Strategy*: A unified team, using a consistent strategy with the needed internal and external relationships and alliances is more likely to succeed. It is not necessarily a matter of how big the organization is, but rather the degree of unity, sound execution, and common purpose. The strategy comes to life through the daily, weekly, and monthly tactics manager-leaders put in place and act upon.
- *Positioning*: Organizations must take advantage of opportunities, but also protect what has been achieved so far in terms of brand recognition, market share, and customer good-will. Moving into new markets, launching new products or services, or pursuing new customers while neglecting existing ones is a sure way to fail eventually.
- *Energy and Directing*: An organization's momentum is determined by the energy the enterprise possesses and the soundness of the direction the leadership team provides. Creativity and proper timing cannot be overstated in giving an organization that edge toward success.
- *Capitalizing on Weaknesses*: Opportunities often surface as a result of the weaknesses that exist in the marketplace, whether it is because other organizations have neglected those sectors, or there is a change in the socio-economic environment that no one has noticed.

- *Management and Maneuvering*: Going head to head with another organization, employee, manager, or supplier is not always the best strategy. Direct conflict can be self or mutually destructive. Instead, manager-leaders should know when adaptability, flexibility, change, and negotiation are needed to ensure success.
- *Variation in Approach*: An organization must be able to change tactics to address evolving changes so that the strategy can succeed. Flexibility in the face of changing circumstances is essential for success.
- *Situational Positioning*: When manager-leaders engage in strategic planning, they must consider the three main forms of resistance for ongoing success: distance, dangers, and barriers. How big is the gap between where we are and where we want the organization to go? What are the risks that could impede our ability to get there and what are the obstacles that, if not removed, will impede our progress? There are advantages and disadvantages to every decision; so actions, whether related to human resources, finances, compliance, operations, or otherwise, must be weighed in terms of the merits and demerits of each.
- *Business Intelligence*: Every organization must invest in the gathering, analysis, distribution, and response to competitive intelligence about products, customers, competitors, and any other relevant aspect of the environment needed to support the organization in making decisions.

General Characteristics of Top Organizations

There has been a noticeable increase in the "Top 100 Companies to Work For" lists. This reflects a growing interest in identifying winning attributes that differentiate poor, from average, from exceptional organizations. So, what are some of those attributes that separate exceptional organizations from the rest? The following provides some examples:

Must Have:

- Defined career paths
- Length of service recognition
- Meaningful succession plans
- Meaningful formal and informal feedback
- Engagement surveys
- Retirement savings programs
- Tuition reimbursement
- Health benefits
- Program for high-potential employees
- Bonus programs aligned with performance and organizational objectives
- Community involvement
- Competitive compensation
- Awards based on employee and team contributions
- Recruiting incentives
- Development programs

High-Value:

- Flexible work schedules
- Mentoring and coaching programs

- Paid leave
- Employee Assistance Program
- Exercise facilities

Innovative:

- Job sharing
- Sabbatical leave and learning program
- Circle of interest social forums, such as book clubs, outing clubs, volunteering

Well run organizations are typically characterized by four key general characteristics, which are as follows:

- Adaptability: It includes creating a culture that drives and embraces change, a relentless focus on customer needs, and fostering constant learning.
- Mission: It is characterized by having a strategic direction with a clear mission, vision, goals, and objectives.
- Consistency: It is exemplified by having core values that everyone agrees on, getting everyone involved, and coordinating and integrating the multiple aspects of the organization.
- Involvement: It is focused on employee empowerment, team orientation, and constant development of employee capabilities.

As can be seen, these four elements promote equilibrium between flexibility and stability, while also considering internal and external needs. When organizations establish and maintain clarity and alignment among these elements, they enjoy high levels of performance. As these elements weaken through confusion, uncertainty, and lack of reinforcement and leadership, performance suffers.

Internal auditors should evaluate performance using multiple metrics, which include the following:

- Profitability, such as high Returns on Investment (ROI), Return on Assets (ROA), and Return on Equity (ROE)
- High Quality
- Employee and Customer Satisfaction
- Creativity and Innovation
- Sales Growth and Increased Market Share

Summary

A key ingredient in achieving effectiveness and operate efficiently is to have a well-defined structure that addresses the needs of the organization. Although traditionally organizations have used a tall pyramid structure with a clear command and control approach to management, modern organizations are increasingly adopting flatter and matrix structures, which are more dynamic, flexible, and responsive to stakeholder needs. This structure, and the organizational charts that visually depict the arrangement, should be revisited periodically to determine it continued usefulness, and make necessary improvements.

Internal auditors should include an evaluation of their organizations' structure and ability to change. The answer will provide valuable insights about the ability to operate at its maximum capacity creating value for its stakeholders.

QUESTIONS

1. List and describe the three most common types of organizational structure.
2. Which organizational structure, while typically providing greater clarity about roles and responsibilities, often slows operational responsiveness?
3. Which structure is most often used when operations are relatively stable and there is a low rate of change?
4. Which two structures often provide the greatest opportunities for workers to learn from each other thus facilitating the transfer of knowledge laterally in the organization?
5. Why are org charts commonly reviewed by internal auditors?
6. Why is Variation in Approach important to the success of organizations and what are the implications for internal auditors?
7. Relate the three main forms of resistance to Situational Positioning and how awareness of this impacts risk assessments.
8. List five attributes that characterize exceptional organizations and explain their significance to operational auditors.
9. Explain why employee involvement is important for operational effectiveness.
10. Develop an operational audit program that includes procedures to determine if a unit is effectively balancing flexibility and stability.

Chapter 16

Conclusion

Inspecting and detecting problems is good. Preventing problems is better.

Using Operational Audits to Help Reposition the Internal Audit Function

When we examine the changing role of internal audit as it relates to people, processes, and technologies, it becomes apparent that we are entering a new era. This new phase in our history is characterized by change, increased expectations and demands, ever-changing risks, and an overwhelming amount of data and competitive pressures that can collectively or in isolation cripple an organization very rapidly. Internal auditors are tasked with assessing and making appropriate recommendations for improving the governance processes in their organizations, evaluating the effectiveness and contributing to the improvement of risk management processes, and assisting their organizations in maintaining effective controls. To do this, auditors need independence, objectivity, clarity of mind, and effective tools. They must be guided by the goal of promoting continuous improvement throughout the organization and to accomplish this, they must constantly perform gap analyses. They must also energize and encourage their organizations to mobilize through the practice of change management principles.

Adding value and being perceived as trusted advisors to their organizations are perhaps the highest aspirations of internal auditors around the world. Operational auditing is a key contributor to achieving that goal. This can be achieved by

- Helping their organizations establish the right strategic direction to achieve their mission
- Identifying opportunities to work faster, cheaper, and better
- Anticipating positive and negative events that can enable or hinder future success
- Encouraging stakeholders within and outside the organization to act ethically

The operational improvements will translate into stronger financial results, and by achieving its goals over the long term, the organization will safeguard its sustainability. This entry into the realm of auditing strategic initiatives and risks requires internal auditors to recruit SMEs who are knowledgeable about how the company's risk profile is changing.

How can this be accomplished?

Developing Operational Talent

PWC's 2015 State of the Internal Audit Profession identifies four significant factors enabling internal audit contribute to strategic initiatives

1. A risk focus on the right risks at the optimal time in the process
2. A talent model that includes developing business acumen and offers valuable insights
3. Proper business alignment with ERM and the other two lines of defense
4. Proficient use of technology and data analytics to provide valuable insights into the business and strengthen overall risk management

The number and complexity of external drivers for change are influencing the way internal audit operates, and the function should evolve to make sure it maintains it relevance.

KPMG's Internal Audit: Top 10 Key Risks in 2016 identifies internal audit talent recruitment and retention as one of the key considerations that internal auditors should evaluate as part of their overall strategy. Finding qualified individuals is challenging. Recruitment efforts have long expanded beyond the recruitment of accountants with public accounting experience and CPA credentials. The internal audit profession has realized that internal auditors do more than review accounting procedures, verify financial figures, and confirm that internal procedures have been followed. Recruitment efforts should incorporate the impact that greater involvement in the business's strategic initiatives has. Internal competency assessments are required to perform a gap analysis and determine what skillsets are lacking. With this information, CAEs can determine which areas need improvement and search for SMEs to supplement the existing competencies and expand the audit work beyond compliance.

Internal audit must recruit individuals with different backgrounds who can think about risk creatively, and hire employees from the organization who have operational experience and subject matter expertise. External recruitment often includes job banks, recruiters, referrals, and corporate webpage postings. Social media, especially LinkedIn, has also become a formidable avenue to identify new talent. Until those auditors are hired, internal audit can leverage the resources from third parties who can provide cosourcing services. Once hired, an important action has to be the expansion of training and development programs that go beyond traditional compliance topics and build skills in other business objectives and methodologies.

Transformation: Becoming Trusted Advisors

Becoming a trusted advisor to the board and management has long been presented as a strategic goal of internal auditors. This designation implies that the internal auditor is no longer seen merely as the corporate cop who moves around the organization searching for instances o noncompliance. As internal auditors go beyond compliance and accounting-focused work, they can become trusted advisors when they do the following:

- Perform risk-based audits that probe topics important to the achievement of business objectives
- Effectively identify the root cause of operational issues and use facts and figures to support statements
- Leverage their deep knowledge and experience in diverse business areas
- Practice participative auditing techniques that result in collaboration with audit clients during the planning, fieldwork, and report-preparation phases of engagements
- Eloquently present the benefits of recommendations in terms of improving the control environment, but more importantly, how they reduce risk exposures and support efforts to achieve business objectives
- Share knowledge, insight, case studies, updates, and other facts that demonstrate their personal investment in the well-being of the organization even when an audit is not underway
- Acting with a sense of urgency and always conducting themselves professionally

Becoming a trusted advisor is not something that happens by accident. It is not something that is gained automatically after a long tenure in the organization. Becoming a trusted advisor is the result of consistently delivering what the client values, being right about issues, making useful and pragmatic recommendations, and being fair in the evaluation of business processes while acknowledging the context in which issues confront the organization. This does not mean the auditor loses independence or objectivity, but rather that they are fair, competent, and credible.

Eventually the client trusts the auditor to practice sound auditing techniques based on effective research and grounded in facts. The client comes to trust the auditor to tell the truth and rely on the veracity of communications shared with them. It can be described as: If the auditor said it, it must be true.

At the highest level the relationship becomes one of partnership not only related to ongoing operations, but one where the client asks for advice before making important decisions. This transforms the relationship from one of detection and correction of issues, into one of deterrence, prevention, and preemptive actions to anticipate risky situations. When this happens, the auditor is being sought, not avoided, and can be described as one where the auditor is the client's trusted advisor.

Applying Consulting Skills Effectively during Operational Audits

As the internal auditor's role and practices evolve, the value of what they provide increases as well. Initially, the auditor provides information, facts, and figures related to the result of their reviews. Over time, the auditor becomes more adept at providing solutions to the problems identified. In other words, the auditor doesn't merely provide a list of problems, but those issues are accompanied by useful and pragmatic recommendations.

Management, as owners of the programs and processes within the organization, is responsible for the implementation of recommendations. I have found that clients appreciate the effort made to discuss corrective action, how it can best be implemented, and who is best suited to perform the enhanced or additional activities. The final decision rests with management, and quite often they know what needs to be done, who will do it, and when. But to the extent that the auditor can share insights and remind management about the implications in terms of segregation of duties, access controls, performance metrics for monitoring, and workflow leveling, this can help make the implementation more successful, sustainable, and with fewer unintended consequences.

The facilitation of learning helps to build institutional knowledge and the capacity to make better decisions in the future. It is a form of coaching that can enhance leadership and managerial know-how. Collectively it results in an improvement in organizational effectiveness.

Operational Excellence and Cultural Transformation: Role of Internal Audit

Among the key focus areas for internal audit are cybersecurity, ensuring compliance, dealing with bribery and corruption at home and abroad, producing efficiently and effectively, managing third-party relationships, helping the organization capture and manage data through data analytics, and maintaining strategic alignment between internal audit and the business. Many internal audit departments are well on their way to meeting these challenges, while others are just beginning their journey. In the end the goal can be summarized as helping the organization act faster, cheaper, and better.

Bibliography

Boyer, K. K., Frohlich, M., and Hult, G. T. (2005). *Extending the Supply Chain: How Cutting-Edge Companies BRIDGE the Critical Last Mile into Customers' Homes.* New York, NY: American Management Association.

Cannon, D. ITIL. (2011). *Service Strategy* (2nd ed.). Norwich, UK: The Stationery Office.

Carpenter, G. and White, P. (2004). Sustainable development: Finding the real business case. *International Journal for Sustainable Business, 11*(2), 2-51–2-56.

Christopher, M. (1998). *Logistics and Supply Chain Management: Strategies for Reducing Cost and Improving Service* (2nd ed.). New York, NY: Prentice Hall.

Cobb, A. T. (2006). *Leading Project Teams: An Introduction to the Basics of Project Management and Project Team Leadership.* Thousand Oaks, CA: Sage Publications.

De Feo, J. A. and Barnard, W. (2005). *Juran Institute's Six Sigma Breakthrough and Beyond: Quality Performance Breakthrough Methods.* New York, NY: McGraw-Hill.

Donaldson, T. (1996). Values in tension: Ethics away from home. *Harvard Business Review,* September–October, 1–12, Reprint #96502.

Drucker, P. (1999). *Management Challenges for the 21st Century.* New York, NY: Harper Collins.

Fugate, S. B. and Mentzer, J. T. (2006). Supply chain management coordination mechanisms. *Journal of Business Logistics, 27*(2), 129–161.

Gilly, S. (1997). "The development of management and organizational thinking in Anthony Tarantino (2008)." *Governance, Risk, and Compliance Handbook: Technology, Finance, Environmental and International Guidance and Best Practices.* Hoboken, NJ: John Wiley and Sons. https://books.google.com/books?id= 3aUyqPxYw10C&pg=PA93&lpg=PA93&dq=sue+gilly+the+development+of+management+and+organiza-tional+thinking&source=bl&ots=syeaExi1BD&sig=ACfU3U1YxMB82IZoWQy68K9RlBgNBIVouA&hl= en&sa=X&ved=2ahUKEwib4bG9z5_vAhUso1kKHblZBKEQ6AEwAnoECAMQAw#v=onepage&q=sue %20gilly%20the%20development%20of%20management%20and%20organizational%20thinking&f=false

Harry, M. and Schroeder, R. (2002). *Six Sigma: The Breakthrough Management Strategy Revolutionizing the World's Top Corporations.* New York, NY: Doubleday.

Hartman, L. (2002). *Perspectives in Business Ethics* (2nd ed.). New York, NY: McGraw-Hill Irwin.

Hosmer, L. (2006). *The Ethics of Management* (5th ed.). Boston: McGraw-Hill Irwin.

Hunnebeck, L. (2011). *ITIL Service Design* (2nd ed.). Norwich, UK: The Stationery Office.

Jacoby, D. (2009). *Guide to Supply Chain Management: How Getting It Right Boosts Corporate Performance.* New York, NY: Bloomberg Press.

Johnson, C. E. (2007). *Ethics in the Workplace: Tools and Tactics for Organizational Transformation.* Thousand Oaks, CA: Sage Publications.

Kendrick, T. (2004). *The Project Management Tool Kit: 100 Tips and Techniques for Getting the Job Done Right.* New York, NY: American Management Association.

Kotter, J. P. (1995). Leading change: Why transformation efforts fail. *Harvard Business Review,* March–April, Reprint 95204.

Lawrence, A. T., Weber, J., and Post, J. E. (2011). *Business and Society: Stakeholders, Ethics, Public Policy* (11th ed.). Boston: McGraw-Hill Irwin.

Liker, J. K. (2004). *The Toyota Way: 14 Management Principles from the World's Greatest Manufacturer*. New York, NY: McGraw-Hill.

Lloyd, V. (2011). *ITIL Continual Service Improvement (Best Management Practices)*. Norwich, UK: The Stationery Office.

Martin, J. W. (2014). *Lean Six Sigma for Supply Chain Management: A 10-Step Solution Process* (2nd ed.). New York, NY: McGraw-Hill.

McKeller, J. M. (2014). *Supply Chain Management Demystified*. New York, NY: McGraw-Hill.

Mead, R. (1999). *International Management*. Malden, MA: Blackwell Publishers.

Murdock, H. (2011). *10 Key Techniques to Improve Team Productivity*. Altamonte Springs, FL: The IIA Research Foundation.

Post, J. (2002). *Business and Society: Corporate Strategy, Public Policy, Ethics* (10th ed.). New York, NY: McGraw-Hill Irwin.

Rance, S. (2011). *ITIL Service Transition (Best Management Practices)*. Norwich, UK: The Stationery Office.

Rhode, D. L. (2006). *Moral Leadership: The Theory and Practice of Power, Judgment, and Policy*. San Francisco, CA: John Wiley & Sons.

Sawyer, L. (1988). *Sawyer's Internal Auditing: The Practice of Internal Auditing*. Altamonte Springs, FL: The Institute of Internal Auditors.

Steinberg, R. (2011). *ITIL Service Operation (Best Management Practices)*. Norwich, UK: The Stationery Office.

Tarantino, A. (2008). *Governance, Risk, and Compliance: Technology, Finance, Environmental, and International Guidance and Best Practices*. Hoboken, NJ: John Wiley and Sons.

Treviño, L. K. and Nelson, K. A. (2014). *Managing Business Ethics: Straight Talk about How to Do It Right* (6th ed.). San Francisco, CA: John Wiley & Sons.

Trompenaars, F. (1993). *Riding the Waves of Culture*. London: Nicholas Brealey.

Velasquez, M. (2006). *Business Ethics: Concepts and Cases* (6th ed.). Upper Saddle River, NJ: Prentice Hall.

Wilkins, A. M. and Mooningham, B. (2013). *Internal Auditor Magazine*. Volume LXX: IV, August.

Index

MTO, Make to order (MTO)
MTS, Make to stock (MTS)

N

National Vulnerability Database (NVD), 76
New York Stock Exchange (NYSE), 106
Nitpicking, 234; CCCER/5C model
NVD, National Vulnerability Database (NVD)
NYSE, New York Stock Exchange (NYSE)

O

OECD, Organization for Economic Cooperation and
    Development (OECD)
OFAC, Office of Foreign Assets Control (OFAC)
Office of Foreign Assets Control (OFAC), 242
Open-ended questions, 46, 50–51
Operational auditing, 3, 9, 33, 61, 347; Audit evidence
        types; Internal auditing
    beyond accounting, 12
    actions without purpose, 5
    advantages, 62
    broken process, 62
    enterprise risk assessment, 36
    fieldwork, 40
    follow-up, 57–58
    identifying operational threats and vulnerabilities, 17
    internal auditors, 37–39
    interviewing, 4
    life cycle of audits, 33
    metrics, 58–61
    objectives of, 33–35
    people, processes, and technology, 61–62
    phases of, 35
    planning, 36–37
    questions, 62
    reporting, 55–57
    to reposition internal audit function, 347
    risk factors, 38–41
    impact of risk factors on risk profile, 38
    role of, 8–9
    8 Es model, 89
    skills required for, 18
    steps for audit programs, 39
    understanding nature of internal controls, 4
Operational review outcomes, 231
Operational risk types, 67
Operational talent development, 348
Organization, 199
    focus areas of, 103
    managers in, 271
    waste reduction, 175–177
    organizational climate, 145–146
    organizational culture, 114
Organizational structure, 339
    Characteristics of top organizations, 343

    Flexibility and stability, 343
    Organizational (org) charts, 342
        Types, 340
    Organization for Economic Cooperation and
            Development (OECD), 203
    Outsourcing, 82; Risk assessments
    Overproduction, 176, 200–201

P

P&G, Procter & Gamble (P&G)
Paper-based filing systems, 203
Paperless office, 203
Pareto chart, 153; Tools
Pareto principle, 153
Parts per million (PPM), 221
Patagonia, 101
Payable, 317
PDCA, Plan-Do-Check-Act (PDCA)
Performance evaluation process, 266; Change
        management
Personal devices, 324
Personal Health Information (PHI), 203
Personal Information Protection and Electronic
        Documents Act (PIPEDA), 84
Personally identifiable information (PII), 127, 203
Personnel risks, 119; Control frameworks
PERT, Program Evaluation and Review
        Technique (PERT)
PHI, Personal Health Information (PHI)
PII, Personally identifiable information (PII)
PIPEDA, Personal Information Protection and Electronic
        Documents Act (PIPEDA)
Plan-Do-Check-Act (PDCA), 259–260; Change
        management
PM, Project management (PM), Project manager (PM)
PMI, Project Management Institute (PMI)
PMO, Project Management Office (PMO)
PO, Purchase order (PO)
Point of sale (POS), 80
Poka Yoke, 190–192, 234; CCCER/5C model; Tools
    attributes, 191
    principles, 192
    ways of mistake-proofing processes, 191
Political risk, 120; Control frameworks
POS, Point of sale (POS)
PPM, Parts per million (PPM)
Pricing, 305–307; Auditing business functions and
        activities
Process map, Flowcharts
Process model, Flowcharts
Procter & Gamble (P&G), 100
Program Evaluation and Review Technique (PERT), 280;
        Project phases
Project, 273–274
    life cycles, Project phases
Project management (PM), 261, 273, 293; Project phases